THE OFFICE OF

AMBASSADOR

IN THE MIDDLE AGES

THE OFFICE OF AMBASSADOR IN THE MIDDLE AGES

BY DONALD E. QUELLER

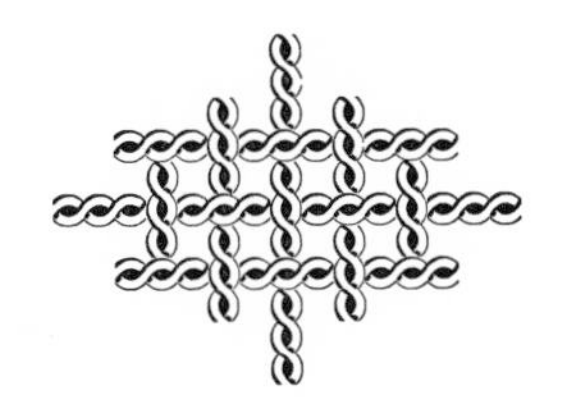

PRINCETON, NEW JERSEY
PRINCETON UNIVERSITY PRESS
1967

Library of Congress Catalog Card Number: 67-11034

Printed in the United States of America by
Princeton University Press

to Gaines Post

with respect and affection

ABBREVIATIONS

A.S.M.	Archivio di Stato, Milano
A.S.F.	Archivio di Stato, Firenze
A.S.V.	Archivio di Stato, Venezia
C.	*Codex*
C.C.R.	*Calendar of the Close Rolls Preserved in the Public Record Office*
C.P.R.	*Calendar of the Patent Rolls Preserved in the Public Record Office*
C.R.	*Close Rolls of the Reign of Henry III*
D.	*Digestum*
Decret. Greg. IX	*Decretales Gregorii IX*
Decretum	*Decretum Gratiani*
E.H.R.	*English Historical Review*
H.F.	*Recueil des historiens des Gaules et de la France*
M.G.H., Capit.	*Monumenta Germaniae historica, Legum sectio II: Capitularia regum Francorum*
M.G.H., Const.	*Monumenta Germaniae historica, Legum sectio IV: Constitutiones et acta publica imperatorum et regum*
M.G.H., Dipl. reg. imp. Germ.	*Monumenta Germaniae historica, Diplomata regum et imperatorum Germaniae*
M.G.H., LL.	*Monumenta Germaniae historica, Leges*
M.G.H., Script. rer. Germ., N.S.	*Monumenta Germaniae historica, Scriptores rerum Germanicarum. Nova Series*
M.G.H., Script. rer. Mer.	*Monumenta Germaniae historica, Scriptores rerum Merovingicarum*
M.G.H., SS.	*Monumenta Germaniae historica, Scriptores*
O.E.D.	*Oxford English Dictionary*
R.S.	*Rerum Britannicarum Medii Aevi scriptores* (Rolls Series)
Sext.	*Liber Sextus*

PREFACE

The study of medieval diplomatic history, in general, and of diplomatic institutions, in particular, has not received the scholarly attention which would seem to be warranted by such an important area of activity. M.A.R. de Maulde La Clavière's old, massive, and erudite *La diplomatie au temps de Machiavel*, which is actually broader in chronological scope than the title indicates, has been for almost three-quarters of a century the dominant work in the field. Despite the author's vast learning, it suffers from conceptual weakness and a tendency toward anachronism. François L. Ganshof's volume in Renouvin's *Histoire des relations internationales* devotes three chapters to the techniques of diplomacy which represent a broad culling of information from secondary materials. Taken for what it purports to be, it is a useful work, but it is not a major scholarly effort by this eminent medievalist. Much more successful is Garrett Mattingly's *Renaissance Diplomacy*. Only lightly endowed with scholarly apparatus, it is nevertheless a learned work. Mattingly is amazingly accurate even in treating subjects upon which he had relatively little data—and upon which other noted scholars have gone badly astray. One may supplement his work or criticize his emphasis, as I do in the case of the resident ambassador, but what he has chosen to do has been done with exquisite insight and precision. I had at one time thought of limiting the present study to the period before 1436, the date of Bernard du Rosier's treatise on the ambassador upon which Mattingly leans heavily, but I have overlapped Mattingly's work somewhat, and my study has developed an emphasis and style quite different from his. Other authors have treated well other highly limited topics. G. P. Cuttino's *English Diplomatic Administration, 1259–1339*, which traces the rise of the office of *custos processuum*, is an excellent example of a specialized monograph. So is Joycelyne G. Dickinson's study of the Congress of Arras. Many more examples could be given of good and bad monographs, some of them supplanted by more recent works, or of general treatments of the history of diplomacy which have little or nothing to say concerning diplomatic institutions, but enough has been said here to indicate the large gap which the present work is designed, in part, to fill.

The subject of this study is the evolution of the office of the ambassador from the late twelfth century until the end of the fifteenth. It is founded upon a variety of types of sources. Absolutely basic are the diplomatic documents themselves: letters of credence, powers, instructions, reports, and, to a lesser extent, treaties, truces, and other conventions. Not all such documents for a period of over three centuries could be examined, of course, but the footnotes will reveal that a considerable sampling of unpublished and published documents from various places has been used. The bulk of the diplomatic documents, it is true, has been drawn from Venice, Flanders, and England. A great Italian city-state, a powerful county, and a national monarchy are thus abundantly represented. Not many differences in the development of the office of the ambassador are found in these various lands or in others from which a smattering of evidence has been drawn. Uniform development of the ambassadorial office is what we should expect among states which exchanged ambassadors, for the very nature of ambassadorship, as contrasted, for example, to chancellorship, demands a certain uniformity of practice among states. The intensive use of diplomatic documents of different provenance, I am sure, would have added little of value. Chronicles have been used as supplementary sources, especially when the author was an experienced diplomat, such as Villehardouin or Commines. Maulde La Clavière also used these types of sources liberally (although I believe he relied more upon chronicles than official documents), but his failure to use legal sources prevented him from reading his documents with a technical eye and led to his misunderstanding of the juridical character of various envoys. I have therefore placed heavy reliance upon legal sources, the *Corpus juris civilis*, the *Corpus juris canonici*, and various less official writings by lawyers. Treatises on diplomacy are rare and of doubtful value, although some use has been made of those by Bernard du Rosier and others who had some diplomatic experience. Such esteemed theoreticians as Thomas Aquinas and Christine de Pisan simply did not know very much about diplomatic practice, although they are occasionally cited as authorities. Doubts sometimes even arise whether the experts on ceremony at the Roman *curia*, such as Johannes Burckhard, actually report what was customarily done, rather than what they would have liked done. I have tried to write not a theoretical account based on theoretical works, but an account of how envoys actually were employed based upon diplomatic sources. Legal and theoretical works have been used only insofar as they enlighten the diplomatic sources.

The occasional *dicta* of medieval lawyers and theoretical writers on sovereignty and the *droit d'ambassade* and the more lengthy arguments of modern authorities who follow them are simply not relevant to diplomatic practice in the Middle Ages. They do not enlighten, but obfuscate; they contradict what the official documents conclusively prove—that diplomatic agents with whatever title were sent and received for pragmatic reasons without regard to sovereignty. No doubt there was developing a concept of sovereignty, but it had no significant bearing upon the right to send or receive ambassadors or other diplomatic envoys. The diplomatic game was open to anyone who had sufficient power at his command to enter it. Today, after living for several centuries under the influence of the concept of sovereignty, we have ambassadors to the United Nations, which, if I understand the concept of sovereignty (and I am not sure that anyone does), is not a sovereign power. Grotius himself recognized that in the course of a civil war one people might almost become two for purposes of international affairs.[1]

The modern scholar also runs the risk of error if he tries to distinguish sharply between diplomatic and political institutions or between public and private ones. The scholarly mind has a tendency to classification that was alien, it seems to me, to the practice of the Middle Ages. Medieval rulers, churchmen, lawyers, merchants, and others took such devices as they found available and used them for whatever purposes they thought suitable without much consideration for classification.

Such a device was *plena potestas,* the use of which in diplomacy is a central theme of this study. Its introduction in the late twelfth century transformed the medieval diplomat who received it from a mere messenger into an agent with authority to bind his principal. Sometimes the diplomatic plenipotentiary received the broadest and most unrestricted powers to commit his principal, but as the frequency of communication between principals or between principal and agent increased, it became common practice to withhold *plena potestas* until the principal had approved any draft conventions made by his envoys.

Every professional historian tries, insofar as possible, to grasp medieval diplomatic practice on its own terms, to avoid distorting the data to make it conform to his own preconceptions and those of his own time and place. Maulde La Clavière, too fine a scholar to deny his data, sometimes was guilty of judging medieval practices which did not conform to his preconceptions as extraordinary or even bad. No historian studying an age long past, of course, can enter into the mind of that age with complete success. He cannot really, as Collingwood would have him do, rethink the thoughts of the writers of his documents and the thoughts of those whose acts are described in them. The historian is of necessity a man of his own age, and his frames of reference are in large part those of his culture. The historian cannot really get inside the mind of Villehardouin, although he can make an effort, through immersion in the sources and literature on the Fourth Crusade, to view events as Villehardouin viewed them. It is his twentieth-century mind that attempts to rethink those thoughts, however,

[1] Hugo Grotius, *De jure belli ac pacis libri tres,* James Brown Scott, ed.; I, reproduction of edition of 1646; II, trans. by Francis W. Kelsey *et al.* (Washington, 1913–1925). Lib. II, Cap. XVIII, Sec. II; I, 295.

and it cannot be made a *tabula rasa.* It is good that it cannot. Not without reason do statesmen appeal to history for a truer evaluation of their acts than their contemporaries can give. Removed from the passions of the day, sometimes provided with data unknown to contemporaries, standing on the shoulders of his predecessors, and equipped with a more comprehensive view of the nature of man and society, the historian would lose much if he merely rethought past thoughts. Yet, cognizant that he cannot escape his frames of reference—nor would he wish to do so—the historian must be empathic enough to attempt to reconstruct the frames of reference of the past and to understand them. Then, recognizing these as his own constructions with all their limitations, he should bring to bear upon his subject every resource of his mind formed by his life in the present and his study of the past. However inadequately, this is what I have attempted to do.

My chief interest has been to determine how diplomatic representation was used in the Middle Ages to conduct relations among states. The discovery of new devices, such as *plena potestas,* offered new opportunities to overcome conditions that hampered diplomatic activity, such as the slowness of transportation and communication. A society undergoing great economic and political changes, on the other hand, adapted its diplomatic techniques to suit the changed conditions. A greater intensity of diplomatic relations and the possibility of more frequent communication between principal and representative resulted in a more restrained use of *plena potestas* and a greater dependence of the ambassador upon the will of his principal. As diplomatic contact among states became ever more frequent, the *ad hoc* representative became imperceptibly a resident ambassador. This transformation, in turn, worked another in the functions of the ambassador, for the resident, less adequately informed of the intentions of his principal than the *ad hoc* envoy, became less useful for purposes of negotiation but more important for gathering information. Thus the institution of the diplomatic representative reacted to changes in the society of which it was a part and to changes within itself in order to remain functional and to comport more adequately with the ever evolving patterns of society.

Since I have employed in my study of the ambassadorial office documents from all over Western Europe for a period of over three centuries, I suspect that I have not avoided errors insofar as I have touched upon the substantive history of international relations. For these I apologize in advance and recall to the reader to whose specialty I may have done violence that my concern is basically with whatever my documents show concerning the institution of ambassadorship.

PREFACE

I have had some difficulty in attempting to find a principle for the consistent handling of medieval proper names. One cannot easily tell when a place name has become a surname. As a place name it might be translated from the Latin to the vernacular, but more restraint should be exercised in translating surnames. Some given names are customarily translated. Others have no translations. Under which name a medieval author should be listed in the bibliography has been a problem sometimes, but not always, settled by usage: e.g., "Durandus, Gulielmus," but "Gratia Aretinus." I have tried not to be haphazard in these matters, but I am not sure that I have succeeded.

It is my pleasant duty to express my gratitude for Fulbright fellowships to Belgium and Italy and for a Rockefeller Foundation fellowship for study in Venice. Without the archival work which they allowed, this study would have been badly truncated, if not impossible. I am deeply appreciative, not only for the opportunities provided, but for the expressions of confidence which these grants implied. I am also grateful to the University of Southern California for a succession of small research grants which have greatly facilitated my work. I owe much to the helpfulness of archivists and librarians beyond number, but especially to those of the Archivio di Stato di Venezia, the Rijksarchief of Ghent, the Bibliothèque Royale, and the Archives du Royaume of Brussels, where I worked for considerable periods. The staff of the library of the University of Southern California has also been most helpful, especially Miss Marion Schulman, who has shown a great talent for identifying mangled references.

It is a particular pleasure publicly to offer my thanks to the historians under whom I have studied. Gaines Post gave me my start on the subject, has consistently made available to me his great knowledge of representative institutions, and has always encouraged me with his friendship and example. Charles Verlinden was especially helpful in introducing me to archival research in Belgium, and has continued to earn my gratitude by reading manuscripts and suggesting European journals in which they might be published. I am also grateful for the tutelage of the late Robert L. Reynolds and the interest and encouragement of the late Garrett Mattingly. If the present work earns the approbation of such scholars as these, I shall have achieved my aim.

DONALD E. QUELLER

CONTENTS

THE OFFICE OF AMBASSADOR IN THE MIDDLE AGES

CHAPTER I

THE *NUNCIUS*

In the very dim and distant past when war and diplomacy were born as twins, primitive societies communicated with one another their intentions, desires, and demands by means of messengers. In the course of millenia various societies have invested diplomatic message-bearers with diverse names and different ceremonial trappings, but the basic function of the messenger has remained the same. In medieval Latin Europe, a variety of titles were employed to designate one carrying a diplomatic communication from one ruler to another.

The most commonly used title in the Merovingian age, according to Professor F. L. Ganshof, who has made a detailed study of Merovingian envoys, was *legatus* or some variant of that basic word, although other names, such as *nuncius* and *missus* are also found.[1] In subsequent centuries *legatus* remained in use, although by the thirteenth century it is more commonly found in narrative sources than in official diplomatic documents. [2]

Nuncius, although a term by no means unknown to the Merovingians, came into its own in the twelfth century.[3] In the thirteenth century it prevailed over the other titles for a message-bearing envoy and subsequently began to share its place of prominence with the newer terms *ambaxator* and *orator*. Notice must be taken of a special connotation of the word *nuncius* for Venetian envoys of the High (approximately 1000–1300) and

[1] François L. Ganshof, "Merowingisches Gesandtschaftswesen," in *Aus Geschichte und Landeskunde. Forschungen und Darstellungen. Franz Steinbach zum 65. Geburtstag gewidmet von seinen Freunden und Schülern* (Bonn, 1960), p. 167. Variants include such titles as *legatarius* and *commissarius.*

[2] For the tenth, eleventh, and early twelfth centuries, see the frequent and indistinguishable uses of *legatus* and *nuncius* in Cosmas of Prague, *Chronica Boemorum*, B. Bretholz and W. Weinberger, eds., in *M.G.H., Script. rer. Germ., N.S.* (Berlin, 1923), II, 41, 54, 56, 63, 91-93 (*legatus*), and 117, 153 and 206 (*nuncius*). Also *apocrisarius* for a papal emissary, p. 124. For the tenth century, M.A.R. Maulde La Clavière, *La diplomatie au temps de Machiavel*, 3 vols. (Paris, 1892–1893), I, 297, n. 3. For the twelfth century, *Urkunden zür älteren Handels-und Staatsgeschichte der Republik Venedig*, G. L. Fr. Tafel and G. M. Thomas, eds. (Wien, 1856–1857), 3 vols., in *Fontes rerum austriacarum*, zweite abtheilung, Banden XII-XIV, I, 107, and *Gli atti del commune di Milano fino all'anno MCCXVI*, C. Manaresi, ed. (Milano, 1919), pp. 319–320, no. CCXXV. For thirteenth-century use in chronicles, see, for example, Jacques de Guyse, *Annales Hannoniae*, De Fortia d'Urban, ed. and trans., 22 vols. (Paris, 1826–1838), XV, 148. *Legatus* did occasionally appear in official documents, even in Venice, where it is extremely rare. A.S.V., Senato, Secreta, IX, 161r (159r). The doubled and sometimes tripled page numbers reflect pagination that has been added to the registers at different times.

[3] Many examples of its use in Manaresi, *Atti . . . di Milano.*

Late (1300–1500) Middle Ages, because only Venetian noblemen could become ambassadors or orators, although many missions—some of great importance—were undertakten by secretaries or notaries of the Republic with the title *nuncii.*

Various other terms were less frequently used for diplomatic envoys. *Missus* appeared at least as early as the Merovingian period and was used now and then thereafter. *Mandatarius* is found more rarely.[4] In French documents or chronicles, *messages* is the exact equivalent of *nuncii.* Either word could be applied to envoys of high status and great responsibility, like the *messages* of Philip III sent to pacify a quarrel between the Count of Flanders and the Bishop of Liège,[5] as well as to low-born messengers. Sometimes no title was given to an envoy, and he was simply described as "our beloved companion" or "our faithful man."[6]

In the variety of terminology there is no significance. All those named above were in essence the same: bearers of messages, written or oral. The broad and equivalent meaning of such words as *legatus, missus,* and *nuncius* is exemplified by a nondiplomatic document from Ottonian Germany referring to *legatis nostris . . . et aliis nunciis nostris.*[7] That an orator was also a *nuncius* is shown by a pair of acts of the Venetian Senate in 1450, the first of which refers to the envoys of a condottiere, the Marquis of Mantua, as *nuncii,* while the second refers to one of these *nuncii* as *orator.*[8]

[4] François L. Ganshof, *Le Moyen Age,* Vol. I in *Histoire des relations internationales,* Pierre Renouvin, ed. (Paris, 1953), 122.

[5] *Monuments pour servir à l'histoire des provinces de Namur, de Hainaut et de Luxembourg,* De Reiffenberg, J. J. De Smet, L. Devillers, Ad. Borgnet, E. Gachet et Liebrecht, eds., 8 vols. (Bruxelles, 1844–1874), I, 14-16. Maulde La Clavière points to the frequent use of *messages* in the fourteenth century for even the most exalted missions and its decline in the fifteenth as a term used for simple messengers. *La diplomatie au temps de Machiavel,* I, 300.

[6] "Documents relatifs aux formes diplomatiques aux XIIIe et XIVe siècles," Frantz Funck-Brentano, ed., *Revue d'histoire diplomatique,* XI (1897), 92; *Gesta Ludovici VIII, Francorum rex, auctore anonymo, ab anno 1223 ad annum 1226* in *H.F.,* XVII, 307, n. c.

[7] *M.G.H., Dipl. reg. imp. Germ.,* V, 508. For interchangeable use of *legatus, missus* (or *messaticus*), and *nuncius,* see A.S.V., Miscellanea di atti diplomatici e privati, busta I, and *Liber iurium reipublicae Genuensis* in *Monumenta historiae patriae,* VII and IX (Turin, 1854 and 1857), I, cols. 883–887. The tendency for *legatus* to occur in narrative, while the same envoys appear in the official documents as *nuncii* or *messages* is shown in Gilles Le Muisit, *Chronicon majus,* J. J. De Smet, ed., in *Corpus chronicorum Flandriae,* 4 vols. (Bruxelles, 1837–1865), II, 185; *Codex diplomaticus Flandriae, 1296–1327,* Thierry de Limburg-Stirum, ed., 2 vols. (Bruges, 1879–1889), I, 1 and 132–149. Du Cange defines *legatus* as the *nuncius* of any private man. Charles du Fresne, sieur du Cange, *Glossarium mediae et infimae latinitatis,* new edition by Leopold Favre, 1883–1887, reprinted, 10 vols. (Paris, 1937–1938), *Legatus.* This usage was unusual at best. I have found no evidence to confirm Cuttino's statement that the difference between a *nuncius* and a *legatus* in the fifteenth century gave the principal the modern choice between "sending a note" or "making a diplomatic representation." George P. Cuttino, *English Diplomatic Administration, 1259–1339* (London, 1940), p. 86. Although I cannot support him on this point and a few others, this is a fine monograph.

[8] A.S.V., Senato, Secreta, XIX, 4v (4v) and 24v (24v).

Another Senatorial decree shows more vividly still the broad scope of the title *nuncius*. It amends an existing regulation which provided that ambassadors going on their missions or returning on merchant galleys should not pay for their passage. Although it had been the original intention of the decree to include all *nuncii*, this had not been clearly stated. The original act, therefore, was clarified by expressly including provisors, syndics, *tractatores*, and all other *nuncii*.[9] No contention is made that all these terms are equivalent. A syndic, for example, is something more than a person sent for the purpose of communication. *Nuncius*, *legatus*, *missus*, *message*, and variants of these may be called the generic terms. All diplomatic envoys were *nuncii* in the broadest sense.

Although this study is directed toward secular diplomacy, confusion may arise unless a word is said concerning the papal legate, for this ecclesiastical functionary carried out the duties of an ambassador of the papacy as well as other functions. The word *legatus* remained current for diplomats of the papacy, as well as of other principals of lesser rank, while *nuncius* was applied in ecclesiastical diplomacy to envoys entrusted with affairs of lesser importance.[10] The Venetian secretary who first described an apostolic legate in the rubric as *nuncio*, then crossed it out and substituted *legato*, was making a legitimate and important distinction among papal diplomats, although in more general usage the terms were identical in meaning.[11]

Nuncius, then, covered a broad spectrum of envoys. At the lower end of this spectrum were the lackeys and other couriers who simply carried letters. Professional or occasional runners of messages might be called *cursores*, *tabellarii*, *fanti*, or *varletti*.[12] The most interesting title for a courier was *coquinus* or *cokinus*. According to Hill, the *cokini*, "kitchen knaves and hangers-on," were first employed in England about the middle of the thirteenth century, when the need for couriers outstripped the number of *nuncii regis* available. They remained in use, perhaps, because they were cheaper, being unmounted and not entitled to robes and shoes. In fact, they became so frequently employed for carrying messages that they became un-

[9] A.S.V., Senato, Misti, XLI, 121r (written over 113) (124r). *Syndici* and *tractatores* will be discussed in a subsequent chapter, *infra*, pp. 33-34. *Provisores* are not of direct concern for the study of diplomacy. Another example grouping orators, provisors, and secretaries under the rubric *nuncii* is A.S.V., Senato, Terra, VI, 99r (100r).

[10] Gondisalvus de Villadiego, *Tractatus de legato*, in *De legatis et legationibus tractatus varii*, edidit Vladimir E. Hrabar (Grabar) (Dorpat, 1906), introduction, p. 53.

[11] A.S.V., Senato, Secreta, rubr. gen., R. II, 29v (33v). It might be added that *legatus* was unusual even for papal diplomats in Venice, where they were also customarily called ambassadors or orators.

[12] Cosmas of Prague, *Chronica Boemorum*, p. 157; *Foedera*, Thomas Rymer, ed., 10 vols. (Hagae Comitis, 1739–1745), I, i, 114: A.S.V., Senato, Secreta, XV, 126r (127r), and XXII, 173v (175v); A.S.F., Signori, Carteggi, Responsive originali, XI, 39r, 50r, and 78r.

available for other duties, forming an inferior class of professional couriers. In the reign of Edward II they sloughed their ignominious title and became known as *cursores*.[13] For ceremonious message-bearing, heralds were sometimes used in the fifteenth century, not only for declarations of war, but for such purposes as the delivery of the ratification of a treaty.[14] In its broadest sense *nuncius* can cover all of the titles given above.

Given the relationship of these various titles to one another, a close examination of their legal significance seems appropriate. Contrasted to the numerous and lengthy discussions of procurators by legists and canonists, little is said by them on the present subject. A few definitions and comments on the *nuncius* can be found, however, and, beginning with Gulielmus Durandus in the thirteenth century, a succession of canonists devoted themselves to treatises on the *legatus*. While much of what these canonists say is limited to the papal legate, much is applicable also to secular *nuncii*.

Durandus provides an excellent definition:

> A legate is, or can be called, whoever has been sent from another . . . either from a ruler or from the pope to others . . . or from any city or province to a ruler or to another . . . or even from a proconsul. . . . On this account a legate is called a substitute for the office of another. . . . But also nuncii whom foreigners send to us are called legates. . . .[15]

Like most definitions, it is not completely true. *Nuncii* sent by foreigners were most often called *nuncii* in the thirteenth century, though they might be called *legati*. Either term used broadly meant someone sent from another. Essentially, however, it is a sound definition, and it was followed with minor variations by other canonists.[16]

The legal effect of sending a *nuncius* or *legatus*—assuming that the envoy was that and no more—was equivalent to sending a letter. Roman law established this equivalence, and medieval legists and canonists resounded

[13] Mary C. Hill, *The King's Messengers, 1199–1377* (London, 1961), pp. 14-15. St. Louis used the *queux* or *coquus* of France for diplomatic missions, but this was by no means a menial office in France. Achille Luchaire, *Manuel des institutions françaises. Période des Capétiens directs* (Paris, 1892), p. 530. The French and the English still mean something quite different by "cook," as anyone who has eaten in the two countries can testify.

[14] Paul-Michel Perret, *Histoire des relations de la France avec Venise du XIIIe siècle à l'avènement de Charles VIII*, 2 vols. (Paris, 1896), I, 504; A.S.V., Senato, Secreta, XXV, 141v (150v); XXXIV, 49v (61v).

[15] Gulielmus Durandus, *Speculum legatorum* (in eius *Speculo iuris*, rubrica *De legato*), in Hrabar, *De legatis*, p. 32.

[16] Alberico de Rosate, *Vocabularius utriusque juris* (Lugduni, 1535), p. cvii; Andreas (de) Barbatia (Siculus), *Tractatus de cardinalibus legatis a latere*, Praeludium, 1, in Hrabar, *De legatis*, p. 42; Gondisalvus de Villadiego, *Tractatus*, pars II, q. v, par. 15; Petrus Andreas Gambarus, *Tractatus de officio atque auctoritate legati de latere* (Venetiis, 1571), p. 2. Gondisalvus de Villadiego states that those sent by private persons are not *legati*, but *nuncii*. *Tractatus*, pars II, q. v, par. 16.

the theme.[17] Azo stated it vividly: "A *nuncius* is he who takes the place of a letter: and he is just like a magpie, and an organ, and the voice of the principal sending him, and he recites the words of the principal."[18] In diplomatic practice the replies returned to rulers sending *nuncii* suggest by their wording that the function of a *nuncius*, like that of a letter, was to communicate a message. A typical example is: "Sire, we have listened well to that which you have sent to us by means of master Giffroi."[19] The letters of credence borne by *nuncii* also suggest the role of a magpie or a living letter, as in this example addressed by Henry III to Frederick II in 1236: ". . . Certain other things concerning our business touching the king of France *we place in the mouth* of our aforesaid *nuncii* for the purpose of explaining to you. . . ."[20]

Why, then, should a *nuncius* be sent instead of a letter borne by some menial or entrusted to a passing merchant or other traveler? The Venetian *Maggior Consiglio* gave one answer in appointing an envoy to Genoa in 1306, pointing out that one could not respond by way of letters in just the same way as by word of mouth.[21] The attitude of the speaker, the intonation of his words, his wording of the message (if that were left to his choice, as it usually was), his response to questions—all these gave the advantage to the use of a *nuncius* possessed of some little discretion. Another reason was added security, for medieval roads were none too secure and it was no difficult matter for a letter to be seized from the bearer, opened and read.[22] The *nuncius* who was more than a simple courier of inferior status also had a vast ceremonial advantage. He represented a much more courteous means of conveying a message than a mere letter. Many times, of course, letters and *nuncii* were used conjointly. What has been said of the advantages

[17] *D.*, 2, 14 (*De pactis*), 2. Wherever the text of the *Corpus juris civilis* is cited, reference is to the edition by Paul Krueger and Theodor Mommsen, 2 vols. (Berlin, 1888-1889). Gulielmus Durandus, *Speculum juris*, 2 vols. (Augustae Taurinorum, 1578), 1, 3, c. *ut autem*, 5; Andrea Alciati, *Iudiciarii processus compendium* (Venetiis, 1544), pp. 30-31; Conradus Brunus, *De legationibus*, quoted in B. Behrens, "Treatises on the Ambassador Written in the Fifteenth and Early Sixteenth Centuries," *E.H.R.*, LI (1936), 622, n. 2.

[18] Azo, *Summa* (Venetiis, 1594), 4, 50 (*Si alteri, vel sibi, sub alterius nomine, vel aliena pecunia emerit*), 1.

[19] *Treaty Rolls: Preserved in the Public Record Office*, Pierre Chaplais, ed. (London, 1955——), I, 75, no. 184; ". . . ex hiis quae per eum nobis significastis . . ." Rymer, *Foedera*, I, i, 52.

[20] Chaplais, *Treaty Rolls*, I, 18, no. 42; Rymer, *Foedera*, I, i, 127. Italics mine. Joycelyne Dickinson reports how the English envoys at the Congress of Arras, receiving the last offer of the French in writing, promised only to report it to their king "se in hac parte puros relatores et nuncios constituendo." Joycelyne C. Dickinson, *The Congress of Arras* (Oxford, 1955), p. 153.

[21] A.S.V., Maggior Consiglio, Capricornus, 22r (127r). Letters of credence of Henry III say of his *nuncius*: ". . . quedam negocia nostra specialia ipso commisimus viva voce pocius quam scripto exponenda . . ." *C.R. (1237-1242)*, p. 433.

[22] Rymer, *Foedera*, I, i, 89-90, 106.

of the *nuncius* in no way contradicts Azo. The legal import of the words of a *nuncius* was precisely that of a letter, he was an instrument, and he spoke the words of his principal—though usually not word for word. Yet, as a living letter, he was a more flexible and effective instrument than words fixed upon parchment.

Of course there is a risk attending even the small measure of flexibility represented by the *nuncius*. Baldus and others found it necessary to caution the *nuncius* against overstepping his limitations. He had no activitiy of his own, but was only a bearer of a message. He might not declare or add anything on his own initiative, but only express formally the words of his principal.[23] In the absence of a procuratorial mandate, a *nuncius* could not treat anything, nor, beyond the limitations of his duty, should he be believed.[24] He possessed no will of his own, but was simply a means of transmission of the will of another.[25] The want of a will of his own will be found to distinguish clearly the simple *nuncius* from the *procurator* or the *nuncius* who was also a *procurator*.

Despite the limitations of *nuncii*, they could be employed to make treaties, truces, marriage alliances, and other pacts. The Roman jurisconsult Paul wrote that parties who were not present could enter into conventions by means of letters or *nuncii*.[26] What was necessary to a binding act by means of letters or *nuncii* was a joining of the wills of the principals. Sohm has summed up the question with great precision:

> If I desire to conclude a juristic act on my own behalf, but am prevented by purely physical reasons, I may frequently avail myself of the services of a messenger. The messenger fulfills precisely the same purpose as a letter,

[23] Baldo degli Ubaldi, *Commentaria*, 10 vols. (Venetiis: 1615-1616), ad C. 4, tit. *Si quis alteri vel sibi*, 6, 18-19; Hermolaus Barbarus, *De officio legati*, in Hrabar, *De legatis*, p. 66. The amount of discretion actually allowed to a *nuncius* depended upon the particular diplomatic "style" of the principal, as well as the circumstances. Louis XI, as we might expect, employed his envoys as mere agents of transmission. Antoine Degert, "Louis XI et ses ambassadeurs," *Revue historique*, CLIV (1927), 12.

[24] Mathias de Nuwenburg, *Chronica*, Adolf Hofmeister, ed., *M.G.H.*, *Script. rer. Germ.*, *N.S.*, IV, 393. I cannot subscribe to Ganshof's remark that in the fifteenth century the *nuncius* "eut tendance a être employé plutôt pour les envoyés ayant un message à remettre, une communication à faire que pour ceux habilités à négocier." Ganshof, *Le Moyen Age*, p. 268. There was always this tendency, but within the limits expressed here it could be overcome in the fifteenth century as in earlier centuries. Giasone de Maino, *Repertorium copiosissimum*, in *Omnia Jasonis Mayni Mediolanensis juris consulti clarissimi commentaria* (Augustae Taurinorum, 1573), p. 133.

[25] Michele Carboni, "Sul concetto di 'Nuntiis,'" *Scritti giuridici dedicata a Giampietro Chironi* (Milani, Torino, Roma, 1915), pp. 47–48.

[26] *D.* 2, 14, 2. Baldus' comment that just as letters do not obligate, neither does a *nuncius*, appears superficially to contradict Paul. *Commentaria*, ad *D.* 3, *De negociis gestis*, 6, *Item si*, 4. It must be interpreted, however, in the light of his statement that a pact may be made by means of a *nuncius* or a letter. *Ibid.*, ad *D.* 2, *De pactis*, 1, 11, *Labeo*, 1.

> the purpose, namely, of overcoming the external obstacle of distance. He relieves the sender of the journey, but it is the sender who concludes the juristic act. The messenger is merely the instrument by which the sender expresses *his* will, by which, that is, the sender concludes the juristic act. A messenger is a person who conveys the expression of another person's will, the will, namely, of the person who sends him.[27]

Sohm stresses that the juristically binding act must be completed by an expression of the will of the principal to be bound to such-and-such specific conditions. In entering into a covenant a *nuncius* was not one bit more flexible an instrument than a letter. He could not receive a general power to conclude,[28] but he could conclude an act upon terms already specifically accepted by his principal. For example, Henry III wrote to Raymond Berengar, Count of Provence, that the King's Council had agreed to the conditions for the treaty of marriage between the king and the count's daughter Eleanor. Henry, therefore, was sending solemn envoys to conclude the marriage. Their letters of credence informed the count that he should believe in them without doubt and fulfill the pact, just as if these things were treated and affirmed with the king himself present.[29] All negotiations had been completed; only the formally concluding act remained to accomplish.

In word and deed the *nuncius* represented the person of his principal. As Garrett Mattingly noted, ". . . a *nuncius* speaks in his lord's person, never of himself."[30] Although others have said that a *nuncius* speaks in his master's name, and some documentary support can be found for this assertion,[31] it does not adequately describe the totality of representation or sufficiently differentiate the *nuncius* from the *procurator*. Baldus wrote that the *nuncius* conceives his words in the person of his principal, and proceeded to elaborate upon the magpie and organ analogies: "For just as a magpie speaks through himself, and not from himself, and just as an organ does not have a sound by itself, so a *nuncius* says nothing from his own mind or by his own activity, but the principal speaks in him and through him."[32] Many

[27] Rudolph Sohm, *The Institutes: A Textbook of the History and System of Roman Private Law*, 3rd Eng. edn. (Oxford, 1907), par. 45, p. 219. See also Adolf Berger, *Encyclopedic Dictionary of Roman Law*, in *Transactions of the American Philosophical Society*, N.S., XLIII, 2 (1953), *Nuntius*, p. 602.

[28] De Maino, *Repertorium*, p. 95.

[29] Chaplais, *Treaty Rolls*, I, 30–31, nos. 84, 85, 89, and 90.

[30] Mattingly, *Renaissance Diplomacy*, p. 30.

[31] Behrens, "Treatises on the Ambassador," p. 622; Cuttino, *English Diplomatic Administration*, p. 87, quotes and follows Behrens; A.S.V., Senato, Secreta, XXXIV, 3r (15r) and 188r (199r).

[32] *Commentaria*, ad *C.* 4, *Si quis alteri vel sibi*, 4, 17. See also, *ibid.*, ad *C.* 4, *Si quis alteri vel sibi*, 6, 21, and Bartolus a Saxoferrato, *Commentaria*, in *Opera omnia*, 11 vols. in 6 (Venetiis, 1602-1603), ad *D.* 3, *De procuratoribus*, 1, *Procurator* and *Quamvis*.

letters of credence used in diplomacy request for the envoy the same measure of faith as if the principal himself were present, so that all that the *nuncius* says should be considered as coming from the lips of the principal.[33] Similarly, Philip Augustus requested the Duke of Austria not to release King Richard until the French king had spoken with the duke and the emperor either mouth to mouth or by means of *nuncii*.[34] A *nuncius* did not exist as a distinct legal person, because he always conceived words in the person of the principal. In speech he completely represented another.[35] The corollary was true in legal act. The *nuncius*, lacking legal personality, could not sue or be sued. By his action, which was equivalent in law to the principal's action, the principal entered into immediate relationships with third parties.[36] The representation was sufficiently complete that oaths could be received by a *nuncius* that ought to be performed in the presence of the principal.[37]

The papal legate shows most clearly the total representation of the principal, although in a less obvious manner the secular principal was also completely represented by his *nuncius*. Gregory VII, who formed the office of the medieval papal legate out of antecedent institutions,[38] demanded "that one see in the legate the pope's own face and hear in his voice the living voice of the pope." The legate also enjoyed the ceremonial honors of his exalted principal. When it is said that he wore the papal mantle, it is literally true, and he also rode the white horse and wore the golden spurs.[39] Perhaps because secular rulers did not possess quite the distinctive ceremonial accouterments of the pope, the complete representation of the secular

[33] E.g., A.S.V., Senato, Secreta, xxxiv, 188r (199r).

[34] *Recueil des actes de Philippe Auguste, roi de France*, H. F. Delaborde, ed., 1 vol. (1179-1194) appeared (Paris, 1916), I, 528, no. 440.

[35] Baldus, *Commentaria, D.* 2, *De procuratore et defensore*, 1, *Additio Bald.*, 4.

[36] *Ibid., C.* 4, *Si quis alteri vel sibi*, 6, 21.

[37] *Historia critica comitatus Hollandiae et Zeelandiae*, Adriaan Kluit, ed., 4 vols. in 2 (Medioburgi, 1777-1782), II, 584–585, no. CLXX. Also published in *Groot charterboek der graven van Holland, Zeeland en heeren van Vriesland*, F. van Mieris, ed., 4 vols. (Leyden, 1753-1756), I, 260.

[38] On the development of the papal legate through Gregory VII, see Richard Schmutz, "The Foundations of Medieval Papal Representation," unpublished Ph.D. dissertation (University of Southern California, 1966).

[39] Franz Wasner, "Fifteenth Century Texts on the Ceremonial of the Papal 'Legatus a Latere,'" *Traditio*, XIV (1958), 300. Karl Ruess reports that cardinal-legates employed papal insignia from the eleventh century on. Thirteenth-century evidence indicates that it was used only when "across the sea" or by special privilege, but Ruess doubts whether this distinction was always made. *Die rechtliche Stellung des päpstlichen Legaten bis Bonifaz VIII* (Paderborn, 1912), pp. 204-206. Ruess confirms that from the earliest representation of the pope by legates at church councils the pope was present in the person of his legate (pp. 6-9). See also, Durandus, *Speculum legatorum*, 1, 52, p. 37. Not only the legate, but the *nuncius* of the Apostolic See should be honored as the pope himself. *Ibid.*, 1, 3, p. 33. "Factum tamen a legato per interpretationem dicitur factum sedis apostolicae, quando materia non est specialiter reservata Papae." Gambarus, *Tractatus*, pp. 5-6.

principal by his *nuncius* is not so obvious. Yet in secular *nuncii* also ought to be seen all qualities belonging to their principals, and all honors due to their principals ought to be paid to them.[40] One who harmed a *nuncius* was considered to have harmed his principal.[41]

Much legalistic or idealistic nonsense has been written about the *droit d'ambassade*, the right of sending and receiving diplomatic agents. It is said quite properly that diplomatic rights are correlative to the right of war. He who can make war can also treat, directly or by means of diplomatic representatives. The argument continues, however, that it was the sovereign only who had the right to make war, and, therefore, no subject or vassal could send or receive diplomatic agents, since private war was forbidden. Maulde La Clavière cites Thomas Aquinas and Christine de Pisan to this effect.[42] This seems logical enough, but it is not true, and the pious assertions of theologians and learned females bear little weight in this area. The previously cited definition by Durandus is much more pertinent: "A legate is . . . whoever has been sent from another . . . ; either from a prince, or from the pope to others . . . , or from some city, or province to a prince or to another. . . ."[43] All sorts of principals sent diplomatic agents to all sorts of recipients. The concept of sovereignty is not useful. A government did not make war or desist from war according to rules about sovereignty, but as war or peace served—or seemed to serve—the interests of the state or government. Similarly, diplomatic agents were sent where interest dictated negotiations. The distinction between public and private was extraordinarily difficult to draw in the Middle Ages.

Many examples may be given refuting the notion that the *droit d'ambassade* was limited to sovereigns. A complicated but clear case will show the pragmatic way in which envoys were sent and received in an age when public and private status were hopelessly confused. In the thirteenth century the countess of Flanders was the vassal of the German king for imperial Flanders, although crown Flanders, the more important part of her territory, was held of France. She made war upon William, king of the Romans, of whom she held her imperial fiefs, and who, as Count of Holland, happened to be her vassal for Zeeland. Margaret's forces were defeated and two of her sons captured. She sent legates to seek from William terms for their

[40] Andrea Alciati, *Reliqua . . . opera quae . . . excusa* (Lugduni, 1548), col. 483.

[41] *Ibid.*, citing Baldus, and ultimately resting upon *D.* 11, 7, 8, 5, which, however, speaks specifically of the *procurator*, not the *nuncius*. I have not been able to identify the passage from Baldus.

[42] *La diplomatie au temps de Machiavel*, I, 163. I have two criticisms of this work of massive erudition: the author was too prone to place his knowledge of the Middle Ages into a nineteenth-century frame of reference; the scholarly apparatus is miserably inadequate.

[43] Durandus, *Speculum legatorum*, 1, 1, p. 32.

release, and, although they did not succeed in obtaining terms, they were finally received by the king. Four months later the same legates were sent on behalf of the king of France and the whole land of Flanders, and this time they were successful in learning the conditions upon which the liberty of the captives could be gained.[44] What meaning has sovereignty in this kind of diplomatic tangle? How often were English and French envoys exchanged between 1066 and 1453 upon affairs which touched the English ruler, not as king of England, or sovereign, but as vassal of the king of France? Another Flemish example shows six knights of Flanders in 1295 sending *nuncii* to Philip IV to seek the freedom of Count Guy.[45] In another instance the chancellor of the emperor of Constantinople sent his *nuncius* to Barbarossa.[46] By the mid-fifteenth century in Italy considerable numbers of *nuncii* or orators were sent and received by condottieri, who had little or no status in public law, but who freely exercised rights of war and diplomacy.[47] The Venetians even received an ambassador from a mythical figure, Prester John, "lord of the countries of India." He brought gifts of four leopards, aromatics, and other pleasing things.[48]

Diplomatic envoys could also be sent to all sorts of nonsovereign recipients. They could, of course, be dispatched to meet with the envoys of another ruler.[49] Very frequently kings, nobles, or cities sent diplomatic envoys to the cardinals, often to the entire college with a separate letter of credence for each cardinal.[50] The distinction between diplomatic envoys and others is not easy to make. The Venetian Senate sent a *nuncius* to its own citizens in Naples, ordering them to leave in retribution for the bad treatment of Venetians in that city. On another occasion the *Maggior Consiglio* sent a *nuncius* to a subject town to return the regalia of the late doge to the lagoons.[51] Edward II employed an envoy bearing letters of credence to communicate with the clergy of the archdiocese of Canterbury.[52] It would of course be difficult to argue that every single one of these uses can be called diplomatic. The forms, however, are identical with those used in

[44] Jacques de Guyse, *Annales Hannoniae*, xv, 148-162.

[45] Rijksarchief, Gent, Chronologisch supplement, no. 192; Archives du Nord, Lille, Chambre des comptes, B 1263, no. 3633.

[46] *Historia de expeditione Friderici imperatoris*, A. Chroust, ed., *M.G.H.*, *Script. rer. Germ.*, *N.S.*, v, 29.

[47] E.g., A.S.V., Senato, Secreta, xix, 79v (79v).

[48] A.S.V., Maggior Consiglio, Leona, 127r (131r).

[49] Rymer, *Foedera*, i, iii, 166; Chaplais, *Treaty Rolls*, i, 173-174, nos. 420-421. I find no. 420 in the *Foedera*, but not no. 421, as cited by Chaplais. I have checked the Hague edition, which is convenient.

[50] Chaplais, *Treaty Rolls*, i, 91, nos. 218-219.

[51] A.S.V., Senato, Misti, xxvii, 70v (70v); *Deliberazioni del Maggior Consiglio di Venezia*, Roberto Cessi, ed., 3 vols. (Bologna, 1931-1950), iii, 259.

[52] *C.P.R., Edward II, (1313-1317)*, p. 114.

the sending of an ambassador from one sovereign to another, and it is sometimes difficult to state unequivocally which are diplomatic and which are not. There is no reason to believe that any medieval prince, city, or condottiere would concern himself with such a distinction.

An interesting manifestation of this lack of concern about who had the power to send and receive diplomatic envoys is the way in which envoys picked up letters of credence and messages along the way. Edward I, having received *nuncii* from the king of the Romans, sent them back bearing his own letters of credence, not only to the king, but to other German nobles and ecclesiastics.[53] Replying through the *nuncii* of another, a common practice, had the disadvantage that they were more likely to garble the communication than one's own trusted emissaries.[54] A more cautious method was to offer only a limited response via the *nuncii* of the other party, reserving a full reply for carefully selected *nuncii* of one's own sent after mature deliberation.[55] An envoy often received messages from third parties, sometimes even messages addressed to a fourth. A Venetian envoy to Ussono Cassano received an additional commission upon his return journey from Stephen Voivode of Moldavia to the pope. Stephen also requested from Venice a doctor to cure an ulcer on his leg, and Venice complied.[56] Journeys were long and dangerous in the Middle Ages, embassies were costly, governments were only gradually obtaining increased resources in men and money, and *nuncii* had little discretion anyway, so rulers took advantage of whatever *nuncii* were at hand for conveying their messages.

The functions which *nuncii* actually performed were, if anything, more varied than the persons who sent and received them. The basic function of the *nuncius* was to communicate a message. Many of them were mere letter-bearers, and even important negotiations could be conducted in this way, as were those for the departure from England of Prince Louis in 1217.[57] This was an unwieldy and tedious method. Among the illiterate barbarians of the era of invasions, it is true, the envoy bearing a message by word of mouth was every bit as limited in authority as a letter-bearer. The Hunnish king sent a message to the Eastern emperor via an envoy who memorized and mechanically repeated the words.[58] In a more literate age, however, rulers entrusted oral messages to envoys because, for some

[53] Rymer, *Foedera*, I, iii, 139-140; Chaplais, *Treaty Rolls*, I, 102-103, nos. 239-241.

[54] Rymer, *Foedera*, I, ii, 197; Chaplais, *Treaty Rolls*, I, 72, no. 176.

[55] Chaplais, *Treaty Rolls*, I, 173, no. 419.

[56] A.S.V., Senato, Secreta, XXVII, 3r (13r).

[57] Roger of Wendover, *Flores historiarum*, Henry Hewlett, ed., in *R.S.*, no. 84, 3 vols. (London, 1886-1889), II, 223.

[58] Bruno Paradisi, *Storia del diritto internazionale nel Medio Evo: L'età di transizione (dal sec. V al sec. IX)* (Napoli, 1950), p. 102.

reason, they did not wish to put their thoughts in writing, and so the letter of credence requested the recipient to accept what was communicated on behalf of the sender viva-voce.[59] A combination of letters and oral messages was commonly used, often for the purpose of communicating the basic message in writing and allowing the *nuncius* to explain it.[60] The *nuncius* to whom the mind of his principal had been opened[61] seems to have had somewhat more flexibility than one who had received in his mouth the words of the principal. The recipient might also read that the envoy was well informed, and he might inform himself through him.[62] Whether bearing a letter or interpreting the mind of his principal, however, the *raison d'être* of the *nuncius* was to provide a channel of communication between principals.

An important and delicate function entrusted to *nuncii* was the exploration of possible treaties, alliances, or *condotte*. Preparatory to his expedition beyond the Alps, for example, Henry VII sent letters to Mantua accrediting three *nuncii* and expressing his desire to bring peace to Italy.[63] The Venetian Senate in 1436, at the invitation of two Swiss nobles earlier in the service of the duke of Milan, sent a *nuncius* to explore their expressed desire to serve the Republic against Milan. If the two Swiss were really disposed to do this, they should be requested to send to Venice their own orators or *nuncii* informed of their intention and provided with a sufficient mandate.[64] Another purpose of exploratory missions might be to arrange meetings between the principals themselves. In the earlier Middle Ages final negotiations were almost always carried on by the principals, often on neutral ground, such as the middle of a bridge or a ship anchored in the middle of a river, and with elaborate safeguards against treachery. Legates going back and forth between the principals arranged such a meeting in 921 between Henry the Fowler and Charles of France on a ship in mid-Rhine.[65] This naturally remained in later centuries a task that *nuncii* executed, as when the prior of Valverde la Vega, *nuncius* of Louis IX, agreed with Henry III to a meeting of the two kings at Boulogne-sur-mer, perhaps for the purpose of

[59] *C.R. (1237-1242)*, p. 145.

[60] Rymer, *Foedera*, I, iii, 141; Chaplais, *Treaty Rolls*, I, 104, no. 243. See also Funck-Brentano, "Documents relatifs aux formes diplomatiques," pp. 370-377.

[61] ". . . quibus super quibusdam negociis que vestre serenitati volumus explicari aperuimus mentem nostram." Rymer, *Foedera*, I, ii, 194; Chaplais, *Treaty Rolls*, I, 70, no. 169.

[62] Archives du Royaume, Bruxelles, Trésor de Flandre, I, no. 2106.

[63] *Acta Imperii selecta*, J. F. Böhmer, J. Ficker, eds. (Innsbruck, 1870), p. 422, no. 593.

[64] A.S.V., Senato, Secreta, XIII, 216r (216r). A similar example, *ibid.*, IX, 51r (52r). Also the mission mentioned earlier sent by the Countess Margaret of Flanders to seek the release of her sons. Jacques de Guyse, *Annales Hannoniae*, XV, 148-162.

[65] *Regesta Imperii*, Johann Friedrich Böhmer, ed., new edn. by Mathilde Uhrlirz, II (Sächsiches Haus, 919-1024) (Graz and Koln, 1956), Part 2, p. 7.

arraigning Simon de Montfort before the court of France.[66] Providing for the safety of the principals in such confrontations was also a duty confided to *nuncii*.[67]

In the business of treating, however, it was not necessary for the *nuncius* to give way before the physical presence of the principal. It remains true that the *nuncius* could not negotiate *and* conclude without reference to the principal and the latter's specific consent to be bound. He could, however, negotiate the terms of a potential truce, treaty, or alliance, and a principal could conclude such an act through his *nuncius* just as he could through a letter. Probably the least exacting of these tasks was the prolongation of a truce, the terms of which were already agreed upon and in effect,[68] but such a prolongation is an example of a legally binding act carried out via a *nuncius*. Slightly more complex, perhaps, is the case of prorogation, to which were added requests for payments of money due, hostages to replace those that had died, and the mutual exchange of reparations for violations of the current truce.[69] Moreover, just as an existing truce could be prolonged via *nuncii*, a principal could enter into a new truce by the same means.[70] From a legal point of view, only the tentative character of a truce differentiates it from a treaty, and in the making of the latter *nuncii*, of course, also engaged. They might fulfill only the very limited function of carrying offer and counteroffer between principals who, as in the case of Philip Augustus and Philip of Alsace, count of Flanders, approached each other but did not meet, concluding their peace by means of *nuncii* going back and forth.[71] On the other hand, Edward I responded to offers of friendship from Alfonso of Castile by sending a *nuncius* not only to respond to the Spanish king, but to treat with him.[72] Naturally, such negotiation might extend through a series of missions. A letter of Henry III to the king of Bohemia in 1226 speaks of English *nuncii* who had negotiated at the Bohemian court, their return to England accompanied by an envoy from Bohemia to inform Henry of the wishes of his king, and the return of the

[66] *C.R. (1264-1268)*, p. 552; F. M. Powicke, *King Henry III and the Lord Edward*, 2 vols. (Oxford, 1947), II, 442.

[67] Rymer, *Foedera*, II, i, 38; Chaplais, *Treaty Rolls*, I, 205, no. 518.

[68] Rijksarchief, Gent, Saint-Genois, no. 1215.

[69] Having requested the above, they might prolong the truce if it seemed appropriate. Rymer, *Foedera*, IV, iv, 141-142. Full powers were definitely not granted, despite the authority to take a conclusive act.

[70] Rymer, *Foedera*, I, ii, 141.

[71] *Continuatio Claromariscensis*, to *Flandria generosa auctore monacho S. Bertini*, L. Bethmann, ed., *M.G.H.*, *SS.*, IX (Hannoverae, 1851), p. 328.

[72] He requested the king of Castile to approach Bayonne about the feast of St. John so that the English *messages* could readily find him. This reflects, I think, the exalted status of *nuncii* as representatives, especially since this particular envoy was only a clerk. Chaplais, *Treaty Rolls*, I, 75, no. 184. See also *C.R. (1251-1253)*, pp. 454-455, and *C.R. (1256-1259)*, p. 104.

Bohemian with Henry's oral response.[73] When such negotiations finally resulted in agreement of the principals, *nuncii* could conclude a pact.[74] Letters empowering a *nuncius ad tractandum* did not constitute full powers, however, and did not authorize him to conclude on the basis of his negotiations. If he were authorized in the same document *ad tractandum et complendum*, it would be a very different matter, I think, and we would no longer be speaking of a mere *nuncius*. When *nuncii* of Doge Sebastiano Ziani negotiated a treaty with William II of Sicily providing immunity for Venetian merchants in the *Regnum*, they had to refer the agreement to the doge for its completion.[75] Letters of Edward I appointing an envoy to treat with Robert Bruce, or those deputed by him specifically, advise the envoy that he must refer any agreements to the king.[76] Letters from the same king to the count of Flanders in 1313 constitute an acceptance of the terms negotiated and agreed upon between his envoys and the count.[77] While *nuncii* did not conclude agreements negotiated by themselves and not referred to their principals, they could conclude upon the basis of terms specifically formulated by their principals and only conveyed by the envoys. The Tartar *nuncii* at the Council of Lyons in 1274, for example, bore an offer in letters (in Arabic) promising 20,000 soldiers for a first attack upon the sultan of Egypt and the entire Tartar army for a second assault.[78] Upon this basis they could conclude. To take a different example, Henry III sent *nuncii* to the count of La Marche "for completing those negotiations, which have been treated between us and you by our *nuncii* and yours."[79] Negotiations were carried out by *nuncii*, the terms referred to the principals and approved by them, and the conventions could then be concluded by *nuncii*. Marriage alliances, incidentally, formed a significant portion of the conventions negotiated by *nuncii*.[80]

[73] Rymer, *Foedera*, I, i, 98.

[74] *Ibid.*, I, iii, 141; Chaplais, *Treaty Rolls*, I, 105, no. 246.

[75] Andreas Dandulo, l. 1, p. 301, in Tafel and Thomas, *Urkunden*, I, 171. Another example, *Liber Iurium reipublicae Genuensis*, I, cols. 609-614.

[76] Rymer, *Foedera*, I, iv, 145.

[77] *Ibid.*, II, i, 29.

[78] *Cronica S. Petri Erfordensis moderna*, O. Holder-Egger, ed., *M.G.H.*, *SS.*, XXX (Hannoverae, 1896), 407.

[79] Rymer, *Foedera*, I, i, 100.

[80] Ganshof, "Merowingisches Gesandtschaftswesen," 174. This is worthy of note, since we shall discuss in the next chapter the need for a special procurator or one with *libera administratio* for contracting a marriage. To avoid confusion, one must always remember that the simple *nuncius* without procuratorial powers could only negotiate *or* conclude. Alfred Löhren's statement that Gothic legates in 584 arbitrarily changed a marriage treaty to allow the intended bride to remain for a time in the house of her Frankish father is misleading at best. They did allow her to remain contrary to the covenant of the two kings, but this was at the Frankish king's demand; the legates had no choice. The covenant was not changed, but was unfulfilled.

Ratification of conventions already agreed upon by the principals might also be accomplished by *nuncii*, and this was a legally binding act, though not one requiring much discretion on the part of the envoy. Ratification, indeed, was not a formality accomplished once and for all, but was occasionally repeated to lend additional sanction to diplomatic conventions.[81] *Nuncii* also might be charged with exchanging ratifications done by the hands of the principals.[82] Confirmation of conventions was often carried out in the same ways.[83] If authorized to do so in a sufficiently specific manner *nuncii* could carry out the most solemn acts. "If indeed the principal is absent, the *nuncius* will swear on his soul that the principal has sworn that he will do such a thing and has commanded that so he should swear."[84] In the course of negotiating the Peace of Constance, the envoys of the emperor promised that Frederick "ought to swear himself or through another person to whom specifically he will give the command that he should swear on his soul."[85] No request for full powers was made, although full powers were known at this time, so I think that we may assume that the oath-takers would be mere *nuncii*. Moreover, if I correctly interpret *nominatim parabolam dabit* as "to whom he will give the word expressly," it illustrates very clearly the uses and limitations of the *nuncius*, in this activity as in others. Note that as in any other act of *nuncii* legally binding the principal a direct relationship with the principal was established. He, not the *nuncius*, would suffer the penalties of a perjurer. As the *nuncius* could swear for his principal, so he could receive oaths. The records of the relations of France and Flanders from the treaty of 1226 until Philip the Fair and Count Guy approached the point of rupture are filled with accounts of French *nuncii* receiving the oaths

---

Beiträge zur Geschichte des gesandtschaftlichen Verkehrs im Mittelalter. I. Die Zeit vom vierten bis zum Ende des neunten Jahrhunderts (Marburg, 1884), p. 74. A very brief treatment in which *Bevollmächtiger* is used very loosely. Unlike *nuncius* or *legatus*, plenipotentiary is a highly specific term. On the event of 584, see Gregory of Tours, *Historia Francorum*, Wilhelmus Arndt, ed., *M.G.H.*, *Script. rer. Mer.*, Bk. VI, Sec. 34, I, 274.

81 Ratification of an old treaty by the king of Aragon and a Genoese *nuncius*. *Liber Iurium reipublicae Genuensis*, I, cols. 883-887.

82 Rymer, *Foedera*, V, i, 157. The English ratification was delivered by "Jarretiere le Herault Roy d'Armes d'Angleterre."

83 *Liber Iurium reipublicae Genuensis*, I, cols. 152-153; A.S.V., Miscellanea di atti diplomatici e privati, busta II, no. 63. On *nuncii* of Venetians and crusaders seeking papal confirmation of their treaty in 1201, see Donald E. Queller, "Innocent III and the Crusader-Venetian Treaty of 1201," *Medievalia et humanistica*, fasc. XV (1963), 31-34.

84 "Die Dekretglossen des Cod. Stuttgart, hist. f. 419," Franz Gillman, ed., *Archiv für katholisches Kirchenrecht*, CVII (1927), p. 208, n. 1.

85 Manaresi, *Atti . . . di Milano*, p. 190, no. CXXXV. Examples abound. See Henry S. Lucas, "John of Avesnes and Richard of Cornwall," *Speculum*, XXIII (1948), 98. Despite a plethora of small errors of fact, this article has value. For an early seventh-century example: Fredegarius Scholasticus, *Chronicarum*, Bruno Krusch, ed., Book IV, Sec. 30, in *M.G.H.*, *Script. rer. Mer.* (Hannoverae, 1888), II, 132.

of relatives of the Flemish ruler and nobles and towns of Flanders guaranteeing Flemish adherence to its treaty obligations with France.[86] The same *nuncii* also could have authorization to give and receive security.[87]

Ganshof points out that from the beginning of the Middle Ages one of the important uses of *nuncii* was to summon careless or disloyal allies to the performance of their obligations.[88] In a military alliance, the partner receiving the brunt of the enemy's attack would commonly send *nuncii* to plead with his ally for the support that was his due. Thus the suffering count of Flanders in 1297 pleaded with Edward I that he embark for the continent with a military expedition—to no avail.[89] Two years later, excluded from the settlement between England and France, the count was still sending envoys to Edward to plead his cause, receiving from the king soothing words unsupported by acts.[90] A less trustful ally might seek assurance via *nuncii* from the beginning, as Philip Augustus requested renewed affirmation of King Richard's intention to go on crusade.[91] Or, if hostilities had broken out or were on the verge of doing so, *nuncii* could be sent to recall the other party to his peaceful duties.[92]

Exchange of money could also be brought about by means of *nuncii* in Roman law.[93] Just after the burial of Louis VIII, for example, Arnold of Oudenaarde and Rase of Gavere appeared before the French court on behalf of the countess of Flanders bearing the money that the late king had agreed to accept for the release of Ferrand after twelve years of captivity.[94] On occasion Flemish rulers used *nuncii* to demand the payment of

[86] Alexandre Teulet, Joseph Delaborde, and E. Berger, *Layettes du Trésor des Chartes*, 5 t. in 6 vols. (Paris, 1863-1909), II, 115, nos. 1911-1912; 331-332, no. 2476; 332, no. 2478; 342-346, nos. 2519-2556; 358-361, nos. 2591-2605; 362-371, nos. 2611-2691; 552-553, nos. 3231-3240; 600, nos. 3456-3458; 607, nos. 3476-3478. Charles Duvivier, *Les influences françaises et germaniques en Belgique au XIIIe siècle; la querelle des d'Avesnes et des Dampierres*, 2 vols. (Bruxelles, 1894), II, 70, no. XLVI. A treaty between Flanders and Holland in 1168 provided that if all the supporters of the count of Holland did not come with him for renewing his conventions, the count of Flanders would be entitled to send *nuncii* who should receive those oaths that ought to be made in his presence. Kluit, *Historia critica*, II, 190.

[87] Rymer, *Foedera*, I, i, 45.

[88] "Merowingisches Gesandtschaftswesen," 175.

[89] Rymer, *Foedera*, I, iii, 179; Chaplais, *Treaty Rolls*, I, 185, no. 460.

[90] Kervyn de Lettenhove, *Études sur l'histoire du XIIIe siècle. Recherches sur la part que l'ordre de Citeaux et le comte de Flandre prirent à la lutte de Boniface VIII et de Philippe le Bel* (Bruxelles, 1853), pp. 66–67.

[91] Delaborde, *Actes de Philippe-Auguste*, I, 319, no. 267.

[92] Rijksarchief, Gent, Saint-Genois, no. 825; Frantz Funck-Brentano, *Les origines de la Guerre de Cent Ans: Philippe le Bel en Flandre* (Paris, 1897), p. 170, n. 3. A magnificent book.

[93] Rudolf Düll, "Über Ansätze direkter Stellvertretung im fruhrepublikanischen romischen Recht," *Zeitschrift für Savigny-Stiftung für Rechtsgeschichte, Romanistische Abteilung*, LXVII (1950), 168.

[94] Philippe Mousket, *Chronique rimée*, De Reiffenberg, ed., 2 vols. (Bruxelles, 1836–1838), ll. 27495–27502. Actually, the countess herself was also present. Payments from the count of

their money fief held of England.[95] In 1193 *nuncii* of the emperor received the ransom for King Richard's deliverance.[96] This was another relatively routine task, requiring trustworthiness to be sure, since large sums of money were involved, but demanding little exercise of discretion on the part of the envoy beyond the minimum required to conform to standards of courteous behavior. Baldus pointed out that a *nuncius* dispatched for receiving money in a certain place and at a certain time could not extend the time for payment.[97] Principals might also seek loans by means of *nuncii*,[98] though the *nuncius* either had to be provided by the principal with a specific promise to pay or he could not conclude (though he might negotiate) the loan. The transfer of real property, for example the castle of Douai, could be effectuated by envoys on either side.[99] *Nuncii* could also prove useful for requesting and receiving the delivery of persons.[100]

A very delicate mission was received in 1449 by a Venetian secretary, Bertuccio Nigro, who was sent to Rome with letters of credence to the cardinal-vicechancellor (a Venetian) to seek information concerning those involved along with the king of Aragon in a plot against the Republic organized by Christoforo Chauco, a papal notary. He also had letters of credence to the pope, in case the cardinal-vicechancellor should require license to speak, and to another Venetian cardinal and Cardinal Colonna. A month later he returned to seek additional information and to ask the pope to act against Chauco. An interesting clause cautions him that if he should be approached on any other matter, he should not dare to involve himself, but should listen and inform the Ten. This mission was quite successful, and some time later another envoy was sent to try to persuade the culprit, thought to be in Siena, to come to Venice. This last mission was in vain, but the delivery of Chauco into the hands of the Venetian Republic was soon purchased. In spite of episcopal reluctance to authorize torture, this

---

Flanders to the king of Scotland in 1283 and 1284 not only illustrate the use of *nuncii* to convey such payments, but also the *ad hoc* character of medieval diplomacy. Of the three envoys who made a large payment for Count Guy at Christmastime, 1283, two were well-known Flemish subjects, the third a Scottish merchant, Henry Carwy (Carwyn, Karwin). Two months later King Alexander requested Guy to make another payment to several envoys, one of whom was the same Carwy. Archives du Nord, Lille, Chambre des Comptes, B 403, nos. 2530, 2543, and 2545. Whose envoy was he? According to medieval practice he could represent each alternately or both simultaneously. Diplomacy was not then so neatly schematic as it is now—or is thought to be.

[95] Rymer, *Foedera*, I, i, 152.

[96] *Ibid.*, I, i, 27; Chaplais, *Treaty Rolls*, I, 22, nos. 54–55.

[97] *Commentaria, D.* 45, *De verborum obligatione*, 122, par. *Callimachus*.

[98] A.S.V., Senato, Secreta, XIX, 48v (48v).

[99] Delaborde, *et al.*, *Layettes du Trésor des chartes*, II, 334, no. 2481.

[100] Rijksarchief, Gent, Chronologisch supplement, no. 192; Archives du Nord, Lille, Chambre des Comptes, B 1263, no. 3633; Mieris, *Charterboek van Holland*, I, 148.

means of persuasion was almost certainly applied, and Chauco confessed. Documents on this sordid business go on and on. Eventually, in any case, Nigro returned again to Rome to inform the pope of the case and to ask him to degrade Chauco from his clerical status and to authorize a secular trial. Certain prelates who were acceptable as papal delegates were specified. This, too, was in vain, for Nigro received a final commission to inform the pope that Chauco had died in prison of natural causes.[101]

Propagandizing, fomenting revolts, and attempting to break unfriendly alliances could also be among the functions of *nuncii*. In the formation of the League of Friuli in 1384, Venice sent *nuncii* to Friuli and other towns dependent upon that city and the church of Aquileia urging them to resist foreign encroachment. The patriarch, learning of these secret envoys, objected, but the Senate replied that they had only exhorted his subjects to support him—which appears to be true.[102] On other occasions, however, *nuncii* might be dispatched to stir up a revolt against one's enemies, as the Senate believed the *nuncii* of the duke of Milan were doing against Venice in Brescia in 1427.[103] Secret *nuncii* also were sent to try to divide enemies, as Venice tried to win Francesco Sforza away from the duke of Milan.[104] Pope Gregory IX sent a *nuncius* to Henry III to protest the alliance of the English king with the pope's archenemy Frederick II.[105]

A state which felt itself injured by another might employ *nuncii* to convey a protest, an ultimatum, or a declaration of war. Protests borne by *nuncii* against depredations, such as those caused by naval raids, were common.[106] As Ganshof has said, if conditions became bad enough a message amounting to an ultimatum could be sent via *nuncii*.[107] If relations became still worse, *nuncii* might bear letters declaring war.[108] Heralds and kings of arms in the Late Middle Ages customarily served for transmitting such messages.[109] Froissart, however, reports a declaration of war by Charles V against Edward III borne by a "varlet" of the French king, a person of such menial

[101] A.S.V., Dieci, Misti, XIII, 121v (123v)–123r (125r).

[102] The *nuncius* was instructed that if he found Sacilo already occupied he should feign some excuse for being there and return. A.S.V., Senato, Misti, XXXIX, 19r (22r)–20r (23r). Another *nuncius* sent on a propaganda mission was Gerard of Sotteghem, sent by King John to his native Flanders after Innocent III annulled the Magna Carta. Gaston Dept, *L'influence anglaise et française dans le comté de Flandre au début du XIIIe siècle* (Gand, 1928), p. 159, n. 2.

[103] A.S.V., Senato, Secreta, x, 22r (26r).

[104] *Ibid.*, x, 17r (21r).

[105] Chaplais, *Treaty Rolls*, I, 20, no. 48.

[106] E.g., Rymer, *Foedera*, I, iii, 118.

[107] "Merowingisches Gesandtschaftswesen," p. 175.

[108] *Istore et croniques de Flandre*, Kervyn de Lettenhove, ed., 2 vols. (Bruxelles, 1879–1800), I, 198. In this instance war was avoided, though the message in question amounted to a declaration of war. As in the case of other messages, a declaration of war might be returned via the *nuncius* of the other party. *Historia de expeditione Friderici*, p. 58.

[109] Ernest Nys, *Les origines du droit international* (Harlem, 1894), p. 180.

status that he professed not even to know the contents of the letters he delivered.[110] The use of such an envoy constituted a calculated insult.

From the earliest Middle Ages *nuncii* were often sent in time of war to an ally in order to coordinate efforts against the enemy.[111] In the early thirteenth century Count Ferrand of Flanders, on the brink of war with Philip Augustus, sent Baldwin of Neuport to England to ask the Flemish knights in English service to intercede with John for aid, which they did, obtaining John's promise to send the earl of Salisbury at the head of an expedition.[112] Genoa in 1440 was obligated by treaty to provide 2,000 infantry to Venice against Milan, so the Venetian Senate sent a *nuncius* to exhort and induce the Genoese to dispatch the promised aid. A final clause in the document is revealing of the status and basic function of the *nuncius*, for his mission was to be accomplished "with those words which seem appropriate to the College."[113] On another occasion the Senate invited the king of Hungary to send *nuncii* to Venetian rectors in Spoleto and Sibinico to receive *gratis* the powder for bombards that he needed against the Turks.[114]

A considerable number of envoys were sent by medieval rulers in the interests of private persons, usually, but not always, merchants. A Venetian document of 1384 instructs the notary of the Republic at the Roman court to seek a renewal of papal permission to trade with the sultan of Egypt. To achieve this end he could spend whatever was necessary.[115] Notice the discretion allowed to the notary in the matter of bribes. I find no evidence of procuratorial powers, but neither is there evidence of authority to commit Venice to anything by his own acts, for it seems that the bribes—quite naturally—were to be paid in cash on the spot. On another occasion the Great Council sent a *nuncius* to Germany, since the free movement of merchants had been impeded by the death of the king.[116] Admittedly, overly fine distinctions must be drawn to say that these missions were in the private rather than the public interest, especially in the light of the communal character of much of Venetian trade.[117] Always in fact, the two are interwoven, but some cases lean a little more clearly toward the private side. *Nuncii* were often sent to claim and receive amends for robberies, at-

[110] *Ibid.*, p. 179. Jean Froissart, *Oeuvres*, Kervyn de Lettenhove, ed., 25 vols. in 26 (Bruxelles, 1867–1877), VII, 305–308.

[111] Ganshof, "Merowingisches Gesandtschaftswesen," p. 175.

[112] *Histoire des ducs de Normandie et des rois d'Angleterre, 1181–1218*, F. Michel, ed. (Paris, 1840), p. 126; *Istore de Flandre*, I, 110.

[113] A.S.V., Senato, Secreta, XV, 16r (17r). [114] *Ibid.*, XXII, 3r (5r).

[115] A.S.V., Senato, Misti, XXXIX, 16r (19r).

[116] A.S.V., Maggior Consiglio, Capricornus, 70r (175r).

[117] Frederick C. Lane, "Venetian Merchant Galleys, 1300–1334: Private and Communal Operation," *Speculum*, XXXVIII (1963), 179–205.

tacks at sea, and other injuries inflicted upon private citizens. Even these, of course, could be freighted with public interest in forestalling a general disruption of trade.[118] Sometimes *nuncii* were sent not only to claim and receive amends, but to make reparations for damages inflicted upon the other side as well.[119] That this making of amends through *nuncii* was considered an allowance of somewhat unusual discretion to them is indicated by Edward I's appointment of two envoys to serve him in a joint inquisition with representatives of Philip IV on the mutual raiding of ships in the Channel. Edward's representatives had power to settle those things which were clear, and to refer to him those which were doubtful.[120] It is quite natural that most of these missions in the interest of private citizens should be in favor of merchants, but occasionally others, too, required such assistance. The king of Serbia in 1295 dispatched a *nuncius* to Venice to claim a *vilanus* of a certain Serbian knight who had fallen into Venetian hands.[121] The Venetian government sent so many envoys in the interests of private persons—merchants whose goods had been seized by legal process or otherwise, or who had been required to pay customs or taxes not regarded as customary, or clerics seeking preferment from the papal court, or others—that it acted as early as 1260 to restrict the number of embassies that could be sent for the affairs of private persons at the expense of the Republic.[122] Many subsequent examples exist, however, of missions sent at the expense of the interested persons or on condition that the cost of the embassy be reimbursed to the Republic out of the damages recovered.

Another important use of *nuncii* was to represent their principals acting as third parties in attempting to make peace between others. In 1295, Edward I, constructing a grand alliance against Philip IV, sent the ubiquitous Brabançon knight John of Kuik to the counts of Flanders and Holland to represent the king *viva voce oraculo* in settling their dispute.[123] A variation of this procedure is exemplified by the *nuncii* of Edward

[118] A.S.V., Maggior Consiglio, Magnus, 39v (40v); Rymer, *Foedera,* I, i, 126–127, and I, iii, 118.

[119] *C.R.* (*1227–1231*), pp. 236–237; *C.R.* (*1237–1242*), p. 530.

[120] Rymer, *Foedera,* I, iv, 31.

[121] Cessi, *Deliberazioni del Maggior Consiglio,* III, 384.

[122] *Ibid.,* II, 53.

[123] Rymer, *Foedera,* I, iii, 145; Chaplais, *Treaty Rolls,* I, 110, nos. 258–259. On John of Kuik and his international role, see D. E. Queller, "Diplomatic Personnel Employed by the Counts of Flanders in the Thirteenth Century," *Revue belge de philologie et d'histoire,* XXXIV (1956), 417–418, and Funck-Brentano, *Philippe le Bel en Flandre,* p. 491. *Nuncii* of the same king attempting to mediate between France and Castile. Chaplais, *Treaty Rolls,* I, 62, nos. 153–154; 65, no. 160; 71, no. 171. Nos. 160 and 171 also appear in Rymer, *Foedera,* I, ii, 188 and 194. A clerk of Thomas of Savoy acting as mediator. Samuel Guichenon, *Histoire généalogique de la royale maison de Savoye,* 1st edn. (Lyon, 1660), new edn. 4 t. (Turin, 1778–1780), *preuves,* no. 91.

I who requested of Alfonso of Aragon full powers for Edward to arrange a truce between Aragon and France.[124] Durandus, writing of course of papal legates, specifies opposing themselves to wars and discords as one of their functions and, on account of this, their taking cognizance of disputes between kings.[125]

The functions of the *nuncius*, as has been indicated, were as broad as the uses of letters, although as a "living letter" the *nuncius* was a somewhat more flexible instrument. Even when he had the power to conclude for his principal, a limited and specified discretion could be allowed him. Mention has already been made, however, of Baldus' denial that the *nuncius* for receiving a payment could prorogue the term, although he exempts from this prohibition a *nuncius* appointed for receiving money at any time and place.[126] A more significant illustration of the limited discretion of diplomatic *nuncii* is presented by the commission of Venetian *nuncii* to the emperor Andronicus in 1283. They were to make a truce extending between seven and ten years according to what they thought they could obtain. The conditions, however, were to be those contained in an earlier truce except for those having to do with Marco Sanuto, which were established by the Great Council. They were allowed a maximum of two months for negotiation, after which they had to return home.[127] On the other hand, *nuncii* could freely draft an entire agreement, as did those of England and Scotland in 1429 on the subject of reparations for violations of a truce, but this presumably was not binding until accepted by the principals, either by formal act or by action to fulfill it.[128] A *nuncius* surprisingly had the authority to commit to another what had been committed to him. Edward III in 1344 "opened his mind" to the earl of Derby on the subject of resuming negotiations for a marriage alliance with Castile. The earl, however, did not complete the mission, but committed it to another. The response of the Castilian king was favorable and proctors were dispatched to continue negotiations.[129]

124 Rymer, *Foedera*, I, iii, 8; Chaplais, *Treaty Rolls*, I, 80–81, no. 192.

125 Durandus, *Speculum legatorum*, p. 37. E.g., *legatus* of Innocent III attempting to make peace between Otto of Brunswick and Philip of Swabia. *Regestum Innocentii III papae super negotio Romani Imperii*, Friedrich Kempf, ed., in *Miscellanea historiae pontificiae*, XII (Roma, 1947), 336–337, no. 142; *Das Register Papst Innocenz' III. über den deutschen Thronstreit*, Walther Holtzmann, ed., 2 vols. in 1 (Bonn, 1947), pp. 201–202, no. 142. The papal legate was customarily provided with full powers and was not, therefore, a mere *nuncius*. The full powers, however, would not as a rule be necessary to the mediating function.

126 *Supra*, p. 24; *Commentaria*, *D.* 45, *De verborum obligatione*, 122, par. *Callimachus*.

127 Cessi, *Deliberazioni del Maggior Consiglio*, III, 49.

128 Rymer, *Foedera*, IV, iv, 148–149.

129 Durandus, *Speculum legatorum*, p. 36; Baldus, *Commentaria*, *D.* 17, *Mandati*, 9, par. *Si quis mandaverit*, 3. Rymer, *Foedera*, II, iv, 165–166; *C.C.R.*, *Edward III* (*1343–1346*), p. 449.

Occasionally, of course, a *nuncius* overstepped his authority, and although the principal could not be legally bound in such a case, the consequences could be serious.[130] Sometimes principals took occasion in advance to warn their envoys against overstepping their limitations, and to instruct them that they should inform the opposite party that they might undertake only the specific task committed to them.[131] From time to time, however, an envoy would exceed his instructions. This lack of restraint could be such a minor thing as the indiscretion of a papal *tabellarius*, bearing a letter from the pope to Venice concerning the negotiation of a treaty, who revealed publicly that he was bearing "good news." This and other rumors brought inquiries from the Milanese and Florentine ambassadors and forced the Senate into a premature publication of the treaty.[132] In another instance a series of documents reveals the displeasure of the Senate with Francesco Cauco for making an agreement with the king of Aragon for which he had no mandate.[133] A prudent and modest infraction of instructions, on the other hand, could even have beneficial results. Edward I reported to Adolph, king of the Romans, that the latter's *nuncius* had intimated to the English king on his own account and beyond the message entrusted to him that the day agreed upon for a meeting of the two kings was too early, and Edward therefore sent a *nuncius* to Adolph to negotiate a prorogation of the date.[134] Of course, the acts of a *nuncius* in excess of his authority could be repudiated, as in the case of Francesco Cauco just mentioned, but the repudiation of an envoy was an embarrassing and unpleasant measure. When Bologna repudiated its orator's agreement with Venice that Bologna should return to papal jurisdiction, the Senate accused that city of bad faith in making the *nuncius* the scapegoat for its own vacillation of purpose.[135]

[130] Ganshof, "Merowingisches Gesandtschaftswesen," p. 179; S. Bakhrouchine and E. Kosminski, "La diplomatie du Moyen Age," Vol. I, Part. II, *Histoire de la diplomatie*, Vladimir B. Potemkin, ed., trans. from the Russian edition of 1941 by X. Pamphilova and M. Eristov (Paris, 1946), p. 91.

[131] *The War of Saint-Sardos, 1323–1324. Gascon Correspondence and Diplomatic Documents*, Pierre Chaplais, ed., in Camden Third Series, LXXVII (London, 1954), 183.

[132] A.S.V., Senato, Secreta, XXIX, 97r (107r).

[133] The Senate repudiated his articles of agreement and ordered him not to concern himself in the matter further under severe penalties. Furthermore, ". . . valde gravamus et turbamus contra ipsum, de modo quem tenuit in tractando cum domino Rege, aliquid, absque nostro mandato vel licentia, quia manifeste fuit contra honorem et statum nostrum, et fuit causa etiam manifesta turbandi intentionem nostram, pro qua misimus dexideratum notarium nostrum." A.S.V., Senato, Misti, XXXIII, 76v (76v). Note the *pars non capta*, *ibid.*, 88r (88r). He continued to deal with the king of Aragon, and a move to impose the penalties failed to carry. *Ibid.*, 148v (148v). In fact, the Senate, recognizing the importance of the affair, authorized Cauco to treat "as it seems best to this council." *Ibid.*, 148r (148r). What actually occurred is not clear from these documents, but what is apparent is the confusion caused by the acts of a *nuncius* in excess of his authority.

[134] Chaplais, *Treaty Rolls*, I, 109, no. 254; 110–111, no. 260; Rymer, *Foedera*, I, iii, 145.

[135] A.S.V., Senato, Secreta, X, 218v (222v).

Nuncius, as has been indicated, was a very broad term meaning only someone sent from a principal to another. The *nuncius* was only an organ of communication, a living letter, who could either negotiate and report or conclude, but could not negotiate and conclude, at least not without an intervening reference to the principal and approval by him. Ceremonially, however, the *nuncius* fully represented the person of his principal, and what was done through a *nuncius* was conceived as done directly by the principal. The character and functions of the *nuncius* did not alter significantly over the centuries. The envoys described by Ganshof for the Merovingian age do not differ from the *nuncii* of the late fifteenth century. In the High and Late Middle Ages, however, a radically different diplomatic representation was introduced with the Roman law procurator and titles such as ambassador and orator were given to many *nuncii*, especially to those of high rank. Whether under the more modern titles of ambassador and orator, though, or bearing the more modest designation, the *nuncius* remained a vital alternative in diplomacy throughout the Middle Ages.

CHAPTER II

THE PROCURATOR OR PLENIPOTENTIARY

The limited flexibility of the *nuncius* was no serious handicap in a feudal age when most diplomacy was conducted by the chiefs of state, when diplomatic relations were intermittent and infrequent, and when most diplomatic dealing was with nearby neighbors. As the power, wealth, and governmental efficiency of some states increased, however, diplomatic activity became more frequent and was conducted with more distant powers. The participation of the chief of state, either personally or through the *nuncius*, who was merely an extension of the principal's will, became less practicable, and new devices had to be found for carrying on affairs of state.

After the revival of Roman law in the early twelfth century, a new instrumentality became available for diplomatic use in the form of private law procuration. The procurator was a sort of agent, useful primarily in business affairs or before a court. The identical instrument, however, gradually was found serviceable for governmental administration or diplomacy, all the more since the distinction between public and private law was blurred in the Middle Ages.[1] J. Mervyn Jones speculates that procuration came to diplomacy, not directly from the Roman law, but through Roman influence upon the canon law, and it is quite likely that he is correct.[2] In whatever fashion it was discovered, procuration clearly provided a convenient though somewhat risky solution to the pressing problems of distance and time which beset diplomacy in an age of slow transportation and poor communication so different from our own. Unlike the *nuncius*, the procurator properly empowered could negotiate *and* conclude, thus obviating the need for meetings of the chiefs of state or for an interminable succession of messages sent back and forth between principals or between negotiating

[1] Gaines Post, "Plena Potestas and Consent in Medieval Assemblies," *Traditio*, I (1943), 364, and in Gaines Post, *Studies in Medieval Legal Thought: Public Law and the State, 1100–1322* (Princeton, 1964), p. 103; Ganshof, *Le Moyen Age*, p. 270. In Roman antiquity, of course, the procurator was employed as a provincial governor. The procurator is our proxy.

[2] J. Mervyn Jones, *Full Powers and Ratification* (Cambridge, 1949), p. 68. The theme of this valuable book is that in the age of personal diplomacy from the seventeenth century until the American and French revolutions diplomatic agents armed with full powers committed their principals to formal ratification of their acts, while subsequent to the great eighteenth-century revolutions ratification became discretionary. A later chapter of the present work will deal with the question of ratification in the Middle Ages.

nuncii and principals who had to approve specifically any acts concluded by their representatives. The usefulness of procuration is stressed in an English document of 1235: "... because many things can arise unexpectedly which need a rapid solution and recourse can not easily be had to us concerning the matters touching us in this country."[3]

When procuration first was used for diplomatic envoys is not exactly clear, although it became increasingly common in the latter part of the twelfth century. What is apparent after checking the sources is that a number of references by secondary authorities to procurators or plenipotentiaries from the Merovingian age until the late twelfth century cannot bear scrutiny. Löhren refers to reception of brides through full powers by the Merovingians, but the chronicles cited show no evidence of *plena potestas*, and, as we have seen, marriage alliances could be concluded by simple *nuncii*.[4] Menzel cites the use of *libera potestas* for *missi dominici* of Louis the Pious, but the document in question shows no trace of Roman law forms, but only general instructions.[5] Löhren also cites examples of *Vollmachten* in the late ninth and early tenth centuries, attributing them specifically to Roman-Byzantine influence, but again full powers cannot be documented, even though the *legati* and *missi* concerned did take oaths.[6] Nor is a basis found for Luchaire's statement that Mannases, bishop of Orléans, added full powers to the letters of credence of Louis VII for the Count of Champagne, emissary to Barbarossa in 1162,[7] although this approaches the date that we should expect *plena potestas* to appear in diplomatic documents. Armingaud also wrongly refers to a Byzantine *nuncius* sent as a plenipotentiary to Venice in 1171 or 1172 with returning *legati* of Doge Vitale Michieli II.[8] As late as the Third Crusade we find Barbarossa seeking an envoy from the sultan to treat of peace with him, but failing to specify that such a representative should possess full powers.[9] A few years later

[3] Chaplais, *Treaty Rolls*, I, 25, no. 65.

[4] Löhren, *Geschichte des gesandtschaftlichen Verkehrs*, pp. 74–75; Gregory of Tours, *Historia Francorum*, II, 28; Fredegarius, *Chronicarum*, IV, 30.

[5] Victor Menzel, *Deutsches Gesandtschaftswesen in Mittelalter* (Hanover, 1892), p. 38; *Capitularia regum Francorum*, in *M.G.H.*, *Capit.*, A. Boretius and V. Krause, eds. (Hannoverae, 1883–1897), I, 308–309, no. 151.

[6] Löhren, *Geschichte des gesandtschaftlichen Verkehrs*, p. 76; Hincmar of Rheims, *Annales*, in *M.G.H.*, *SS.*, I (Hannoverae, 1826), 475; *Annales Fuldensis*, *M.G.H.*, *SS.*, I, 388, 415.

[7] Achille Luchaire, "Louis VII—Philippe Auguste—Louis VIII," in *Histoire de France*, Ernest Lavisse, ed. (Paris, 1901), III, i, 41. At any rate, full powers are not indicated by the following sources: Hugo Pictavinus, *Historia Vizeliacensis monasterii*, Martin Bouquet, ed., in *H.F.*, XII, 329–330; *Epistolae illustrium virorum, clericorum vel laicorum ab a. 1060 ad a. 1180*, la Congrégation de S. Maure, ed., in *H.F.*, XVI, 30.

[8] J. Armingaud, *Venise et le Bas-Empire: Histoire des relations de Venise avec l'Empire d'Orient*, extrait: *Des archives des missions scientifiques et litteraires*, T. IVe–2e sér. (Paris, 1868), p. 100. The quotation in note 1 does not substantiate full powers.

[9] *Historia de expeditione Friderici*, p. 84.

Henry VI invested Milanus, judge and procurator of Verona, and Thebaldus, consul of Verona, with Garda, empowering them to place Verona in possession. Böhmer refers to them as *Bevollmächtigen*, but only the word "procurator" indicates this, and in context it is clear that "procurator" is the title of an office in Verona.[10] Armingaud, followed by the learned Baschet, again falsely reports plenipotentiaries of the Byzantine emperor in 1198.[11]

These premature discoveries of the diplomatic plenipotentiary do not belie the existence of procurators for other purposes from about mid-eleventh century.[12] In the 1060's and 1070's evidence appears of full powers in the hands of papal *legati, missi*, and *apocrisarii*.[13] These, however, do not seem to have received diplomatic missions. Venetians and undoubtedly others were clearly employing *plena potestas* in private documents by the 1160's and probably much earlier.

If procuration was found useful in private and ecclesiastical affairs, discovery of its utility in diplomacy cannot have lagged far behind. After all, truces, treaties, and alliances are merely special forms of conventions or contracts,[14] and if procurators could enter into private contracts for their principals (as they could), they could also enter into public conventions. And so in practice we find the bishop of Novara entering into an alliance with the Milanese in 1167 through his procurator.[15] In 1170 a *legatus* of Genoa received *potestatem et mandatum* to treat and to come to an agreement with Manuel Comnenus under the promise that Genoa would support any convention to which he would swear. He did make the treaty and swear to it, and promised that the archbishop, consuls, and commune of Genoa would also swear to maintain it.[16] Though the documentation does not happen to include the word "procurator," there is no doubt that

10 Böhmer–Ficker, *Acta Imperii selecta*, pp. 171-173, nos. 184-186.

11 Armingaud, *Venise et le Bas–Empire*, pp. 124–127. He simply translated the *nuncii* and *missi* in his Latin footnote into French *plenipotentiaires*. Armand Baschet, *Les archives de Venise: Histoire de la Chancellerie Secrète* (Paris, 1870), pp. 393–394.

12 *Die Urkunden Heinrichs III*, H. Bresslau and P. Kehr, eds., in *M.G.H., Dipl. reg. imp. Germ.*, v, 242, 390. The first document dated 1047 is taken from a late fifteenth- or early sixteenth-century copy, and an anachronism could have crept in, but the second dated 1052 is printed from the original document.

13 Cosmas of Prague, *Chronica Boemorum*, pp. 124–125 and 124, n. 2. For stronger and fuller evidence, see Schmutz, "The Foundations of Medieval Papal Representation," pp. 160–219.

14 *D.* 2, 14, 5 and *Casus* in *Glossa ordinaria* to *lex* 5; Post, "Plena Potestas in Medieval Assemblies," p. 366, and Post, *Medieval Legal Thought*, pp. 104–105.

15 Manaresi, *Atti . . . di Milano*, p. 86, no. LVII.

16 *Liber Iurium reipublicae Genuensis*, I, cols. 252–255, CCLXXX. Post concluded that "true corporate proctorial representation" began with Innocent III's summons of procurators from six cities of the March of Ancona to his Curia in 1200. "Roman Law and Early Representation in Spain and Italy, 1150–1250," *Speculum*, XVIII (1943), 211–232. He undoubtedly had in mind political representation, but diplomatic procuratorial representation of a corporate body is at least an interesting forerunner.

the Genoese envoy was precisely that. Frederick Barbarossa's truce of Alessandria in 1175 appears to have been made by procurators of the Lombard League and his other foes.[17] The protocol of the Peace of Constance summarizes Barbarossa's letters, typical of subsequent procurations, granting to his so-called *nuncii* full powers to treat and to conclude a peace and promising to hold firm whatever they swore and to incorporate it in letters sealed with the emperor's seal.[18] It is less clear, but very likely, that the duke of Burgundy possessed full powers for the treaty he made with Genoa for the transportation of Philip Augustus to the Holy Land.[19] Post speculates that the use of procurators for diplomacy spread to the North from Italy, the seat of the revival of Roman law,[20] and so it would seem. All the examples cited above represent either Italian procurators or conventions made in Italy. The first purely northern example I have is that of English envoys empowered to treat and conclude the peace with France in 1193.[21] Otto IV added a Roman law *ratihabitio* clause to the letters borne by his *legati* to the pope in 1198.[22] Although the evidence is somewhat scanty and, in many cases, full powers seem tacked onto the letters of credence of the primitive *nuncius, plena potestas* became well known before the end of the twelfth century. As a sort of landmark in the development of diplomatic plenipotentiaries stands the mission of Geoffrey of Villehardouin and his fellow *messages* on behalf of the chiefs of the Fourth Crusade in 1201. Endowed with *plain pooir*, they stand in marked contrast to *nuncii* with sharply limited discretionary powers. Geoffrey of Villehardouin and his colleagues—not their principals—decided that Venice was the maritime power with which they should treat, and they negotiated and concluded upon terms unforeseen by their principals. They redacted and swore to their treaty, sent it off to the pope to be confirmed, and borrowed money to implement it, all without referring their actions to their principals

17 They acted *vice et nomine omnium civitatum et locorum et personarum societatis Lombardie, Marchie, Venetie et Romanie* to conclude the truce. Manaresi, *Atti . . . di Milano*, p. 133, no. XCIV.

18 *Ibid.*, pp. 191–193, no. CXXXVI; Menzel, *Deutsches Gesandtschaftswesen*, p. 15.

19 *Liber Iurium reipublicae Genuensis*, cols. 355-356, CCCLXXII; summarized in Delaborde, *Actes de Philippe Auguste*, I, 354, no. 292.

20 Post, "Plena Potestas in Medieval Assemblies," pp. 366–367, and Post, *Medieval Legal Thought*, p. 106.

21 We do not have the letters of procuration, but the envoys acted *ex parte regis* by virtue of letters containing a *ratihabitio* clause. Roger of Hoveden, *Chronica*, W. Stubbs, ed., in *R.S.* no. 51, 4 vols. (London, 1868–1871), III, 217.

22 Kempf, *Regestum super negotio Imperii*, pp. 10–13, no. 3. Also printed in Holtzmann, *Register über den Thronstreit*, pp. 13–14, no. 3. This reference was called to my attention by Richard Schmutz, although I had already discovered it in an earlier printing. *Constitutiones et acta regum Germanicarum*, in *M.G.H., LL.*, II, 204; Menzel, *Deutsches Gesandtschaftswesen*, p. 16.

for approval.[23] The advantages and the risks of procuratorial diplomacy should be apparent.

Since the procurator was to become such an important instrument in diplomacy, and since it is from the procurator that the ambassador plenipotentiary derives, it is necessary to examine the nature of procuration in considerable detail. The basic definition by Ulpian is found in the *Digest*: "A procurator is he who administers the affairs of another by the mandate of the principal."[24] It is a term taken from private law, in which the procurator had a great variety of uses. One of these, the management of the property of the emperors, probably served as the transition from the use of procurators in private law to their use in public law as governors of imperial provinces.[25]

Naturally with the revival of Roman law the medieval legists and canonists gained knowledge of procuration. The great Irnerius, oddly enough, changes the definition drawn from the Justinian compilation: "A procurator, indeed, is he who administers the affairs of another, the principal permitting."[26] Other early legists, however, borrow directly from the *Digest*.[27] Under the influence of the legists, canonists also wrote of procurators. Bernard of Pavia repeated what amounted to Ulpian's definition and added a distinction between general and special procurators. He also remarked that there are those who are admitted as procurators without a mandate, and that the effect of procuration is that what is done with the procurator should be regarded as if it were done with the principal.[28] William of Drogheda and Tancred also provide variants of the basic definition.[29] Rich-

[23] See my article, "L'évolution du rôle de l'ambassadeur: Les pleins pouvoirs et le traité de 1201 entre les Croisés et les Vénitiens," *Le Moyen Age*, LXVII (1961), 479–501, for a detailed analysis of the making of the treaty.

[24] *D.* 3, 3, 1.

[25] Herbert F. Jolowicz, *Historical Introduction to Roman Law* (Cambridge, 1952), pp. 348–350.

[26] Irnerius, *Summa Codicis*, Hermann H. Fitting, ed. (Berlin, 1894), 2, 7, *De procuratoribus*, p. 31.

[27] *Petri exceptionum legum Romanorum appendices*, in *Juristische Schriften des früheres Mittelalters*, Hermann H. Fitting, ed. (Halle, 1876), c. 67, p. 162; *Libellus de verbis legalibus*, in *Juristische Schriften des früheres Mittelalters*, c. 29, p. 192. Azo added that the service must be gratuitous. *Summa*, 2, 13 (*De procuratoribus*), col. 85. This was true of mandate in classical law, not of procuration, but before the time of the composition of the *Digest*, mandate and procuration had become confused. Alan Watson, *Contract of Mandate in Roman Law* (Oxford, 1961), p. 8.

[28] Bernardus Papiensis, *Summa Decretalium*, E.A.T. Laspeyres, ed., 1st edn., 1860, reprint (Graz, 1956), 1, 29, 1 and 7, p. 24.

[29] William of Drogheda, *Summa aurea*, XCIX, in *Quellen zur Geschichte des römisch-kanonischen Processes im Mittelalter*, Ludwig Wahrmund, ed., 5 vols. (Innsbruck, 1905–1931), II, ii, 94; Tancred, *Ordo iudiciarius*, 1, 6, 1, in *Pillii, Tancredi, Gratiae libri de iudiciorum ordine*, Fridericus Bergmann, ed. (Gottingae, 1842), p. 114. Tancred has simply incorporated *D.* 3, 3, 1, 1, in the basic definition of *D.* 3, 3, 1.

ard the Englishman, thinking only of those involved in the judicial process, defines a procurator as one who sues or is sued in the name of another.[30] Later canonists present various combinations of the elements already mentioned. The extension of the institution of procuration can also be traced in vulgar law in the *Établissements* of Saint Louis, which cite the basic definition of the Justinian corpus.[31]

Many of the variations in the definitions of the procurator can be comprehended when it is understood that procuration as defined in the sixth century stands at the end of some hundreds of years of evolution, which, like all historical evolutions, followed the obscure logic of the social arena rather than the more clearly structured logic of the schools. The oldest form of procuration was a general representation in all property rights by a friend or a freedman.[32] *Mandatum* was a much more specific form of representation, but over the years relatively broad mandates tended to resemble relatively restricted procurations. With the introduction of the *procurator ad litem*, whose single judicial function made him more akin to a mandatory than a procurator, the *actio mandati* made its appearance in the realm of procuration. Probably on the analogy of the *procurator ad litem*, a *procurator unius rei* was introduced beside the *procurator omnium bonorum*, and the *actio mandati* was also given in this case. At some uncertain point, perhaps even before the development of the *procurator unius rei*, the *actio mandati* was also given against the *procurator omnium bonorum*. By the time of Justinian, mandate and procuration were joined for practical purposes.[33] The variations of medieval legists and canonists on *D*. 3, 3, 1 stem from passages containing reflections of the pre-Justinian law.

A procurator could be appointed personally, by mean of a *nuncius*, or by a letter.[34] This is of considerable interest for the diplomatic use of procuration, especially as emissaries tended to remain on their missions for longer periods of time and eventually became residents. Increasingly in the fourteenth and fifteenth centuries, procurations could not be given personally, for the procurator was already abroad. During this period the

30 Ricardus Anglicus, *Summa de ordine iudiciario*, XVIII, in Wahrmund, *Quellen*, II, iii, 19. Notice that *agere* and *convenire*, however, have common meanings, as well as specific legal ones.

31 *Les Établissements de Saint Louis*, II, ix, Paul Viollet, ed., 4 vols. (Paris, 1881–1886), II, 345.

32 Leopold Wenger, *Institutes of the Roman Law of Civil Procedure*, trans. by Otis H. Fisk from the German edition of 1925 (New York, 1940), p. 91.

33 Watson, *Mandate*, p. 60. Considerations such as these caused F. Serrao to reconstruct *D*. 3, 3, 1, contending that in classical law reference to the mandate of the principal should be omitted, and that the passage should read: "A procurator is he who administers the affairs of another as if he were the principal." *Il Procurator* (Milano, 1947), pp. 13, 19. It is interesting that Irnerius substituted *domino permittente* for *mandatu domini* of *D*. 3, 3, 1.

34 *D*. 3, 3, 1, 1; *Pauli Sententiae*, 1, 3, 1, quoted in Watson, *Mandate*, p. 44.

phrase *licet absentem* appears again and again in the Venetian procurations or *sindicati.*

By any of these means, then, a principal could instruct and authorize his procurator to do something for him. This was the procurator's *raison d'être,* and he was held to execute his mandate faithfully, not only with that diligence which he would bring to his own affairs, but more.[35] He was put in the place of the principal to act for him.[36]

The nature of the procurator is most easily made clear to American readers by substituting the word "attorney"—understood in its broadest significance, and not as coterminous with "lawyer."[37] The *Oxford English Dictionary* declares that "attorney" comes from the Old French *atorné,*[38] a word which can be found in diplomatic parlance, as well as other contexts. In an English-Burgundian confederation of 1297, Burgundian envoys are called *les procureours ou les attornes.*[39] A diplomatic procuration of Edward II in 1312 also empowers his *attournez et Procurours* to deal with Robert of Flanders.[40] A nondiplomatic papal letter of 1259 addressed to Henry III speaks of "a procurator, who in your court is called in the vulgar tongue attorney."[41] A number of diplomatic documents written in Latin prior to the French examples cited use procurator and attorney as synonyms. They come not only from England, but from Flanders and Brabant.[42] These cast no doubt upon the Old French provenance of the word, however, for Latin remained the language of Western European diplomacy until almost the end of the thirteenth century, and then only a few documents written in French (or German or Dutch) appear among those written north of the Alps. Latin retained its strong predominance in Italian diplomacy until the fifteenth century.

[35] Hostiensis, *Summa super titulis Decretalium* (Lugduni, 1548), 1, t. *De procuratoribus, Ad quid teneatur.*

[36] Such expressions as *metoms en nostre liu* are common in diplomatic procurations. Limburg–Stirum, *Codex diplomaticus Flandriae,* I, 210-211, no. 64. Also *Lieutenantz ou Procureurs.* Rymer, *Foedera,* III, iv, 96.

[37] Du Cange gives *procurator* as a synonym for *attornatus.*

[38] *O.E.D.,* I, 553.

[39] Chaplais, *Treaty Rolls,* I, 132–133, no. 354.

[40] Rymer, *Foedera,* II, i, 19.

[41] *Ibid.,* I, ii, 45.

[42] *Ibid.,* I, iii, 46 (in which *negotiorum gestor* is also equated with *attornatus* and *procurator*); Rymer, *Foedera,* Record Commission edition (London, 1816–1869), I, ii, 791 (This document of 2 August 1293 is not found in the Hague edition normally cited here); Reiffenberg, *et al., Monuments,* I, 272, 276–277; *Acta Imperii, Angliae et Franciae ab anno 1267 ad annum 1313,* Fritz Kern, ed. (Tübingen, 1911), p. 74, no. 106. Jean de Sturler discusses *attornati et procuratores* acting as legal and business representatives of Brabançon merchants in England. One, in fact, was a *procuratrix et attornata. Les relations politiques et les échanges commerciaux entre le duché de Brabant et l'Angleterre au Moyen Age* (Paris, 1936), pp. 264-266. The *Modus tenendi parliamentum* in discussing the lay commons describes the elected members as *attornati.* Maude V. Clarke, *Medieval Representation and Consent* (London, 1936), p. 200.

A number of terms which, unlike "attorney," were not synonymous or at least not originally synonymous with "procurator" appear along with the latter or in its place in diplomatic documents. Aegidius de Fuscararius states that a person could act *per se* or through a procurator or a syndic. Sometimes *yconomi*, *actores*, or *defensores* are also used, though they rarely occur.[43] To avoid confusion a brief explanation of these terms will be useful. The syndic, who represents a corporate body (*universitas*) and not an individual person or prelate, is the most significant of these.[44] Corporate representation accounts, of course, for the common appearance of the syndic in the diplomacy of the city-republics of Italy. This was not a regional usage, but a proper legal one, for when a diplomatic plenipotentiary was appointed by a prince like the Duke of Milan or the Marquis of Ferrara, he was called procurator.[45] Another term occasionally seen is *actor*. The actor is distinguished from the procurator and the syndic, because he was appointed for only one cause, while a procurator or syndic might have a less limited authority.[46] The *defensor* was the counterpart of the *actor* for defense. That a somewhat meaningful distinction existed in the early thirteenth century is indicated by Henry III's request of 1219 that if his appointees should not be admitted before Pandulf as procurators, they should be admitted as *actors*.[47] An *oeconomus* represented a secular church, but this is not an important term. Slightly different connotations are given by such titles as *tractatores*, *compositores*, *ordinatores*, and others.[48] Terms which are not—as the lawyer would say—words of art also appear along with the others mentioned above. Such words as *vicarius*, *vicecomes*, and *vicegerens* are merely descriptive of the procurator's role.[49]

In medieval law the distinction between these various forms of representation did not last long. Although Tancred (who died before 1236) recognizes the distinction, he also declares that "the canon calls all such persons procurators."[50] Gratia Aretinus, writing somewhat later, states that Tancred

[43] Aegidius de Fuscararius, *Ordo iudiciarius*, 168, in Wahrmund, *Quellen*, III, i, 239.

[44] True of a prelate acting *suo nomine*. Otto von Gierke, *Das deutsche Genossenschaftsrecht*, 1st edn., 1881, reprinted, 4 vols. (Graz, 1954), III, 205 and 232, n. 145. William of Drogheda, *Summa aurea*, CXLVIII, in Wahrmund, *Quellen*, II, ii, 177.

[45] A.S.M., Registri ducali, no. 183, 3v (6)–4r (7); A.S.V., Senato, Secreta, R (E), 62r. Venice habitually and correctly referred to its own procurators as syndics.

[46] *D.* 3, 4, 6, 1; *Glossa ordinaria, D.* 3, 4, 1, par *quibus*, ad v. *syndicum*.

[47] Rymer, *Foedera*, I, i, 76–77.

[48] *Lettres de rois, reines, et autres personnages des Cours de France et d'Angleterre depuis Louis VII jusqu'à Henri IV tirés des archives de Londres par Brequigny*, J. J. Champollion-Figeac, ed., I (Paris, 1839), 334.

[49] Boncompagnus, *Rhetorica novissima*, 3, 2, A. Gaudenzi, ed., in *Bibliotheca juridica Medii Aevi*, Augustus Gaudentius, ed., 3 vols. (Bononiae, 1888–1901), II, 259; Rijksarchief, Gent, Saint-Genois, no. 868.

[50] Tancred, *Ordo iudiciarius*, 1. 7, 4 (pp. 125–126) and 3, 2, 4 (p. 205) in Bergmann, *Libri de iudiciorum ordine*.

had shown the differences among the procurator, syndic, and *actor*, "but today there does not seem to be any difference other than verbal."[51] Thus a gradual amalgamation took place and the ground was prepared for the well-known declaration of Hostiensis: "But according to our laws it is plain that we do not give great force to names, for whether he is called procurator, or syndic, or *economus*, or ass, or even if no name is expressed, it doesn't matter as long as the mind of the person constituting him is clear."[52] This colorfully expressed doctrine prevailed. Nonetheless the clerks who composed diplomatic documents continued to pile redundancy upon redundancy—*ambassiatores, oratores, procuratores, commissarios, actores, factores, negotiorum gestores et nuncios speciales.*[53] To be sure that no applicable title would be left out, the clerk sometimes added "and by whatever name he can better be called."[54] This phrase, in fact, became standard in Venetian procurations.

The interchangeability of procurator and attorney is further emphasized by the fact that, as in Anglo-American law there are attorneys-at-law and attorneys-in-fact, in Roman law and canon law there are procurators *litis* and *negotiorum*. All Romanists agree that originally the only procurator was the *procurator omnium bonorum*, whose responsibility it was to look after the property interests of his principal. It is sharply debated whether or not the *procurator litis* was classical,[55] a debate into which it would be presumptuous and useless to enter. Procurators for legal representation before a court and for conducting other affairs were both recognized in the period of concern to us. We also find mention of a third type *ad impetrandum.*[56] The belief of several modern writers that diplomatic procurators were originally and predominately representatives at law is harmful to an understanding of diplomatic procedure.[57] It is the *procurator negotiorum*, as a matter of fact, with which diplomacy is almost always concerned. The *procurator litis* was appointed for such purposes as suing and being sued,

[51] Gratia Aretinus, *Summa de iudiciario ordine*, 1, 8, 2, in Bergmann, *Libri de iudiciorum ordine*, p. 348; Gierke, *Das deutsches Genossenschaftsrecht*, III, 341, n. 303.

[52] Hostiensis, *Summa*, 1, *De procuratoribus*, rubric, *quis dicatur procurator.*

[53] Rymer, *Foedera*, IV, iv, 187.

[54] Böhmer–Ficker, *Acta Imperii selecta*, p. 690, no. 985.

[55] Serrao, following Frese, takes the negative. *Il Procurator*, p. 17. Buckland finds it difficult to accept this view. W. W. Buckland, *A Textbook of Roman Law from Augustus to Justinian*, 2nd edn. (Cambridge, 1932), p. 709, n. 9. Watson accepts it as classical, but not early—"some time before Julian." *Mandate*, pp. 9, 60.

[56] Johannes Bononiensis, *Summa notarie*, p. 605. I have not seen this work, but owe the reference to Professor Post. Rudolf von Heckel contrasts the procurator *ad impetrandum*, functioning before the papal chancery, to the *procurator ad agendum* or *ad causas*, functioning before the court. "Das Aufkommen der ständigen Prokuratoren an der päpstlichen Kurie im 13 Jht.," *Miscellanea Francesco Ehrle*, II (Roma, 1924), p. 313.

[57] Cuttino, *English Diplomatic Administration*, pp. 86–87; Ganshof, *Le Moyen Age*, pp. 270, 275–276.

responding, contesting, taking appropriate oaths in court, making exceptions, replicating, introducing witnesses, hearing sentence, appealing, and the like. This is not the stuff of which diplomacy is made. *Procuratores litis* are occasionally found in legal proceedings which are closely related to diplomacy, such as the litigation over the legitimacy of the two broods of Margaret of Flanders, the D'Avesnes and the Dampierres, or the English procurators in Paris contesting the possession of disputed lands.[58] Or, conversely, they may be found engaged in diplomatic activity which borders upon judicial. Such were the procurators of Flanders and Hainaut in late 1293 and early 1294 appearing before *enquêteurs* of Philip to argue concerning infractions of the truce achieved through the intervention of the king.[59] Procurators appearing before arbitrators of interstate disputes also partook of this judicial character.[60] These mark the exception, however, and not the rule.

A procurator could be appointed for one specific task or for all the affairs of his principal, for a specific time, for an indefinite time, or in perpetuity.[61] One appointed for a specific task or for a specific time was known as a special procurator, otherwise he was a general procurator.[62] Of course, the general procurator was earlier. The *procurator unius rei* may have been introduced by analogy with the *procurator litis*. At any rate, the date of its acceptance is another of those problems debated among Romanists.[63]

There were a great many things that a general procurator *per se* could not do. He could not alienate the goods of his principal.[64] He could not discharge a debt, nor enter into a composition upon a disputed debt, nor settle a disputed claim by *transactio*.[65] He could not enter into any pact,

[58] Duvivier, *Influences*, II, 48, no. CXCIX; Rijksarchief, Gent, Chronologisch supplement, no. 246; Archives du Nord, Lille, B 1266, no. 4200; Chaplais, *Treaty Rolls*, I, 190, no. 475.

[59] "Recueil de documents inédits relatifs aux relations du Hainaut et de la France de 1280 à 1297," Etienne Delcambre, ed., *Bulletin de la Commission Royale d'Histoire*, XCII (1928), 75–99, nos. XXV-XXVI; Rijksarchief, Gent, Saint-Genois, no. 697.

[60] E. Poncelet, "La guerre dite 'de la Vache de Ciney,'" *Bulletin de la Commission Royale d'Histoire*, 5e sér., III (1893), 292-293; A.S.V., Senato, Misti, XXVIII, 92v (92v).

[61] *D.* 3, 3, 1, 1; *D.* 3, 3, 1, 3–4.

[62] Magister Arnulphus, *Summa minorum*, L, in Wahrmund, *Quellen*, I, ii, 52–53. A similar distinction is made between special and general agents in Anglo-American law. *Black's Law Dictionary*, 1st edn., 1891, 4th edn. (St. Paul, 1951), *agent*, p. 86.

[63] Serrao, following Albertario, holds the distinction to be postclassical. *Il Procurator*, pp. viii, 15, 18–19; Watson declares this false, fixing the introduction by the time of Paul. *Mandate*, p. 60.

[64] *D.* 3, 3, 63; Rogerius, *Summa Codicis*, II, viii, G. B. Palmieri, ed., in Gaudenzi, *Bibliotheca juridica*, I, 29.

[65] *Glossa ordinaria, Decret. Greg. IX*, 1, 3, 28 (*Nonnulli*), ad v. *speciali mandato*; Magister Arnulphus, *Summa minorum*, in Wahrmund, *Quellen*, I, ii, 54; William of Drogheda, *Summa aurea*, in Wahrmund, *Quellen*, II, ii, 100; *D.* 3, 3, 60; Rogerius, *Summa Codicis*, II, viii, in Gaudenzi, *Bibliotheca juridica*, I, 29; *Glossa ordinaria*, *C.* 2, 13, 10, ad v. *plenum; Decret. Greg. IX*, 9, 1, 43, 9; *Sext.* 1, 19, 4; Durandus, *Speculum juris*, 1, 3, 1, 4–5.

and most specifically not into a marriage contract, a peace, or an arbitration.[66] Taking or receiving an oath was forbidden.[67] In fact, it is rather difficult to perceive what a general procurator could do that would be of much concern to diplomacy. General procurations are very rare.[68] Some that are called general are not. For example, the commune of Frosinone granted *liberum et generale mandatum* to *sindicos, procuratores, actores et nunptios speciales*[69] to submit their castle to the pope's jurisdiction and protection. The document goes on to grant them *liberum et generale mandatum* for making pacts, provisions of whatever kind, obligations and conventions with the pope.[70] This is probably not really a general mandate, although even if it is, by virtue of its *liberum et generale mandatum* it does not fall under the prohibitions just listed. It seems that the clerks were deliberately confusing the two types. By mid-fifteenth century the *Foedera* contains example after example of the phrase *mandatum tam generale quam speciale.*

What made procuration a valuable instrument for diplomacy was that a procurator with *plena potestas* could negotiate and conclude. What was done by a procurator had exactly the status in law as if it had been done by the principal.[71] Post has shown that the plenipotentiary *per se* was regarded as *sufficienter instructus*, and did not need to refer to his principal.[72] From time to time diplomatic procurations contain expressions like *super hiis finaliter concordandum*,[73] although such words were not necessary to grant conclusive authority to a properly empowered procurator. Mention has already been made of the *plain pooir* of the crusader-envoys of 1201. Sent merely to obtain transportation for the crusading army, they accepted Enrico Dandolo's offer of active Venetian participation in the crusade in return for a share of the conquests. They concluded a treaty on this basis, sent it to Rome for confirmation, and borrowed money to carry it out. The account

[66] Durandus, *Speculum juris*, 1, 3, 4–5; *Sext.* 1, 19, 4; *D.* 3, 3, 60; *Decret. Greg. IX*, 9, 1, 43, 9; *Coutumes d'Anjou et du Maine*, F, 260, K, 120, quoted in J. Fourgous, *L'arbitrage dans le droit français aux XIIIe et XIVe siècles* (Paris–Toulouse, 1906), p. 75, n. 3.

[67] Durandus, *Speculum juris*, 1, 3, 1, 4–5; *Sext.* 1, 19, 4.

[68] A.S.V., Sindicati, I, 24r. A general procuration for a *sindicum, procuratorem et nuncium specialem* (in spite of this last, it is a general procuration, I think) in the Roman *curia.* It is basically for nondiplomatic affairs.

[69] This bastard term *nunptios speciales* generally seems to indicate a special procurator, although the procuration cited in n. 71 may be general. The term does not, in any case, appear to designate a *nuncius* as contrasted to a procurator.

[70] Archivio secreto vaticano, AA. Arm. I-XVIII, no. 3699.

[71] *Sext.* 5, 12, *De regulis juris*, 72; *Bernardi Summa Decretalium*, 1, 29, p. 24.

[72] "Plena Potestas," pp. 383–407, and *Medieval Legal Thought*, pp. 127–160. A procuration of Henry III in 1255 reads: "nuncios nostros proprios super premissis sufficienter instructos cum plena potestata (*sic*) vobiscum super hiis ex parte nostra tractandi plenius et expendiendi omnia predicta, prout inter vos et nuncios nostros convenire poterit, ad vestram presentiam transmittemus . . ." *C.R.* (*1254-1256*), p. 376. The words *sufficienter instructos*, however, were not at all necessary.

[73] Rymer, *Foedera*, II, iv, 14, and v, i, 47.

of Villehardouin, a member of the embassy and its spokesman, proves conclusively that the principals had no knowledge of what their envoys were doing until their return, nor did they expect any. Responsible representatives had been empowered at their discretion to make covenants binding upon their principals, and they did so.[74] The crusader-Venetian treaty of 1201 is an early and spectacular example of the conclusive nature of *plena potestas*, but it is by no means isolated. For example, the English king ordered his constable of Bordeaux to make payments to allies which he hoped to gain through the negotiations of envoys he was then dispatching with full powers. The procurators would inform the constable directly of the amounts to be paid without reference to the king.[75] In another instance, the king commanded his ministers and subjects in Aquitaine to be obedient to agreements which might be made by his plenipotentiaries with the king of France.[76] The value of envoys possessing power to negotiate and conclude was inestimable in this period of slow communications. Without *plena potestas* an envoy either had to return to his own government or he had to send messengers as the situation developed. This was the handicap under which ancient and earlier medieval diplomacy had labored.[77] The intensification of diplomatic activity in the High and Late Middle Ages lent itself readily to a more flexible pattern. Full powers were requested of the opposite party,[78] and where they should have been granted and were not, complaints were likely to follow.[79]

Extreme freedom of the procurator to bind his principal by his own discretionary act was more common in the thirteenth century than later. In procuration a device had been discovered which obviated slow-moving negotiations through *nuncii*. As diplomatic activity intensified in the fourteenth and fifteenth centuries, as communications between principals and representatives became more frequent, and as resident representatives became separated by miles and months from the minds of their principals, this freedom was restricted. Full powers continued to be granted, but the discretion allowed to the envoy was usually more limited.

The procurator did not possess the same representative character as the *nuncius*, although in a somewhat different sense he was a representative. The question is confusing for two reasons: (1) the concept of representation is not easily definable, and (2) the evidence is not entirely consistent.

In a passage immediately following upon the one quoted in the previous

[74] Queller, "L'évolution du rôle de l'ambassadeur," pp. 479–501.

[75] Rymer, *Foedera*, II, ii, 95.

[76] Chaplais, *Treaty Rolls*, I, 255–256, no. 652; Rymer, *Foedera*, II, ii, 134.

[77] Harold Nicolson, *The Evolution of Diplomatic Method* (London, 1954), p. 11. I believe that Menzel, *Deutsches Gesandtschaftswesen*, pp. 13–14, is quite wrong on this point.

[78] A.S.V., Senato, Secreta, XIII, 67v (67v).

[79] Rymer, *Foedera*, I, i, 132; I, iii, 69.

chapter, Sohm gives his definition of representation. It is not entirely satisfactory, but it is useful in bringing out the factors to be considered.

> Suppose, however, that in employing another to do business for me, I have no intention of concluding the transaction myself. In that case, I shall give the other person authority to act on my behalf, to act in my name. . . . My intention is that the negotiations conducted with the person whom I have authorized to act in my stead, shall decide the result, and shall be regarded in the same way as though they had been carried on by myself on my own behalf. The business of the authorized representative is not merely to save me a journey, but to conclude the juristic act for me, to decide as to the will to be expressed, and then to express that will and thereby conclude the juristic act. Therein lies the essence of representation . . . the will expressed by a representative—the will to conclude a juristic act in my stead—is *his* will, and his alone. I express no will whatever. A representative, then, is a person who concludes a juristic act by the expression of his own will, but with the intention that the act just concluded shall have the same effect as though it had been concluded, not by him, but by another. Representation is the conclusion of a juristic act by one person with the intention that it shall operate directly for another person; in short, the conclusion of a juristic act by one person *in the name of another.*[80]

The *nuncius* met some of Sohm's criteria, but others he did not. The *nuncius* acted so as to bring his principal into direct relationship with another, but he represented the *person* of his principal and expressed only the principal's will, not his own. In some ways, according to Sohm's definition, the *nuncius* was more representative than the procurator, in some ways less. Representation, it seems, is not to be summed up so neatly as Sohm attempted, but rather it has a variety of forms, of which nunciatorial representation was one.

Some authorities describe the procurator as a representative, while others expressly deny him that description.[81] Both groups are not so much wrong as unclear concerning the criteria at issue. What has already been said about

[80] Sohm, *Institutes*, par. 45, pp. 219–220. Representation in this sense was alien to classical Roman law. The suggestion that it is an Hebraic contribution based upon the doctrine that one's messenger is equivalent to oneself and the doctrine of vicarious sin and atonement appears to me farfetched. N. Isaacs, "The Influence of Judaism on Western Law," in *The Legacy of Israel*, planned by I. Abrahams and ed. by Edwyn R. Bevan and Charles Singer, 1st edn., 1927 (Oxford, 1948), p. 396.

[81] Menzel, *Deutsches Gesandtschaftswesen*, p. 19, "Vertreter seines Absenders war . . ." Behrens, "Treatises on the Ambassador," p. 622, declares the procurator an agent, not a representative. Cuttino, *English Diplomatic Administration*, pp. 86–87, follows Behrens. *Black's Law Dictionary*, 3rd edn. (St. Paul, 1933), *agent*, par. Synonyms, p. 80, gives "representative" as a synonym for "agent." (The section on synonyms was omitted from the 4th edn.)

the procurator demonstrates clearly that he acted not by the will of another, but by his own. Baldus qualifies this with a "generally,"[82] and it is true, as we shall see, that a procurator can be appointed as a mere message bearer, although in this case his powers would seem to be superfluous. It was, after all, the power to speak and act on the basis of his judgment and will so as to bind his principal that gave to the procurator an advantage in flexibility over the *nuncius*.

A criterion of representation stressed by Sohm is that the representative must act in the name of another. This is precisely the description of the procurator given by Richard the Englishman, and Baldus lends his strong authority to the same position.[83] Throughout the mass of medieval procurations run phrases indicating that the procurator acts for his principal and in his principal's name. Sometimes it is "in our place and in our name," and therefore he is sometimes called *noz lieu tenantz*.[84] Some were sent "for representing us . . . and in our name."[85] There the words of representation actually appear, but it is clear that although the procurator can be called a representative, this was a considerably different kind of representation than that of the *nuncius*.

Many legal texts and procurations contain the implication that the principal was not present in the person of his procurator, although the effect of the acts of the procurator should be the same as if the principal himself were present.[86] One of the ways in which Baldus distinguishes the procurator from the *nuncius* is that the procurator speaks in his own person.[87] In a few documents, however, a hint of representation of the person of the principal does appear. One speaks of something that must be done in the presence of the parties, who ought to be there, either through themselves or through procurators.[88] Another document, Charles VI's procuration for the queen and the duke of Burgundy to act for him in concluding the Treaty of Troyes, expressly appoints them to represent his person.[89] *D.* 11, 7, 8, 5, holds that one whose procurator is prohibited from employing a burial place should be considered to have been prohibited himself. Also a gloss to the

[82] Baldus, *Commentaria*, ad *C.* 4, *Si quis alteri vel sibi*, 6, 18.

[83] Ricardus Anglicus, *Summa de ordine iudiciario*, XVIII, in Wahrmund, *Quellen*, II, iii, 19; Baldus, *Commentaria*, ad *C.* 4, *Si quis alteri vel sibi*, 6, 18.

[84] Rymer, *Foedera*, II, iii, 68; Chaplais, *Treaty Rolls*, I, 219, no. 554. ". . . by our authority and in our place." Rymer, *Foedera*, I, ii, 207.

[85] Archivio secreto vaticano, AA. Arm. I-XVIII, no. 3699.

[86] Chaplais, *Treaty Rolls*, I, 258, no. 656; *M.G.H.*, *Const.*, III, 489, no. 509; Ganshof, *Le Moyen Age*, p. 270.

[87] Baldus, *Commentaria*, ad *C.* 4, *Si quis alteri vel sibi*, 6, 21; Gondisalvus de Villadiego, *Tractatus*, 3, 1, 19.

[88] Reiffenberg *et al.*, *Monuments*, I, 14–16.

[89] Rymer, *Foedera*, IV, iii, 170.

canon law says that a syndic of a corporation or a college sustains the person of that body, although Durandus interestingly enough amends the statement by substituting "place" for "person."[90] Some considerable element of confusion is therefore found on this question, but in the vast majority of cases the procurator is said to act in the name or the place or by the authority of his principal, and not as representative of his person. The truth of this statement is illustrated by the procurator's use of his own seal or those of his deputies to redact a document in the name of his principal.[91] It is also indicated by the use of the procurator's own money to pay his principal's debts.[92]

Confusion is reflected again when we examine oaths taken by procurators, although here the evidence is on the side of more complete representation, for the procurator customarily takes an oath "on the soul" of his principal.[93] Perhaps this can be explained by a feeling that an oath was a rather weak straw upon which to lean, which is certainly true. Durandus and William of Drogheda both declare that a syndic should swear on his own soul,[94] but this may be a result of the corporate nature of the syndic's principal.

A final test of the representative character of the procurator is the nature of the relationship brought about between the principal and the procurator, on the one hand, and third parties, on the other. Unlike the agent in Anglo-American law, the procurator in Roman law originally could not succeed in bringing his principal into direct legal relationships with third parties. Rather he himself entered into such relationships on behalf of his principal.[95] There occurred, however, a trend toward giving an action to or against the principal, i.e., direct representation was introduced. The time at which this occurred is somewhat debatable, but it was true in postclassical law, at any rate.[96] Traces of the older indirect representation, however, seem to

[90] *Decret. Greg. IX*, 1, 39, 1, ad v. *generaliter*; Durandus, *Speculum juris*, 1, 3, *De actore* (p. 234, col. 1, in the Frankfort, 1612, edn.).

[91] Rymer, *Foedera*, III, ii, 84. In this instance the authorization to use his own seal or that of his deputies is given to the Prince of Wales. Only the expression of this authority is unusual, however, for a procurator would quite normally use his own seal. The occasional use of blank documents with pendant seals of the principals is quite another matter, which will be discussed subsequently.

[92] *Glossa ordinaria* to *D.* 46, 3, 87, ad. v. *solutum*. In practice this was unusual in diplomatic affairs, since procurators were as reluctant as anyone else to risk their own cash, but it was perfectly lawful.

[93] Manaresi, *Atti . . . di Milano*, no. 152–153, CX; Limburg–Stirum, *Codex diplomaticus Flandriae*, I, 114, no. 30; Chaplais, *Treaty Rolls*, I, 96–97, nos. 228–230; Rymer, *Foedera*, I, iii, 196. Examples abound.

[94] Durandus, *Speculum juris*, 1, 3, *De actore* (p. 234, col. 1, in the Frankfort, 1612 edn.). William of Drogheda, *Summa aurea*, CXLIX, in Wahrmund, *Quellen*, II, ii, 178.

[95] Watson, *Mandate*, p. 78.

[96] Buckland, *Textbook of Roman Law*, p. 710; Wenger, *Institutes*, pp. 91-92; Serrao, *Il Procurator*, p. 99.

have survived, for Baldus gives as another criterion for distinguishing the procurator the acquisition of an action by the principal in an oblique manner, rather than a direct action immediately obtained.[97] Documentary support for this view of indirect representation can also be found. In 1337 procurators of Edward III busied themselves in lining up allies against the king of France, promising sums of money in return for support, obligating themselves and their own goods. At their request Edward promised to hold them indemnified for any losses they might suffer as a consequence.[98] In an interesting document of 1365 an English plenipotentiary who had received lands on behalf of his master from the king of France according to the terms of peace sought redress to prevent the treasurer and the barons of the Exchequer from having him distrained for the issues of those lands, since he had delivered them immediately to the king.[99] Obviously, there was at least a suspicion that the legal effect of the conveyance had not been to place the lands immediately in the hands of the king of England, but, for the moment, in those of his envoy.

In spite of these ambiguities and difficulties, I think that we must regard the procurator as a representative of his principal, although a different sort of representative than the *nuncius*. The procurator customarily and characteristically spoke and acted upon the basis of his own will, and was by no means a speaking letter. He spoke and acted in the name of his principal, at least in the vast majority of cases, although there is an occasional hint of representation of the person. Most of the evidence, again, suggests that through the acts of the procurator the principal was placed in direct legal relationships with third parties, although some evidence does indicate the survival of traces of an earlier indirect representation. The contrast between procuratorial and nunciatorial representation is fairly clear. The *nuncius* was a more absolute and personal representative, suitable where the immediate and direct role of the principal was to be emphasized, as on ceremonial occasions in diplomacy. The procurator was a more free and flexible representative, more useful in negotiations.

Since procuration was an institution of private law borrowed for diplomatic and other governmental affairs, it is not surprising that procurators or syndics could be sent and received by anyone competent to conduct his own affairs. Merchants themselves sometimes sent procurators to deal with princes concerning trade, or at other times merchants and their states

[97] Baldus, *Commentaria*, ad *C.* 4, *Si quis alteri vel sibi*, 6, 21.

[98] Note, parenthetically, that they made conventions *de voluntate nostra*, as well as *pro Nobis et Nomine nostro*. Rymer, *Foedera*, II, iii, 188. Another example from 1442. *Ibid.*, v, i, 113.

[99] *C.C.R., Edward III (1364–1368)*, p. 128.

joined to send procurators representing both the public entity and the private persons.[100] Princes, on the other hand, might send procurators to deal with another state or with private persons as circumstances dictated.[101] Once again the medieval willingness to blur the line between public and private is noteworthy. As in the case of the *nuncius*, therefore, we find diplomatic procurators sent and received by all sorts of people. Diplomacy was not a game exclusively for sovereigns.[102]

Even more than private persons, however, rulers are beset by so many duties that only a few can be performed personally. The procurator, who could act for a principal when the principal could not be on the spot, offered considerable attraction. The procurator's *raison d'être* was to do those things which the principal could do if he were present.[103] Reference has already been made to the fact that principals actually spoke in terms of being present "by a procurator."[104] What a procurator was empowered to do was contained in his mandate, and his function was to carry out his mandate with strict diligence.[105]

Since anything that a man could do himself could be done by a properly empowered procurator, the diplomatic uses of procuration were legion. Occasionally, indeed, procuratorial powers were given when no evident need for them existed. A procurator might be appointed for explaining something, for making excuses, or simply for carrying and perhaps explaining a written message.[106] The use of procuration in these cases is hard to explain, for it seems that a *nuncius* would have served as well.

The delivery and receipt of official documents by means of procurators was not necessarily identical in nature to the bearing or receiving of a message,

[100] Rymer, *Foedera*, I, iv, 70; Cessi, *Deliberazioni del Maggior Consiglio*, III, 77.

[101] *Documents historiques inédits tirés des collections manuscrites de la Bibliothèque Royale et des archives ou des bibliothèques des departements*, Jacques J. Champollion–Figeac, ed., 4 vols. (Paris, 1841–1848), I, 518–519, 528, 556.

[102] The weakness of the concept of sovereignty in diplomacy is also illustrated by the use of foreigners as envoys and, in particular, by granting of procurations to procurators of another principal in order to conclude some affair of common interest. Examples from mid-thirteenth to mid-fifteenth centuries: Chaplais, *Treaty Rolls*, I, 27, no. 72; Rymer, *Foedera*, IV, iii, 101; A.S.V., Sindicati, II, 62r. Opposing sides might also appoint a joint procurator as mediator, like Florent, Count of Holland, appointed by both sides along with their particular procurators. *M.G.H.*, *Const.*, III, 489–492, nos. 509–512.

[103] *Decretum*, 2, 5, 3; *D.* 3, 3, 35, 3; William of Drogheda, *Summa aurea*, CII, in Wahrmund, *Quellen*, II, ii, 97.

[104] Reiffenberg *et al.*, *Monuments*, I, 15.

[105] Hostiensis, *Summa*, 1, *De procuratoribus*, *Quod sit eius officium;* Tancred, *Ordo iudiciarius*, 1, 6, *De procuratoribus*, 6, in Bergmann, *Libri de iudiciorum ordine*, p. 120; Watson, *Mandate*, pp. 178–179.

[106] Rymer, *Foedera*, I, i, 114; *Table chronologique des chartes et diplômes concernant l'histoire de Belgique*, Alphonse Wauters, ed., 11 vols. (Bruxelles, 1866–1907), VI, 420; Archives du Nord, Lille, Chambre des Comptes, B 1263, no. 3708.

for this was an age of legal formalism and the transfer of a document constituted the completion of a legally binding act. Thus Henry III employed procurators to deliver, at the request of Louis IX, certain documents concerned in the Treaty of Paris of 1259.[107] A host of documents arose out of the failure of the count of Hainaut in 1295 to provide for the exchange of documents with procurators of the count of Flanders as a result of a contested arbitral decision.[108]

Nothing could be clearer in Roman law than the ability of procurators with a special mandate or *libera administratio* to pay or collect debts for their principals.[109] Examples of procurations to collect debts are much more common than those for paying. Each was equally valid at law, but people are understandably more eager to collect than to pay.[110] Occasionally, however, we hear that a procurator made payment.[111] If a procurator received payment or other things owed his principal, he could give quittance.[112] A procurator could even be empowered to appoint another as a receiver.[113] Possession of lands could be transferred through procurators, and implicitly or expressly this might include the allegiance of vassals with fiefs within the transferred lands.[114] Rule over the state itself, in fact, could be so conveyed.[115] Moveable goods could be bought or received or sold or otherwise alienated.[116] A procurator could also be employed to borrow money.[117] Like a *nuncius*, naturally, a procurator could complete by delivery or receipt an agreement

[107] Chaplais, *Treaty Rolls*, I, 41, no. 108 and 43, no. 111. The first also in Rymer, *Foedera*, I, ii, 49.

[108] Archives du Nord, Lille, Chambre des Comptes, B 1263, nos. 3680-3703; Rijksarchief, Gent, Saint-Genois, no. 768.

[109] *D.* 3, 3, 58-59; 3, 3, 63; 46, 3, 87; 2, 14, 11; 46, 3, 12; 50, 17, 180; Baldus, *Commentaria*, ad *D.* 3, *De negotiis gestis*, 25, *Si ego*, 3, stresses that a general mandate alone was insufficient.

[110] Archives du Nord, Lille, Chambre des Comptes, B 403, no. 3087 bis, and B 1262, no. 3314; Reiffenberg *et al.*, *Monuments*, I, 260-261, 272-273; A.S.V., Maggior Consiglio, Magnus, 43v, Capricornus, 58r (163r), and Fronesis 26v (26v); Rymer, *Foedera*, IV, iv, 129-130.

[111] Rymer, *Foedera*, I, ii, 109.

[112] Chaplais, *War of Saint Sardos*, p. 141; Rymer, *Foedera*, II, i, 21; III, iii, 39; II, iii, 152 equals *C.C.R. Edward III (1333-1337)*, pp. 714-715.

[113] Reiffenberg *et al.*, *Monuments*, I, 276-277.

[114] Chaplais, *Treaty Rolls*, I, 49, no. 122; I, 137-138, no. 362; I, 157, no. 388; A.S.V., Sindicati, II, 48r.

[115] Mandate of the town of Frosinone for subjecting itself to the papacy. Archivio secreto vaticano, AA. Arm. I-XVIII, no. 3699; mandate of Emperor Lewis IV for submission and surrender of the empire to the pope. Mathias de Nuwenburg, *Chronica*, p. 191. The pope and the college did not take this seriously, but formally it was all right.

[116] Cessi, *Deliberazioni del Maggior Consiglio*, I, 68; A.S.V., Maggior Consiglio, Presbiter. Somehow I have omitted to copy the page number, but the document can easily be found by its date, 27 November 1310. *D.* 3, 3, 63.

[117] Rijksarchief, Saint-Genois, no. 310; Duvivier, *Influences*, II, 364, no. CCXII, and 367-370, no. CCXV. The former, the mandate, was really a blank parchment, filled out and predated by the procurator. *Infra*, pp. 130-136.

entered into by the principal, but what is noteworthy is that he could also be the negotiator of such agreements.[118]

Again like *nuncii*, procurators were employed to set up meetings between their principals for negotiations at the highest level or for such acts as the performance of homage and fealty,[119] but I think we may infer that when such a meeting was arranged by a procurator with full powers the agreement to meet had the nature of a binding convention, even though the procurator had been left free to negotiate the time, place, and conditions of the session.

When things went badly between states, a protest carried by a procurator might be the first step toward improving relations—or a last step before breaking them. The Venetians never hesitated to dispatch procurators when other states or citizens of other states raised obstacles against Venetian merchants.[120] A procurator might be sent to protest truce violations or the infringement of any other right of his principal.[121] On the one hand protests shade into accusations, on the other into appeals.[122] Of course the same document which authorized a procurator to protest could also empower him to negotiate the rectification of grievances.[123]

Preeminently, procurators were appointed to negotiate agreements,[124] because for many lesser tasks *nuncii* were sufficient. The powers granted might be quite special, as in the case of Venetian syndics authorized to enter a covenant with Ancona concerning the extradition of fugitives and the goods carried away by them.[125] Slightly more freedom of action was given to Louis IX's procurators dispatched to Genoa to obtain galleys and supplies for his crusade to Tunis, for they could deal either with the government or with private citizens.[126] A *condotte* was simply a special kind of contract for military service. Hearing that ten or twelve Catalan galleys might be

[118] Buckland points out that when he was only a courier, not a negotiator, the procurator was really no more than a *nuncius*. W. W. Buckland, *The Main Institutions of Roman Private Law* (Cambridge, 1931), p. 169.

[119] Chaplais, *Treaty Rolls*, I, 202, no. 509; 228-229, nos. 583-584; 234, no. 611; 235-236, no. 614; Rymer, *Foedera*, II, i, 4, 194 and 197; II, ii, 93.

[120] Cessi, *Deliberazioni del Maggior Consiglio*, III, 296.

[121] Delcambre, "Recueil de documents . . . relatifs aux relations du Hainaut et de la France," p. 101. A procurator was sent to protest on behalf of the Count of Flanders the attempt of the Count of Hainaut to intrude his candidate into the bishopric of Tournai. Rijksarchief, Gent, Saint-Genois, no. 644.

[122] Delcambre, "Recueil de documents . . . relatifs aux relations du Hainaut et de la France," p. 115; Archives du Nord, Lille, Chambre des Comptes, B 1397, nos. 2515-2517; Rijksarchief, Gent, Saint-Genois, nos. 439-440, 442, 445; *ibid.*, Chronologisch supplement, no. 146.

[123] Chaplais, *Treaty Rolls*, I, 252-253, nos. 646-647.

[124] Hostiensis, *Summa*, 1, *De transactionibus*, *Quis potest transigere*. Menzel, *Deutsches Gesandtschaftswesen*, pp. 13-14, is quite wrong on the character of *bevollmächtigen Gesandten*.

[125] A.S.V., Spiritus, 111r (112r).

[126] Champollion-Figeac, *Documents historiques inédits*, I, 518-519, 528, 556.

available under the command of the brother of the king of Aragon, and fearing lest the enemies of the Republic might obtain them, Venice sent full powers to its envoy to negotiate for them. In the Senate's instructions to him, by the way, he was authorized to spend only a certain amount, and less if he could—a fairly typical instruction in matters of this sort.[127] Another type of convention was a truce, and procurators naturally could prorogue truces as well as make original ones.[128] A more definitive settlement could also be negotiated by plenipotentiaries in the form of a treaty.[129] Very considerable freedom might be allowed to these negotiators, and this flexibility was especially desirable when negotiations were to take place at a great distance. Venice sent a syndic to the king of Bohemia and Poland in 1331 for entering into whatever conventions seemed appropriate to him on the matter of merchants and merchandise.[130] Despite the reputation of the Venetian Republic for bureaucratic government, Venetian diplomacy was as wide-open and freewheeling as that of any other medieval state. A syndic was sent to the king of Hungary in 1349 empowered to make conventions or pacts obligating the Venetians in whatever way was opportune. It is true that they were instructed to say that they had no mandate to agree to cross with him into Apulia, and this was to be added to their commission or instructions, which were otherwise extremely vague.[131] Therefore, if any treaties made by procurators "by some certain impediments, failed to come into effect and to the desired end,"[132] the fault lay in circumstances, not in any legal disability of procurators to do anything that their principals could do. As procurators could make truces and treaties, they could also be authorized to make one or the other at their discretion and as circumstances dictated.[133] Frequently, too, plenipotentiaries were sent "fishing" for allies, so that even the parties with whom they were to deal were not specified.[134] The freedom

[127] A.S.V., Senato, Secreta, xi, 153r (154r), 176r (177r)–177r (178r). He did not succeed, and was subsequently authorized to employ galleys owned by private persons and to form a *condotte* with Bernardus Senteles. *Ibid.*, 208r (207r).

[128] Chaplais, *Treaty Rolls*, i, 111, no. 261; 112-114, nos. 266-273; 169, no. 404; 170-171, nos. 407-408; 255, no. 651; Rymer, *Foedera*, i, iii, 149, 155, 158, and 159; Limburg-Stirum, *Codex diplomaticus Flandriae*, i, 321, no. 132; 323-324, nos. 134-135; 326-329, nos. 137-139.

[129] Chaplais, *Treaty Rolls*, i, 111-112, nos. 263-264; Rymer, *Foedera*, i, iii, 150; F. Guessard, "Pierre de Mornay, chancelier de France," *Bibliothèque de l'École des Chartes*, v (1843-1844), 146-147, *pièces justificatives*, 167-168; Limburg-Stirum, *Codex diplomaticus Flandriae*, i, 31-41.

[130] A.S.V., Sindicati, i, 10r.

[131] A.S.V., Senato, Misti, xxv, 55r (55r), 54v (54v), 31v (31v).

[132] Chaplais, *Treaty Rolls*, i, 160, no. 394.

[133] *Ibid.*, i, 83, no. 197; 126-127, nos. 324-327; Rymer, *Foedera*, i, iii, 8, 174.

[134] Böhmer–Ficker, *Acta Imperii selecta*, p. 404, no. 554, and p. 483, no. 694. Or loosely specified. Rymer, *Foedera*, v, iii, 14-15. Or particular powers might be given for treating with certain specified persons—the count of Hainaut, the count of Guelders, the bishop of Liège, the bishop of Utrecht, the nobles of Burgundy—and a more general procuration designed for add-

which procurators enjoyed in making conventions is illustrated by Edward I's answer to an inquiry concerning conventions allegedly made by his procurators. He did not know whether or not they had done so, but would inform the count of Hülchrath when he learned.[135] It is true that as diplomacy became increasingly modern the authority of the plenipotentiary to bind his principal to far-reaching obligations without reference or consultation tended to be restricted or withheld. Improved diplomatic communications made the use of such powers less necessary, although the juridical position of the procurator with *plena potestas* remained unchanged and he could continue to receive great discretionary authority.

Like *nuncii*, procurators could be used to convey a declaration of war. The well-documented defiance of the count of Flanders to Philip the Fair in 1297 may provide a clue as to the reasons for using the one rather than the other. In fact, the two abbots sent by Guy are called *messages* and, in a Latin inventory, *nuncii*, but they are appointed to speak "de par nous, et en nostre non," that which they see will appertain to that matter. This statement is followed by a *ratihabitio* clause. True, their powers were strictly limited to the matter of the defiance contained in letters under the count's small seal, but the abbots were not mere message bearers.[136]

Since procurators—and other envoys—were not only exposed to the common dangers of the roads but to ill treatment because of their involvement in controversial matters, they naturally preferred to travel under a safe-conduct.[137] Procurators as well as principals could issue safe-conducts to their counterparts on the other side if they had a special mandate or *libera administratio*.[138]

Disputes which could not be settled by negotiation could be submitted by procurators to arbitration.[139] This was a favorite medieval method of attempting to settle controversies, and given the terms and conditions of the arbitral settlement by his principal, a *nuncius* could also appoint arbiters; but a procurator could be appointed to negotiate and, if that failed, to enter into an arbitration upon conditions judged satisfactory to him.[140] The

ing any possible allies not covered in the particular powers. Chaplais, *Treaty Rolls*, I, 128-130, nos. 334-347; Rymer, *Foedera*, I, iii, 174.

135 Chaplais, *Treaty Rolls*, I, 174, no. 423; Rymer, *Foedera*, I, iii, 171.

136 Limburg-Stirum, *Codex diplomaticus Flandriae*, I, 132-133, no. 40. Called *messages*, *ibid.*, I, 132-146, nos. 40-41. Called *nuncii*, *ibid.*, I, 1 and 146-149, no. 42. Funck-Brentano, *Philippe le Bel en Flandre*, pp. 201-203, reports their address to Philip.

137 Safe-conducts will be discussed in a later chapter.

138 Chaplais, *Treaty Rolls*, I, 120, no. 294; Rymer, *Foedera*, I, iii, 165; II, ii, 203; III, iii, 38, 45, 110.

139 Raoul Naz, *Dictionnaire de droit canonique* (Paris, 1935), I, cols. 871-872 and 874. I am not here distinguishing between arbiters and arbitrators.

140 Chaplais, *Treaty Rolls*, I, 94, no. 226; Rymer, *Foedera*, II, iii, 165.

negotiators on each side were sometimes authorized to select a neutral party to settle disputed points upon which they could not agree.[141] Just as a procurator in a court of law received judgment in the name of his principal, so procurators were also appointed to receive arbitral decisions.[142] This was not an act requiring any discretionary authority, but was analogous to the act of a *procurator litis* in private law. Rather similar to procurators empowered to appoint arbitrators were those authorized to appoint inquisitors to settle any disputes between the principals.[143] Inquisitors had a more limited task than arbitrators—the assessing of the amount of damages or the fixing of a boundary, for example.

Procurators were employed to give and receive guarantees of adherence to covenants. A procurator with special mandate or *libera administratio* could guarantee his principal's performance of his obligations by taking an oath on the principal's soul.[144] That, at any rate, is the common formula, although in a few early examples we find the plenipotentiary swearing that he will make his principal swear, which appears to emphasize the originally indirect or oblique character of procuratorial representation. In one of these cases copied into the document is the procuration itself, in which the principal, Barbarossa, promises to hold firm whatever his procurators, for making the Peace of Constance, will accept by oath.[145] In strictly juristic terms, therefore, the emperor's personal oath would be superfluous, but extralegal factors are also involved. For greater sanction the oath of the principal was sometimes desired. Authorizing procurators to take oaths on his soul was certainly not unknown to Barbarossa at an even earlier date, witness the truce between the emperor and the Lombard League in 1177.[146] Such authorization became commonplace. Incidentally, procurators were even used to take oaths on behalf of principals who were present, for kings customarily refused to swear before their inferiors, except for coronation oaths.[147] Procurators also

141 *C.R. (1256-1259)*, pp. 118-120; Rymer, *Foedera*, v, iii, 24.

142 Chaplais, *Treaty Rolls*, i, 148-149, nos. 373-375; 153, no. 381; Rymer, *Foedera*, i, iv, 11 and 18.

143 Reiffenberg *et al.*, *Monuments*, i, 30-31.

144 *Sext.* 1, 19, 4; Durandus, *Speculum juris*, 1, 3, 1 (*Ratione igitur*), 4-5; Magister Arnulphus, *Summa minorum*, li, in Wahrmund, *Quellen*, i, ii, 54; *Ordo judiciarius "Scientiam,"* xxi, in Wahrmund, *Quellen*, ii, i, 41; De Maino, *Repertorium*, p. 79, no. 14. Menzel, *Deutsches Gesandtschaftswesen*, p. 13, reports a time when plenipotentiaries did not possess authority to take oaths for their principals. This is incorrect.

145 Manaresi, *Atti . . . di Milano*, pp. 191-193, no. cxxxvi. Legates, presumably plenipotentiaries, of Milan and Piacenza in 1200 swore to make their principals swear to uphold the alliance they had just formed. *Ibid.*, pp. 325-327, no. ccxxx.

146 *Ibid.*, pp. 152-153, no. cx.

147 Pierre Chaplais, "The Making of the Treaty of Paris (1259) and the Royal Style," *E.H.R.*, lxvii (1952), p. 237 and p. 241. On at least one occasion Countess Margaret of Flanders imitated this royal custom, perhaps because William of Holland was both her lord and her

were empowered to receive oaths in the names of their principals.[148] Letters guaranteeing adherence to the agreements made by them were also given by procurators.[149] So were pledges of a financial guaranty.[150] When financial pledges for adherence to conventions were given by others, procurators could be empowered to promise to hold them indemnified for any losses.[151]

In a truce or a peace made by procurators, they might stipulate fines and promise restitution for damages caused by its violation.[152] When occasion for the invocation of such clauses arose, procurators were again appointed (or they might have been named in the truce or treaty) to amend infractions.[153] It is easily understandable that such investigations or hearings sometimes involved the procurators of a ruler and those of injured private persons.[154] Very similar to this and to arbitration was the appointment of procurators or commissioners to settle boundary disputes and, perhaps, to exchange lands.[155]

Granting and seeking pardon or absolution were among the powers of procurators. Especially when plenipotentiaries were appointed to make peace following a war in which vassals had been arrayed against their lord, it was desirable for the lord's procurators to have power to pardon transgressions against his rights.[156] Procurators, of course, could also seek absolution for wrongs committed by their principals.[157]

The most solemn acts, such as contracting and completing—everything, in fact, short of consummating—a marriage alliance, could be done by procurators. Canon law authorized contracting a marriage under a special mandate, and it was commonly done.[158] The procurator, moreover, could

---

vassal. *Oorkondenboek van Holland en Zeeland*, L. Ph. C. van den Bergh, ed., 2 vols. (Amsterdam, 1866-1873), I, 276, no. 514; Kluit, *Historia critica*, II, 584, no. CLXX; Van Mieris, *Charterboek van Holland*, I, 259. Her predecessors Ferrand and Jeanne, however, personally swore to uphold the Treaty of Melun before the French king, their feudal lord. Edouard Le Glay, *Histoire de Jeanne de Constantinople, comtesse de Flandre et de Hainaut* (Lille, 1841), p. 174.

148 Émile Varenbergh, "Épisodes des relations extérieures de la Flandre au Moyen Age: Trois filles de Gui de Dampierre," *Annales de l'Académie d'Archéologie de Belgique*, XXIV, 2e sér., t. IV (1868), 629, no. II; Chaplais, *Treaty Rolls*, I, 114-115, no. 275; Rymer, *Foedera*, I, iii, 155.

149 Rymer, *Foedera*, IV, iii, 78, and V, iv, 25-26.

150 A.S.V., Maggior Consiglio, Spiritus, 111r (112r).

151 Cessi, *Deliberazioni del Maggior Consiglio*, III, 33-34.

152 Chaplais, *Treaty Rolls*, I, 127, nos. 328-329; Rymer, *Foedera*, I, iii, 174.

153 Rymer, *Foedera*, I, ii, 3, and III, i, 58.

154 Rijksarchief, Gent, Saint-Genois, no. 394.

155 Archives du Royaume, Bruxelles, Trésor de Flandre, I, no. 2102; Archives du Nord, Lille, Chambre des Comptes, B 1263, nos. 3707-3709; Reiffenberg *et al.*, *Monuments*, I, 32-33; Chaplais, *Treaty Rolls*, I, 219, no. 554.

156 Chaplais, *Treaty Rolls*, I, 157, no. 389; Rymer, *Foedera*, II, iv, 114, and III, i, 6.

157 Archivio secreto vaticano, AA. Arm. I-XVIII, no. 3704.

158 *Sext.* 1, 19, 9; *C.P.R. Henry III (1247-1258)*, p. 230; Varenbergh, "Trois filles," pp. 625-627, no. I.

carry out the marriage ceremony *per verba de presenti*, actually standing in for the bride or the groom. Frederic II's famous counselor, Peter della Vigna fulfilled this role for him in the emperor's marriage with Isabella, sister of Henry III, exchanging consent and exchanging rings with the bride.[159] Dowery could also be granted and promise of dowery received from the other party.[160] As in his other dealings, the procurator need not be restricted by terms already accepted by the principal, but could enjoy the freedom to negotiate. Negotiating for an adoption of a person by another as his heir was also entrusted to procurators.[161] As a mark of honor procurators were requested and dispatched to hold and receive infants being baptized. I find it rather interesting that a corporate entity, the commune of Venice, could be represented in this role.[162] Notice that in these solemn acts of marriage, baptism, oaths, and the like, the procurator seems to be more of a ceremonial and personal representative than he is in negotiating truces and treaties "in the name" of the principal.

Homage was occasionally performed or received by the use of procurators, although it was generally recognized that this constituted an infraction of the highly personal character of the feudal relationship.[163] Commines (Commynes) objects that the king acted "against all reason" in granting the request of Ludovico il Moro that his nephew, the duke of Milan, be admitted to homage for Genoa by proxy.[164] Royalty, becoming increasingly conscious of its exalted position as the Middle Ages progressed, grew understandably reluctant to bend the knee in homage before a lord, though it was not at all squeamish toward the benefits of vassalage. Procuration

[159] Chaplais, *Treaty Rolls*, I, 1-3, no. 1; 3-4, no. 4; 6, no. 9; Rymer, *Foedera*, I, i, 120 and 123; *C.R. (1234-1237)*, p. 167. *Per verba de presenti* means "by words of the present tense." Maulde La Clavière states: "Le mariage 'per verba de presenti' . . . signifie un mariage vrai. Pour mieux en accentuer le caractère définitif, non seulement l'ambassadeur passe l'anneau nuptial au doight de la mariée, mais il se livre respectueusement à quelque démonstration matérielle de prise de possession: baiser le mariée, mettre une jambe dans son lit . . . ; procès verbal en est dressé." *La diplomatie au temps de Machiavel*, III, 334. On the basic point he is quite right. He is probably also correct on the symbolic acts, but I could not find the primary sources. This is a fundamental criticism of this learned work: the documentation is totally inadequate.

[160] Chaplais, *Treaty Rolls*, I, 1-3, no. 1; 3-4, no. 4; 6, no. 9; 136, no. 359; Rymer, *Foedera*, I, i, 120-123; I, iii, 206; III, i, 39-40; *C.C.R., Edward III (1346-1349)*, p. 590; *C.P.R., Henry III (1247-1258)*, p. 219.

[161] Rymer, *Foedera*, IV, iii, 98.

[162] A.S.V., Sindicati, I, 188v and 226v. For the baptism of the son of the king of Poland the syndics were three Poles, two noblemen, and the vice-chancellor. Even in fifteenth-century Italy the title of ambassador was not used for these baptismal representatives, but rather syndic and procurator.

[163] Theo Luykx, "De strijd van Margareta van Constantinopel, gravin van Vlaanderen en Henegouwen, voor het behoud van hare rijksgebieden," *Gedenkschriften van de Oudheidkundigen Kring van het Land van Dendermonde* (1950), pp. 7-8.

[164] Philippe de Commynes, *Mémoires*, B. de Mandrot, ed., 2 vols. (Paris, 1901-1903), II, 118-119.

could allow a monarch to accept those benefits without personally performing an act of subordination. Richard II made it clear in his instructions to an embassy to France that he was prepared to perform simple homage for Guienne, though he would not perform it personally and would not appear at the court of France except by a procurator.[165] Although the reason is not made explicit, English rulers had appointed procurators to perform homage for French fiefs much earlier.[166] In 1438 we find the bishop of Münster naming a procurator to perform homage and fealty to Henry VI and to accept any fiefs that the king might bestow in return.[167] A treaty between the king of England and the archbishop of Cologne contains a provision permitting the archbishop to perform homage by a procurator.[168] Although this was contrary to feudal custom, and a lord probably had the right to demand personal performance of homage, there is no doubt that the lord also had the right to accept it by proxy if it pleased him. Sometimes the plea of the vassal was based upon the dangerous state of the roads.[169] The lord could, if he preferred, obviate such a difficulty by sending a procurator of his own to receive homage in his place.[170] The sentiment that homage ought to be performed personally by the vassal was stronger than any feeling that it should be received personally by the lord. A single document from the *Archivio Vaticano* dating from the beginning of the reign of Peter IV of Aragon reveals much concerning the performance and reception of homage and fealty by procurators. According to the terms of the grant of Corsica and Sardinia by Boniface VIII, James II had performed homage and fealty in person to that pope, although when it had been necessary to renew the same king's homage and fealty to succeeding popes, performance by procurators had sufficed. In his turn Alfonso III had performed the ceremonies personally according to the conditions of the original enfeoffment, but he had not performed them before the pope, John XXII, but before the archbishop of Alessandria, acting in the name and in the place of the pope. By procurator, however, he renewed his oaths to Pope Benedict XII, John's successor. Peter confesses that he also is obligated to perform homage

[165] *Proceedings and Ordinances of the Privy Council*, Sir N. H. Nicolas, ed., 7 vols. (London, 1834-1837), I, 19-21. Called to my attention by Professor Charles Leon Tipton.

[166] Chaplais, *Treaty Rolls*, I, 229-232, nos. 586-589, 594-596, 599-602; Rymer, *Foedera*, II, i, 175. These documents, except for the last, which is identical with the first, represent slightly different forms giving the same power in the same instance. This may indicate some doubt as to the acceptability of the procedure. Another instance: "Documents concernant l'Angleterre et l'Écosse anciennement conservés à la Chambre des Comptes de Lille (XIIe-XVe s.)," Pierre Chaplais, ed., *Revue du Nord*, XXXVIII (1956), pp. 190-191, no. 2.

[167] Rymer, *Foedera*, V, i, 51.

[168] *Ibid.*, IV, ii, 159-161.

[169] Chaplais, *Treaty Rolls*, I, 175, no. 424; Rymer, *Foedera*, I, iii, 155.

[170] Luykx, "Strijd van Margareta voor het behoud van hare rijksgebieden," pp. 7-8, n. 20; Rymer, *Foedera*, II, iii, 117; III, i, 177.

and fealty personally to Benedict, but the pope has graciously consented to receive it through Peter's procurator on condition that the king perform his oaths personally within a year.[171]

Fealty was considered a somewhat less solemn act than homage, and it sometimes happened that a lord would accept fealty by a vassal's procurator, though he would require a promise that the vassal would subsequently perform homage in person.[172] A corporate body could obviously not perform fealty personally, and so it was not much of a concession to accept it by the act of a syndic instead of the chief magistrate.[173] In fact it might be even more satisfactory to the lord, since the syndic would be appointed by the commune specifically for that purpose, whereas a chief magistrate might possibly be acting in this instance without a specific mandate. Fealty, of course, could also be received by a procurator.[174] Where homage was also required, the procurator might be assigned to accept fealty but extort a promise from the vassal to perform homage personally at a later date.[175] Both could be accepted, of course, at the will of the lord.[176] The feudal defiance or renunciation of homage, the *exfestucatio*, could be performed by a procurator.[177] It would, in fact, take a bold man to perform it personally.

Procuration was useful also as a device by which neutral parties might mediate disputes. In many cases the disputants were allies, and the procurator was engaged in the important and delicate task of patching up a crumbling alliance, perhaps by asking the disputants to submit their controversy to arbitration.[178]

One of the powers that a procurator might receive was that of issuing procurations himself.[179] If both parties to a dispute authorized their procurators to issue a procuration to settle the dispute to some third party, the effect would be similar to an arbitration, though words of arbitration might never appear.[180]

[171] Archivio secreto vaticano, AA. Arm. I-XVIII, no. 462.

[172] Chaplais, *Treaty Rolls*, I, 251, no. 643; Rymer, *Foedera*, II, ii, 119; I, ii, 62.

[173] *Acta Imperii inedita*, Eduard Winkelmann, ed., 2 vols. (Innsbruck, 1880-1885), II, 70-71, no. 76.

[174] Rymer, *Foedera*, I, ii, 129; *C.C.R.*, *Edward I (1272-1279)*, p. 2.

[175] Chaplais, *Treaty Rolls*, I, 101, no. 235; I, 167, no. 396; Rymer, *Foedera*, I, iii, 139; II, iii, 110.

[176] *Supra*, pp. 49-51; A.S.V., Senato, Secreta, XXXVI, 90r (102r).

[177] Marc Bloch, "Les formes de la rupture de l'hommage dans l'ancien droit féodale," *Nouvelle revue historique de droit française et étranger*, XXXVI (1912), pp. 143-158.

[178] Chaplais, *Treaty Rolls*, I, 63-64, no. 157, and 131-132, nos. 349-353; Rymer, *Foedera*, I, ii, 186; I, iii, 175; II, i, 165.

[179] Archivio di Stato, Mantova, Archivio Gonzaga, 2881 (Copialettere I, c. 4.).

[180] Chaplais, *Treaty Rolls*, I, 78-79, no. 189; 80-81, no. 192; 83-84, no. 198; Rymer, *Foedera*, I, iii, 8, 11 and 12.

A principal could grant to his procurator authority to substitute another for himself.[181] Watson disputes Sanfilippo's thesis that this was possible only if it was not excluded by express consent of the parties or by the special nature of a procuratorial assignment requiring a high degree of skill in the mandatory. Watson finds no distinction between tasks requiring special skills and others, and the grant of this authority to diplomatic procurators in the Middle Ages certainly lends support to Watson's contention—at least for that late period.[182] When substitution occurred it was expressly authorized, and at least one document can be cited—not a diplomatic one, unfortunately—in which a procuratorial act was declared null by a principal on the grounds that his procurator had not received power to delegate his authority.[183] It would appear, therefore, that this power must be expressly granted, or, if not given by special mandate, at least granted by means of *libera administratio*.

Watson points out that the only text which has been thought to restrict the discretion that could be granted to the mandatory does not, in fact, do so. He further argues that if there had originally been rules restricting the uncertainty of mandate, these would have had to be relaxed with the union of mandate and procuration, especially procuration *omnium bonorum*, where the procurator had very wide discretion.[184] Freedom to do "what seems to them to be advantageous," to pay "whatever sum appears appropriate," and other like phrases are not unusual in medieval procurations.[185] The crusader-envoys of 1201 provide an excellent example of procurators with broad discretion. They received full powers to treat for transportation "in whatever seaport, wherever they should go," and it was the envoys themselves who decided upon Venice as their destination. They accepted the Venetian offer of participation in the crusade, giving in return a promise of half the conquests. Whether the secret codicil to the treaty specifying Egypt as the destination of the crusade was done on their initiative, or whether they had instructions on this is not known.[186] In any event, the

181 Baldus, *Commentaria*, ad *D.* 17, *Mandati*, 9, *Si quis mandaverit*, no. 1; Post, "Plena Potestas in Medieval Assemblies," p. 362; Post, *Medieval Legal Thought*, p. 100.

182 Watson, *Mandate*, p. 183; Cessi, *Deliberazioni del Maggior Consiglio*, I, 169; Chaplais, *Treaty Rolls*, I, 95-96, no. 227; Rymer, *Foedera*, I, ii, 46 and I, iii, 196; G. P. Cuttino, "The Process of Agen," *Speculum*, XIX (1944), 166.

183 Rijksarchief, Gent, Saint-Genois, no. 640.

184 Watson, *Mandate*, pp. 96-99.

185 *C.R. (1256-1259)*, pp. 326-327; Chaplais, *Treaty Rolls*, I, 256-257, nos. 654-655. Documents for the same matter, *ibid.*, I, 257-258, nos. 656-657, mention "a certain sum of money." Löhren claimed to find exceptional cases in the early Middle Ages of diplomatic envoys with discretion to do what they thought best, though the supposed evidence of Roman law plenipotentiaries at such an early date has been shown to be weak. *Geschichte des gesandtschaftlichen Verkehrs*, p. 67.

186 Geoffroi de Villehardouin, *La conquête de Constantinople*, Edmond Faral, ed. and trans.,

discretionary powers of these envoys were remarkable. Venice, too, sometimes sent envoys out to conclude alliances wherever they might find them.[187] It was not really unusual for English monarchs to issue powers for concluding alliances "with whatever nobles and other persons, of whatever kingdom or land, state, dignity or condition, and with whatever communes and corporations." Sometimes these broad powers included authorization to agree upon fiefs or other remuneration to be granted in exchange for the alliances. Even marriage alliances could be negotiated in this broadcast fashion.[188]

Although a mandate, as we have seen, could be couched in the broadest terms, a procurator was obligated to remain within the limitations of his mandate, broad or narrow. Since the obligation under a mandate rested upon consent, the terms of the mandate expressing the limits of that consent should not be violated.[189] As Hostiensis put it, the mandate should be served with "exact faithfulness."[190] Against the terms of his mandate a procurator was powerless, and if he presumed to exceed his powers his acts were not binding upon the principal.[191] *C.* 2, 12, 10, poses a problem in this regard.

---

2 vols. (Paris, 1938-1939), Secs. 13-31. On the choice of destination, see Roberto Cessi, "Venezia e la quarta crociata," *Archivio veneto*, ser. 5, XLVIII-XLIX (1951), p. 10 and p. 14, n. 1. Louis Bréhier, *L'église et l'orient au Moyen Age* (Paris, 1928), p. 151, paraphrases Villehardouin inexactly, obscuring the freedom of the procurators. Villehardouin's polite speeches to the Venetians should not refute his earlier assertion of procuratorial independence. Nor should the oaths of the envoys in support of the treaty. Villehardouin, *Conquête de Constantinople*, I, 217, Appendix I, 2; Jean Longnon, *Recherches sur la vie de Geoffroy de Villehardouin, suivies du catalogue des actes des Villehardouin* (Paris, 1939), no. 60, p. 182; Tafel and Thomas, *Urkunden*, I, 358-362. Jules Tessier, *Quatrième Croisade. La diversion sur Zara et Constantinople* (Paris, 1884), pp. 57-59, argues rather persuasively that no decision as to the destination of the crusade could be reached by the crusaders at Compiègne because the majority of the leaders favored Egypt, while to the rank and file this was odious. Hence, he believes, the decision was left to the envoys. In this connection it is worth noting that the envoys represented only the three leaders, Baldwin of Flanders, Thibaut of Champagne, and Louis of Blois, not the crusading army as a corporate body.

187 Cessi, *Deliberazioni del Maggior Consiglio*, I, 198; A.S.V., Sindicati, 12r.

188 Chaplais, *Treaty Rolls*, I, 89-90, no. 213, and 258, no. 658; Rymer, *Foedera*, I, iii, 146 (on p. 153 is evidence that they did make a treaty subsequently ratified); I, iii, 174; II, ii, 113; II, iii, 165; III, i, 111. "Ad tractandum cum aliquibus Nobilibus de Regno Franciae, seu aliis, cum quibus, pro honore nostro melius viderint fore faciendum . . . super Matrimonio, seu sponsalibus, inter Johannem, Filium et Heredem Edmundi nuper Comitis Kantiae defuncti, Consanguineum nostrum carissimum, et aliquam filiarum dictorum Nobilium, seu aliam Generis, Morum, et Corporis Elegantia praepollentem, contrahendo. . . ." Rymer, *Foedera*, II, iii, 111. This is the broadest authorization for making a marriage alliance that I have seen, though many allow the procurators to contact marriage with any one of the daughters (or sons) of a specified king or other important personage.

189 *D.* 17, 1, 1; *D.* 17, 1, 5, 1; *Inst.* 3, 26, 8.

190 *Summa*, I, *De procuratoribus*, 11.

191 William of Drogheda, *Summa aurea*, CII, in Wahrmund, *Quellen*, II, ii, 97-98; *Établissements de Saint Louis*, 2, 9, Viollet ed., II, 345-347; *Glossa ordinaria, Decret. Greg. IX*, 1, 43, 9, ad v. *Fines mandati excesserit*. An English procurator appearing before the seneschal of Perigord and Cahors in 1324 immediately read into the record the interesting disavowal that he

It begins with an incontrovertible statement that if a special procurator has exceeded his mandate, what he has done should not prejudice the principal. It continues, however, that if he has *plena potestas* for suing, the matter settled by judgment should not be annulled, since the principal retained the right to sue the procurator for any damages he suffered through his fraudulent or wrongful act.[192] This last clause seems to say that a principal could be bound by an act of his procurator in violation of the mandate, but probably it does not. That a procurator acts *fraude vel dolo* does not mean that he exceeds his mandate, but only that he does not act in the best interests of his principal within it. The notion of exceeding the mandate, contained in the first part of *C.* 2, 12, 10, ought not to be carried over into the second part, which treats of another matter. Common sense dictates that the mere possession of full powers for one purpose would not permit a procurator to bind his principal by acting upon some matter unrelated to the purpose for which the full powers were granted. The *Decretals* offer evidence to this effect, for a procuration with full powers for suing was held insufficient even for responding.[193] In diplomatic negotiations, therefore, careful notice was taken of the extent of the powers borne by procurators.[194]

Instances in medieval diplomacy in which principals repudiated the acts of procurators in excess of their mandates are extremely rare, even though we know that envoys did often exceed their mandates.[195] After all, diplomats were usually men of great skill and good faith laboring under serious handicaps in attempting to negotiate at points remote from contact with their principals. If they knowingly or inadvertently exceeded their powers, it was usually to the advantage of the principal that they should do

did not intend "aliquid dicere, proponere, nec requirere, per quod posset in aliquo pre(j)udicari nec derogari juri dicti domini sui regis et ducis nec honori nec jurisdiccioni ejusdem nec privilegiis suis que habet seu potest habere . . . quod, si aliquid faceret seu requireret per quod contrarium in aliquo facere videretur, illud vult pro non dicto, requisito et proposito haberi et habet . . ." Chaplais, *War of Saint Sardos*, p. 28.

[192] *C.* 2, 12, 10: "Si procurator ad unam speciem constitutus officium mandati egressus est, id quod gessit nullum domino praeiudicium facere potuit, quod si plenam potestatem agendi habuit, rem iudicatam rescindi non oportet, cum, si quid fraude vel dolo egit, convenire eum more iudiciorum non prohiberis."

[193] *Decret. Greg. IX*, 1, 38, 10, and *Glossa ordinaria* ad v. *respondendum*. Post has shown that *plena potestas* has to do not with the breadth or extent of the authority committed to the procurator, but with its "depth," i.e., the power to act *conclusively* within the limitations given. "Plena Potestas in Medieval Assemblies," pp. 363-364, and *Medieval Legal Thought*, p. 102. A careful distinction should be drawn between exceeding one's mandate and exceeding one's instructions. Instructions might be written or oral and, if written, intended for the eyes of the opposite party or not. If a procurator exceeded his instructions, but acted within his mandate, the act was binding upon the principal.

[194] Champollion-Figeac, *Lettres*, I, 48. Sometimes the procurators themselves insisted upon the limitations of their mandates. English ambassadors refused to treat anywhere except at Bruges. *The Anglo-French Negotiations at Bruges (1374-1377)*, Edouard Perroy, ed., in *The Camden Miscellany*, XIX (Camden Third Series, LXXX), (London, 1952), 25, no. XXX.

[195] See the surprising Venetian law on procurators who exceeded their mandates. *Infra*, p. 107.

so. Even if the principal considered that he had been prejudiced by the excessive acts of his procurators, the problems raised by repudiation of such acts might outweigh the damages suffered, so he often allowed them to stand or even formally ratified or confirmed them. In the negotiation of the treaty of Corbeil, however, Aragonese procurators had agreed to surrender the county of Foix, even though they had not received power to do so. James I chose to ratify everything that his ambassadors had done with the exception of this article, retaining his rights over the county.[196] In another instance, Countess Margaret of Flanders repudiated an alleged agreement made by her *bailli* and the count of Holland concerning tolls on the lower Scheldt, contending that this was beyond the *bailli*'s mandate.[197] A document touching Anglo-Castilian negotiations in 1325 seems to contradict all that has just been said, for the English envoys protested that they could not extend themselves further, since they had already made promises beyond what was contained in their mandates.[198] Either one of two interpretations, however, will serve to bring this case under the general rule that procurators could not act to bind their principals beyond the powers granted to them. First and less likely, *mandatis* may be used in a common and generic sense meaning orders—or even instructions. *Mandare*, after all, is a rather broad term. More likely *mandatis* is used in the legal sense, and the statement of the English procurators implies that their king would have to approve their promise in excess of their mandates before he could be bound. Of course, the English procurators may have possessed unshown procurations belying their words. The negotiation was over the price to be paid for aid, and in money matters especially it was not unusual for a series of procurations to be issued in different amounts in the hopes that the opposite party could be persuaded to accept something less than the real maximum as a final offer. At any rate, the tenet that procurators could not bind their principals beyond the terms of their mandates must be accepted.

Closely related to the question of exceeding the limitations of the mandate is that of acting after a mandate has been revoked. To be effective in absolving the principal from responsibility for the acts of his procurator, the revocation must be made known to the other party, but if this has been accomplished the procurator can no longer act to bind the principal.[199] Thus, as part of the procedure of breaking relations with France in 1297, Guy

[196] Charles Jean Marie, Baron de Tourtoulon, *Don Jaime I, el conquistador, rey d'Aragon, conde de Barcelona, señor de Montpeller, segun las crónicas y documentos ineditos*, 2 vols. in 1 (Valencia, 1873), II, 252. Dr. Iris Wilson called my attention to this in a seminar paper, "James I and the Treaty of Corbeil," presented in 1959.

[197] Leopold A. Warnkoenig, *Histoire de la Flandre jusqu'à l'année 1305*, A. E. Gheldolf, trans., 5 vols. (Bruxelles, 1835-1864), I, 361, no. XXI.

[198] Chaplais, *War of Saint Sardos*, pp. 214-217, no. 178.

[199] Tancred, *Ordo iudiciarius*, 1, 7, 6, in Bergmann, *Libri de iudiciorum ordine*, pp. 121-123;

of Flanders sent letters, read aloud by Pierre Flotte, revoking the procurations that he had given for negotiating with the king.[200] Incidentally, just as a procurator could be empowered to substitute another for himself, so could he be authorized to revoke such a substitution and to resume the negotiations himself.[201]

Embassies were normally made up of more than one envoy, which gives rise to the question of the possibility of conclusive action without the participation of all those named in the mandate. Since journeying was slow and sometimes dangerous, sickness or death might often prevent such full participation. Maulde La Clavière reached the false conclusion that when an embassy included several members action could still be taken without the participation of all provided that the head of the embassy was one of those taking an active part.[202] It could be arranged in this manner, to be sure, but in fact no single envoy was usually designated as the head of the mission. The law of procuration is abundantly clear on this matter, and diplomatic procurations follow it with great precision. If two procurators are appointed together without the addition of the words *in solidum*, then one should not be admitted without the other. If they are appointed *in solidum*, however, the one who first undertakes the affair is recognized, and the other cannot intervene. If it is desired, however, that the other should subsequently be permitted to act, it should be specified in the procuration that the condition of the one occupying should not be better.[203] At the will of the principal any number of variations could be incorporated in these multiple procurations. Reliance upon a majority is rare but does occur. A given number of those named—four, three, two —might be given authority to act. Some procurations naming several envoys including one or two bishops specify that four, three, or two of

---

William of Drogheda, *Summa aurea*, CII, in Wahrmund, *Quellen*, II, ii, 100; Martinus de Fano, *Formularium*, XLVII, in Wahrmund, *Quellen*, I, viii, 17.

200 Wauters, *Table chronologique*, VI, 553. The procurators, as well as the members of the count's council present in Paris, were ordered not to go before the king as lord or judge. Funck-Brentano, *Philippe le Bel en Flandre*, p. 203.

201 Rymer, *Foedera*, II, iii, 191.

202 *La diplomatie au temps de Machiavel*, II, 99. This is a common type of error in the above work, generalization on the basis of only one of several possibilities.

203 *Sext.*, 1, 9, 6. The necessity of the *in solidum* clause if all were not present is illustrated by Innocent III's complaint to King John in 1213 that three English procurators were powerless to act without the other three appointed. Rymer, *Foedera*, I, i, 53. Apparently Edward I's mandate for four procurators to hear Boniface VIII's arbitral judgment in 1302 was also of this sort—lacking an *in solidum* clause. When two of the four excused themselves, Edward wrote to the pope "that to avoid delay in the business by their absence, he appoints the two others as his proctors therein." *C.P.R. Edward I* (*1301-1307*), p. 24. See also: Champollion-Figeac, *Lettres*, I, 45, no. XXXV.

them may act, so long as one of them is one of the bishops.[204] The variety of possible arrangements is well illustrated by an English procuration of 1300 naming six envoys. If all cannot be present, full powers are given to Amadeus of Savoy, Henry de Lacy, and Othon de Grandson, or two or one of them. If none of these three can be present, however, full powers are withdrawn from the others.[205] There is no fixed rule concerning the locus of authority among multiple envoys, but by use of the proper formulas the principal could arrange it as he pleased.

Occasional allusion has been made to differences between the *nuncius* and the procurator, but a more systematic contrasting of the two offices may dispel some of the confusion which modern writers and the documents themselves have contributed. Some authors appear to perceive no distinction, while others are not clear as to what the differences were or why both terms were often used of the same envoys.[206] Still others tend to denigrate the *nuncius* and procurator, especially in the fifteenth century with the rise of the ambassador, an envoy wrongly believed by them to be used only by sovereigns, great princes, or independent communes.[207] Even Mattingly, who is quite clear on the distinction between *nuncius* and procurator, sees their decline and the rise of a distinct ambassadorial office before this actually occurred.[208]

That modern authors working from medieval diplomatic documents should confuse *nuncii* and procurators is quite understandable, since they are named in the documents and even in legal manuals apparently indiscriminately. The same envoys might be called *nuncii et procuratores* in one document and simply *procuratores* in another.[209] Even where the appointment was quite clearly that of a *procurator litis*, an attorney-at-law, the terms *nuncius* and procurator were used without discrimination.[210] Other

204 Chaplais, *Treaty Rolls*, I, 89, no. 212; I, 135-136, no. 358; I, 145-146, no. 368; I, 251-252, nos. 644-645; Rymer, *Foedera*, I, iii, 131 and 206, and I, iv, 2.

205 Chaplais, *Treaty Rolls*, I, 146, no. 369; Rymer, *Foedera*, I, iv, 3.

206 Henry S. Lucas, "The Machinery of Diplomatic Intercourse," in *The English Government at Work, 1327-1336*, James F. Willard and William A. Morris, eds. (Cambridge, Mass., 1940), I, 310ff.; Von Heckel, "Aufkommen der ständigen Prokuratoren," pp. 300-301; Clarke, *Medieval Representation and Consent*, pp. 309-310; Cuttino, *English Diplomatic Administration*, p. 87.

207 Ganshof, *Le Moyen Age*, p. 270; Behrens, "Treaties on the Ambassador," pp. 621-622. What Behrens says of the scholastic lawyers of his period is true, but their distinctions were not applied consistently in practice, even in Rome.

208 Mattingly, *Renaissance Diplomacy*, p. 30. Discussion of the ambassador, however, must be postponed until the next chapter.

209 Rymer, *Foedera*, I, i, 117.

210 Duvivier, *Influences*, II, 347-348, no. CXCIX. For a series of thirteenth-century documents appointing legal representatives of the masters of Paris and using *nuntius* and procurator indiscriminately, see Gaines Post, "Parisian Masters as a Corporation," *Speculum*, IX (1934), p. 432, n. 1, and p. 436, n. 6; Post, *Medieval Legal Thought*, p. 41, n. 8, and p. 47, n. 113.

terms, such as "commissioner" and "deputy," were gratuitously added.[211] The use of *nuncius* and *sindicus* by the Venetian chancery, however, was quite clear, and here they were never used as synonyms. True, the same envoy might bear both titles (or he might be *ambassador* and *sindicus*), but *sindicus* was quite properly reserved for an envoy with full powers and was always applied when *plena potestas* was granted. The same clarity cannot be attributed to most of the legal and notarial manuals.[212] Yet the distinction is really quite clear. *D.* 3, 3, 1, 1, points out that one who is appointed to bear a thing or a letter or a message is not appropriately called a procurator.[213] Baldus lists the differences carefully: a procurator speaks in his own person, a *nuncius* in the person of the principal; a procurator acts on his own judgment and by his own activity, but a *nuncius* has no activity of his own. A *nuncius* could not do or say anything on his own. He further states that one can no more say that a procurator is a *nuncius* and a *nuncius* a procurator than one can say a procurator is a letter and a letter a procurator.[214] Long before Baldus, Aegidius de Fuscararius explained the confusion: "So in this document, which says: 'his *nuncius* and procurator,' there seems to be a contradiction, for there is a difference between a *nuncius* and a procurator because the *nuncius* ought to form his words in the person of his principal, but not in his own person. . . . But the procurator ought to speak in his own person. . . ." This inconsistency of putting into the mandate "*nuncius* and procurator," according to Aegidius, "is tolerated by custom."[215] Therefore, in the opinion of Aegidius and in my own, the legal distinction between the two offices was clear, although the words were used confusedly. Long ago, however, it had been laid down by Hilary of Poitiers that the thing ought not to be subject to the word, but on the contrary, the word to the thing.[216] Perhaps

[211] Rymer, *Foedera*, IV, iv, 99. In fact, these terms became commonplace from the late fourteenth century.

[212] *Lo Codi*, 2, 27, 3. (I have borrowed this reference from a manuscript note by Professor Post.) *Summa notariae annis MCCXL-MCCXLIII Aretii composita*, L, Carolo Cicognario, ed., in Gaudenzi, *Bibliotheca juridica*, III, 295; *Summa notariae Belluni composita*, XXXII-XXXVI, Arthuro Palmerio, ed., in Gaudentius, *Bibliotheca juridica*, III, 361-362; Durandus, *Speculum juris*, 1, 3, 4, 11.

[213] In spite of this, Azo, Durandus, and Baldus all state that "to a great extent, every *nuncius* is a procurator, but not every procurator is a *nuncius*." Azo, *Summa*, 4, *Si alteri, vel sibi, sub alterius nomine, vel aliena pecunia emerit*, 1; Durandus, *Speculum juris*, 1, 3, *De procuratore, ut autem*, 5; Baldus, *Commentaria*, ad *C.* 4, *Si quis alteri vel sibi*, 6, 17. They are fitting *nuncius* within the limits of the broad basic definition of *D.* 3, 3, 1: "A procurator is he who administers affairs by the mandate of the principal." This subsuming of *nuncius* under procurator is not very helpful, it seems to me, as can be seen by reading the rest of *D.* 3, 3, 1.

[214] Baldus, *Commentaria*, ad *C.* 4, *Si quis alteri vel sibi*, 6, 17-19; ad *D.* 3, *De procuratoribus et defensoribus*, 1, Additio 5.

[215] Aegidius de Fuscararius, *Ordo iudiciarius*, XIII, in Wahrmund, *Quellen*, III, i, 23-24.

[216] Hilary, bishop of Poitiers, *De Trinitate*, in *Patrologia latina*, J. P. Migne, ed., 221 vols. (Parisiis, 1841-1864), x, col. 107.

this was where the canon lawyers found this enlightened doctrine.[217] As Hostiensis said, as long as the intention of the principal is clear, it does not matter whether the envoy is called "ass."[218]

We have then two distinct offices, useful for different purposes, which might or might not be combined in the same persons.[219] Unlike the simple *nuncius*, the procurator could act and speak in his own person on behalf of his principal. Since he could negotiate and conclude without reference to the principal, the use of the procurator was indicated when it was desired to allow some flexibility to a trusted negotiator. For most ceremonial purposes, on the other hand, the symbolic representation of the *nuncius* was more suitable.

217 *Glossa ordinaria* to *Decret. Greg. IX*, 1, 38, 9, ad v. *intentio*. "Sic patet quod quando verba generalia sive dubia ponuntur in huiusmodi instrumentis procurationis, recurrendum est ad intentionem constituentis. . . . Et illa est causa quia verba debent de servire intentioni, non intentio verbis."

218 Hostiensis, *Summa*, 1, *De procuratoribus*, rubric *quis dicatur procurator*.

219 Rymer, *Foedera*, II, i, 27-28, provides an example of three envoys sent by Edward II to the French court as procurators at law and to the French king as diplomatic *nuncii*. Two separate documents were used in this case.

CHAPTER III

THE AMBASSADOR

Bernard du Rosier, whose *Ambaxiator brevilogus* appeared in 1436, wrote that "ambassador" was a modern name unknown to the ancients. His first attempt to trace the etymology of the word possesses the abundance of imagination and the poverty of knowledge of an Isidore of Seville. It has its origin, he says, in the custom of sending two or more envoys; *ambaxiatores*, therefore, is derived from *ambo*. Of course a single envoy was often dispatched in fact, and when more than one was sent, three or more was probably as common as two. His alternative suggestion comes nearer the mark, for he says that "ambassador" might come from the character of the office which requires the ambassador to go about (*ambire*) the world.[1] The *Oxford English Dictionary* derives the word from *ambactiare*, "to go on a mission," and refers to the Salic and Burgundian laws where *ambactia* and *ambaxia* are used to mean "charge, office, employment."[2] Sir Harold Nicolson finds "ambassador" first used in Latin in *The Gallic Wars* and traces its origin to a Celtic word meaning "servant."[3]

The introduction of a chapter on medieval ambassadors with a discussion of the derivation of the word is no mere pedantic exercise, for the main theme of this chapter will be that the fundamental meaning of "ambassador" until the end of the Middle Ages was precisely "one sent on a mission." He was not necessarily one endowed with specific legal powers or status, and his mission was not invariably diplomatic. An embassy (Lat., *ambaxiata* or variants, Fr., *ambassade* or variants) was the mission or task so assigned.[4] The verbal form *ambasciare* similarly means "to undertake a mission." Du Cange cites a document of Charles the Bald in 877, a grant to a monastery made at the request of the Empress Richildis, whose name appears after his own at the foot of the document: *Domina Richildis imperatrix ambasciavit.*[5] Du Cange declares that this means "intervened," and so in con-

[1] Bernard du Rosier, *Ambaxiator brevilogus*, in *De legatis et legationibus tractatus varii*, Vladimir E. Hrabar, ed. (Dorpat, 1906), pp. 4-5.

[2] *O.E.D.*, I, 267, *Ambassade*. There are many variant spellings given, which should not bother anyone accustomed to medieval documents. I call attention only to an occasional initial "e," as in the modern "embassy," and a rare initial "i."

[3] Nicolson, *Evolution of Diplomatic Method*, p. 33. J. J. Jusserand, "The School for Ambassadors," in *The School for Ambassadors and Other Essays* (New York and London, 1925), p. 9, also equates it with *servitor*.

[4] For example, the *ambaxiatores* of Emperor Henry VII to Genoa *portantes Ambaxiatas infrascriptas. . . . Et est eorum Ambaxiata talis*. Menzel, *Deutsches Gesandtschaftswesen*, pp. 44-45.

[5] Van den Bergh, *Oorkondenboek*, I, 17, no. 20.

text it surely does. Literally, however, the phrase means that the empress received the mission of obtaining the grant from the emperor. Even in the fifteenth century *ambaxator* and *ambasciata* had not become specific words of diplomatic art. The Venetian *Maggior Consiglio* in 1413 acted to increase the penalty against notaries employed by the government and used by the nobles in elections for performing *ambasiatas* and carrying *cedulas* (writings, probably telling or asking the recipients to vote for certain persons) to the electors.[6] Subsequent discussion will reveal many other nondiplomatic tasks of ambassadors. Maulde La Clavière found much evidence of this unspecific usage:

> ... the names of ambassador, orator, messenger are applied to every person charged with a temporary mission of a public character having in view a peaceful settlement. They will call ambassador an envoy of the duke of Orléans to his Piedmontaise land of Asti, the envoys of Isabelle of Bavaria before the estates of Dauphiné, the deputies of the Swiss cantons to the federal diet, the agents of the Swiss government among the Swiss in the pay of foreign countries; they will give the same appellation to every royal envoy, even princely, in the interior of the country; they will go so far as to apply it, in matters of war, to certain captains who negotiate a capitulation, and even to the commandant of a peaceful army of occupation. The expression has the same elasticity as the institution. In Italy the word *ambasciata* signifies any commission whatsoever.[7]

Often, especially in the later Middle Ages, we encounter *solemnes ambaxatores*, and this term also has no very specific meaning—certainly no technical significance. Du Cange does not even give an example of *solemnis* used in diplomacy. Synonyms are *illustris, clarus, insignis, celebris*, and *spectabilis; solemnis* is used to dignify lords of the court, a physician, a town—and even a mill![8] In this chapter, therefore, we are dealing with extremely loose terms and shadowy institutions, and the fault of some writers has been to make them more precise than the facts allow.

The consensus of historical opinion is that the use of "ambassador" in diplomacy stems from thirteenth century Italy.[9] Extant evidence essentially supports this view, although it rests upon a relative paucity of diplomatic documents prior to that time. Even the rich collections of Venice and England become abundant only in the thirteenth century. Milan possesses

[6] A.S.V., Maggior Consiglio, Leona, 221v (226v).

[7] Maulde La Clavière, *La diplomatie au temps de Machiavel*, I, 304.

[8] Du Cange, *Glossarium*, VII, 514-515, *solemnis* and *solempnis*.

[9] Mattingly, *Renaissance Diplomacy*, p. 29, Ganshof, *Le Moyen Age*, p. 268, Nys, *Origines du droit international*, p. 317.

quite a fine collection of documents from the twelfth century, though, and in them the first appearances of diplomatic ambassadors date from 1198 and 1199. In early 1198 the consuls of Milan treated with *Iohanes Rusca et Berterus de Carrobio consules Cumarum et cum eis Iohanes de Papa, eiusdem civitatis ad hoc legatus sive ambaxator. . . .* In March of 1199 *nuncii et ambaxatores* of Alessandria, Vercelli, and Asti committed the quarrels of their cities with the Marquis of Montferrat to arbitration by *nuncii et ambaxatores* of Milan and Piacenza. A month later we read of Milanese ambassadors receiving safe-conduct for merchants of their city passing through the lands of the commune of Tortona.[10] In the registers of the *Maggior Consiglio* in Venice from 1232, the date at which that series of documents begins, and throughout the thirteenth century "ambassador" is commonly used. Prior to the beginning of this series Venetian evidence is generally lacking, although a nonregistered treaty of 1230 was made with Venice by the *podestà* and ambassadors of Ferrara.[11] Such collaboration of ambassadors with magistrates was not uncommon in this period. A Genoese document of 1239 shows ambassadors of Lucca engaged in treaty-making.[12] Collections of imperial acts also provide examples of thirteenth-century ambassadors in Italy. Consuls of Castel Fidardo swore in 1228 to uphold a pact with the doge of Venice before the latter's "legate and ambassador." Ambassadors of Venice and Genoa made a treaty against the emperor in 1238. The *podestà* and ambassadors of Imola in 1220 sought from Frederick II confirmation of the acts of his chancellor in favor of their city against Faenza. Ezzelino da Romano sent ambassadors to receive from Cremona the balance of a loan that had been agreed upon by ambassadors of that city.[13] Between 1198 and 1240, then, we have widespread evidence of the use of ambassadors in northern and central Italy.

As vernacular documents became more common in the later fourteenth and fifteenth centuries, the word appeared in its various vernacular forms. Indeed, as this happened it tended to disappear in Latin documents, yielding there to the humanistic "orator," especially in Italy. As early as the thirteenth century *ambassadeur* became habitual in French.[14] English did not become either a learned or a diplomatic language as early as Italian or

[10] Manaresi, *Atti . . . di Milano*, p. 300, no. CCIX (note that the ambassador accompanies two consuls); pp. 303-308, nos. CCXII-CCXVI; pp. 312-313, nos. CCXIX-CCXX; pp. 324-325, no. CCXXIX; pp. 490-491, no. CCCLXVIII. (No. CCXIV is an account of the reception of full powers by ambassadors of Asti.)

[11] A.S.V., Miscellanea di atti diplomatici e privati, busta II, no. 91.

[12] *Liber Iurium reipublicae Genuensis*, I, cols. 986-987, no. DCCLIII.

[13] Winkelmann, *Acta Imperii inedita*, I, 160, no. 183; I, 490-491, no. 611; II, 689-690, no. 1028; Böhmer–Ficker, *Acta Imperii selecta*, p. 671, no. 964.

[14] Maulde La Clavière, *La diplomatie au temps de Machiavel*, I, 301.

French. The first use of the word in English vernacular noted in the *Oxford English Dictionary* is in Chaucer (1374).[15] Only rarely, even in the fifteenth century, did diplomatic documents appear in English dress, although there is an indenture of 1397 using *ambassatairs* and another of 1451 employing *ambassatours*.[16]

Brief mention has already been made of the humanistic term "orator," which had its origins in antiquity where it gained the sanction of Virgil and Ovid. It seems to have signified especially, as one might expect, an envoy with an oral message. There is little evidence of its use in the Middle Ages prior to the rise of the cult of classical learning.[17] When it returned to use there was absolutely no difference in meaning between "orator" and "ambassador," but the former was deemed more learned and elegant than the latter. In the abundant diplomatic documents in the Venetian archives for the first half of the fifteenth century, the two words are used interchangeably but are usually not used together. Clerks and lawyers, as we have seen, do not shy away from redundancy if there is the remotest chance of a distinction between terms, so we may take this as evidence that they were exactly synonymous. By the middle of the fifteenth century "ambassador" tends to disappear in favor of "orator" in Venetian documents.

In order to understand the meaning of "ambassador" we must turn again to the word *legatus*, already discussed in the first chapter. Corrections, marginal notes, notations *in dorso* and revised versions of manuscripts can often be very revealing. A thirteenth-century revision of the *Continuatio Anonymi* to *Ottonis Morenae Historia Frederici I*, first written in the 1160's, for example, changes the earlier *legati* to *ambaxatores*.[18] With the popularity of "orator" in the fifteenth century, it too came to be used synonymously with "legate."[19] Like *orator, legatus* had the sanction of antiquity and of the humanists. Étienne Dolet, who was burned to death in 1546, left behind him a book entitled *Liber unus de officio legati vulgo ambassiatorem vocant*,[20] indicating the relationship of these two terms under the

[15] *O.E.D.*, I, 267, *Ambassador.*

[16] Rymer, *Foedera*, III, iv, 136-137; v, ii, 32.

[17] Maulde La Clavière, *La diplomatie au temps de Machiavel*, I, 294; V. Serguiev, "La diplomatie de l'antiquité," I, i, in *Histoire de la diplomatie*, Vladimir E. Potemkine, ed., trans. from the Russian edn. of 1941 by X. Pamphilova and M. Eristov (Paris, 1946), p. 50. Ruess does claim to have found one use of *oratores* for papal legates prior to 1050. *Die rechtliche Stellung des päpstlichen Legaten*, pp. 40-41.

[18] *M.G.H., Script. rer. Germ., N.S.*, VII, 186, 205 and 212. *Einleitung*, p. xxviii, on date of the revision.

[19] A.S.V., Senato, Secreta, XX, 31v (32v); A.S.F., Signori—Carteggi—Missive—Legazione e Commissarie—Elezioni e Istruzioni a Oratori, XXI, 28v. Documents of July 9 and 10.

[20] Ernest Nys, "Les origines de la diplomatie et le droit d'ambassade jusqu'à Grotius," *Revue de droit international et de législation comparée*, XVI (1884), 172.

impact of humanism. Bernard du Rosier asks himself whether *legatio* and *ambaxiata* differ, and if so in what way. He replies brusquely that they differ only in name, for the office is the same. The ancients, he says, used *legati* for messengers destined for any task in any place. Moderns generally reserve *legati* for papal envoys, while others are commonly called ambassadors.[21] On their identity the fifteenth-century scholar was absolutely correct, although he introduced a sharper distinction between the ecclesiastical and secular uses than is justified by the evidence. Not only are fifteenth-century secular diplomats often called *legati*,[22] but it is only in the late fifteenth century that Venetian documents consistently apply *legati* or *nuncii* rather than *ambasciatores* or *oratores* to papal diplomats.

Now if "ambassador" and "orator" are equivalent to "legate," then according to the earlier discussion,[23] they ought also to be the same as *nuncius*, and so they are frequently used. Louis IX sent *nuncii et ambaxatores* in 1246 to arrange transportation for his first crusade.[24] Through the fourteenth and fifteenth centuries this practice of redundancy continued.[25] Admittedly, the mere use of the two terms in juxtaposition does not prove them synonyms, for *nuncius* and *procurator* also appear together, but as a real conjunction of offices, not a mere redundancy. An ambassador and a *nuncius* were not distinct, however. An *ambasciata* was received by *nuncii* of the imperial electors.[26] A letter of Edward II to James II of Aragon refers first to *nuncii* that the latter was sending to England, later calls them ambassadors.[27] Two separate Venetian documents of the fifteenth century refer to the same envoy of the patriarch of Aquileia as *orator* and later *nuncius*.[28] Professor Ganshof was quite right, therefore, in equating *ambassador, orator, nuncius*, and *legatus*.[29] Sometimes all these titles and others were strung together. English ambassadors to France in 1488, for example, were called

[21] Bernard du Rosier, *Ambaxiator brevilogus*, p. 3; Mattingly, *Renaissance Diplomacy*, p. 29. Nys denies that the *legati* of Roman law were the same as ambassadors. They were deputies of a province or a town before the emperor. "Le droit d'ambassade jusqu'à Grotius," XVI, 170. In the first place his statement about Roman usage is not universally true. Secondly, the sending of legates by subordinates is not unlike the medieval use of legates from vassals or cities to lords. Nys was too much dominated by concepts of modern diplomacy.

[22] Mattingly, *Renaissance Diplomacy*, pp. 29-30.

[23] *Supra*, pp. 4-5.

[24] Champollion-Figeac, *Documents historiques inédits*, II, ii, 52, no. XXVIII.

[25] E.g., Rymer, *Foedera*, II, iii, 188; III, i, 85; IV, ii, 57.

[26] *Ibid.*, III, i, 34.

[27] Chaplais, *Treaty Rolls*, I, 241, no. 626; Rymer, *Foedera*, II, ii, 45.

[28] A.S.V., Senato, Secreta, XVI, 132r (132r) and 143v (143v).

[29] Ganshof, *Le Moyen Age*, p. 268. Behrens, "Treatises on the Ambassador," pp. 622-623, finds the writers who use *ambassador* and *nuncius* interchangeably to be confused. He also writes that the lawyers tended to confuse *nuncius* and *legatus*, while the papal masters of ceremonies tended to confuse *nuncius* and *procurator*. In fact, the medieval people concerned with diplomacy knew what they were about and understood their terminology quite clearly.

Ambassiatoribus, Oratoribus, Nunciis, Legatis, et Commissariis—and also received the full powers of a procurator.[30] To find the above words mingled with *procurator* and its synonyms, or near synonyms, indeed is very common.[31]

While it is quite true that *ambaxator, orator, nuncius,* and *legatus* were broad, equivalent, and nontechnical terms, special meaning did apply to *legatus* and *nuncius* as used by the papal chancery and to *ambaxator* and *orator* as employed by Venetian clerks. Papal diplomacy, in general, lies beyond the scope of this study, but it is impossible to exclude it altogether. The papal court alone appears to have placed in order a hierarchy of its representatives in the decretal classes of the middle and late thirteenth century. At its apex was the *legatus a latere*, a dignity usually reserved for cardinals, who represented the very person of the pope and received important missions of a diplomatic, political, financial, or religious character. At a slightly lower level were the *legati missi*, usually of episcopal or archiepiscopal rank and possessing less extensive powers than the *legati a latere*. Finally there were the *legati nati*, prelates exercising legatine authority attached to their sees.[32]

Until almost the very end of the Middle Ages, however, the chanceries of secular states referred to papal diplomats in secular terms. In 1375, Bernabò Visconti wrote to Ludovico Gonzaga concerning papal *ambaxiatores* who had come to Milan to form a truce.[33] "Orators" of Pope John XXIII requested the sending of English representatives to the Council of Constance.[34] Secular terms for papal envoys were also customarily used in Venice. The register of the Senate even labels as "orator" an emissary sent in 1429 to seek the imposition of a tenth on prelates and clergy under Venetian rule for the defense of Hungary against the Turks. The mission of this *orator* seems only marginally diplomatic, yet the commonly used word for a secular diplomat was applied to him.[35] Only about the mid-1460's do Venetian documents begin consistently to designate papal diplomats as legates. An interesting Milanese *ordine* of 1468 regulating the reception of ambassadors suggests that the Milanese style remained quite close to the Venetian. A provision dealing with orators of the pope goes on to speak

30 Rymer, *Foedera*, v, iii, 189.

31 Three random samples from thirteenth, fourteenth, and fifteenth centuries: A.S.V., Miscellanea di atti diplomatici e privati, busta III, no. 124; Rymer, *Foedera*, III, iii, 6; A.S.V., Senato, Secreta, XXXII, 81v (81v).

32 Schmutz, "The Foundations of Medieval Papal Representation," p. 1, n. 1.

33 *Documenti diplomatici tratti degli Archivj Milanesi*, Luigi Osio, ed., 3 vols. in 6 parts (Milano, 1864-1877), I, i, 173-174, no. CXVI.

34 Rymer, *Foedera*, IV, ii, 91.

35 A.S.V., Senato, Secreta, XI, 1rv (2rv).

of all cardinals, even if they should not be legates, in such a manner that the equivalence of "orator" with "legate" of the pope is clear.[36] Secular powers, then, continued to use secular terms for papal legates until the late fifteenth century, and the practice of the papal chancery was not customarily followed elsewhere.

The papacy also availed itself of envoys called *nuncii*, inferior in rank to the legates. Incumbents might be archbishops or bishops or clerks of less elevated standing. According to Bernard du Rosier they were not sent for the purpose of the church, but of a person (the pope?) and they did not bear the papal dignity.[37] In the fifteenth century they were sometimes specially endowed with the powers of a *legatus a latere* and about 1460 they tended to replace legates below that highest rank.[38] Thus in papal diplomacy *legatus* and *nuncius* possessed special meanings, although either one might be covered by the secular words *ambaxator* and *orator*.

A special usage of the word *ambaxator* in Venice also requires notice. In the registers of the *Maggior Consiglio* for the thirteenth century, *ambaxator* and *nuncius* seem to be used interchangeably. For example, a consul was sent to Tunis for a year in 1281, ". . . and he ought to be *nuncius* to the said king of Tunis . . ." to seek a payment due to certain of his countrymen. ". . . the said payment ought to be made to that ambassador for those who ought to receive it."[39] By the middle of the fourteenth century, however, a social distinction was introduced. The titles *ambaxator* and *orator* were generally reserved for Venetian patricians, while governmental notaries or secretaries, who received many diplomatic missions, either were called simply *notarius* or *secretarius* or else *nuncius*.[40] When in 1419 the king of Poland sought to act as intermediary in a Venetian dispute with the king of the Romans (and Hungary), the Senate noted its previous unsuccessful attempts to gain a peace or truce through its ambassadors, but agreed to send a notary, Francesco de la Siega. He was a very distinguished commoner who rose through such responsibilities to the Grand Chancellor-

[36] A. Maspes, "Prammatica pel ricevimento degli ambasciatori inviati alla corte di Galeazzo Maria Sforza," *Archivio storico lombardo*, XVII (1890), 148.

[37] Bernard du Rosier, *Ambaxiator brevilogus*, p. 5.

[38] Ganshof, *Le Moyen Age*, p. 269; Vincent Ilardi, "Fifteenth-Century Diplomatic Documents in Western European Archives and Libraries (1450-1494)," *Studies in the Renaissance*, IX (1962), 88.

[39] Cessi, *Deliberazioni del Maggior Consiglio*, II, 128. A thorough study of the consular office would be useful, although a number of specialized studies have been written. This is not the place to discuss it, although it will be necessary later in this chapter to consider the theory that the resident ambassador had his origins in the Venetian consuls, especially in Apulia or Constantinople.

[40] E.g., the College should send either an orator or a secretary. A.S.V., Senato, Secreta, XVI, 199r (199r).

ship, the highest dignity possible to a Venetian commoner. He received powers and discretionary authority comparable to those that might have been accorded to an ambassador, although, because of his social status, he did not receive that title.[41] On an earlier occasion in 1402, the Senate refused the request of the king of the Romans that it send an ambassador to Rome to support his own ambassador in his quest for imperial coronation on the grounds that Venice was already represented there by a chancellor or secretary who should fulfill that function.[42] Once again the Senate was unable promptly to dispatch an orator to Rome, "for our nobles refuse to go on account of the dangers of the way." Considering the matter to require celerity, therefore, the Senate named a *nuncius*, resolving, however, to elect an orator presently.[43] A general act of 1353 on ambassadorial expenses explains another major reason for the distinction between ambassadors and *nuncii*. Because of his higher social status and greater ceremonial value, an ambassador incurred much greater expenses for retinue, housing, servants, entertainment, and the like than did a *nuncius*.[44]

Ambaxator, not *nuncius*, is the word that takes on special meaning in Venice. *Nuncius* remains the generic term for an envoy. This is made very clear by an act of 1390 amending an earlier act that had provided that ambassadors should not have to pay any fare when traveling on Venetian galleys. No mention had been made of provisors, syndics, and other *nuncii*, although the intention had been to cover all *nuncii*. ". . . henceforth the order should be extended and should be understood generally of all ambassadors, provisors, syndics, tractators and all other *nuncii* of our commune."[45] Sometimes in fourteenth- and fifteenth-century documents con-

[41] *Ibid.*, vii, 99r (100r)–100r (101r). Ten years later the Senate rejected a proposal to send an ambassador to Milan and again dispatched the same public servant. *Ibid.*, xi, 43r (44r)–46r (47r).

[42] *Ibid.*, i, 49v (50v).

[43] *Ibid.*, xiii, 75r (75r). A similar example. *Ibid.* x, 22v (26v), and 25v (29v)–26r (30r).

[44] A.S.V., Senato, Misti, xxvi, 126rv (127rv). The French observer who wrote the "Traité du gouvernement de Venise" acutely noted: "Quelquefoys la Seigneurie, al lieu desdiz ambassadeurs, envoye quelque secretaire de la chancelerie, lequel en toutes choses resemble ausdiz ambassadeurs, excepté qu'il n'est pas appellé ambassadeur, mais est appellé secretaire, et mayne avecques luy plus petit train que lesdiz ambassadeurs, lequel train de secretaire est de quatre chevaulx pour le moins et de plus huyt." "Traité du gouvernement de la cité et seigneurie de Venise," in Perret, *Relations de la France avec Venise*, ii, 292-293. Maulde La Clavière incorrectly assumed that the Italian states used secretaries in place of ambassadors only at courts of the second rank. *La diplomatie au temps de Machiavel*, i, 366, n. 4.

[45] A.S.V., Senato, Misti, xli, 121r (written over 113) (124r). An orator and a secretary of the marquis of Mantua, A.S.V., Senato, Secreta, xviii, 165r (167r), referred to jointly as *nuncii* in the Rubriche, ii, 77r (81r). "No *orator* or other *nuncius*." A.S.V., Senato, Secreta, xxii, 160v (162v). ". . . as much orators, as provisors, secretaries, and other *nuncii*, who henceforth will go abroad for the service of our *Signoria* . . ." A.S.V., Senato, Terra, vi, 99r (100r).

cerning Venetian diplomats the two terms are simply linked, *ambaxatores et nuncii*.[46] There was no real confusion, however, for as Mattingly said, "The greater dignity covered the less."[47]

There do exist a few cases in fourteenth- and fifteenth-century Venice, however, where commoners or clergy did receive designation as ambassadors or orators. In the fourteenth century several envoys called ambassadors were actually notaries or the chancellor.[48] The early date might account for the unusual designation in these cases, but there are later examples. In 1408, because of lack of security and want of time, the Senate could not appoint a noble for an embassy to England, so a religious was appointed as a "solemn orator."[49] In 1483 two lawyers were assigned, respectively, to the two orators about to go to the emperor and his son, the duke of Burgundy. The orators were instructed to treat the two lawyers as orators and the letters of credence and instructions were to be made in the names of either of them.[50] The very wording of the document, however, indicates its exceptional character, and the reservation of the word "ambassador" for noble envoys from Venice was the general rule.

Although other states did not use the term *ambaxator* as specifically as was the custom in Venice, there can be no doubt that in the Middle Ages one designated as ambassador by any court in Western Europe was understood generally to be of some considerable social standing. Maulde La Clavière declares that in France the secretary to an embassy had the rank of ambassador, and he notes the objections raised in 1505 by the pontifical master of ceremonies, Burckhard, and the Venetian ambassador, Giustiniani, to the treatment of Guillaume Budé as an ambassador.[51]

Persons bearing various other titles also served as ambassadors on occasion. "Commissary" became fairly common in the later Middle Ages, especially in documents originating from the English court.[52] The use of this term did not signify a status less than that of an ambassador or orator, for the Treaty of Troyes was made by the queen of France and the duke of Burgundy as *commissairs* (English language document) of Charles VI.[53] On

[46] Winkelmann, *Acta Imperii inedita*, II, 540, no. 849; A.S.V., Senato, Secreta, I, 73v (74v).

[47] *Renaissance Diplomacy*, p. 31. Recall, however, that the distinction in meaning between *ambassador* and *nuncius* was not everywhere as clear as in Venice.

[48] A.S.V., Maggior Consiglio, Novella, 75r (86r), and Capricornus, 8v (122v).

[49] A.S.V., Senato, Secreta, III, 125v (125v). Master Paul of the Order of the Hermits of Saint Augustine, professor of liberal arts and theology, and provincial of the province of Lombardy, was also appointed ambassador in 1413. A.S.V., Sindicati, I, 196v.

[50] A.S.V., Senato, Secreta, XXXI, 41r (41r).

[51] Maulde La Clavière, *La diplomatie au temps de Machiavel*, I, 370.

[52] Rymer, *Foedera*, IV, i, 198; *C.C.R. Henry V (1419-1422)*, p. 108; *C.C.R. Henry VI (1447-1454)*, p. 451.

[53] *C.C.R. Henry V (1419-1422)*, p. 108.

the other hand, Nys reports that the Venetian Senate, not wishing to send ambassadors to England, commissioned two merchants who were in London to act as *suboratores*. We also read of the *Maggior Consiglio* sending to Rome in 1303 a *Vice Ambaxatoris*.[54] Although the consuls were not fundamentally diplomatic officials, diplomatic tasks were frequently assigned to them, especially when it was a matter of seeking the release of merchants or their goods, demanding damages, and other tasks closely related to their basic function.[55] Also officials whose fundamental task was military, like castellans, provisors, and *locumtenentes*, could receive diplomatic functions.[56]

The modern notion that only a sovereign state could be represented by an ambassador was as inchoate in the Middle Ages as the concept of sovereignty itself. It is true that such authorities as Behrens, Cuttino, and Ganshof declare that in the fifteenth century the modern rule prevailed at the papal court. All those not possessing sovereignty, they say, were limited to representation by procurators or *nuncii*.[57] The preeminent authority upon which they rely is Bernard du Rosier, whose knowledge of diplomacy was indeed great and who had held a number of offices in the papal curia. Rosier limited the custom of sending ambassadors to "the greater princes of the age by birth, the commune of any city and the three estates of a country or kingdom." He also would restrict the activity of ambassadors to major causes.[58] Certain scraps of more empirical evidence tend to support this view. The papal master of ceremonies, Johannes Burckhard,

[54] Nys, "Le droit d'ambassade jusqu'à Grotius," xvi, 56. He refers to Sanuto's *Diarii* under the year 1496. I was unable to discover such a statement by Sanuto during that year. A.S.V., Maggior Consiglio, Magnus, 58v (58v).

[55] A.S.V., Maggior Consiglio, Magnus, 62v; Fronesis, 95r (96r); Spiritus, 77r (78r); Senato, Secreta, xvii, 68r (66r). In the last case the representative was the *vicedominus*.

[56] A.S.V., Senato, Secreta, vi, 153v (154v); viii, 30r (31r); viii, 92v (93v).

[57] Behrens, "Treatises on the Ambassador," p. 619, though he is careful to point out that other courts were not so meticulous in terminology; Cuttino, *English Diplomatic Administration*, p. 85, simply follows Behrens; Ganshof, *Le Moyen Age*, pp. 269-270. One is immediately led to query whether the duke of Burgundy was sovereign and entitled to an ambassador—as, of course, he was in fact. Maulde La Clavière cites the expulsion from the pontifical chapel by the master of ceremonies of envoys from Rhodes and Bologna because they were from subjects of the pope, and therefore *nuncii*, not orators. Also representatives of the bishop of Liège. Envoys from Rhodes, however, were accepted as ambassadors before the Turk. *La diplomatie au temps de Machiavel*, i, 170, and 296, n. 1. James IV of Scotland in 1490 sent a procurator to Rome to discuss with the pope the defense of Europe against the Turk, clearly diplomatic matter of the highest sort. *Calendar of State Papers and Manuscripts, Relating to English Affairs, Existing in the Archives and Collections of Venice, and in Other Libraries of Northern Italy*, R. Brown, *et al.*, eds., 38 vols. to date (London, 1864-1947), i, 188, no. 568. Maulde La Clavière's discussion of *nuncius* and procurator (*La diplomatie au temps de Machiavel*, i, 295-296) is very confused.

[58] Bernard du Rosier, *Ambaxiator brevilogus*, pp. 5-6. As early as the 1350's, Alberico de Rosate wrote: "Ambassiator est legatus principis in arduis negotiis." *Vocabularius*, p. xxi.

whose authority on these matters must stand extremely high, wrote under 1489 that the pope summoned to his presence all of the orators in the city, *viz.*, "of the emperor, of the kings of the French, of the Spanish, of the Neapolitans and of Hungary, of the dukes of Milan and Ferrara, and of the Florentine commune."[59] Mattingly, whose *Renaissance Diplomacy* is in considerable measure an exposition of the ideas of Rosier, is not quite as willing to accept the words of the fifteenth-century author without qualification. He finds that the usage of "ambassador" was "increasingly restricted to the major diplomatic agents of the major diplomatic powers," a guarded position with which it would be exceedingly difficult to quarrel.[60] In France, Maulde La Clavière found a transformation in the *droit d'ambassade* in the fifteenth century: at its beginning this right belonged to almost everybody, but at its end it was an exclusively royal right. He recognizes, however, that this was not the case in Italy, pointing to the independent diplomacy of subject Genoa.[61] A few documents of an official character appear to lend support to the sharp distinction between ambassadors or orators and envoys of nonsovereign powers. A number of early fifteenth-century documents refer to English envoys as ambassadors dealing with *délégués*, *commys*, and others of lesser title representing Flanders, Burgundy, the Teutonic Order, and the Hanseatic League.[62] All these documents—specifying that the royal emissaries are ambassadors, the nonroyal something else—seem to affirm the modern definition of ambassador as the diplomatic representative of a sovereign state.

A very great amount of evidence exists, however, to indicate that this development was extremely rudimentary and that it did not consistently prevail anywhere, even at the papal curia, before the sixteenth century. Ambassadors were sent and received by the very widest variety of persons and corporate bodies and for all sorts of important and relatively trivial affairs.

Nonsovereign vassals continued to name ambassadors even in the fifteenth century, although the idea of sovereignty was clearly growing. The German electors sent *solempnes ambasiatores* to Boniface IX to secure the deposition of the emperor,[63] but what shall we say of the orator of "thirty-one counties

[59] Johannes Burckhard, *Liber notarum ab anno MCCCCLXXXIII usque ad annum MDVI*, Enrico Celano, ed., in *Rerum italicarum scriptores*, XXXII, 2 vols. (Citta di Castello, 1906-1911), I, 274.

[60] Mattingly, *Renaissance Diplomacy*, p. 30.

[61] *La diplomatie au temps de Machiavel*, I, 189.

[62] Chaplais, "Documents concernant l'Angleterre et l'Écosse," pp. 194-195, no. 10, and pp. 200-201, no. 23; Rymer, *Foedera*, IV, i, 192; *C.C.R. Henry IV (1405-1409)*, p. 62.

[63] *Gesta archiepiscoporum Magdeburgensium*, *Continuatio altera*, Guill. Schum, ed. *M.G.H.*, *SS.*, XIV, p. 450. A letter of Boniface IX quoted in note 10 refers to the envoys, however,

of Germany" received in Venice in 1449?[64] Or of the ambassadors of the dukes of Berry, Orleans, and Bourbon; the counts of Alençon and Armagnac; and the sire de la Bret sent to England in 1412 to throw off the allegiance of their principals to France and to offer liege homage to England?[65]

Not only lay vassals owing allegiance to another, but also ecclesiastics subject to the pope remained capable in the fifteenth century of representation by ambassadors. Because of the highly representative character of a papal legate, it may not be surprising to find a cardinal-legate dispatching orators.[66] The college of cardinals itself, however, could be represented by an orator as occasion demanded,[67] yet the college did not claim sovereignty or lack of dependence upon the pope, although any regulations of the papal curia governing the sending of ambassadors must surely have been known to the cardinals.

Cities and other corporate entities subject to another power also employed ambassadors.[68] Treviso, recently submitted to Venetian dominion, sent its own ambassador to the duke of Austria in 1350, and as late as 1495 subject Cyprus sent its orator to the sultan with the tribute owed to him.[69] For such a mission it is obvious that Cyprus alone, and not the Republic of San Marco should be represented, but if a hierarchy of diplomatic titles had become very firmly established it would seem that he might have been endowed with some less honorable designation. Philippe de Commines cites ambassadors of the three estates of the provinces belonging to Mary of Burgundy before Louis XI.[70] We even find an ambassador sent by the Guelf party in Florence, although this occurred in the thir-

---

as *nuncii*. Ganshof specifically excepted the imperial electors from the category of non-sovereigns denied the droit d'ambassade. *Moyen Age*, pp. 269-270.

64 A.S.V., Senato, Secreta, xviii, 119r (121r).

65 *C.C.R. Henry IV (1409-1413)*, p. 339. An order to customs officials of Southampton to allow *ambassiatores* of the count of Alençon to ship certain items for the use of the count. *Ibid.*, p. 291; Rymer, *Foedera*, iv, ii, 19. Also an ambassador of the duke of Bavaria to Venice in 1376. A.S.V., Senato, Secreta, L, 29v.

66 A.S.V., Senato, Secreta, i, 118r (119r).

67 *Ibid.*, xv, 11r (12r).

68 Martinus Gar(r)atus (de Caratis sive Caraziis) Laudensis, *Tractatus de legatis maxime principum*, q. xxv, in Hrabar, *De legatis*, p. 49, says that a city subject to a prince cannot send a legate to another prince without the permission of its own prince. This can be taken as a germ of the modern notion in the fifteenth century. The very title of the treatise, however, indicates that those other than princes could send legates. I join Angelini in cautioning that the modern concepts of independence and *droit d'ambassade* should not be read back into the Middle Ages. Sergio Angelini, *La diplomazia comunale a Perugia nei secoli XIII e XIV* (Firenze, 1965), p. 6.

69 A.S.V., Maggior Consiglio, Novella, 5r (16r). At other times Treviso sent ambassadors to Venice. A.S.V., Dieci, Misti, Registro, xxvi, 179v (208v), filze, ix, 145.

70 Commynes, *Mémoires*, Chap. xvi, Liv. v, i, 423.

teenth century when most authorities would concede a very loose usage of the term.[71] Bartolus used the word "ambassador" as a synonym for the syndics representing their cities in a provincial parliament.[72] The monks of St. Edmund's Abbey sent ambassadors to the king in 1301 to obtain his permission for the election of a new abbot, certainly not an affair of great international significance.[73] The early date of this "embassy" may also be cited to prove its irrelevance to the question of the restriction of the usage of "ambassador" in the fifteenth century, but then what of the orators of the Dominican convent of SS. Giovanni e Paolo (Zanipolo) in Venice addressed to the Council of Ten? Their mission concerned strictly domestic matters and its date was 1458.[74] All sorts of nonsovereign or dubiously sovereign corporate entities, it seems, could send ambassadors from the thirteenth through the fifteenth centuries.

Private citizens also sent ambassadors, either upon public or private affairs. Ambassadors were sent by certain important citizens of Mantua to Frederick II to offer him the allegiance of the city.[75] In November, 1318, the Venetian *Maggior Consiglio* consented to send an ambassador to the king of Germany to claim restitution for a merchant robbed in that country. Four months later—the ambassador had apparently never departed—the merchant himself was given money to send a "sufficient person," later called an ambassador, for the same purpose.[76] A very interesting Venetian document of 1428 deals with the reception of orators from two Albanian nobles requesting that their principals be accepted as Venetian subjects. They were turned down on the grounds that the peace between Venice and the despot recognized them as subjects of the latter. The right of the subjects of a foreign prince to send ambassadors, however, was not questioned, and the word "ambassador" is used repeatedly in the document.[77]

Documentation abounds for the reception by sovereigns of envoys called ambassadors or orators from their own subjects. The German emperor had many dealings with ambassadors of those who actually were his subjects. Some were sent to him by cities within the empire for the confirmation

[71] Kern, *Acta Imperii, Angliae et Franciae*, pp. 175-185, no. 251, letter of October 15, 1281.

[72] Bartolus à Saxoferrato, *Commentaria*, in *Opera omnia*, 11 vols. in 6 (Venetiis, 1602-1603), ad *C.* 10, 65 (*de legationibus*), 5.

[73] . . . nuntios seu ambassadores . . . *Memorials of St. Edmund's Abbey*, T. Arnold, ed., in *R.S.*, no. 96, 3 vols. (London, 1890-1896), II, 299.

[74] A.S.V., Dieci, Misti, XV, 149v (150v).

[75] Rolandinus Patavinus, *Cronica in factis et circa facta marchie Trivixane* (*1200 cc.-1262*), A. Bonardi, ed., Lib. IV, Cap. 4, in *Rerum italicarum scriptores*, VIII, i (Bologna, 1905-1908), p. 58.

[76] A.S.V., Maggior Consiglio, Fronesis, 8v (8v) and 14r (14r). Incidentally, he was required to repay the commune from the first monies recovered.

[77] A.S.V., Senato, Secreta, x, 115v (119v).

of their privileges. Ambassadors of Savona even appeared before Charles IV to act as lawyers in a judicial appeal.[78] Innocent IV assured ambassadors of subject Mantua that he would not make peace with Frederick II without protecting the interests of the dependents of the church.[79] On the ecclesiastical rather than the political side of papal affairs, in 1383 and 1429 newly elected bishops of Eichstadt sent *ambasiatas* to Rome for their confirmations.[80] Ambassadors of the duke of Albany also made a treaty in 1483 with ambassadors of the English king for the purpose of gaining the Scottish throne for the duke.[81] Venice received a very large number of ambassadors or orators from dependent cities.[82] Some dealt with the very subject of dependency, requesting the sending of a new *podestà* or rector.[83] Others dealt with various and sometimes minor administrative concerns: the abolition of a law prohibiting burials within the city of Parenzo; the terms of office of Venetian officials in Bergamo and Crema; complaints against Venetian officials by Padua, Verona, Treviso and Friuli; the salary and expenses of the count of Trau; revision of a ruling on the import on grain in Verona.[84] So many ambassadors came to Venice from dependent cities that in the late fifteenth century the Senate and the Council of Ten acted to limit their number, their salaries, and the frequency of their visits in the interest of the public purses of those cities.[85] That a transition toward the modern concept that ambassadors should be exchanged only among sovereign and juridically equal states was occurring, however, is indicated by the Milanese *ordini* of 1468 on the reception of ambassadors. Genoese orators, "although they are subjects," should be treated just like those of Bologna, Lucca, and the Swiss confederation because of the excellence and reputation of their city.[86] Although the dependent state retained the *droit d'ambassade*, it was clearly held to be an exception.

[78] Winkelmann, *Acta Imperii inedita*, I, 160, no. 183; I, 340-341, no. 389; I, 465, no. 580; II, 469, no. 750; II, 600-601, no. 924; II, 766, no. 1100. The representatives of Savona were called *ambaxiatores procuratores actores et nuncii*. *Ibid.*, II, 571-573, no. 891.

[79] *Ibid.*, I, 559-560, no. 705.

[80] *Gesta episcoporum Eichstetensium continuata*, L. Bethmann and G. Waitz, eds., in *M.G.H.*, SS., XXV, 602, 607-608.

[81] Rymer, *Foedera*, V, iii, 127-128.

[82] A.S.V., Senato, Misti, XXII, 3r (3r); Senato, Secreta, II, 129r (129r), 181r (181r), 184r (184r), 192r (192r); Maggior Consiglio, Ursa, 112r (118r); Maggior Consiglio, Stella, 136rv (140rv).

[83] A.S.V., Maggior Consiglio, Leona, 220r (225r); Maggior Consiglio, Ursa, 81r (87r).

[84] A.S.V., Maggior Consiglio, Spiritus, 75v (76v); Regina, 81r (87r) and 84v (90v); Clericus Civicus (Copia, 1681), pp. 700-704; Senato, Misti, XXII, 38r (38r); Secreta, XXXI, 90r (90r).

[85] A.S.V., Senato, Terra, IV, 135r (136r); Dieci, Misti, XXII, 53r (89r); XXV, 84r (119r); filze, VI, 23.

[86] Maspes, "Ricevimento degli ambasciatori," p. 149.

Just as ambassadors or orators were received from persons or corporate bodies not sovereign, so they were dispatched to a wide variety of recipients. Some embassies were assigned to more than one destination with a noticeable difference in rank among those to whom they were sent. In the late thirteenth century the Venetian *Maggior Consiglio* sent a solemn ambassador to negotiate upon security of the roads for Venetian merchants with various nonsovereign persons, as well as the king of Germany, and others who seemed to the ambassador important for this purpose.[87] The practice was not limited, however, to the formative period of the thirteenth century or to the Italian city-states, which might be expected to take a liberal view toward sovereignty and the *droit d'ambassade*. An English circular embassy of 1416 was directed to Aragon, the princes of Germany, the Hanseatic League, and Genoa.[88]

Ambassadors could be received by diplomatic representatives as well as their principals. Papal legates not only sent ambassadors, but received them.[89] Ambassadors could also be received by representatives of secular rulers.[90] The very vague meaning of "ambassador" is illustrated by a thirteenth-century Venetian act concerning the reception of envoys. *Nuncii* should be sent to the visitors to inquire of the purpose of their coming, and the number of these "ambassadors" sent to meet them should be four.[91] Such ambassadors never departed from Venice.

The rise of the *condottiere* introduced an additional important factor, though not sovereign, into the already confused scheme of medieval diplomacy. These chiefs conducted their own diplomacy, although they were not heads of territorial states in many cases. The Venetian *Secreta* is full of ambassadors sent to *condottiere*. During Sforza's career as mercenary chieftain there is perhaps as much diplomatic activity directed toward him as toward any state. He even has his own heading in the rubrics, *Gentes Armigerum et Comes Franciscus*. Venice actually sent an orator to its own army—an army, of course, composed of quasi-independent *condottieri*.[92] Like Venice, Florence also sent ambassadors to its stipendiaries.[93]

Far from limiting the exchange of ambassadors to states equal in law, the sending of ambassadors to vassals and subjects was not at all uncom-

[87] Cessi, *Deliberazioni del Maggior Consiglio*, III, 370-371. An early fifteenth-century ambassador to the emperor, princes, and counts of Germany. A.S.V., Senato, Secreta, II, 22v (22v).

[88] Rymer, *Foedera*, IV, ii, 183-185.

[89] *Deliberazioni del Consiglio dei Rogati (Senato) Serie "Mixtorum,"* Vol. I a cura di R. Cessi e P. Sambin, Vol. II a cura di R. Cessi e M. Brunetti (Venezia, 1960-1961), I, 371, no. 138.

[90] Kern, *Acta Imperii, Angliae et Franciae*, pp. 188-189, no. 255.

[91] Cessi, *Deliberazioni del Maggior Consiglio*, III, 59.

[92] A.S.V., Senato, Secreta, XVII, 64r (62r); XVIII, 83r (85r) and 85-86 (87-88).

[93] A.S.F., Signori, Missive, Prima Cancelleria, X, 67r (71r).

mon. In the mid-fifteenth century deposed consuls of the city of Luneburg requested the emperor to send ambassadors to restore them to office. The German kings also had not hesitated to send ambassadors to their subordinates for investing them with their rights and receiving fealty from them.[94] Venice sent ambassadors for receiving fealty and even for recalling one of its own governors of a dependent territory to face investigation for misconduct.[95] In a Florentine law dealing with the election of ambassadors, specific exception is made of ambassadors sent within Florentine territory.[96] "Ambassador" is quite like *nuncius*, meaning someone sent to someone else. One of the more interesting examples is furnished by the Venetian habit of dispatching ambassadors to its own newly elected doge if that dignitary happened to be outside of the city at the time of his election. Large numbers of ambassadors, twelve and more, were sent to salute him and to accompany him in honor to Venice.[97]

Despite the assertions of various scholars with which we began this discussion of those who might send and receive ambassadors, it does not seem that ambassadors or orators were restricted to sovereign (or even major) princes, independent communes, and the like. Even in the relatively highly organized papal curia, and as late as 1488, we have the incomparable authority of Johannes Burckhardt that orators were received from lesser princes and communities.[98] A late fifteenth-century jurist, Johannes Bertachinus, speaks of an *ambasiato* litigating before judges and arbitrators.[99] As late as the early sixteenth century we find Machiavelli as "orator in Capri to a convent of Brothers Minor."[100]

The meaning of the word "ambassador" and the question of the right to send and receive ambassadors have been discussed at some length. It has been discovered that the word had no specific and technical significance and that it could be used to indicate a person sent by anyone or to anyone. It was, however, most commonly used for diplomatic envoys, and there

[94] *Gesta archiepiscoporum Magdeburgensium, Continuatio altera*, Guill. Schum, ed., *M.G.H., SS.*, XIV (Hannoverae, 1883), p. 470; *Continuatio monachorum Sancti Petri*, to *Annales Sancti Rudberti Salisburgensis*, W. Wattenbach, ed., in *M.G.H., SS.*, IX (Hannoverae, 1851), 842; Winkelmann, *Acta Imperii inedita*, II, 444-446, no. 716.

[95] A.S.V., Maggior Consiglio, Spiritus, 105r (106r); Maggior Consiglio, Magnus, 74v. Milan also sent embassies to dependents. A.S.M., Archivio Sforzesco, Milano, busta 657.

[96] Maulde La Clavière, *La diplomatie au temps de Machiavel*, III, 426.

[97] A.S.V., Maggior Consiglio, Novella, 79v (90v), 112v (123v), 187r (198r); Leona, 231v (236v).

[98] Burckhard, *Liber notarum*, I, 230.

[99] Joannes Bertachinus, *Repertorium*, v° *Ambasiator*, in Hrabar, *De legatis*, p. 71.

[100] Alfred von Reumont, *Della diplomazia italiana da secolo XIII al XVI* (Firenze, 1857), p. 9. Perhaps, though I doubt it, the decree of Charles V in the sixteenth century restricting the use of ambassadors to crowned heads and the Republic of Venice put a sudden end to the loose usage described above, but this question goes beyond the chronological limitations of the present work.

were some indications by the end of the thirteenth century of its evolution toward its present significance. Another major question to be considered in these centuries of transition to the modern state system is the development of the distinction between *ad hoc* ambassadors and resident ambassadors. A great portion of the study previously devoted to medieval and Renaissance ambassadors has concentrated upon the question of the earliest appearance of the resident ambassador. Unfortunately, this quest, like others of its sort, hinges upon a semantic question, in this case what we mean by "resident ambassador."

Garrett Mattingly's *Renaissance Diplomacy* sets the terms of the discussion with clarity and reviews the evidence in a masterly way. Mattingly saw the significant departure in the development of the resident ambassador in his assignment to remain at his post until recalled in general charge of the interests of his principal.[101] More recently, Professor Paolo Selmi of Padua has succeeded in refining the definition of a resident: The institution of resident ambassador ". . . begins to exist when one has the institution of a permanent *officium* of which the ambassador, provided with a general mandate, is the titulary during his assignment; and when the existence of such an *officium* is not diminished if it should be temporarily deprived of a titulary, when such a vacancy creates the necessity of nominating a successor."[102] Selmi has contributed something of value with his insistence upon the continuation of the *officium* even in the temporary absence of a titulary. While Selmi is very successful in defining a resident, however, it is a resident *ambassador* that we are seeking. It is lack of clarity on this point which requires the rejection of the proposals of several scholars. Mattingly cleared away the confusion of some of his predecessors who fixed upon certain procurators as the first resident ambassadors by showing that the diplomatic procurators were not residents, and the resident ones were not diplomats.[103] The deficiency in all the candidates proposed for the honor before Mattingly is simply that they were not fundamentally diplomats, although they did occasionally perform diplomatic functions. This was Mattingly's objection to the *apocrisiarii* or *responsales* of the popes at Constantinople as early as the sixth century.[104] He also re-

[101] *Renaissance Diplomacy*, p. 64. See also Behrens, "Treatises on the Ambassador," p. 621. The Venetian Senate in 1471 discussed sending two ambassadors to Rome, who "should remain in the curia for the purpose of executing our mandates from time to time . . ." (That the action was deferred is not important for our purposes.) A.S.V., Senato, Secreta, xxv, 56r (65r).

[102] Paolo Selmi, "L'inizio ed il primo sviluppo della diplomazia stabile della Repubblica di Venezia, unpublished thesis (Padova, 1960), p. 5.

[103] Mattingly, *Renaissance Diplomacy*, p. 67.

[104] Otto Krauske, *Die Entwicklung der ständigen Diplomatie* (Leipzig, 1885), pp. 7-8; A. Pieper, *Zur Entstehungsgeschichte der standigen Nunciaturen* (Fribourg-en-Brisgau, 1894), p. 2;

jected Fincke's Aragonese procurators at the Roman court[105] and Cuttino's English procurators at Paris in the fourteenth century.[106] Examples of resident representatives of this type—i.e., basically attorneys, not diplomats—can be multiplied at some length. Appeals from the vassals of the count of Flanders to their French overlord became so common in the thirteenth century that the count had to maintain resident procurators in Paris to defend his interests. Countess Margaret and Count Guy maintained two houses there, comprising the *hôtel de Flandre*, which might wrongfully be construed as a permanent embassy. Some business in fact took place there which was diplomatic in character. Guy's recall of his procurators in 1297, however, clearly indicates that their principal function was to appear as lawyers before the royal court.[107] I have no doubt that they performed diplomatic functions from time to time, but so did merchants and others, whom we should not call ambassadors. The bishop of Tournai also maintained an establishment in Paris.[108] Guy of Flanders had himself represented by a resident at Rheims before the archbishop, as did the count of Artois at Thérouanne.[109] These thirteenth- and fourteenth-century examples of resi-

---

Ruess, *Die rechtliche Stellung des päpstlichen Legaten*, p. 30 and pp. 41-42; Mattingly, *Renaissance Diplomacy*, p. 65.

[105] *Acta Aragonensia: Quellen zur deutschen, italienischen, französischen, spanischen, zur Kirchen-und Kulturgeschichte aus der diplomatischen Korrespondenz Jaymes II, 1291-1327*, 3 vols. (Berlin and Leipzig, 1908-1922), I, ccxvi ff.; Luis Weckmann, "Les origines des missions diplomatiques permanentes," *Revue générale de droit international public*, LVI (1952), 178; Garrett Mattingly, "The First Resident Embassies: Medieval Italian Origins of Modern Diplomacy," *Speculum*, XII (1937), 425; Mattingly, *Renaissance Diplomacy*, pp. 65-67. Also see Willy Andreas, *Staatskunst und Diplomatie der Venezianer. Im Spiegel ihrer Gesandtenberichte* (Leipzig, 1943), pp. 19-23.

[106] Cuttino regarded his English procurators only as precursors of resident ambassadors. *English Diplomatic Administration*, pp. 96-99. Mattingly stressed that the legal character of these representatives implied recognition of a superior legal jurisdiction, but he did not deny that they occasionally performed diplomatic functions. *Renaissance Diplomacy*, pp. 66-67. Lucas also saw them in this light. "Machinery of Diplomatic Intercourse," pp. 317-318. In any event, the knowledge they had of affairs in France enabled them to provide invaluable information to nonresident diplomatic procurators. Ganshof, *Le Moyen Age*, p. 270. For an example of a procuration clearly exemplifying the legal character of these representatives, see Champollion-Figeac, *Lettres*, I, 340-341.

[107] Funck-Brentano, *Philippe le Bel en Flandre*, p. 12. Rijksarchief, Gent, Gaillard, no. 350, is a receipt for the salary of one of these procurators during a *parlement* of 1292; Georges Huisman, "Un compte de réparations effectuées à l'hôtel du comte de Flandres à Paris (1374-1376)," *Bulletin de la Société de l'Histoire de Paris et de l'Ile de France*, XXXVII (1910), 258; documents analyzed in Louis Prosper Gachard, *La Bibliothèque Nationale à Paris. Notices et extraits des manuscrits qui concernent l'histoire de Belgique*, 2 vols. (Bruxelles, 1875-1877), II, pp. 331 and 333; Archives du Nord, Lille, Chambre des Comptes, B 1457, nos. 3622-3623; Limburg-Stirum, *Codex diplomaticus Flandriae*, I, 131, no. 39.

[108] Armand d'Herbomez, "Philippe le Bel et le Tournaisiens," *Bulletin de la Commission Royale d'Histoire*, 5e sér., III (1893), 95-96.

[109] Archives du Nord, Lille, Chambre des Comptes, B 1564, no. 92; B 1593, no. 236; Funck-Brentano, *Philippe le Bel en Flandre*, p. 18.

dents prove only that judicial business sometimes became so intense as to demand a resident lawyer. Diplomatic dealing at this time was much less frequent and when some matter did not seem to require the sending of an *ad hoc* envoy it might be entrusted to a resident lawyer if one were available.

The traditional and conservative view is that the resident ambassador appeared first in Italy in the mid-fifteenth century.[110] Mattingly adheres to this view, but his contribution lies in rejecting false claimants and in tracing a gradual evolution over the preceding century, beginning in 1341 with a Gonzaga representative "whom we retain continually in Germany for keeping an eye on (*explorandis*) the movements of the Bavarian."[111] A series of documents from the registers of the Venetian Senate may be cited usefully to illustrate an early resident ambassador—but without making any claim for priority. The series begins with the commission of Geronimo Contareno, orator to Rome, 25 September 1431: ". . . we have sent you to his Beatitude to reside there in our name and you can employ yourself about all things which can occur in any way whatsoever pertaining to us and our Republic . . ." Here we find the general mandate and assignment without a fixed term. On 30 March 1432 the Senate provided for the election of Contareno's successor, stipulating that he could not be held in the post more than six months, at the end of which time he might return to Venice without license. On 21 June, Andrea Donato, the newly elected orator, received his commission, very similar to Contareno's. On 29 December the Senate agreed that Donato, having stayed in Rome beyond his term, ought to be permitted to return home. It was "necessary to provide another ambassador in his place." Here is an explicit reference to Selmi's requirement of the necessity of nominating a successor. Three appointees refused, however, and Donato remained. On 10 February 1433 poor Donato was still on the job, although he was again assured that he could return home without leave before Easter after carrying out his new instructions. He reported from Rome on 25 and 29 May, however, and the Senate responded on 5 June without any mention of his repatriation. He did come back to Venice in June with proposals of the pope and the emperor, and on 30 June was reelected to return the Senate's

[110] Carlton J. H. Hayes, "Medieval Diplomacy," in *The History and Nature of International Relations*, Edmund A. Walsh, ed. (New York, 1922), pp. 86-87; Ganshof, *Le Moyen Age*, pp. 272-274; Cuttino, *English Diplomatic Administration*, p. 19.

[111] *Renaissance Diplomacy*, pp. 71-82. The document is given in Alessandro Luzio, *L'Archivio Gonzaga di Mantova: La corrispondenza familiare, amministrativa e diplomatica dei Gonzaga*, 2 vols. (Verona, 1922), II, 78. *Explorator* is the Latin word for "spy." Luzio also points out that genuine resident embassies first appear in the mid-fifteenth century. *Ibid.*, II, 81. Also Romolo Quazza, *La diplomazia gonzagescha* (Milano, n.d.), p. 11.

response. He accepted on 1 July, refused on the fourth, was again elected under great pressure on the fifth and accepted. On 11 August, at the request of the pope and the emperor, the Senate commanded him to accompany the emperor to the Council of Basel and not to depart from there without the specific instructions of the Senate.[112] This example does appear to meet the most rigorous requirements for a resident ambassador, although several approximately contemporary examples might also be given.

Mrs. Clifford has recently presented rather tentatively a new candidate for the honor of being the first resident ambassador in Othon de Grandson, experienced diplomat of the most exalted sort, who spent the greater part of ten years in the early fourteenth century at Avignon on the business of the English king.[113] Her argument that he was not a mere legal procurator before the papal court is compelling, but Selmi's discerning requirement that a resident ambassador must hold an office which is conceived to exist even in the absence of an incumbent would exclude the distinguished subject of Clifford's biography.

Selmi's unpublished thesis is the latest representative of a school of thought which finds the origin of the resident ambassador in the Venetian consuls. This school of thought is founded upon the scholarship of Fausto and Nicolà Nicolini. In a *Festschrift* article appearing in 1926 the former asserted that even before the formal establishment of a resident orator at Naples in the fifteenth century the Venetian consul in that city since 1257 had borne marked resemblance to a resident ambassador. He was not elected upon the spot by councils of the Venetian merchants there, but by the Senate in Venice; he had to be a patrician; his term was limited to two years; he received a fixed salary and a special allowance for obtaining information and sending couriers; he had precedence over other Venetian consuls in the Regno and was frequently called "consul general of Apulia"; he also had a permanent house in Naples. He had originally been designated *consul Trani*, for Trani was the center of commerce, but Nicolini shows that in 1340 the Senate reminded its consul that he was required to spend nine months of the year at Naples, which housed the royal court. This, plus the Senate's urging that the consul remain near the king, keep his eyes open and continue to report on royal activities, led Nicolini to believe that the consul was exercising the functions of a resident ambassador.[114] There can be no doubt that he was a resident and that he did per-

[112] A.S.V., Senato, Secreta, xii, 25r (31r); 73v (79v)–74r (80r); 95r (101r); 145v (151v); 159r (165r); 182r (189r); 184v (191v); 193v (200v).

[113] Esther Rowland Clifford, *A Knight of Great Renown: The Life and Times of Othon de Grandson* (Chicago, 1961), pp. 208-209, 224-225.

[114] Fausto Nicolini, "Frammenti veneto-napoletani," estr. dal vol. *Studi di storia napoletana*

form some of the functions of an ambassador, but Nicolà Nicolini cannot therefore justly claim that the 1926 article demonstrated that he became "a veritable and proper resident ambassador."[115] In fact, some of her own evidence can be turned against her argument. She points out that in 1283 the consul was ordered to spend nine months of the year at Trani, three at Naples *in curia regis et principis*. In 1296, however, he was ordered that the three months should be spent before the court of the duke of Calabria, Robert of Anjou, because Charles II had delegated the administration of justice to his son.[116] An ambassador, at least in the modern sense of the word, does not normally appear before a court of justice—in fact, this is considered a totally inappropriate place for him to be. A consular official, however, representing the commercial interests of his countrymen, would find proximity to the court of justice for a portion of his time, at least, essential to the performance of his functions. Roberto Cessi, the dean of Venetian historians, in an article in the *Enciclopedia italiana* follows the Nicolini, although he does stress very strongly and appropriately the clear distinction in origin and character of the offices of the consul and the ambassador in the thirteenth and early fourteenth centuries.[117] A number of students of Venice, on the other hand, have found in the *baiulo* at Constantinople the first resident ambassador,[118] although a detailed argument in support of this claim awaits the conclusion of Selmi's work.

There is abundant evidence that consuls did engage in diplomatic activity and even some suggesting a merging of the offices of consul (or *baiulo*)

in onore di Michelangelo Schipa (Napoli, 1926), pp. 4-7. Notice, however, that the documentation for most of these points is of the fifteenth century. Also, not all of these elements are necessarily characteristic of the Venetian ambassador. See my forthcoming study, *Early Venetian Legislation on Ambassadors*.

115 Nicolà Nicolini, *Il consolato generale veneto nel regno di Napoli (1257-1495)* (Napoli, 1928), p. 59.

116 *Ibid.*, pp. 30-31.

117 Roberto Cessi, "Ambasciatore," *Enciclopedia italiana* (1929 edn.), II, ii, 782-783.

118 Baschet, *Les archives de Venise*, p. 283; Nys, *Origines du droit international*, pp. 310-311; Andrea Da Mosto, *L'Archivio di Stato di Venezia*, 2 vols. (Roma, 1937-1940), II, 25; Raimondo Morozzo della Rocca, *Dispacci degli ambasciatori al Senato. Indice* (Venezia, 1959), p. ix. Where these authors place the date of transition from consul to ambassador is not always clear. I am not prepared to argue against any date after 1500, but I would then, of course, deny any claim to primacy as resident ambassador. In 1268 the *Maggior Consiglio* required that ambassadors must give up to the state all gifts made to them in their embassies. Cessi, *Deliberazioni del Maggior Consiglio*, II, 101. The rubric of a lost act of 1271, however, declares: "Quod Baiulus Constantinopolis non possit recipere donum ab Imperatore, postquam exiverit de regimine, nec pro unum annum post etc." While I do not think that this actually proves that the *baiulo* in 1271 was not deemed to be covered by the act concerning ambassadors of 1268, I do believe that such an interpretation is rather strongly suggested. Maulde La Clavière was wrong insofar as the *baiulo* of Constantinople is concerned in saying that the consuls did not represent the state. *La diplomatie au temps de Machiavel*, III, 296-298. Cf., A.S.V., Dieci, Misti, XXIII, 47v (77v).

and ambassador. In 1414 the consul of Apulia was granted authority by the Senate to negotiate with the king for the withdrawal of certain *condottieri* who were his subjects from aiding Padua in return for money to be paid to the king. This clearly had nothing to do with his consular function.[119] In 1302 a *nuncius* about to depart for Constantinople was informed that if he were for any reason unable to fulfill his mission he could delegate it to the *baiulo* who was also about to depart.[120] It is not uncommon to see the same patrician elected *ambassiator et baiulus Constantinopolis*.[121] Consuls and *baiuli* also were entrusted with ambassadorial functions in places other than those where they resided, which not only proves that they acted as ambassadors, but also suggests that their ambassadorial functions were quite incidental to the fact that they were residents.[122]

Much evidence, to be sure, indicates the distinction between the two offices. On a number of occasions it is quite clear that the *baiulo* and an orator or ambassador in Constantinople are two different individuals.[123] On another occasion we discover the dispatching of a *baiulo* to Armenia delayed because of news which necessitated the sending of an ambassador.[124] Although one man might be appointed ambassador and consul or *baiulo*, the two offices were nonetheless distinct. He might even be able to enter upon his consular office only when his mission as ambassador had been successfully completed. In 1381 two noblemen nominated as ambassador and *baiulo* of Constantinople had already been appointed ambassadors to the marquis of Este and the king of Hungary respectively. Supporters of these nominations argued that they could be approved in spite of a law prohibiting elections from one ambassadorship into another, since they were being nominated as ambassador *and baiulo*, but it was replied that they could not, because the one elected could not become *baiulo* unless his mission as ambassador was achieved. The advocates of the nominations prevailed, but on the basis of arguments which seem to concede the distinction between the two offices of ambassador and *baiulo*.[125] Even the

119 A.S.V., Senato, Secreta, II, 77r (77r). The *baiulo* at Constantinople in 1363 had a *sindicatus* for requesting from the emperor an oath confirming a truce negotiated by his ambassadors. A.S.V., Sindicati, I, 98v.

120 Cessi, *Deliberazioni . . . Rogati*, "*Mixtorum*," I, 78, no. 281.

121 A.S.V., Maggior Consiglio, Ursa, 80v (86v).

122 A.S.V., Maggior Consiglio, Clericus-Civicus, 119v (167v); Senato, Secreta, VI, 142r (143r); XVI, 179v (179v)–180r (180r); Cessi, *Deliberazioni del Maggior Consiglio*, III, 212; Senato, Misti, XXXVIII, 22v (22v); Perret, *Relations de la France avec Venise*, II, 70-72.

123 A.S.V., Senato, Secreta, XXX, 8v (18v); XXXI, 15v (15v). Advocates of the *baiulo* as the first resident orator would argue that the *baiulo* was an "ordinary" ambassador, and that the ordinary or resident ambassador was often supplemented by an ambassador extraordinary.

124 A.S.V., Maggior Consiglio, Fronesis, 49r (49r).

125 ". . . ultra quod misimus te oratorem ut reperiatur ibi persona representans dominium

prestigious *baiulo* of Constantinople did not have as numerous a retinue as an ambassador. In 1451 the entourage of the *baiulo* was raised from three persons and three horses to five persons and four horses.[126] A law of 1371, however, limited ambassadors to four servants, a notary plus his servant, and two stableboys, if the embassy went on horseback. Another decree of 1461 repeated the limitation upon the retinue of an ambassador as no more than eight persons and eight horses.[127] The evidence, in short, leads me to conclude that the consul or *baiulo* was and remained an official whose main functions of jurisdiction over his fellow countrymen and representation of their commercial interests before the government of the land in which they dwelt were quite distinct from the functions of an ambassador. In an age when resident ambassadors were still unusual, however, and appointed only to those courts with which a government conducted a great deal of diplomatic business, a consul might well be entrusted with diplomatic functions and furnished with a special mandate. On such occasions, but only then, he became for the time and the purpose indicated an ambassador.[128]

The origin of the resident ambassador is not to be found in the resident procurator or the resident consul, although these examples may have had some influence upon its development as also may have the resident factors of merchants, but rather in the increasing frequency and duration of *ad hoc* embassies as diplomatic activity intensified. As Reumont put it, the activity became so intense that it was discovered to be more practical and more economical to appoint an ambassador to remain at a much frequented court.[129] This proliferation of diplomatic activity in the fifteenth century is illustrated by the daily deliberations of the Venetian Senate in 1443 concerning the appointment of ambassadors to diverse parts.[130] The great

nostrum actura ea que in dies expedient, ob bonam pacem et amicitiam que nobiscum Excellentia dicti domini intercedit, fungeris etiam officio Baylatus loco illius bayuli, cui debimus licentiam repatriandi . . ." (1486). A.S.V., Senato, Secreta, XXXIII, 48r (58r); Maggior Consiglio, Magnus, 72v; Leona, 146r (151r); Pien Collegio, Notatorio, I, 74 and 95 at top of page, 110 at bottom.

126 A.S.V., Maggior Consiglio, Ursa, 176v (182v).

127 A.S.V., Senato, Misti, XXXIII, 104v (104v); Senato, Terra, IV, 165v (166v).

128 Francesca Antonibon, *Relazioni a stampa di ambasciatori veneti* (Padova, 1939), p. 25; Luigi Firpo, Description of *Relazioni di ambasciatori veneti al Senato*, in *Catalogo 91, Jura et Medievalia, Bottega d'Erasmo* (Torino, 1963), p. 22.

129 Reumont, *Diplomazia*, p. 5. Admittedly, Reumont saw this development only in the sixteenth century. See also Antonibon, *Relazioni di ambasciatori veneti*, p. 11. Andreas traces this, in turn, to the instability of Renaissance diplomacy. "Das Ständigerwerden des Gesandtschaften wurde Erfordernis eines unbeständigen Zeitalters!" *Staatskunst und Diplomatie der Venezianer*, p. 35.

130 ". . . quotidie occurrit pro arduis et importantissimis causis ad statum nostrum pertinentibus per Consilium Rogatorum fiunt deliberationes mittendi ambassiadores ad diversas partes . . ." A.S.V., Maggior Consiglio, Ursa, 143v (149v).

difficulty experienced in finding suitable persons willing to accept numerous and frequent embassies also may have led to a desire to reduce the number of appointments by establishing resident ambassadors.[131] In addition to cost and convenience, another factor that would make the resident embassy preferable to frequent *ad hoc* embassies was unobtrusiveness. A new embassy attracted attention: everyone could speculate that something of significance was afoot. Sometimes, indeed, pseudocircular embassies were used merely to cover up the embassies' real purpose.[132] The presence of a resident ambassador, on the other hand, was unexceptional by definition. He could much more easily carry out his tasks without attracting unwanted attention.

As diplomatic activity intensified and embassies became more frequent, they also tended to be of greater duration.[133] At least as early as 1269, Venetian ambassadors were required to remain at their posts until granted permission to repatriate themselves, and it tended to become increasingly difficult to obtain such permission.[134] A transitional stage is suggested by the deliberations of the Venetian Senate on 19 August 1443 concerning its orator before Francesco Sforza. Sforza wanted the Venetian envoy to return to Venice to report his views, but the Senate preferred that he remain at his post. The Senate determined to dispatch a secretary to its ambassador, urging that the news to be communicated by Sforza and the ambassador should be sent by the secretary's hand. If Sforza should insist, however, the ambassador might return to Venice leaving the secretary in his place for the time being.[135] Clearly there was no indication of an office of resident ambassador here, but just as clearly the Senate wished to be continuously represented for an extended period of time. Very much earlier, in 1316, we have an example of an embassy of four ambassadors sent from Venice to the papal *curia* with permission to leave one of their number there to deal with the great quantity of business Venice had with the pope. A commission was established for the next six months to take charge of papal affairs, to instruct this ambassador or to send others in his place.[136] This, too, suggests the extended duration and generalized respon-

[131] *Infra*, pp. 158-160.

[132] Maulde La Clavière, *La diplomatie au temps de Machiavel*, I, 316-317.

[133] Cuttino, *English Diplomatic Administration*, pp. 96-97.

[134] Cessi, *Deliberazioni del Maggior Consiglio*, II, 233; Perret, *Relations de la France avec Venise*, II, 289; A.S.V., Senato, Secreta, XVI, 86r (86r); *Supra*, pp. 78-79.

[135] A.S.V., Senato, Secreta, XVI, 32r (32r).

[136] A.S.V., Maggior Consiglio, Clericus-Civicus, 70v (118v). In 1303 the *Maggior Consiglio* granted permission for an ambassador to Rome to remain there at the expense of the Commune. *Ibid.*, Magnus, 58v. An orator to the emperor in 1484 was instructed to remain there at the will of the emperor. A.S.V., Senato, Secreta, XXXII, 23v (23v).

sibility that was to become characteristic of the resident ambassador. It is in the increasing frequency with which *ad hoc* ambassadors were sent and the increasing duration of their missions that the origin of the resident ambassador should be sought, and not, except by way of incidental influence, in other resident, but nonambassadorial offices.

As the *ad hoc* envoy was transformed into a resident, a transformation also occurred in the relative importance of his functions. The chief function of the temporary envoy was either negotiation or the communication of messages, although acquisition of miscellaneous but useful information was never scorned in an age which lacked the facilities available to us for the distribution of news.[137] The resident ambassador, however, often out of touch with happenings at home and poorly informed by his own government, yet wonderfully situated for gathering information for his government from abroad, rarely had power to negotiate, but functioned chiefly to keep his government informed.[138] In fact, even today the resident ambassador has not supplanted the ambassador *ad hoc*. While the resident continues at his post handling routine matters and providing vast quantities of information to his government, most important negotiations are undertaken by special ambassadors appointed for the occasion.[139]

[137] Fritz Ernst, "Über Gesandtschaftswesen und Diplomatie an der Wende vom Mittelalter zur Neuzeit," *Archiv für Kulturgeschichte*, XXXIII (1950), p. 90.

[138] Maulde La Clavière, *La diplomatie au temps de Machiavel*, I, 308, and III, 136 and n. 2.

[139] Ernst, "Gesandtschaftswesen und Diplomatie," p. 92; Maulde La Clavière, *La diplomatie au temps de Machiavel*, I, 294, 313, 366; J. R. Hale, "International Relations in the West: Diplomacy and War," *The New Cambridge Modern History*, I, G. R. Potter, ed. (Cambridge, 1957), p. 268.

CHAPTER IV

FUNCTIONS OF THE AMBASSADOR

Just as an ambassador could be sent or received by all the various sorts of persons or corporations who could send a *nuncius*, so an ambassador could be assigned any of the functions previously assigned to *nuncii*. Just as there are hints of the later notion that ambassadors should be sent and received only by sovereign or major powers, however, so there are incipient differences in the missions assigned to *nuncii* and ambassadors. Strictly speaking, the two words were synonymous, yet new nuances were making an appearance.

Bernard du Rosier explained the uses of ambassadors:

> The causes of sending ambassadors are as various as the developments which occur: for the honor of the divine cult and of the apostolic see, for the unity of the catholic church, for promoting the causes of the Christian faith; for the glory of the imperial highness; for maintaining the rights of kingdoms; for offering obedience to superiors; for aiding fathers and fatherlands; for peace and justice; for friendship; for courting good will; for settling wars; for initiating and strengthening truces; for removing tyrants; for reconciling and leading back schismatics and rebels; for guiding benevolent subjects; for consoling the desolate; for avoiding scandal; for extirpating heresies; for repressing vices and implanting virtues; for any hard, threatening necessities which occur; for all and singular purposes which tend to the good of the commonwealth of any kingdom, principality, ecclesiastical or worldly power, of any city, land, place or country, it is praiseworthy to send ambassadors. Unpraiseworthy, indeed, for declaring and introducing wars, disputes, quarrels, dissensions and scandals, profaning sacred things, occupying the rights and dominions of others, encouraging heretics and schismatics, for defending any other vice, for encouraging wrongful treaties and illicit alliances, and for making excuses for sins.[1]

Like the *nuncius*, the ambassador often served as a message bearer—a living letter.[2] Often the function of the ambassador is expressed as expos-

[1] Bernard du Rosier, *Ambaxiator brevilogus*, pp. 6-7.

[2] ". . . nobis convenientius visum fuit hoc per vos oretenus, quam per literas facere . . ." A.S.V., Senato, Secreta, xiv, 80r (81r); xvi, 189v (189v)–190r (190r); Chantal de Tourtier, "Un ambassadeur de Louis de Gonzague, seigneur de Mantoue: Bertolino Capilupi," *École française de Rome. Mélanges d'archéologie et d'histoire*, lxix (1957), 338-339.

ing the mind or the intention of his principal. Savonarola wrote that the ambassador should be eloquent in presenting those things which are committed to him, neither diminishing, nor adding.[3] Since the mission of the ambassador was usually to improve relations and to assuage difficulties, he should not use comminatory language unless specifically ordered to do so. If threat or denunciation happened to be his purpose, his character as a message-bearer was emphasized by employing a notary to record his words. For the ambassador to go beyond his instructions in this matter was most surely to invite repudiation.[4] Often the ambassador was sent to complain of wrongs against his state or its subjects.[5] Rather less frequently ambassadors were dispatched to excuse their state for wrongs committed against another, e.g., a Venetian mission in 1459 for apologizing to the Duke of Mutina for the arrows shot at him as he was departing from Venice.[6] Sometimes, also, the ambassador served as a mere bearer of letters or other documents, or he might bear something else, such as tribute.[7]

As the words of Bernard du Rosier suggest, a considerable miscellany of tasks exceeding mere message-bearing, some of them requiring various measures of initiative and discretion, fell to the lot of ambassadors. Florentine ambassadors in the mid-fourteenth century were set to Pisa to seek the extradition of two would-be subverters of the Florentine government and to obtain Pisan agreement that that city would not receive bandits or rebels against Florence.[8] On the other hand, an ambassador might seek the release from captivity of a subject of his principal. In fact, one state might send its ambassador as a mediator seeking the release of some foreigner.[9] An ambassador might serve as a mediator, not only between two foreign states, but in the domestic affairs of a foreign power.[10] Occasionally ambassadors received quasi-judicial assignments to investigate and adjudicate alleged violations of truces or treaties.[11] A mission of a Venetian orator to Rome in 1463 sounds more strange to modern ears: he was to seek determina-

[3] Giuseppe Vedovato, *Note sul diritto diplomatico della repubblica fiorentina* (Firenze, 1946), p. 10.

[4] Maulde La Clavière, *La diplomatie au temps de Machiavel*, II, 310; Commynes, *Mémoires*, I, 4-8, Liv. I, Chap. I; 80, Liv. I, Chap. XII.

[5] A.S.V., Maggior Consiglio, Magnus, 93r (94r); Senato, Misti, XVI, 100r (100r).

[6] A.S.V., Dieci, Misti, XV, 179v (180v).

[7] Winkelmann, *Acta Imperii inedita*, I, 412-413, no. 495; Rymer, *Foedera*, IV, i, 92; A.S.V., Dieci, Misti, XXVI, 179v (208v); filze, IX, 145.

[8] A.S.F., Signori, Missive, Prima Cancelleria, X, 20r (22r).

[9] A.S.V., Dieci, Misti, XXII, 82r (118r). For the release of the daughter of Galeazzo Visconti's wife, 1308. A.S.V., Maggior Consiglio, Presbiter, 1r (2r).

[10] A.S.F., Dieci di Balia, Legazioni e commissarie, Istruzioni e lettere missive, I, 41.

[11] *C.C.R. Henry IV (1409-1413)*, p. 403. In one case "commissioners" were named to adjudicate infringements of a truce, but were required to refer and report to the ambassadors who had negotiated it. Rymer, *Foedera*, V, ii, 82.

tion by a papal legate of the rival claims of Venice and Padua to possession of the true body of Santa Lucia.[12] An ambassador might receive incidental assignment of tasks only peripherally related to his main function. A Venetian ambassador to the sultan in 1302 received authority to order all Venetians in Alexandria and elsewhere within the sultan's lands to depart if his plea for indemnification of wronged Venetians went unheeded. Such authority had two purposes: protection of Venetian citizens and economic pressure upon the sultan. In 1387 we find a Genoese ambassador in England acting as *mainpernor* for a countryman. A rather strange peripheral assignment was entrusted to Venetian ambassadors sent to Constantinople to collect a sum of money from the sultan in 1285, for they were instructed to invest the money according to their best judgment.[13]

In addition to these public functions it was not at all uncommon for ambassadors to receive missions of a somewhat private nature. Ambassadors were frequently sent to Rome in order to obtain ecclesiastical preferment for subjects or servitors of a prince or a commune.[14] An orator might also be asked to intervene before the pope or the *curia* for other purposes, and on occasion the person seeking the favor might be required to bear the cost of the embassy.[15] The imposition of private tasks upon Venetian *nuncii* going to Rome became such a serious problem that as early as 1238 the *Maggior Consiglio* prohibited that any private business should be undertaken by such *nuncii* without the consent of the doge and the majority of his council and the Forty, and that even if this consent were obtained the public matters must be handled first.[16] We know of some of the private tasks imposed upon a fourteenth-century Mantuan ambassador: letter-carrying, buying things, making visits for friends. The bishop wanted a fine new or used Spanish saddle and complete harness for a mule. Someone else wanted a canonicate in the cathedral of Parma. On one occasion he had so many little tasks to fulfill for friends that he listed them under the rubric, *Memoria amicorum*.[17] The types of missions described above are really no

[12] A.S.V., Senato, Terra, v, 48r (49r).

[13] Cessi, *Deliberazioni . . . Rogati, "Mixtorum,"* I, 57, no. 201; *C.C.R. Richard II (1385-1389)*, p. 338; Cessi, *Deliberazioni del Maggior Consiglio*, III, 100.

[14] Rymer, *Foedera*, II, i, 111; IV, ii, 31. In the first, the desired promotion might have been incidental business, but in the second it is stated as the object of the mission.

[15] A.S.V., Senato, Secreta, xx, 40v (41v)–41r (42r); Marino Sanuto, *I diarii*, F. Stefani, G. Berchet, N. Barozzi, eds., 42 vols. (Venezia, 1879-1894), II, col. 404; Cessi, *Deliberazioni . . . Rogati, "Mixtorum,"* I, 192, no. 171; Angelini, *La diplomazia comunale a Perugia*, App., no. 2, p. 56.

[16] Cessi, *Deliberazioni del Maggior Consiglio*, II, 44; Giulio Cesare Buzzati, "Diritto diplomatico veneziano del sec. XIII," in *Studi giuridici dedicati a Francesco Schupfer* (Torino, 1898), II, 226.

[17] De Tourtier, "Bertolino Capilupi," p. 330.

different than those assigned to *nuncii* and there is no need to illustrate further the similarities of function. Whatever could be done by a *nuncius* could also be done by an ambassador.

There are, however, two diplomatic functions, the gathering of information and the enhancement of ceremonial, which acquire a new emphasis with the advent of the ambassador. They are not new, for *nuncii* also gathered news and performed ceremonial roles, but they do gain new importance.

As diplomatic contacts became more frequent, the opportunities for acquiring information of interest to the government at home increased. Since the birth of diplomacy it has probably always been true that an important result of a mission was the news, much of it unrelated to the mission in question, which the envoy brought or sent back to his government. Although the gathering of information by diplomatic envoys was a very imperfectly developed process, its relative importance was great in an age when other means of obtaining news—tourism, the press, scientific and technological devices, etc.—were either more imperfectly developed or entirely lacking. The *ad hoc* envoy before the rise of the resident ambassador, it is true, had only rather limited opportunities for systematic gathering of information. His attention was customarily focused upon the negotiation or other assignment which was his specific mission.[18] As early as the thirteenth century, however, well before the rise of the resident ambassador, the Venetian *Maggior Consiglio* required that returning ambassadors report in writing not only upon the results of their missions, but also upon any other items of interest to Venice that they picked up along the way.[19] As the frequency of diplomatic relations increased and as the duration of embassies became longer, the opportunities for the acquisition of information valuable to the government at home became much greater. When finally the resident ambassador appeared, his opportunities for gathering news in the land of his residence were excellent, while his knowledge of the state of affairs at home and of the mind of his government was less current and complete than that of the *ad hoc* envoy. A change in emphasis thus occurred: the primary function of the resident ambassador became the acquisition and transmission of information, while negotiation became secondary and continued often to be entrusted to *ad hoc* ambassadors. As it happens, the intensification of diplomatic activity which led to the birth of the resident ambassador took place during just that period when "orator" and "ambassador" were gaining currency.

[18] Ernst, "Gesandtschaftswesen und Diplomatie," p. 90.
[19] Cessi, *Deliberazioni del Maggior Consiglio*, II, 102.

No reader is likely to be unaware of the reputation of Venetian ambassadors as gatherers of news. An ambassador who kept the Senate well informed was richly praised: ". . . on account of the diligent notice of all news which, according to your custom, you have given to us, we especially praise you and we justly commend you, who truly have omitted nothing which pertains to the office of a faithful, prudent and diligent orator."[20] To its orator keeping the death watch over the king of Naples in 1496, the Senate wrote that it wished to be informed of the inclination of the lords, magnates, and people by the most swift messengers, not daily, but hourly.[21] Stingy as the Senate was concerning the expenses of its representatives, special concessions were often made concerning the cost of messengers sent with news to Venice.[22] In a decree of 1478 the Senate bitterly complained against orators "who . . . do not write what they hear from the princes and potentates to whom they have been sent, which is among the first of the offices of a true and faithful orator. . . ."[23]

Trafficking in news became an important function of ambassadors. So vital to the reputation and the success of an orator was his possession of information that by the end of the Middle Ages a government was reluctant to communicate with another by means of the foreign ambassador accredited to it, but rather by its own ambassador accredited to the foreign government. He thus gained credit as a dispenser of information. To charge a foreign ambassador with some communication was a high mark of honor.[24] This is in marked contrast to an earlier period when diplomatic intercourse was less frequent and one envoy often served the needs of both parties. Maulde La Clavière points out that an ambassador who wished to keep his government well informed had to be well informed by it. To obtain information he had to be able to give some. The Venetian ambassador in Paris in 1514, Dandolo, became furious with the Senate when the brother of the French ambassador to the Republic was informed of happenings in Venice before he was.[25] Mantuan ambassadors prided themselves on being so well informed that sometimes even the Venetian ambassadors sought information from them.[26] Since the papal curia was the court at which more ambassadors

[20] A.S.V., Senato, Secreta, xxx, 52v (62v).

[21] *Ibid.*, xxxvi, 74v (86v).

[22] F. Nicolini, "Frammenti veneto-napoletani," p. 5, n. 7. The Senate conceded to the consul of Apulia, as to his predecessor, authority to spend whatever should be necessary for messengers.

[23] Senato, Secreta, xxviii, 104v (115v).

[24] Maulde La Clavière, *La diplomatie au temps de Machiavel*, iii, 118-119.

[25] *Ibid.*, iii, 113-116. A Milanese ambassador in Venice in 1414 obtained considerable secret information from the Senate in exchange for information that he possessed concerning the situation of the King of the Romans. A.S.V., Senato, Secreta, v, 180v (182v).

[26] Quazza, *La diplomazia gonzaghesca*, p. 27.

gathered than anywhere else, it is not surprising that it was the great center for the exchange of information.[27]

Ambassadors sometimes readily crossed the nebulous line between legitimate gathering of information and espionage and other ill-reputed activities. In a well-known passage Philippe de Commines advises that even ambassadors sent by unfriendly powers should be received honorably, but that trusted persons should be assigned to accompany them, because one can then know who approaches them and can keep malcontents from bringing information to them. Moreover, he advises that they should be heard and quickly licensed to depart, since it is not safe to keep enemies about. Even in time of war, dealings with ambassadors from the enemy should not be broken off, however. Instead, for every ambassador that is received, two should be dispatched. Even if the other side tires of the exchange and wishes to break off, one should continue to send ambassadors at every opportunity, because there is no way to send a spy so good and so sure and with such opportunity for seeing and hearing. If you can send two or three, the recipient will find it very difficult to prevent one or another from picking up information of profit. He has discussed this matter at some length, he says, because he has known so much mischief and so many intrigues brought about by ambassadors.[28] Elsewhere he writes of the coming and going of ambassadors, "some for intelligence, and some to debauch their respective subjects, and make what pernicious bargains they could, and all under the specious pretence of amity and friendship."[29] Bernard du Rosier's admonition that ambassadors should not inquire into the secrets of states and the dispositions of kingdoms, "for this in no way belongs to the office of ambassador,"[30] must be regarded as bookish nonsense. The suspicion that an ambassador was a legalized spy was never far from men's minds. Friar John of Plano-Carpini and Friar Benedict of Poland, emissaries to the

[27] Cuttino, *English Diplomatic Administration*, p. 99.

[28] Commynes, *Mémoires*, Chap. viii, Liv. iii, i, 221-223.

[29] *Ibid.*, i, Chap. xvi, Liv. i, 96. Ambassadors, of course, were not the only sources of diplomatic information. Merchants, whether citizens or foreign, physicians resident in another state, private citizens prepared to betray their own states, and others contributed to the flow of information. In the Venetian records we often find approaches made to Venice through Venetian citizens. About 1450, Geronimo Barbadico was the intermediary for a number of people wishing to give, sell, or trade information to the Senate. The Senate would discuss the matter and order Barbadico to respond in his private capacity. Sometimes, of course, a person was sent specifically and secretly as a spy to seek information. A.S.V., Dieci, Misti, xvii, 108r (150r). Ludovico Gonzaga and his sons, warning King Robert of Sicily of the intentions of Louis the Bavarian, state that they learned of them through a certain *nuncius* of theirs, whom they retained in Germany permanently for spying upon the movements of the king. It is not possible to ascertain certainly from the document whether this *nuncius* was a diplomatic envoy or not. Winkelmann, *Acta Imperii inedita*, ii, 811-812, no. 1152.

[30] Bernard du Rosier, *Ambaxiator brevilogus*, p. 23.

Mongol khan, dissuaded him from sending envoys back with them. In the first place, they feared lest the Mongols would be encouraged by the wars and dissensions among Europeans to march against them. In the second, they feared that the emissaries were intended as spies.[31] The Venetian Senate in 1392, having discovered that visiting ambassadors lacked sufficient mandates, concluded "that their intention is not good in wishing to have concord with us, rather they have come deceitfully and slyly for learning of our affairs."[32] Venetian representatives abroad were justly treated with equal suspicion. The *deliberazioni* of the Senate in 1451 reveal that their secretary in Genoa had become unwelcome and suspect.[33]

Naturally, then, rulers often were less than eager to receive ambassadors. As the frequency and duration of missions increased and the office of the resident ambassador evolved, the danger of spying became more and more apparent. Pope Martin V, for this reason, sought to repress the residents. Notification through a papal chamberlain should be sufficient to terminate an ambassador's privileges on the spot, and even in the absence of such notification an embassy should be understood to have terminated six months from its reception.[34] Ferdinand the Catholic also regarded ambassadors as spies and intriguers, and did not want them to remain long in his territories.[35] Henry VII of England was also reluctant to receive them, and for good reason, since his own instructions to ambassadors reveal little interest in negotiations, but rather lists of questions to which he demanded detailed answers.[36] Sanuto records a *relazione* of a Venetian secretary in Constantinople in 1496 to the effect that the Turk did not wish to accept a *baiulo*, because he did not want a spy. Two and a half years later the *relazione* of an ambassador revealed that the Turk would accept a *baiulo* elected from the community of merchants, but that he did not want one sent as a spy from Venice.[37]

Attempts were made to isolate ambassadors who were received and to limit their access to information. The jealousy and precaution shown toward ambassadors by the Byzantines is well known, especially from the famous

[31] George Vernadsky, *The Mongols and Russia* (New Haven, 1953), pp. 64-65.

[32] A.S.V., Senato, Secreta, R (E), 72r.

[33] A.S.V., Senato, Secreta, XIX, 48v (48v). The Ten in 1494 ordered the orator in Rome to cease sending his secretary or other emissary to receive secret communications from the cardinal of St. Peter in Chains, for although the information was welcome, the suspicions that Venice was plotting against France were not. A.S.V., Dieci, Misti, XXVI, 75v (103v)–76r (104r).

[34] Maulde La Clavière, *La diplomatie au temps de Machiavel*, III, 362-363, and 363, n. 1.

[35] Nys, "Le droit d'ambassade jusqu'à Grotius," XVI, 61.

[36] *Ibid.*, XVI, 61 and 66; Jusserand, "The School for Ambassadors," p. 33.

[37] *Diarii*, I, col. 399, and II, col. 700. On the other hand, if ambassadors were sent to one's enemies, and not to oneself, there was cause for concern. Louis XI complained that Venice sent ambassadors so rarely to him, but so often to Burgundy. Nys, *Origines du droit international*, p. 306.

account of his embassy by Liutprand of Cremona. Mary C. Hill reports that in thirteenth- and fourteenth-century England messengers were assigned to accompany foreign envoys, not only to offer respect and to reinforce the king's safe-conduct, but to check the envoy's movements and contacts.[38] Venice in later years tried in various ways to restrict ambassadorial spying. Nobles having a position in the government were forbidden in 1451 to have any dealings with foreigners touching affairs of state (ambassadors are among those specifically mentioned) or to give audience in their houses to them. If they want to entertain foreigners, they must obtain license from the *Signoria* or from the heads of the Council of Ten. The chancellor and all notaries assigned to the College or the Ten were placed under the same restrictions.[39] Apparently this was ineffective because in 1481 the Ten issued another decree. No member of the Senate, the College, or the Secret Councils should speak of affairs of state to ambassadors or other foreigners inside his house or elsewhere.[40] Molmenti mentions a long series of acts attempting to restrict espionage on the part of ambassadors from the end of the period considered here until the fall of the Republic.[41]

Ambassadors were expected to be able to report on such things as the condition of the routes, the locations of streams and bridges, the forces of the state to which they were sent or those through which they passed, and possible adverse alliances. The same secretarial *relazione* of 1496, reporting that the sultan did not wish to receive a *baiulo*, provides ample reason for that wish: the *relazione* itself is full of information concerning the Turkish military and naval forces.[42] The Venetian orator in Montferrat in 1453 was instructed to try to find out where Charles VII was and if he had undertaken or was about to undertake anything. He should also try to determine whether the duke of Orléans or the bastard were likely to enter into Italy against Sforza, and if so, when and with how many men.[43] Bartholomeus Barberius, Milanese orator in Venice in 1468 had been seen every day taking a position in the ducal palace where he could spy upon what was said and done and who was coming to the *Signoria*. Nothing had been said to him, however, since he did no more than observe from a public place.

[38] *King's Messengers*, p. 95.

[39] Pompeo Molmenti, "Le relazioni tra patrizi veneziani e diplomatici stranieri," in *Curiosità di storia veneziana* (Bologna, 1919), pp. 45-46.

[40] Published in Samuel Romanin, *Storia documentata di Venezia*, 10 vols. (Venezia, 1853-1861), VI, 116. Molmenti corrects the eighteenth century dating of Vetto Sandi. "Relazioni tra patrizi veneziani e diplomatici stranieri," pp. 38-39. Maulde La Clavière is wrong on the amount of the fine. *La diplomatie au temps de Machiavel*, II, 319, n. 2.

[41] Molmenti, "Relazioni tra patrizi veneziani e diplomatici stranieri," pp. 47-52.

[42] Sanuto, *Diarii*, I, cols. 397-400. It happens that Alvise Sagudino, who gave the *relazione*, was not a *baiulo*, but a secretary.

[43] A.S.V., Senato, Secreta, XIX, 224r (224r).

Since then, however, he had been discovered at Chioggia observing and counting the troops about to be sent to Lombardy. It was proposed and defeated in the Council of Ten that he should be arrested and put to torture.[44] Often it was diplomatic information that the ambassador sought. In 1466 the Venetian Senate demanded of its orator in Hungary that he should make secret inquiries whether the king had entered into any negotiation with the Turks. If he had sent any envoy to the Turks the ambassador should inform them of his condition, estate, and character. Five weeks later, not having heard from the ambassador, the Senate reprimanded him for his lack of diligence.[45]

The line between the legitimate gathering of information and espionage is difficult to draw, but diplomatic envoys often became involved in intrigues far from ambiguous. The Venetian secretary and the Milanese *commissarius* at Genoa in 1496, for example, served as intermediaries between their governments and an adventurer who offered to burn up two of three French ships either in the port of Villefranche or at Nice. The two governments agreed to the proposal and to splitting the cost of 400 ducats.[46] Renaissance ambassadors, and especially those of Venice, have a romantic reputation for dealing in assassination. Evidence on this subject, however, is even more scanty than one might expect. Le comte de Mas Latrie's study of political poisoning in Venice does not cite a single instance in which an ambassador was involved.[47] Louis XI, however, expressed fears that Nicolò Canal, a dismissed but not departed Venetian ambassador, was trying to have him poisoned.[48] In at least one well-known instance, Venetian ambassadors did engage in a plot to have enemies of the Republic assassinated. In 1406 the Senate wrote to its ambassadors in Florence that they should accept the offer made by an unknown person through Francesco Bevazano, their notary, to do away with Brunoro della Scala and Ubertino and Marsiglio Carrara. The ambassadors could promise up to 10,000 ducats for the killing, and beyond this they could offer 50 ducats a year pension for life.[49] Although more examples might be found by a more thorough search, it does not seem that ambassadors commonly participated in assassinations.[50]

[44] A.S.V., Dieci, Misti, xvii, 59r (101r). It is the index which reveals his name.

[45] A.S.V., Senato, Secreta, xxii, 167v (169v)–168r (170r), and 173v (175v).

[46] A.S.V., Dieci, Misti, xxvii, 29v (70v)–30r (71r); filze, x, 110.

[47] *De l'empoisonnement politique dans la république de Venise* (Paris, 1893).

[48] Perret, *Relations de la France avec Venise*, i, 431-432.

[49] A.S.V., Senato, Secreta, iii, 47v (47v). The Senate had earlier put a price on the Carraresi. Italo Raulich, *La caduta dei Carraresi, signori di Padova* (Padova-Verona, 1890), p. 110 and n. 1. Also Alice M. Allen, *A History of Verona* (London, 1910), pp. 326-336.

[50] The registers of the *Dieci* to the end of the fifteenth century contribute nothing on this subject.

On occasion ambassadors sought to subvert subjects of the state to which they were accredited. In 1427 the Venetian Senate believed, at any rate, that *nuncii* of the duke of Milan were trying to stir up a revolt in Brescia.[51] Commines reports that Louis XI sent his barber on a trumped-up mission to Mary of Burgundy with the real purpose of bringing about an uprising in Ghent. He approached privately some persons whom he thought most tractable, offering that all their old privileges should be restored and new ones added. The upshot of his bungling job, according to our author, was that he left Ghent in haste to forestall being thrown into the river.[52]

Bribery appears to have been a very common activity of ambassadors, especially those of Venice. An ambassador to the Turk received 500 ducats "to expend on those persons with whom he will have to treat for peace and other matters committed to the said ambassador."[53] Ambassadors to Pope Martin V and to the king of the Romans were allowed to spend up to 10,000 ducats on those persons whom they thought most suitable.[54] In the 1430's document after document mentions bribes to the imperial chancellor, Gaspar Slick.[55] Marco Dandolo could expend up to 5,000 ducats to corrupt the Hungarian nobility, but the Senate subsequently reconsidered the customs and conditions of the Hungarian nobility and authorized an additional 5,000 ducats in the hope that he might corrupt the queen and several of the chief barons of the kingdom.[56] In earlier negotiations with Hungary, Venetian ambassadors were allowed to spend up to 5,000 ducats on bribes. To add insult to injury, any money saved on bribes could be added to the 50,000 to 60,000 ducats that they were permitted to offer the king.[57] The Venetians caught Commines, as French ambassador, trying to corrupt one of the captains of the duke of Milan, who was informed of this attempt.[58] Bribery is not clearly separable from legitimate gifts. By means of Commines, Louis XI had many persons at the English court in his pay—including the English king. It is reflective of the mores of the age that only Lord Hastings refused to give a receipt.[59] A Venetian ambassador to the Turks had an allowance to be spent for gifts of silver for the chancellor and of

[51] A.S.V., Senato, Secreta, x, 22r (26r).

[52] Commynes, *Mémoires*, Liv. V, Chap. xiv, i, 408-409.

[53] A.S.V., Senato, Secreta, vi, 93r (94r). Four hundred ducats authorized for the chancellor of the duke of Burgundy. *Ibid.*, xxv, 141v (150v). Two to three hundred ducats to be offered to favorites of Emperor Maximilian. Dieci, Misti, xxvii, 50v (92v); filze, x, 191. Property worth 100 ducats and 50 ducats a year, respectively, to the chancellor of Francesco Sforza and one Contucio. Senato, Secreta, xiv, 19r (20r).

[54] A.S.V., Senato, Secreta, vii, 6r (7r).

[55] *Ibid.*, xii, 182r (189r); xiv, 51rv (52rv); 79r (80r); 84v (85v).

[56] *Ibid.*, x, 119r (123r).

[57] *Ibid.*, iv, 119r (118r).

[58] Maulde La Clavière, *La diplomatie au temps de Machiavel*, iii, 350, n. 1.

[59] *Ibid.*, ii, 344-345.

cloth for other courtiers.[60] The Venetians well knew the difficulty in distinguishing ceremonial gifts from bribes, as we shall see.[61] This was not new in Renaissance diplomacy. At the end of the thirteenth century Flemish envoys in Rome were paying off the famous Cardinal Matthew of Aquasparta, who held a pension of the count.[62] They complain of the high cost of doing business in Rome because of the necessity of offering great gifts.[63] Clearly corruption played a greater part in medieval and Renaissance diplomacy than it does today—or, at any rate, it was a more gross and more personal corruption.

It is quite clear that one of the undercover functions of the ambassador was to serve as a center or clearinghouse for the gathering of information and the attraction of proposals subversive to the government to which he was accredited or to some other government. The Council of Ten wrote to the Venetian ambassador in Naples in 1494 that it belonged to his office "to hear all those referring or proposing anything to you and diligently to inform us of whatever comes to your attention. . . ." A certain Joannes Jacobus Trivultio had expressed his desire to serve Venice.[64] One would like to know just what service he had in mind. Subversive proposals quite naturally were usually expressed in euphemistic terms. In Zaccaria Contarini's *relazione* in 1492 of his mission to France, he gives a list of pensioners of the king of France whom he holds certain to be more willing to serve Venice than the king. The list is headed by the duke of Lorraine, who had this communicated expressly to the ambassador by one of the duke's secretaries. Then as now, a man "much deprived of the honor and reputation that he had," as Contarini said of another on his list, was a prime candidate for espionage or subversion.[65] The Ten in 1451 alerted the orator in Siena to expect to be approached by Schalabrinus de Volterra, a soldier in the company of a *condotierre* employed by Sforza. He wished to sell information concerning a dangerous plot against the Republic. He had previously been unable to contact the ambassador and had communicated with the Ten through a Venetian noble found in Perugia. The ambassador was authorized to promise even more money than the amount demanded if the news was worth it, but he could not buy the in-

[60] A.S.V., Senato, Secreta, x, 175r (179r).

[61] Venetian ambassadors were required to deliver to the state any gifts offered to them. *Infra*, pp. 204-206.

[62] Kervyn de Lettenhove *Études*, pp. 62-63.

[63] *Ibid.*, pp. 31-32; Kervyn de Lettenhove, *Histoire de Flandre*, 6 vols. (Bruxelles, 1847-1850), I, 305-308; Funck-Brentano, *Philippe le Bel en Flandre*, pp. 281-282.

[64] A.S.V., Dieci, Misti, XXVI, 71r (99r)–71v (99v).

[65] *Le relazioni degli ambasciatori veneti al Senato durante il secolo XVI*, Eugenio Albèri, ed., 15 vols. (Firenze, 1839-1863), serie I, IV, 21.

formation without approval of the Ten.[66] In 1489 the Ten reprimanded the orator in Hungary for communicating secret information from an unnamed informer to anybody other than the Ten. He should assure the informer that his services are and will be appreciated and that they will be kept most secret, as he understandably desires.[67] On another occasion the Ten wrote to the orator in Genoa that he should employ two spies (*exploratores*), neither one knowing of the other, and send them to Lyons and beyond to try to learn of the comings and goings of the king of France, his plans, and any preparations for war. He was sent 100 ducats for the purpose.[68] In this last case the ambassador was not to be merely the recipient of information or proposals, but was to take the initiative.

Much diplomatic skulduggery, as is well-known, surrounded the captivity of Djem, brother of the sultan. At the end of 1488, Domenico Trevisan, orator in Rome, communicated to the Ten that Francesco, nephew of Innocent VIII, had quite openly offered to deliver Djem to Venice upon the death of the pope. The Ten instructed Trevisan to express its gratitude for the offer.[69] After the accession of Alexander VI, the new pope demanded of the Venetian orator the name of the Ten's informant on the possibility of Djem's escape from papal custody—probably the aforementioned Francesco. The Ten replied that he should refuse:

> . . . once having given our faith to the person from whom we have had this most secret information with the promise never to reveal it, as is customary in matters of this kind, we do not see in what way we can—and much less ought—to break and violate our faith once it has been pledged. This is a thing our republic has never wished to do at any time or in any case, nor will it, since it has always recognized that in the inviolable observation of this principally consists the foundation and conservation of our state. By means of this principal through the ages we have experienced very great profit and convenience. . . .[70]

Actually, Venice did not want Djem's escape from papal custody, and so instructed its orator in 1492 to reject offers to procure it.[71]

A closely related activity of the orator was counterespionage. In 1478

[66] A.S.V., Dieci, Misti, XIV, 92v (96v). Another example, *ibid.*, XVIII, 74r (129r).

[67] Vladimir Lamansky, *Secrets d'état de Venise* (St. Petersburg, 1884), pp. 198-199. Letters published. A note indicates that they were sent in cipher.

[68] A.S.V., Dieci, Misti, XXVI, 197r (226r); filze, IX, 227.

[69] *Ibid.*, XXIV, 47v (86v)–48r (87r); filze, IIbis, 148.

[70] Lamansky, *Secrets d'état de Venise*, p. 250. In 1451 the Senate sent a secret *nuncius* to hear information that the widow of the duke of Milan wished to say to them. A.S.V., Senato, Secreta, XIX, 65v (65v).

[71] Lamansky, *Secrets d'état de Venise*, pp. 252-253.

the Ten wrote to the Venetian orator to the pope that it was common knowledge that Venetian secrets were being written to Rome. It is said that he knows something concerning this, so he is ordered to write by his own hand all that he knows, believes, suspects, or conjectures of this leakage of secret information. They want to know by whom it was written and to whom, when and by what messengers it was carried, and the reasons for his beliefs and suspicions. His report should be sworn by him and detailed in character.[72] On an earlier occasion Venetian orators in Rome were instructed to use every means to obtain from *cubicularii*, *camerarii*, or others information concerning Venetian secrets disclosed in Rome.[73] In 1496 the Venetian orator in Milan received from the duke information about Venetian secrets sent into France. As a result two informants were imprisoned in Venice.[74]

Since ambassadors dealt with so much secret information, the revelation of which would be harmful to the state and could cost the lives of informers, precautions had to be taken to prevent ambassadorial records from falling into the wrong hands. The Venetian orator in Rome in 1496 was ordered to have the registers of his letters and the letters received from Venice prepared for destruction, if it should be necessary in order to prevent them from coming into the possession of foreigners.[75] Sanuto reports an ambassador in France who burned all his records by order of the government a few years later.[76] An act of the Great Council of 1401 required that ambassadors upon their return had to turn over to the government all the letters which had been addressed to them, lest these should at some time fall into the hands of others.[77]

It is obvious that an ambassador who became a turncoat could inflict incalculable harm upon the state. Evidence of such treachery is rare, however. After all, every precaution would be taken to conceal a betrayal. In 1498 one Francesco Capinsacho, formerly orator of the lord of Rimini, revealed to the Council of Ten what he knew about his master and Rimini. The Ten then provided that his account should be read in the Senate, al-

[72] A.S.V., Dieci, Misti, XIX, 79r. A similar document of 1494, except that the information that secrets were revealed came from the orator and there is no indication that he had yet acquired any further knowledge of the matter. A.S.V., Dieci, Misti, XXVI, 127r (156r); filze, VIII, 254.

[73] *Ibid.*, XV, 192v (193v), 14 November 1459.

[74] *Ibid.*, Dieci, Misti, XXVII, 9v (50v); filze, X, 4. See also the missions of Bertuccio Nigro, Venetian secretary, to Rome to try to discover the citizens involved in a plot with the king of Aragon and a papal protonotary. *Ibid.*, XIII, 121v (123v)–123r (125r). *Supra*, pp. 19-20.

[75] *Ibid.*, XXVI, 127r (156r); filze, VIII, 254.

[76] *Diarii*, VII, col. 736.

[77] A.S.V., Maggior Consiglio, Leona, 118v (122v)–119r (123r).

though his name should be concealed.[78] No indication of betrayal of the Republic by a Venetian ambassador has been discovered, despite the bitterness of some ambassadors at their compulsory and costly service and considerable evidence of mismanagement and indiscretion. Nicolà Nicolini points to the nonpatrician secretary accompanying an ambassador as a means of controlling the latter's loyalty—indeed, as a sort of spy upon him.[79]

Virtually all of the evidence of ambassadorial espionage and other skulduggery comes from the fifteenth century, but this is not especially indicative of moral degeneration in the Quattrocento. Rather it reflects the increased importance of information-gathering among the functions of ambassadors as the resident ambassadorship was gradually evolving.

The second new emphasis was upon the ceremonial function of envoys. The Late Middle Ages was a period of "a thousand formalities," and it is not surprising that diplomatic envoys played a ceremonial role.[80] In documents dealing with the appointment of ambassadors we find more frequently such expressions as *occasione onorandi festum suum*.[81] Marriage ceremonies, especially, great events that they were in the lives of princes and the affairs of state, required the presence of ambassadors (in numbers which tended to increase) representing states friendly to those becoming allied through marriage. Venice, for example, in 1362 sent to the court of each of the contracting parties two ambassadors who were to join together subsequently at the place of the wedding to represent the Republic on that occasion. They bore scarlet robes as gifts of Venice to the bride and the groom.[82] Reluctance to send ambassadors or orators to grace a wedding would tend to indicate a coolness toward at least one of the parties.[83] Another great event requiring ceremonial orators from the Italian city-states was the journey of a king of the Romans to Rome for his imperial coronation. It was customary to honor the emperor-elect with orators to accompany him on his way.[84] Various congratulatory messages were also borne by ambassadors or others. It was deemed more complimentary to send an ambassador, but long distance involving great expense rendered the use of some functionary, such as the captain of a galley, quite acceptable

[78] A.S.V., Dieci, Misti, xxvii, 168r (210r); filze, xii, 81.

[79] Nicolini, *Il consolato generale veneto nel regno di Napoli*, p. 48.

[80] Johan Huizinga, *The Waning of the Middle Ages*, 1st edn. in Dutch, 1919; trans. and adaptation from 2d edn. by F. Hopman, 1924, reprinted (New York, 1954), p. 9.

[81] A.S.V., Maggior Consiglio, Clericus-Civicus, 71r (119r).

[82] A.S.V., Maggior Consiglio, Novella, 82v (93v).

[83] A.S.V., Senato, Secreta, xvi, 69v (69v) and 86v (86v). The Senate reversed itself and sent the desired orators for the marriage of the marquis of Este despite its strained relations with his prospective father-in-law, the king of Aragon.

[84] *Ibid.*, xix, 91r (91r).

in lieu of an ambassador appointed solely for the purpose.[85] The death of a friendly prince or a member of his family was another of those climactic events surrounded with solemn pageantry and calling for an embassy to share the grief and offer condolences.[86] Almost all ambassadors in the High Middle Ages had a ceremonial role to play, even thought it might be incidental to more mundane objectives. The Florentines were particularly apt to have their ambassadors, already engaged upon some mission, stop at other courts along the way with letters of credence and courteous words. Two ambassadors sent in 1480 to Rome and to Naples to offer congratulations on the new peace, for example, were also to proffer congratulations or gratitude to Siena, to the duke and duchess of Calabria and to the grand constable and all the cardinals.[87] Sometimes, of course, ceremonial embassies received political missions in addition. A ceremonial appearance could pave the way for forming new friendships or renewing old ones.[88] The ceremonial value of an orator is indicated by a Venetian document of 1443. The doge of Genoa had requested an orator of the Senate, even though Venice was already represented in Genoa by a secretary. The Senate agreed to send one "in order to enhance the reputation of his Excellency, and that all should know that we are inclined, not only to conserve our good friendship and union, but also to augment it from good to better, and to have that care of his state that we have of our own."[89]

It is clear, therefore, that the ambassador was becoming the most solemn type of diplomatic representative.[90] Buzzati and Antonibon, basing their conclusions upon Venetian evidence, contend that as early as the thirteenth century the ambassador completely represented his government or state. From his reading of fifteenth- and sixteenth-century treatises on ambassadors, Behrens also concluded that one of the characteristics of the ambassador was to personify the dignity of the principal. Maulde La Clavière adds that whether a prince was present in his own person or in that of his ambassadors did not make any difference, and the same would be true, of course, if the principal happened to be a city or other corporate body.[91]

85 A.S.V., Senato, Misti, XVI, 73v (73v).

86 A.S.V., Senato, Secreta, XXXVI, 171v (183v).

87 A.S.F., Signori—Carteggi, Missive—Legazioni e commissarie—Elezioni e istruzioni a oratori, XXI, 2r–6r.

88 Winkelmann, *Acta Imperii inedita*, II, 822-823, no. 1163.

89 A.S.V., Senato, Secreta, XVI, 1r (1r).

90 Cuttino, *English Diplomatic Administration*, p. 85; Ganshof, *Le Moyen Age*, p. 270. "Ambassador" did continue, however, to be used very loosely at times.

91 Buzzati, "Diritto diplomatico veneziano," p. 231; Antonibon, *Relazioni a stampa di ambasciatori veneti*, p. 11, n. 1; Behrens, "Treatises on the Ambassador," p. 620; Maulde La Clavière, *La diplomatie au temps de Machiavel*, II, 286-287.

Some of the diplomatic documents themselves make this representation of the person of the principal most explicit.[92] When in 1422 a Castilian orator and an English procurator (the bishop of Chichester, a person of high status in his own right) came to blows over precedence, the character of personal representative possessed by the Castilian caused the pope to judge in his favor.[93] That ambassadorial representation could continue after the death of the principal[94] does not belie its personal character, for even in a monarchical state it was the person of an institution, not merely an individual that was represented.

Whatever ambassadors said or did was held to be done by those who had sent them.[95] A Florentine ambassador in 1447, wishing to offer his own opinion on a certain matter, specified that "he spoke as Andrea, not as ambassador."[96] In any ceremony the ambassador could stand for the person of his principal. The orator of Ferdinand and Isabella, for example, received for the queen the papal rose.[97] In 1510, Venetian ambassadors had to submit to penance and receive absolution for the Republic. The papal master of ceremonies, Paris de Grassis, reports the precedents. All had been struck with switches, some on their bare shoulders, others without removing their garments, some vigorously during the chanting of three entire psalms, some gently. The master of ceremonies suggested a very gentle whipping for the Venetian envoys, but Julius II excused them from this humiliating ceremony and imposed upon them instead the visiting of seven churches.[98] An ambassador could also represent his state as godfather at a baptism.[99] The degree to which the ambassador represented his principal is indicated by Baldus' assertion that one who killed an ambassador was guilty of *laesa maiestas*.[100] In this personal representation there is nothing really new. What has been said above closely parallels what was earlier

[92] A.S.V., Dieci, Misti, XIV, 4r (7r); Senato, Secreta, XXXIII, 48r (58r).

[93] Ganshof, *Le Moyen Age*, p. 270. Maulde La Clavière distinguishes *nuncii* or *oratores*, simple delegates, who act in the name of the pope, from *legati*, substitutes or representatives of the pope, who act in their own name. *La diplomatie au temps de Machiavel*, I, 298. I think this is confused on both legal and ceremonial representation.

[94] Maulde La Clavière, *La diplomatie au temps de Machiavel*, III, 366.

[95] Dolius, *Glossae*, no. 5, in *Iuris interpretes saec. XIII*, E. M. Meyers, ed. (Neapoli, 1924); Bernard du Rosier, *Ambaxiator brevilogus*, p. 24.

[96] A.S.F., Signori—Missive—Originali, IV, 7v. See also the Mantuan ambassador's response to the bishop of Zagreb indicating that he was not instructed on the issue raised, but offering his own opinion. Archivio di Stato, Mantova, Archivio Gonzaga, 533 (E. V. 3).

[97] Burckhard, *Liber notarum*, I, 300.

[98] Nys, *Origines du droit international*, p. 186. The implications of this act are fascinating, not only for the intensity of the representation of the principal by the envoy, but for the concept of a corporate personality capable of penance and absolution.

[99] A.S.V., Sindicati, II, 39v. Recall earlier reference to procurators who performed this function, although the representative character of the procurator was not the same as that of the ambassador. *Supra*, p. 49.

[100] *Commentaria*, ad *Libros Decretalium*, 1, *De officio legati*, 1, 7; Gambarus, *Tractatus*, p. 16.

said of the *nuncius*.[101] The only difference was not in the nature of the representative character of the *nuncius* and the ambassador, but in the gradually emerging superiority in status and ceremonial value of the latter. This representative character is the unspoken presupposition behind the interminable discussions of the ambassador's personal status, equipment, clothing, retinue, and the like by the fifteenth- and sixteenth-century writers on the ambassadorial office.[102] At issue was the honor and dignity of the principal.

Although it is true that the ceremonial and information-gathering functions of ambassadors became more and more prominent, negotiations continued to be carried on by their means. In the later Middle Ages, however, rulers except for the pope only rarely participated actively in negotiations with ambassadors sent to them.[103] Instead they usually dealt with visiting ambassadors through *tractatores* or *praticatores*, who resembled ambassadors appointed to meet with ambassadors of another power on neutral ground, except that the *tractatores* remained at home. The resemblance is so close, however, that on rare occasions the words ambassador and *tractator* were used interchangeably.[104] A ruler, of course, could elect to deal directly with ambassadors, and often such direct access to the ruler was sought by them. Some Venetian emissaries in 1348 were instructed to seek words directly with the ruler, but if he could not or did not wish to hear them, they should accept *tractatores*.[105]

Whether the situation was one of dealing directly with the ruler or with *tractatores* or ambassadors, however, a considerable amount of jockeying over the showing of powers, if any, or the opening of negotiations was not unusual. Each side usually tried to get some idea of how far the other was prepared to go before revealing its own intentions.[106] Some debate might also occur over the admissibility of documents presented as evidence

[101] *Supra*, pp. 9-11.

[102] Behrens, "Treatises on the Ambassador," p. 620.

[103] Maulde La Clavière, *La diplomatie au temps de Machiavel*, III, 94-95.

[104] Cessi, *Deliberazioni del Maggior Consiglio*, III, 59. See my article, "Early Venetian Legislation Concerning Foreign Ambassadors," *Studies in the Renaissance*, XII (1965), pp. 10-12, on laws governing *tractatores*.

[105] A.S.V., Senato, Secreta, A (B).

[106] *Ibid.*, XXXVII, 42r (56r). See also the description of long days of haggling between French and English ambassadors in 1418 over which side should open, what language should be used, the accurate redaction of verbal offers into writing—all broken by long periods of uncomfortable silence when neither side was willing to say anything. Rymer, *Foedera*, IV, iii, 70-75. There was a certain presumption that visiting envoys should open. Maulde La Clavière, *La diplomatie au temps de Machiavel*, III, 54. An interesting Venetian document of 1422 reveals that the Venetian *tractatores* failed to request that the visiting ambassadors reveal their powers at the outset, and the Senate concluded that, after negotiations had progressed somewhat, a belated demand for the visitors' procuration might imply an overeagerness on the part of Venice to come to terms. So they decided to let it pass. A.S.V., Senato, Secreta, VII, 51v (52v).

of the rights of one party or the other. A Venetian document of 1428 reveals a dispute between its ambassador and that of Milan over the use of copies of authentic and original documents and of witnesses against the writings.[107] There is also a rather good and lengthy account of the sparring between English and French envoys over what was to become the treaty of 1415. At the time this document was written neither side was prepared to make a commitment, and one may suppose that the ambassadors were not then empowered to do so.[108]

Like the *nuncius*, the ambassador, *qua* ambassador, did not possess the power to conclude. In the course of negotiations it might be demanded of an ambassador whether he possessed such authority, and the reply often was that he did not and must either go or send to his principal to inform him of the status of negotiations, for without the knowledge and mandate of the principal he could proceed no further.[109] This represents no oversight, but a conscious effort on the part of the principal to maintain control over negotiations. It is a more cumbersome, but much more cautious method than that exemplified by procurators empowered to conclude treaties with whatever states and upon whatever terms seemed good to them. Venetian ambassadors were instructed again and again to learn what the other party had to propose, then to write to Venice and await instructions.[110] Sometimes the ambassador himself returned home to consult with his principal.[111] The instructions of Venetian ambassadors often state that they should reply to certain openings that they have nothing in their mandates. This lack of powers provided a valuable protection to the ambassador and was a convenient device for gaining time for consideration or simply for stalling.[112] Negotiations thus often stretched into a series of negotiations, one embassy preparing the ground for a later one.[113] If an ambassador's proposals or demands were not well received, he might be instructed to refuse to accept the response as final. On the other hand, he might have instructions to communicate to the opposite party that a failure to

[107] A.S.V., Senato, Secreta, x, 187rv (191rv).

[108] Rymer, *Foedera*, iv, ii, 106-109.

[109] A.S.V., Senato, Secreta, ix, 172r (170r); A.S.F., Signori, Carteggi—Missive—Legazione e commissarie—Elezioni e istruzioni a oratori, xxi, 30v. Of course, an ambassador might have full powers to conclude, but yet take refuge behind his lack of powers to make certain concessions demanded by the other party. Perret, *Relations de la France avec Venise*, ii, 102.

[110] A.S.V., Maggior Consiglio, Magnus, 8r; Senato, Secreta, i, 62r (63r); xxxi, 1r (1r).

[111] A.S.F., Signori—Legazioni e commissarie: Risposti verbali di oratori, ii, 79r.

[112] Delay was not always on the side of the visiting ambassador. A Neapolitan ambassador in Venice caught the Senate by surprise with an unexpectedly strong affirmative reply to a very tentative feeler concerning an alliance. The Senate was unquestionably favorable to the proposed alliance, but had not expected things to move so rapidly, and was not yet prepared to take the next step. A.S.V., Senato, Secreta, v, 86v (88v).

[113] Rymer, *Foedera*, v, iv, 87.

respond favorably to his demands within a given time should be reason for his repatriation and an assumption that the other party intended war.[114]

Commines gives us a picture of the physical setting and the actual procedure of a high level and full dress negotiation of French ambassadors with the duke of Milan and his allies. The ambassadors were received by the duke and the duchess in their quarters, and they then proceeded to the duke's chamber where two rows of seats had been placed face-to-face, the one for Commines and his colleagues, and other for the duke and his allies or their ambassadors. On the one side only the duke spoke, but the French were inclined to speak all at once, which caused the duke to appeal repeatedly for better order. Everything agreed upon had to be formed into articles, so whenever agreement was reached upon any subject it was put into writing by a secretary on each side, then read aloud by each, one in Italian, the other in French. This was repeated at the next meeting, so that a running account could be kept of the areas of agreement.[115] The same author gives a treaty of peace which reveals something of the outline of negotiations, for the grievances communicated by the Burgundian ambassadors to the king of France are given with the recommendations of the ambassadors and the answers and concessions given by the king to them.[116]

From fifteenth-century Venetian documents it appears that an ambassador seeking a treaty commonly bore with him a draft treaty. The other party might agree to treat upon the basis of the draft, might demand modifications of it before agreeing to treat, might in turn send its own draft treaty to Venice, or, of course, it might decline to enter into negotiations. On the other hand, the first draft of a proposed convention might come from the other party. The Venetian provisors negotiating the surrender of Padua in 1405 had begun to negotiate upon the basis of a Paduan draft which the Venetian Senate found so inconsistent with the instructions of the provisors that it commanded an end to negotiations upon that basis.[117]

By the fifteenth century the typical result of a successful negotiation by ambassadors was a series of *capitula* or a "minute" embodying the agreements achieved. This was not yet a treaty, for the power to conclude was by that time not normally given until the principal had approved the agreements. A succeeding step might be the dispatch of plenipotentiaries em-

[114] A.S.V., Senato, Secreta, XXIX, 15r (25r)–15v (25v).

[115] Commynes, *Mémoires*, Liv. VIII, Chap. XVI, II, 322.

[116] The treaty is given in translation in Philip de Commines, *The Memoirs*, Andrew R. Scoble, trans., 2 vols. (London, 1889-1890), I, 130-145. It is not included in the B. de Mandrot edn. normally used here nor in Philippe de Commines, *Mémoires*, J. Calmette and G. Durville, eds., 3 vols. (Paris, 1924-1925).

[117] A.S.V., Senato, Secreta, II, 146r (146r). Notice that the negotiators of the proposed surrender are the provisors, or military authorities, not ambassadors.

powered to conclude, or, if the original envoys had not returned home, the sending of full powers for them to conclude.[118]

Up to this point we have largely ignored the fact that the ambassador, like the *nuncius*, might also have received procuratorial powers. An ambassador was not *per se* a plenipotentiary, but he could be both an ambassador and a plenipotentiary. The effect of full powers, of course, was to authorize the ambassador to conclude.[119] When Louis XI lamented the lack of full powers of the ambassador of George Podiebrad to treat upon the spot concerning an anti-Turkish alliance excluding the pope, he intended to signify his willingness to enter immediately into a binding alliance.[120] By the time the word "ambassador" was in common usage, it is true, the extremely broad discretion frequently allowed to diplomatic procurators of an earlier period had become uncommon. The fourteenth- and fifteenth-century ambassador usually submitted a draft or *forma capitulorum* containing the commitments he wanted to make: after consideration of the terms the principal subsequently authorized the conclusive act.[121] In the Venetian *Sindicati*, they often appoint syndics such-and-such a person or persons, their ambassador or ambassadors, *licet absentes*. These words are an indication that the *sindicatus* is being granted to an ambassador who has already been negotiating abroad, has reported, and is awaiting full powers to conclude. If the mandate to conclude was not forthcoming, the agreements made by ambassadors came to nought.[122] It was possible, of course, to give full powers to an ambassador at the outset of his mission, and this was more commonly done for missions to distant places in consideration of the slowness of communication.

An ambassador endowed with full powers could do anything that any other procurator or syndic could do. The functions of ambassador and procurator were not exclusive, but complementary. Above all, he could enter into binding conventions. He could prorogue an old alliance or enter into

[118] Rymer, *Foedera*, IV, ii, 144; A.S.V., Senato, Secreta, XIII, 200r (200r).

[119] "Par quoy soit Besoing, pour le Bien des dites Matieres, Donner toute planiere Puissance a noz Ambaxadeurs a ce qu'ilz puissent donner Conclusion qui soit ferme et estable es dites Matieres." Rymer, *Foedera*, V, ii, 179. Maulde La Clavière's discussion of special powers in which the principal promises to ratify, but reserves that right to himself, as opposed to full powers, which are opposed to the nature of diplomacy and therefore seldom used, is based upon a complete misunderstanding of full powers, special mandate, and the *ratihabitio* clause. *La diplomatie au temps de Machiavel*, II, 92-93. Moreover, his distinction between documents written in Latin and those in the vernaculars is not valid.

[120] Perret, *Relations de la France avec Venise*, I, 392-393.

[121] A.S.V., Senato, Secreta, I, 33v (34v)–34r (35r), and XVII, 170r (168r).

[122] In 1444, because the military situation had changed since an apostolic orator had negotiated a peace, the pope not only refused to grant a mandate to conclude, but recalled his orator. A.S.V., Senato, Secreta, XVI, 109r (109r); 111r (111r); 111v (111v); 116r (116r).

a new one.[123] He could make conventions for the settlement of boundary disputes, for freedom of the roads, or for the carrying out of joint military or naval expeditions.[124] He could make a peace or a truce or enter into an arbitral proceeding, or he could have discretion to choose among the above alternatives and others.[125] Implied in these powers was the additional authority to agree to penalties for noncompliance.[126] The ambassador could also receive full powers for making documents and performing all solemnities connected with such agreements, including taking oaths upon the soul of his principal.[127] On the other hand, full powers were sometimes given merely for discussing terms and reporting to the principal, but not for concluding.[128] From a juridical point of view there appears to be no necessity for such powers, since an ambassador lacking *plena potestas* could do the same. In the course of practical negotiation, however, the possession of even such limited powers might be advantageous, especially prior to the point at which their precise terms would have to be revealed.

It is also somewhat surprising to find orators receiving full powers to perform acts of subordination before another. Ambassadors plenipotentiary were appointed for performing homage, for submitting their principals as clients to more powerful states, for offering lordship over their states to others, and for submitting to others and requesting a *podestà*.[129] Al-

[123] A.S.V., Senato, Secreta, XVI, 108v (108v); *Liber iurium reipublicae Genuensis*, I, cols. 1402-1410, no. DCCCCLV; Winkelmann, *Acta Imperii inedita*, II, 849-852, no. 1171; Rymer, *Foedera*, III, ii, 135; V, i, 65. The last also in *C.C.R. Henry VI (1435-1441)*, pp. 357-358.

[124] A.S.F., Signori—Carteggi—Rapporti e relazioni di oratori, III, 3r; A.S.V., Maggior Consiglio, Presbiter, 117r (118r); *Calendar of State Papers. Venetian*, p. 327, no. 893.

[125] Rymer, *Foedera*, III, i, 94. This included power to renounce English claims to the throne of France and all rights that the English king claimed in France. A.S.V., Senato, Secreta, XXIII, 11v (13v). As it happens, these particular instructions were addressed to the *Capitaneus Culphi*, a military commander. He had authority to include in the truce the king of Hungary, the ally of Venice, but he could not make a peace, since the Senate was not yet fully informed concerning the affairs of that king. Maulde La Clavière pointed out that in exceptional circumstances a "sovereign" could make a truce, not only in his own name, but in that of sovereign allies or of his own children. *La diplomatie au temps de Machiavel*, II, 88. Cessi, *Deliberazioni . . . Rogati*, "*Mixtorum*," I, 46, no. 163. Rymer, *Foedera*, III, i, 69; Winkelmann, *Acta Imperii inedita*, II, 882-883, no. 1231.

[126] De Maino, *Repertorium*; Bertachinus, *Repertorium*, pp. 72 and 75.

[127] A.S.V., Senato, Secreta, XIX, 204rv (204rv); Winkelmann, *Acta Imperii inedita*, II, 637-638, no. 977. Ambassadors took oaths for their principals more often than Maulde La Clavière believed. *La diplomatie au temps de Machiavel*, III, 237. In conventions and oaths undertaken by ambassadors endowed with *plena potestas*, the texts of the procuratorial letters were commonly included. *Ibid.*, III, 196.

[128] Rymer, *Foedera*, III, ii, 209; IV, ii, 66; and IV, iv, 45-46. Perret, *Relations de la France avec Venise*, I, 528. The first document cited is a procuration for Geoffrey Chaucer and two other envoys to Genoa.

[129] Archivio secreto vaticano, AA. Arm. I-XVIII, 462; A.S.V., Senato, Secreta, I, 86r (87r) (In this document stating his authority to submit Cyprus to Venice, he is not specifically called ambassador, but does receive that designation in surrounding documents.); Nys, *Origines du droit international*, p. 329; Cessi, *Deliberazioni del Maggior Consiglio*, III, 11 and 17. Am-

though we tend to think of the orator as a diplomat exclusively concerned with dealings between juridical equals, an orator could even receive a procuration *ad litem* for pleading as a lawyer before a court.[130]

Ambassadors or orators with full powers were also named for ecclesiastical matters which seem to moderns somewhat strange tasks for diplomats. In 1416, Henry V appointed English ambassadors to the Council of Constance for reforming the church.[131] The duke of Milan in 1490, hearing of the serious illness of Innocent VIII, sent procuratorial powers to his orators in Rome so that they could intervene in his name in procuring the succession of a new pontiff.[132] The Venetians on one occasion appointed an ambassador plenipotentiary to demand from the patriarch of Aquileia the return of certain relics taken from Grado and to give quittance for the same.[133]

It was implied that greater powers included the lesser unless the latter were specifically denied, for, as Bernard du Rosier put it, ". . . it is better to bring back something than nothing. . . ."[134] The powers for making peace, for example, always implied the lesser powers to enter an armistice for the duration of negotiations.[135]

Some ambassadors, on the other hand, were inclined to assume that the lesser powers included the greater, and thus, exceeding their mandates, they introduced a most disrupting factor into diplomacy. Venice has a great name for the efficiency of its administration of diplomacy and for the tight control exercised by the Senate over it, yet the Republic had a great deal of trouble with overly ambitious ambassadors. In 1418 the Senate wrote to its ambassador at Constance, who was attempting to negotiate a truce with the king of the Romans, that it was astonished he had entered into negotiations on certain matters without their mandate and beyond what had been conveyed to him in letters. If he had not yet sealed such agreements as he described in letters to the Senate, he should not do so, using whatever excuse he could contrive.[136] In 1470 the Senate was most annoyed with Filippo Corrario, ambassador to King Ferdinand the Bastard, for entering into conventions beyond his mandates. They dispatched another ambassador, Bernardo Justiniani, to remedy matters, while refusing to accept the *capitula* that Corrario had negotiated. The king, not at all

bassadors of the dominant state might also obtain full powers for negotiating and concluding such agreements. A.S.V., Senato, Secreta, I, 148r (149r).

130 A.S.V., Sindicati, II, 76.

131 Rymer, *Foedera*, IV, ii, 168.

132 A.S.M., Registri ducali, LXXXIII, 40v (80)–41r (81).

133 A.S.V., Sindicati, I, 87r.

134 *Ambaxiator brevilogus*, p. 20.

135 Maulde La Clavière, *La diplomatie au temps de Machiavel*, III, 170.

136 A.S.V., Senato, Secreta, VII, 15r (16r).

pleased with these developments, urged them not to send the new ambassador and insisted that he was not disposed to see one iota of the agreements removed or changed. This seemed unbearable to the Senate, which preferred to break off negotiations completely, so they sent Justiniani in spite of the king's objections. Eventually a satisfactory agreement was indeed reached, but the episode illustrates the embarrassment into which an overly zealous orator could lead his state.[137] Somewhat different was the case of the Venetian orator sent to offer the king of Hungary 60,000 ducats for his fight against the Turks. He sought the aid of other Christian states as a condition, but the Senate reprimanded him and ordered him to make the offer forthwith and unconditionally.[138] A succession of such problems led the Senate in 1478 to complain of the most harmful custom that had grown up among ambassadors of presuming to undertake matters not committed to them and of speaking and responding beyond what they received in their mandates. This was so widespread that the Senate enacted a decree imposing penalties upon ambassadors who should dare henceforth to exceed their mandates. The Senate saw in this excess an act of pride on the part of ambassadors, ". . . what is even worse, they do not hesitate without any reverence to wish to appear wiser than their betters and superiors. . . ."[139] This may be too severe, and a more sympathetic view might take into account the ambassador's problems in this age of slow communications. Distant from Venice, not sufficiently informed by letters from home,[140] and under pressure to act, ambassadors understandably tended to do whatever they thought best.

Sometimes also we find complaints against the insufficiency of ambassadorial mandates. The Venetian Senate, after examining the powers of an ambassador of the count of Pavia in 1404, found that he was not authorized to offer the terms which he had presented to that body. The manner in which such a situation was met could be significant in the overall course of a negotiation. In the case just mentioned, the Senate first debated and rejected a proposal that they should inform the ambassador that they found his mandate insufficient, and if he offered to send for a sufficient mandate,

137 *Ibid.*, XXIV, 110v (114v)–111r (115r); 105r (109r); 109r (113r); 113rv (117rv).

138 *Ibid.*, XXII, 2v (4v)–3r (5r).

139 *Ibid.*, XXVIII, 104v (115v). The "Traité du gouvernement de Venise" notes this prohibition, but adds that in exceptional cases ambassadors may go beyond their orders for the evident utility of the Commune. To do anything without the express order of the *Signoria*, however, was a very dangerous thing. In Perret, *Relations de la France avec Venise*, II, 289. Perugia also legislated against ambassadors going beyond their instructions. Angelini, *La diplomazia comunale a Perugia*, p. 38. Even French ambassadors under Richelieu were apt to exceed their powers, if we believe the cardinal himself. Baschet, *Les archives de Venise*, pp. 328-329.

140 Ambassadors and governments both complain about the failure of each to keep the other fully informed. *Infra*, pp. 136-138.

it should be responded that he might do as he wished. Instead they voted to inform him that whenever he should have a sufficient mandate they would listen to him and respond as would appear just to them.[141] The accepted response appears to offer more encouragement than the rejected one. A question was raised in early 1405 about the powers of an ambassador sent to Venice by the cardinal-legate of Bologna because the nature of the legate's own powers were not revealed. Because Francesco Foscari testified that he had seen the papal bull granting most ample powers to the legate and because legates who were vicars for governing always had full powers for all purposes, however, the Senate continued negotiations with the ambassador.[142] On rare occasions, then, minor flaws could be overlooked.

On other occasions it was not some petty flaw in a mandate that hampered negotiations but a deliberate withholding of full powers either completely or for certain purposes. In 1419, for example, Venetian negotiations with the king of the Romans and Hungary broke down because the royal ambassadors had *plena potestas* only for affairs of the Empire.[143] In 1475 an interchange between Venice and the Turks resulted in an informal and very uneasy armistice, but nothing more, since the Senate had carefully and properly withheld from its orator the authority to submit to the territorial demands it anticipated from the Turks.[144] When ambassadors from Ferrara appeared in Venice in March 1405 lacking full powers, the Senate "marvelled not a little that they came without a *sindicatum*, because that does not correspond to the requests that we made."[145] One solution to such a problem was to dispatch one's own ambassador with full powers to the other principal, although this placed one at the disadvantage of appearing eager to conclude.[146] Sometimes, naturally, an ambassador lacking full powers was not indicative of any reluctance to come to a conclusion or any distrust of the other party, but only an initial move in a contemplated series of exchanges which should finally result in the sending of plenipotentiaries.[147] Or the initial move might be made by the host government to a resident—in this particular case not an ambassador, but the Venetian *baiulo* at Negropont. A resident, though he could be given full powers for a

[141] A.S.V., Senato, Secreta, II, 12v (12v). On another occasion the Senate employed the excuse of an insufficient mandate to rid themselves of ambassadors thought to be sent to Venice only for the purpose of spying. *Ibid.*, R (E), 72r.

[142] *Ibid.*, II, 84v (84v); 84v (84v)–85r (85r); 85v (85v)–86r (86r).

[143] *Ibid.*, VI, 22v (23v). In another document this limitation of powers is called *impertinens. Ibid.*, 20v (21v).

[144] *Ibid.*, XXVII, 14v (24v); 15rv (25rv).

[145] A.S.V., Senato, Secreta, II, 95v (95v).

[146] *Ibid.*, II, 10r (10r).

[147] *C.C.R. Edward II (1323-1327)*, pp. 253-254.

specific purpose, did not normally possess them, so he could only send quickly to his government for instructions. On this occasion the Senate instructed him to say that he had no mandate, but that Venice was awaiting word from its ally, the king of Hungary, after which they expected to send him full powers for making peace.[148]

The Gonzaga princes conducted a most devious diplomacy—as did many others—in which ambassadors possessing full powers were actually instructed not to conclude according to the terms of their procurations. In 1383 an ambassador from Mantua wrote to Francesco Gonzaga asking for two letters, one to be shown, the other revealing his true intentions.[149] Luzio asserts that the Gonzaga orators had orders not to come to any conclusion before receiving a prearranged sign from the prince certifying his assent. The document cited does, indeed, provide that the ambassador should receive half of a "sign," the other half of which should be kept by the princes. Even if the princes themselves should appear on the spot indicating their favor toward the project, the ambassador should not conclude without the other half of his "sign."[150] That this was done more than once and by others than the Gonzaga, I have no doubt, but that Gonzaga orators were customarily dispatched under these conditions cannot safely be asserted from a single document.

In spite of occasional examples of devious methods in diplomacy, it must be borne in mind that these instances represent aberrations from the norm. If dealings in the realm of private law rest upon mutual trust and confidence, in spite of the subjection of the parties to the authority of a common tribunal, how much more must relations among powers which recognize no common tribunal do the same. Most of the activities of the ambassador were routine, commendable, and appropriate for furthering the objectives of both parties. While Bernard du Rosier may have been overly sanguine concerning the virtues of ambassadors, Nicolò Machiavelli was surely overly cynical.

148 A.S.V., Senato, Secreta, XXI, 142 (144).

149 Archivio di Stato, Mantova, Archivio Gonzaga, 439 (E. II. 3). This document reveals quite a contest over revealing the powers of the Mantuan envoy.

150 Luzio, *L'Archivio Gonzaga*, II, 79, and n. 3; Archivio di Stato, Mantova, Archivio Gonzaga, 2881 (Copialettere I, c. 4). Of course, if a properly empowered orator acted in conformity with his powers, but against his secret instructions, his acts were no less binding upon the principal from a juridical point of view. This remained true in the time of Hugo Grotius. *De jure belli ac pacis*, I, 224, Lib. II, Cap. XI, Sec. XII.

CHAPTER V

LETTERS AND REPORTS

The contents of the medieval "diplomatic pouch" must be examined now that the development of the different types of envoys from the message-bearing *nuncius* through the procuratorial plenipotentiary to the Renaissance ambassador or orator has been described. While barbarian rulers at the dawn of the Middle Ages sent envoys without letters merely to mouth memorized messages,[1] civilized states such as those of the High Middle Ages conducted their relations by means of envoys whose powers depended upon the letters entrusted to them.[2] The documents borne by the envoy determined his status before the party to whom he was sent and in his own eyes. Additional important documents passed between the envoy and the principal during the course of the mission. Finally the returned envoy delivered an oral or written report on the outcome of his embassy. No list of ambassadorial documents can be complete, for effective bureaucratic government makes use of forms, categories, and precedents without becoming enslaved by them. As occasion demanded, letters not falling within any customary category were used, and at other times a single document might incorporate the functions of two or more of the conventional letters. The most common letters and reports, however, include: letters of credence, letters of procuration, instructions, evidentiary documents, letters of safe-conduct, instructions during the course of the mission, dispatches, reports, and the unique—or virtually unique—Venetian *relazioni*.[3]

Through the thirteenth century an envoy often was the bearer of a single document revealing his status and powers, but it became increasingly common for him to possess several types of documents, slightly varying versions of the same document, and documents of one type or another addressed to various persons. These originated in the office of the chancellor, and that official naturally came to have a considerable influence in foreign affairs.[4]

[1] Paradisi, *Storia del diritto internazionale*, p. 102.

[2] Durandus, *Speculum legatorum*, p. 34; Cuttino, *English Diplomatic Administration*, p. 85; Ganshof, *Le Moyen Age*, p. 275.

[3] Treaties, truces, and other conventions have been omitted here as pertaining to the history of diplomacy generally and not specifically to the ambassadorial office. Suffice it to mention that they were in essence private law contracts.

[4] Luchaire, *Manuel*, p. 522; Ganshof, *Le Moyen Age*, p. 124. Maulde La Clavière sought to establish a firmer rule concerning the language in which a document was written than I find substantiated by the documents themselves. *La diplomatie au temps de Machiavel*, II, 69-71. He does indicate exceptions. In general, it is true, the more formal documents, such as conventions or even letters intended for the opposite party, were likely to be in Latin, while the less

It was customary, of course, to preserve a copy of at least the more important documents—which is fortunate indeed for the historian, since the widely scattered originals have not often survived.[5]

The letter of credence was the document commonly required to constitute a *nuncius* or an ambassador.[6] The same envoy might carry a procuration or other documents, but if his mission was simply to carry a message or to fulfill some other straightforward task, a letter of credence would suffice.[7] As a general rule it was stated that an ambassador should not be believed without letters of credence[8]—although, as we shall see, there were exceptions to the rule. In contrast to the procuration, which, of course, came into use only after the revival of Roman law, letters of credence possessed a hoary tradition. Ganshof has found them used in Merovingian diplomacy as early as the late sixth and early seventh centuries.[9] They continued in use for the same purpose throughout the period under consideration and until the present.

The form of letters of credence was quite simple. They always included the name and titles of the sender and the name and titles of the recipient of the embassy,[10] unless, of course, they happened to be letters patent of general application. This last was rare in diplomatic usage, but not unknown. The order of the names depended upon the relative rank of the parties. The heart of the document was the clause of supplication, which named the envoy and requested that his message be received as from the sender. A date and place clause was included, and the letters concluded with

---

formal documents, especially those intended only for correspondence between the envoy and his government, went earlier into the vernaculars. It varied from place to place. Mantuan diplomatic correspondence went into the vernacular earlier than Venetian, perhaps because its diplomacy was more confined to Italy, perhaps for some other reason.

[5] One English procuration of 1297 by chance gives us the distribution of its four copies: one to the king; one to the count of Holland, to whom the mission was sent; one to the chancellery; and the fourth to the envoys. Chaplais, *Treaty Rolls*, I, 125-126, no. 322.

[6] Mattingly, *Renaissance Diplomacy*, p. 38 and n. 4. Papal *nuncii* bore letters of credence identical in character with those of secular princes. Guillaume Mollat, "La diplomatie pontificale au XIVe siècle," in *Mélanges d'histoire du Moyen Age dédiés à la mémoire de Louis Halphen* (Paris, 1951), p. 509. E.g., Rymer, *Foedera*, I, i, 7; III, ii, 80; III, iv, 112. Maulde La Clavière points out that a mere courier bearing a message from an ambassador to his principal might be given letters of credence. *La diplomatie au temps de Machiavel*, III, 150.

[7] Dickinson, *Congress of Arras*, xvi-xx, although the author does not give as much information upon the differences between letters of credence and procurations as might be desired.

[8] Bertachinus, *Repertorium*, p. 74.

[9] Ganshof, "Merowingisches Gesandtschaftswesen," p. 177.

[10] Not to address the recipient by his proper titles, of course, was a calculated insult, as when Philip IV addressed Guy of Dampierre as marquis of Namur, *se gerenti, ut dicitur, pro comite Flandrie*. On the back of the document a scribe subsequently wrote: . . . *dura est; non salutat Rex eos nec vocat ipsum Dominum Guydonem, Comitem, sed Guydonem de Dampetra.* Limburg-Stirum, *Codex diplomaticus Flandriae*, I, 152, no. 44.

the usual signs of validation, i.e., signatures or seals.[11] A clause of salutation was frequently present, and a clause setting forth the reasons for sending the envoy was sometimes included.

The effective clause, however, was the clause of supplication, which in its barest form requested the recipient to "deign to believe (the envoys) upon those matters which they expose to you on behalf of us."[12] Ganshof cites letters of Edward II in 1309 requesting the pope to hear the very voice of the king in the speech of his envoys.[13] On another occasion the recipient is asked to believe "as if I were speaking to you with my own mouth."[14] Security, of course, was one of the reasons for using a *nuncius* or an ambassador rather than a letter, and the clause of supplication sometimes states that the sender has placed his secrets in the mouth of the envoy.[15] Occasionally letters of credence state that the sender has opened his mind to the envoy, which implies a little more than a message-bearing magpie, an instrument of communication, to be sure, but at least a *rational* living letter, capable of explaining and elaborating the thoughts of his principal.[16] Often, of course, the recipient is asked not only to believe, but to do something requested by the sender.[17]

That letters of credence could do no more than establish a means of communication between principals, however, is made quite clear by Bartolus. When they are very general, he says, requesting that you give full faith to the bearer in those things which he will say to you, then by the force of those letters the bearer can do nothing to prejudice the rights of the writer, for they are only commendatory letters. They do no more than state that the bearer is a faithful person whom you can trust. Even when the letters state that the recipient should consider the bearer fully informed concerning the intention of the sender, they do not contain any authority to obligate the sender to any agreement. If such an envoy should enter into a contract in his principal's name, the latter would not be bound, for the envoy would have exceeded his mandate. Even if the envoy declares that his principal

[11] Instructions of a Venetian ambassador to the sultan in 1480 mention at the end: *La lettera de credenza del Signor havemo facto bollar doro per più honorificentia . . .* A.S.V., Senato, Secreta, xxix, 92v (102v).

[12] "Liste analytique des documents concernant l'histoire de la Belgique qui sont conservés au *Record Office*," Ernest van Bruyssel, ed., *Bulletin de la Commission Royale d'Histoire*, 3e sér., i (1859), 115.

[13] *Le Moyen Age*, p. 275.

[14] Kern, *Acta Imperii, Angliae et Franciae*, p. 9, no. 16.

[15] *C.R. (1237-1242)*, p. 501. This letter of credence happens not to be diplomatic, but the form did not depend upon the use.

[16] Chaplais, *Treaty Rolls*, i, 70, no. 169; Rymer, *Foedera*, i, ii, 194.

[17] Chaplais, *Treaty Rolls*, i, 172, nos. 413-418, and 245, no. 636; Rymer, *Foedera*, i, iii, 165; ii, ii, 92.

has made him a procurator for entering into a compact, he ought not to be believed in attributing to himself this or any office without letters expressly granting authority to contract.[18] Subsequent writers follow the authority of Bartolus.[19]

Multiple letters of credence were often carried, even in the very early Middle Ages, addressed to various influential persons of the court of the recipient of the embassy.[20] In particular, it was customary for a *nuncius* or an ambassador to have letters of credence for the queen and to ask permission of the king during the first audience with him to be received by her.[21] The reception by the queen usually was a mere matter of courtesy, but could be of considerable substantive importance. Since letters of credence were customarily in the form of letters close, a circular embassy required separate letters of credence addressed to the various persons whom the envoy was to visit.[22] An English embassy of 1297 had letters for the archbishop of Cologne, the archdeacon of Cologne, the duke of Brabant, the count of Holland, the count of Flanders, the count of Hainaut, the bishop of Liège, the bishop of Utrecht, the duke of Lorraine, the count of Guelders, the count of Savoy, and the count of Bar.[23]

The discovery that envoys could be sent without letters is surprising, albeit the occasion was rare and possessed an ambiguous character. In 1499 the Milanese ambassador in England wrote to Ludovico Sforza of the arrival without letters of a secretary of the king of the Romans, who was received by the king and returned extremely satisfied.[24] The Venetian Senate in 1390 first passed a measure providing that a *nuncius* with *literis credulitatis* be sent to acknowledge formally the accession to power of Francesco di Carrara the Younger. An amendment was passed, however, decreeing that he should go without letters.[25] The Florentines received in 1459 an *assertus orator* to the pope from the king of France lacking letters.[26] Reluctance to address letters of credence to a government that was not recognized was one reason for their omission. The count of Charolais was much insulted in 1466 when Louis XI sent him ambassadors with only an

[18] Bartolus, *Commentaria*, ad *D.* 45, tit. *De fideiussoribus et mandatoribus*, 25. Notice the nontechnical use of *mandatum*.

[19] Bertachinus, *Repertorium*, p. 71; Gondisalvus de Villadiego, *Tractatus*, III, i, 28 and 31.

[20] Ganshof, "Merowingisches Gesandtschaftswesen," p. 177.

[21] Maulde La Clavière, *La diplomatie au temps de Machiavel*, II, 367.

[22] *Ibid.*, II, 106. During the course of his mission an ambassador might receive a letter of credence addressed to his own principal. This could be called a *recréance* or *quasi-créance*. *Ibid.*, III, 363.

[23] Chaplais, *Treaty Rolls*, I, 178-179, nos. 433-445.

[24] *Calendar of State Papers. Venetian*, pp. 281-283, no. 791.

[25] A.S.V., Senato, Secreta, R (E) 59v.

[26] A.S.F., Signori—Legazioni e Commissarie: Risposti verbali di oratori, I, 52v.

oral credence.[27] Similarly in 1476 the emperor sent envoys requesting aid of the duke of Milan, who had not yet received his investiture. Since the emperor declared himself unwilling to wound the duke by failure to use his proper titles, letters were omitted. Quite naturally the duke replied that his aid could be expected only after he received the desired investiture.[28] Another reason for omitting letters of credence was the reluctance of the sender to appear to act in any official capacity, as when the Venetian Senate sent one David the Hebrew, a subject from Crete, as a private person to feel out the Turks concerning peace.[29] Danger to the ambassador might also be a motive for the lack of letters, as illustrated by the dispatch of Andrèa Badoer to London by the Council of Ten in 1509. Since the ambassador spoke English, he was traveling incognito as an Englishman. Upon his arrival in England he should first announce himself to the Venetian consul as ambassador, then to the king. He was not given credentials for fear that they would cause his arrest. His instructions were sent separately to the consul by way of Germany, but even so letters of credence were not sent with the instructions because their seal might attract attention. (Instructions did not require a seal.) Credentials would be sent by yet another means, but meanwhile the consul should orally communicate to the king that Badoer was the ambassador and should be believed.[30] It was only upon infrequent and somewhat equivocal occasions, though, that the accustomed letters of credence were wanting.

Letters of credence were not considered essential, however, if the envoy was provided with a procuration.[31] This was true, at any rate, during the century or so after the introduction of procuration into diplomacy, although as the office of the ambassador developed it became customary for the envoy to receive letters of credence to which letters of procuration might be added.

An envoy who was intended to conclude a juristic act in the name of his principal had to be provided with a procuration or mandate—the two terms were synonymous. Maulde La Clavière believed that the importance of the procuration was formal, rather than real, since there was no tribunal competent to enforce upon the principal commitments made by his procurator.[32] Nothing could be more incorrect—unless, perhaps, one wishes

[27] Maulde La Clavière, *La diplomatie au temps de Machiavel*, II, 109.

[28] *Ibid.*, II, 109.

[29] A.S.V., Senato, Secreta, XXIII, 148r (150r). Also see *ibid.*, 8r (10r); 10r (12r); XXIV, 34v (43v).

[30] *Calendar of State Papers, Venetian*, pp. 336-338, no. 922. The document is a letter to the consul in London containing the *commissione* (or instructions) and sent by way of Germany.

[31] Cuttino, *English Diplomatic Administration*, p. 110.

[32] *La diplomatie au temps de Machiavel*, II, 86-87.

to exclude every legal concept and form from the realm of diplomacy, for the same argument can be applied to the use of all agreements made between parties not subject to a common tribunal. Even rights in private law cannot always be enforced by the competent court, for example, a judgment against a defendant who is judgment-proof. Legal concepts do have a place in diplomacy, and rights among states do have real meaning, even though the determination and enforcement of those rights may be encompassed with difficulties largely obviated in private law by the existence of the commonly recognized court. The mandate of a procurator was of the very greatest importance. Without a mandate he could not conclude, even if he declared, as Bartolus said,[33] that his principal had made him a procurator for the purpose of entering into a compact. Baldus added that a procuration had to be established through letters of the principal, and not through witnesses to an oral commission of procuratorial powers.[34] When the procurations of English envoys to Castile were lost at sea with certain of the envoys in 1344, the remaining envoys had to await new letters of procuration before continuing on their mission.[35] The care customarily taken in examining procurations is, in itself, indicative of their real importance.

Among certain modern writers on medieval diplomacy there has been some confusion of terms in describing the contents of the diplomatic pouch. Lucas simply failed to distinguish between letters of credence and procurations.[36] Cuttino, on the other hand, makes a distinction between letters of procuration and letters of attorney, whereas "procurator" and "attorney" were actually synonymous.[37] For the purposes of the medievalist, on the other hand, the debate over a distinction in classical law between procurators and mandatories may be avoided. The same may be said for the highly restrictive definition of mandate which would limit it to a special mandate.[38] We are concerned with the very real distinction between letters of credence and procurations.

[33] *Supra*, pp. 112-113.

[34] Baldus, *Commentaria*, ad *D.* 3, tit. *De procuratoribus et defensoribus*, 65, additio Bal., *Si procurator*.

[35] Rymer, *Foedera*, II, iv, 170; *C.C.R.*, *Edward III* (*1343-1346*), p. 484.

[36] "Machinery of Diplomatic Intercourse," pp. 309-310. The editor of the *C.C.R.*, *Edward III* (*1333-1337*) incorrectly calls plenipotentiaries (plenipotentiaries *were* procurators) the envoys named in a letter of credence of 7 June 1333. Nowhere does the document contain any of the signs of full powers, although the envoys are called *plenius informatos*, which is quite another thing. Pp. 115-116. The full document is given in Rymer, *Foedera*, II, iii, 94.

[37] *English Diplomatic Administration*, pp. 111-112. *Supra*, p. 32. On the difference between letters of credence and procurations and the confusion between them, see Donald Queller, "Thirteenth-Century Diplomatic Envoys: *Nuncii* and *Procuratores*," *Speculum*, XXXV (1960), 196-213. On the deliberate contamination of forms, see Menzel, *Deutsches Gesandtschaftswesen*, pp. 16-17.

[38] See Serrao, *Il Procurator*, p. viii and pp. 13-15; Berger, *Dictionary*, p. 654.

Legal and notarial manuals are full of procuratorial formulas which the lawyer or notary could copy, inserting the proper names and titles and making other minor alterations as necessary. Considering the sources in which these are found, it is not surprising that most of them are exemplars for the creation of *procuratores litum* or attorneys-at-law, either general or special.[39] General mandates for conducting business affairs are given also.[40] Our concern for diplomacy, however, is largely with the special procuration for nonjudicial affairs, and models for such procurations are also to be found in the formularies. A very skeletal example will suffice to illustrate the bare necessities:

> I Ja. constitute you B. my procurator for receiving so many *denarii* which so-and-so owes to me, or for buying such a horse for so much and for receiving such a quittance from so-and-so in my name. And I will hold firm and fast whatever you do. *Quae omnia etc.* (Clause of validation, date, place, *etc.*)[41]

Numbers 505 through 508 of Series B 1561 of the Archives du Nord also contain a fragmentary formulary from the chancery of Countess Margaret and Count Guy of Flanders. Included are models for dispatching procurators to Rome for both judicial and other affairs, for nonjudicial matters only, and specifically for borrowing money. Faced with any of these situations or a similar situation, the clerks could simply make any necessary modifications in copying these formulas.

Although a procuration could be long and complex, its form was basically simple and a very brief document sometimes was quite adequate. A combination of the requirements given in several legal sources may provide an outline of a procuration.[42] Not all of the elements given by each of

[39] *Summa notariae Aretii composita*, nos. XLIX, L, LI, in Gaudentius, *Bibliotheca juridica*, III, 295; *Summa notariae Belluni composita*, nos. XXXIV and XXXV, in Gaudentius, *Bibliotheca juridica*, III, 361-362; Magister Arnulphus, *Summa minorum*, nos. L and LI, in Wahrmund, *Quellen*, I, ii, 53; *Curialis*, nos. LXXIV, LXXVI, LXXVII, and LXXVIII, in Wahrmund, *Quellen*, I, iii, 24-25; Martinus de Fano, *Formularium*, nos. XLIII and C, in Wahrmund, *Quellen*, I, viii, 16 and 40; *Rainerii Perusio Ars notaria*, G. B. Palmieri, ed., I, XXXXVI, in Gaudentius, *Bibliotheca juridica*, II, 40. In French law, see Philippe de Beaumanoir, *Coutumes du Beauvoisis*, Am. Salmon, ed., 2 vols. (Paris, 1889-1890), I, 76, no. 140.

[40] Martinus de Fano, *Formularium*, no. XCVIII, in Wahrmund, *Quellen*, I, viii, 39-40. There are also examples of general mandates *ad causas et negotia*. Durandus, *Speculum juris*, 1, 3, 4 (*ut autem*); Rolandinus Passagerii, *Summa totius artis notariae* (Venice, 1574), I, 214v-215r. I have not seen this last volume, but have taken the reference from a manuscript note made by Professor Post. He refers to it in Post, "Plena Potestas in Medieval Assemblies," p. 362, n. 39, but does not quote the document. (Post, *Medieval Legal Thought*, p. 100, n. 43.)

[41] Martinus de Fano, *Formularium*, no. XCIX, in Wahrmund, *Quellen*, I, viii, 40; also no. XLIV, in Wahrmund, *Quellen*, I, viii, 16-17.

[42] *D.* 3, 3, 65; Tancred, *Ordo iudiciarius*, in *Pillii, Tancredi, Gratiae libri de iudiciorum ordine*, Fridericus Bergmann, ed. (Gottingae, 1842), p. 125; Magister Arnulphus, *Summa*

them were actually essential. Moreover, since the authors had in mind primarily procurations for attorneys-at-law, necessary adjustments should be made for attorneys-in-fact. The name of the principal and of the procurator should obviously be given. The cause (for diplomatic procurations interpret as "purpose") for which he is appointed, against whom and before whom he is appointed (interpret both of these as "to whom he is dispatched") must be mentioned. William of Drogheda states that one must specify whether he is appointed to a given day or for the whole cause, whether for one cause or several, and whether, if a general procurator, he has *libera administratio* or not, but these are not essential to the simplest procurations. Generally a *ratihabitio* clause, promising to hold firm whatever the procurator will do, is included.

Turning from the legal writings to diplomatic practice, a very simple example may be given, a procuration by Henry III in 1250:

> Henry, by the grace of God king of England, lord of Ireland, duke of Normandy, of Aquitaine, and count of Anjou, to Blanche, by the same grace illustrious queen of France, his beloved relative, greetings and a disposition of sincere affection. You should know that we have given full power to the venerable father Philip, elect of Lyons, and to our beloved and faithful Richard, earl of Cornwall, our brother, and Peter of Savoy, for extending the truce between the lord Louis, illustrious king of France, your son, and us until a term of sixteen years, or until a more distant term according to what they see to be expedient; we will hold firm and acceptable whatever they will have done upon this matter. In testimony of which we have caused to be made these our letters patent. Witnessed by myself. At Westminister, the eighth day of March, in the thirty-fourth year of our reign.[43]

The significance of procuratorial full powers has already been indicated in the chapter on the procurator. Full powers could be granted in various ways. Bartolus indicates that a procurator who has received *plena potestas* or *libera administratio*, or whose mandate states that "he can do all things that his principal can," has *plena potestas*.[44] Some say that one who has a special mandate has *plena potestas*. Rational order emerges from the con-

---

minorum, no. L, in Wahrmund, *Quellen*, I, ii, 53; William of Drogheda, *Summa aurea*, no. CVII, in Wahrmund, *Quellen*, II, ii, 102-103; *Glossa ordinaria* to *Decret. Greg. IX*, 1, 38, 13, ad v. *Mandato procuratoris*.

[43] Champollion-Figeac, *Documents historiques inédits*, I, 82.

[44] *Commentaria*, ad *C.* 2, 12, 10. Baldus also seems to support this interpretation. *Commentaria*, ad *C.* 2, 12, 10. I recognize the partial tautology here, and will try to explain its significance as the argument proceeds.

fusion of legal texts and official documents if *plena potestas* is interpreted as a generic term covering the legal authority to conclude in the name of another by an act of the representative's will. Special mandate, express mention of *plena potestas* and *libera administratio* are specific ways of granting that authority. *Libera administratio* could be granted, moreover, by the use of those exact words or similar ones, by the clause quoted from Bartolus, or by a *ratihabitio* clause.[45]

The portion of this interpretation that causes the most difficulty is that *plena potestas* is acquired by a special mandate. Two consecutive documents of 1286 in the *Treaty Rolls* lend support to it. In the first, Alfonso of Aragon grants full powers to his procurators to grant full powers in turn to Edward I to arrange a truce between Aragon and France. Nothing is said concerning a special mandate. In the second document, however, the procurators themselves describe the preceding document as a special mandate.[46] No other documentation is as convincing as this, but a number of other diplomatic documents offer supporting evidence. The Treaty of Lierre of 1294 mentions the procurators of Guy of Flanders "having a special mandate and also *potestatem* from the aforesaid count for the said matter."[47] Other procurations grant special mandates for making alliances, marriages, affirming, extending and supplementing treaties, and requesting and receiving homage and fealty, all lacking expressions indicating *plena potestas*, *libera administratio*, *ratihabitio*, *etc*., and yet all clearly intended to grant the power to conclude.[48]

As stated above,[49] it is not certain that truly general mandates were ever used in diplomacy, but, even if they were, the procurator so appointed could enjoy the broader range of powers of the general procurator without falling under the disabilities previously ascribed to him. An express grant of *plena potestas* conveyed the power to conclude.[50] Another means by

[45] In my article, "Thirteenth-Century Diplomatic Envoys," p. 206, n. 31, I wrote that *Liber Sextus*, 1, 19, 4, suggested that *libera potestas* constituted a special mandate. This was based upon a misreading.

[46] Chaplais, *Treaty Rolls*, I, 80-82, nos. 192-193.

[47] Émile Varenbergh, *Histoire des relations diplomatiques entre le comté de Flandre et d'Angleterre au Moyen Age* (Bruxelles, 1874), p. 230, no. XIII. This work earlier appeared in parts in *Messager des sciences historiques de Belgique* from 1869 to 1873.

[48] Rymer, *Foedera*, II, iv, 55; III, iii, 53; III, iii, 75; IV, iii, 45. Also see William of Drogheda, *Summa aurea*, no. CVIII, in Wahrmund, *Quellen*, II, ii, 103-104; Aegidius de Fuscararius, *Ordo iudiciarius*, no. XI, in Wahrmund, *Quellen*, III, i, 19-20.

[49] *Supra*, p. 36.

[50] Rymer, *Foedera*, IV, ii, 4. This procuration is for a specific negotiation, but it empowers the procurators to perform "alia quaecumque, etiam predictis expressatis majora, et quae mandatum exigerent etiam magis speciale, et generaliter, ad, omnia et singula, quae Nosipsi . . . facere possemus, si presentes et personaliter interessemus, sine exceptione vel retentione quacumque, faciendum . . ."

which a general procurator could obtain the power to conclude, even in those areas where a special mandate was otherwise required, was by a grant of *libera administratio*. The expressions *libera potestas*, *generalis administratio*, *plenum mandatum*, and other similar ones appear to signify the same. Various combinations of these expressions and combinations of them with *speciale mandatum* were also used.[51] The clause, "He can do all things that his principal can," is not ordinarily used alone to grant conclusive powers, although it is very common in combination with other words or clauses which have that effect. On the authority of Bartolus, however, we should concede its efficacy.

Bartolus does not mention, though, another means by which full powers could be granted, a clause promising that whatever was said or done by the procurator would be held firm by the principal. As Post has pointed out, Francesco Tigrini in the fourteenth century held that this *ratihabitio* clause had the effect of granting *libera potestas et administratio*.[52] So did Andrea Alciati in the sixteenth century,[53] although others, according to Post, did not. The evidence that it did convey full powers, in fact, is overwhelming. According to a gloss to *Decretales*, I, 43, 9, a procurator with a general mandate could not *transigere* (as we know), but if he had letters *de rato*, he could *transigere*.[54] The importance of including this *ratihabitio* clause in a general mandate intended to give full powers is apparent.[55] An

[51] *Casus* to *D.* 3, 3, 58, and to *D.* 3, 3, 59; *Glossa ordinaria* to *C.* 2, 12, 10, ad v. *plenam potestatem*; Martinus de Fano, *Formularium*, no. XCVIII, in Wahrmund, *Quellen*, I, viii, 39-40; Aegidius de Fuscararius, *Ordo iudiciarius*, no. XI, in Wahrmund, *Quellen*, III, i, 19-20; Durandus, *Speculum juris*, I, iii (*De procuratore*), c. *ut autem* 11; William of Drogheda, *Summa aurea*, nos. CVII and CVIII, in Wahrmund, *Quellen*, II, ii, 102-104; *Sext.*, 1, 19, 4; De Maino, *Repertorium* p. 159; Kluit, *Historia critica*, II, 1007; Winkelmann, *Acta imperii inedita*, II, 848, no. 1190; Chaplais, *Treaty Rolls*, I, 117-118, nos. 282-287; I, 156-157, no. 387; I, 258-259, no. 659; A.S.M., Registri ducali, no. 183, 12v (24). Baldus points out that *libera administratio* ought never to be presumed to be conceded. *Commentaria*, ad *D.* 3, 3, 60.

[52] Post, "Plena Potestas in Medieval Assemblies," p. 358 and n. 13; Post, *Medieval Legal Thought*, p. 94 and n. 17. Bartolus discusses the question, and, though contested, he appears to hold that the *ratihabitio* was equivalent to full powers. *Commentaria*, ad *C.* 2, *De procuratoribus*, 10. He also points out that it was not permissible to promise to hold firm whatever the procurator did "legitimately" or to impose any other restrictive clause. *Commentaria*, ad *D.* 3, *De procuratoribus*, 25, 3. He was undoubtedly correct, for I have never seen a *ratihabitio* clause containing such a restriction. The clause does often declare that the principal will hold firm whatever the procurator does concerning "the above matters," a reasonable restriction which would be implied, even if not expressed.

[53] Andrea Alciati, *Index locupletissimus D. Andreae Alciati super commentariis Codicis Iustiniani imperatoris* (Lugduni, 1536), p. 482.

[54] Ad v. *generale mandatum*. ". . . licet haberet generale mandatum, transigere tamen non poterat . . . Sed si clausula de rato fuit apposita: tunc videtur, quod transigere possit, aliter non; quod adiectio illius clausulae aliquid operatur argumentum." The *casus* to *Decret. Greg. IX*, 1, 36, 3, says virtually the same.

[55] *D.* 3, 3, 65, and, especially, *Glossa ordinaria* to *D.* 1, 38, 13, ad v. *Mandato procuratoris*: "In mandato enim procuratorio debet contineri praecipue . . . quod ratum habebit quod cum eo

exemplar from the First Chartulary of Flanders lends additional credence to Tigrini's opinion, since it gives a general mandate with a *ratihabitio* clause, followed by a denial that by virtue of these letters anyone could contract a loan. A mere general procurator, it is clear, could not borrow money, so unless the *ratihabito* clause had the effect of *libera administratio* the restriction would be meaningless.[56] The equivalence of *ratihabitio* with mandate is also indicated by a letter of Richard II referring to the mandate of procurators of the Master General of the Teutonic Order as their *ratihabicione*.[57] Among modern scholars V. Menzel and J. G. Edwards lend their authority to Tigrini's and Alciati's position, although neither of them has approached the question via the legal texts, but, respectively, by way of diplomatic and parliamentary use of procurations.[58] Full powers granted in any of the ways described above allowed a procurator to possess a freedom of action and authority to conclude which, in combination, were utterly impossible to the *nuncius*.

The ubiquity of legal and notarial manuals containing forms for procurations and the existence of models for procurations in chanceries indicates that considerable care was usually taken in the composition of these documents. The law, however, was not excessively formalistic, which may account for a great deal of the variety in wording that is found. A gloss to the *Decretales* states that when general or doubtful words are contained in a procuration one should recur to the intention of the principal,

---

actum erit." When it is stated in *D.* 46, 3, 12, 4, "rati enim habitio mandato comparatur," a subsequent ratification of the act of one lacking a mandate is intended, but in a very real sense it is also true of the *ratihabitio* contained in a mandate. Beaumanoir wrote: "Nule procurations ne vaut riens se cil qui fet le procureeur ne s'oblige a tenir ferme et estable ce qui sera fet ou dit par son procureeur." Beaumanoir, *Coutumes*, I, 78, Chap. IV, Par. 143. See also Bartolus, *Commentaria*, ad *D.* 3, *De negotiis gestis*, 10. Serrao stated that the acts of the procurator passed into the economic and juridical sphere of the principal *solely* on the basis of the *ratihabitio*. *Il Procurator*, p. 97. Power to conclude, however, was sometimes granted without the *ratihabitio* clause. Rymer, *Foedera*, I, ii, 25. Still clearer, special mandates of the English and Castilian kings in 1411 for proroguing a truce, both lacking expressions of full powers and *ratihabitio*. Nonetheless, the truce was extended with express reference to the above documents as the source of the procurators' authority. *Ibid.*, IV, i, 198-199. This provides further proof that *plena potestas* was acquired through a special mandate.

[56] Archives du Nord, Lille, Chambre des Comptes, B 1561, no. 505. See an extremely general mandate with *ratihabitio*. Rymer, *Foedera*, I, i, 56. Mistakenly called letters of credence in the headnote.

[57] *The Diplomatic Correspondence of Richard II*, Edouard Perroy, ed., in Camden Third Series, XLVIII (London, 1933), 68, no. 102.

[58] Menzel, *Deutsches Gesandtschaftswesen*, p. 16; J. G. Edwards, "The Plena Potestas of English Parliamentary Representatives," *Oxford Essays in Medieval History Presented to Herbert Edward Salter* (Oxford, 1934), p. 153, n. 8. Maulde La Clavière, *La diplomatie au temps de Machiavel*, II, 94-95, correctly identifies this clause as crucial, but mistakes the words which make it so. *Parole de roi* is not important, but the promise to hold firm what is said or done is.

"because words ought to serve the intention, not the intention the words."[59] Nonetheless, it is certain that diplomatic procurations were examined for formal adequacy very carefully, for, whereas in private law a commonly accepted judge had authority to determine the intention of the principal,[60] in diplomacy an unclear procuration could lead to endless controversy.

Menzel long ago suggested that when procuration first was introduced into diplomacy a deliberate contamination of forms occurred with key phrases from letters of credence and letters of procuration intermingled in the same document.[61] As lawyers and bureaucrats sought to take advantage of the new institution they simply interwove it with the old forms. Those who bore such mixed letters presumably enjoyed both the representative character of the old *nuncius* and the powers of the new procurator. Additional evidence of formal contamination can be cited. The oaths of the crusader-envoys of 1201 show that their letters contained both words of credence and a *ratihabitio* clause and Villehardouin's description of the letters confirms it. The same is true of letters of Frederick II to Henry III in 1241 concerning his capture of delegates to the anti-imperial council.[62] One example of letters containing both full powers and words of credence has been found as late as 1338, which would have been surprising to Menzel for he believed that custom soon came to preclude this contamination.[63] Many other *nuncii* and ambassadors, of course, received full powers, but these were customarily contained in separate procurations, which might be given simultaneously with the letters of credence or, more commonly in later years, forwarded to the envoys after negotiations had already led to a draft agreement.

Some procurators were provided with multiple procurations on the same matter representing progressive concessions which the principal was prepared to make. By gradually revealing the true extent of his powers, the envoy was often able to extract concessions from the other party with a minimum commitment on his own part.[64] This, at any rate, was his purpose. The most obvious use of progressive powers was in cases involving financial transactions, as in negotiating a marriage alliance and dowery. Henry III's procurators for negotiating the marriage alliance with Eleanor of Provence

[59] *Glossa ordinaria* to *Decretales*, 1, 38, 9, ad v. *intentio*. See also the chapter on procurators, n. 216.

[60] Post, "Plena Potestas in Medieval Assemblies," p. 361; Post, *Medieval Legal Thought*, p. 98.

[61] Menzel, *Deutsches Gesandtschaftswesen*, pp. 16-17.

[62] Villehardouin, *Conquête de Constantinople*, Appendix, I, 218; *ibid.*, Sec. 15; Matthew Paris, monk of St. Albans, *Chronica majora*, H. R. Luard, ed., in *R.S.*, no. 57, 7 vols. (London, 1872-1883), IV, 126.

[63] Böhmer–Ficker, *Acta Imperii selecta*, pp. 526-527, no. 780.

[64] Cuttino, *English Diplomatic Administration*, pp. 108-109.

received procurations authorizing them to accept from the count 20,000, 15,000, 10,000, 7,000, 5,000, or 3,000 marks.[65]

Letters of instruction were not essential to the medieval diplomat, although they became increasingly common.[66] Although it may safely be assumed that oral instructions were given by the principal when written instructions were lacking, not even verbal instructions were essential in a formal or juridical sense. In 1383 a Mantuan ambassador informed the council of the emperor: ". . . my lord, when I inquired concerning the things to be done in this court, said to me: 'You are a wise man. I send you to handle my affairs. It is not necessary that I should tell you what is to be done. . . .' "[67] Whether this was true, or whether the ambassador merely wished to avoid dealing with the council's demand for payment for renewal of Mantuan privileges may be questioned. In any case, such a lack of instructions of any kind would be exceptional, but the document does establish the *possibility* of an uninstructed envoy.

Until the thirteenth century, written instructions were relatively rare except for Byzantine envoys and those of states, such as Venice, strongly influenced by Byzantine procedures.[68] Even in the later Middle Ages the use of verbal rather than written instructions continued, as is apparent from letters of credence naming envoys who have been instructed *viva voce* concerning the intentions of their principals. A Mantuan ambassador of the late Quattrocento—and Mantuan diplomatic technique was in at least one respect more advanced than Venetian[69]—received his instructions verbally from Ludovico II Gonzaga, summarizing them in writing for his own use either at that time or immediately after the audience.[70]

It was, of course, not at all uncommon for instructions of a sort to be inserted in letters of credence or procurations, although this procedure possessed an obvious disadvantage in revealing the intentions of the principal to the opposite party. Where hard bargaining was not involved or where these public instructions were supplemented by separate and secret ones, this was a useful technique never completely abandoned.

The subject of this chapter, however, is the contents of the diplomatic pouch, among which were often included letters of instructions, in addition to letters of credence and procurations. Written instructions were first

[65] Chaplais, *Treaty Rolls*, I, 13, nos. 24-25.

[66] As Post has shown, even a procurator who was required to be "sufficiently instructed" was assumed in that state by virtue of his full powers. *Supra*, p. 36, and n. 72.

[67] Archivio di Stato, Mantova, Archivio Gonzaga, 439 (E. II, 3).

[68] Ganshof, *Le Moyen Age*, pp. 123-124.

[69] Precautions for the security of dispatches. *Infra*, pp. 140-141.

[70] De Tourtier, "Bertolino Capilupi," pp. 326-327. His text was subsequently corrected to

employed in the medieval West no later than the Carolingian period, perhaps earlier.[71] The first extant Venetian instructions date from 1198, addressed by Enrico Dandolo to ambassadors to the emperor at Constantinople. These are very detailed and attempt to foresee a considerable number of problems that the emperor might raise.[72] The Venetians may have employed written instructions much earlier, for the Venetian archives, quite magnificent from the fourteenth century, provide very scanty materials prior to the thirteenth. Throughout Western Europe written instructions became more and more common from the thirteenth century until the end of the Middle Ages.[73]

Letters of instruction were very different in character from either letters of credence or procurations. Whether intended for the eyes of the envoy only or for those of the opposite party also, they were at least ostensibly directed to the envoy, did not obligate the principal, and were not normally sealed.[74] In general detail the envoy was instructed as to what he should do and say, and, perhaps, the manner in which he should do or say it.[75] Where negotiation was the object, instructions should provide guidelines for obtaining the greatest possible concessions from the opposite party by means of the slightest possible concessions by the envoy. Where the more formal documents do not clearly indicate how far the envoy may go in making concessions, or where, for example, multiple procurations provide authority for progressive concessions, instructions should inform the envoy how far and under what conditions he should proceed.[76] Instructions did not grant powers or establish limitations upon powers otherwise granted. Between instructions and powers there is a clear distinction. In one late fifteenth-century instance the Venetian secretary writing in the *Secreta* erred in

---

take into consideration events intervening between his audience with Gonzaga and his departure.

[71] Löhren, *Geschichte des gesandtschaftlichen Verkehrs*, pp. 42-43.

[72] Armingaud, *Venise et le Bas-Empire*, pp. 126-127, n. 1.

[73] According to Menzel, German ambassadors were not regularly provided with written instructions until Henry VII, and then not invariably. *Deutsches Gesandtschaftswesen*, p. 44.

[74] Maulde La Clavière, *La diplomatie au temps de Machiavel*, II, 132.

[75] Bakhrouchine and Kosminski, "La diplomatie au Moyen Age," p. 153; Jusserand, "The School for Ambassadors," p. 34. Baschet, *Les archives de Venise*, p. 395, indicates that earlier instructions were apt to be more specific, while in a later period when couriers came and went with regularity, the original instructions tended to be banal. If a person of the very highest rank, such as a member of a royal family, were serving as ambassador, instructions might be considered inappropriate and be replaced by a memorial or memorandum. Maulde La Clavière, *La diplomatie au temps de Machiavel*, II, 136-137.

[76] Maulde La Clavière, *La diplomatie au temps de Machiavel*, II, 119-120. I cannot, however, agree with this author that "the ideal consists in paying for realities by fine, gracious and friendly words." Diplomatic agreements are effective only if they are and remain mutually advantageous to the parties.

labeling a procuration as *commissione*; he subsequently and appropriately wrote over that word *sindicato*.[77]

Since instructions were less formal instruments than letters of credence or procurations, they tended to be given in the vernacular earlier. The English ambassador empowered to negotiate in 1418 concerning a treaty with the dauphin and the marriage of Henry V and Katherine, for example, has procurations for these two negotiations in Latin, but instructions in English.[78] As the fifteenth century progressed, more and more of the Venetian *commissioni* were written in *Veneziano*.

The contents of instructions vary infinitely, of course, in subject and in amount of detail. English instructions of 1276 for envoys to negotiate a marriage alliance for the daughter of Edward I with the son of the king of Germany contained, in outline, the following: (1) they should thank the king; (2) if asked how much money Edward wants for the marriage alliance, replies are given; (3) they should ask the king to send his son to England for knighting and for consummating the marriage; (4) they should seek delay in sending Edward's daughter to France, because of her youth; (5) they should seek a promise that if the king of Germany should be supplanted as emperor, he should strive for the election of his son; (6) and (7) they should seek securities; (8) they should see the son and make inquiries about him; and (9) they should thank the queen.[79] Some instructions were much more specific. One *commissione* of 1480 occupies 6 pages in a folio register and contains 31 separate items.[80] Yet even with rather specific instructions, considerable latitude might be left to the ambassador.[81] On the other hand, instructions can be found which supply the exact words which the envoys should say.[82] Sometimes the ambassador is instructed

[77] A.S.V., Senato, Secreta, XXXVI, 7r (19r). The *commissioni* of Italian diplomacy are simply instructions, in spite of the fact that they are sometimes described as *mandata*. Maulde La Clavière, *La diplomatie au temps de Machiavel*, pp. 104-105. The author was somewhat confused on this point, although he did recognize that one could not conclude upon the basis of a *commissione*. *Mandatum* was sometimes used in a generic sense for instructions. The word *sindicato* was used consistently and with unusual legal precision by the Venetians instead of *procuratio* since the envoy represented a corporation, the Republic of Saint Mark. Not all clerks were so careful in their terminology. I have seen instructions obviously intended only for the eyes of the envoy labeled *la credence*. Chaplais, *War of Saint Sardos*, pp. 182-184, 192-194.

[78] Rymer, *Foedera*, IV, iii, 67-69. See the interesting comments of Hale on the use of Latin and the vernacular in diplomacy. "International Relations in the West," pp. 270-271.

[79] Rymer, *Foedera*, I, ii, 154-155.

[80] A.S.V., Senato, Secreta, XXIX, 92v (102v).

[81] *Calendar of State Papers. Venetian*, pp. 14-17, no. 47. Although rather specific instructions were given covering various contingencies, and the ambassador was not a plenipotentiary and could not conclude, discretionary phrases run through the *commissione*. ". . . thou wilt do in this matter as shall seem most profitable and fit to thee." ". . . in such adroit and sage manner as shall seem fit to thee."

[82] "Che sunt les paroles ke on doit dire au roy d'Engleterre, u à ces gens, de par le conte de

to make certain concessions demanded by the other party, but grudgingly and after making himself difficult.[83] An ambassador was sometimes advised not to obligate his principal to anything.[84] He could take refuge behind the silence of his instructions on any matter on which he did not wish to commit his principal.[85]

The showing of instructions was considered a manifestation of friendly relations.[86] We know of instructions which were read to the opposite party and others whose wording indicates that they were virtually to be read.[87] The instructions of a Paduan embassy of 1308 were copied into the register of the *Maggior Consiglio* of Venice.[88] Letters of instruction which were to be communicated to the other side served to open negotiations, and the normal response was a note or memoir.[89]

Many instructions, of course, were intended only for the eyes of the envoy, especially as the information-gathering function gained in importance. The well-informed Bernard du Rosier, writing of instructions which should not be revealed, advises the ambassador to use great caution in deciding what should be said and what should be concealed. He ought to be very reluctant to deliver to the other party the original of his instructions, and should not even transfer a copy unless such was the will of the principal.[90] Instructions which were kept secret, of course, might differ considerably from what appeared in instructions which were shown, or in letters of credence or procurations. Sometimes the ostensible purpose of the

---

Flandres." Kervyn de Lettenhove, *Études*, pp. 25-27. Instructions of Venetian orators to the new king of the Romans, Rupert, in 1401 included the essential outline of a speech of welcome and congratulations and excuses to be offered for their lack of a procuratorial mandate. A.S.V., Senato, Secreta, I, 30v (31v)–31r (32r). The Venetian Senate usually left the polite speeches to the ambassador's discretion, but customarily gave rather specific instructions on the substance of negotiations. The first surviving Venetian *commissione* of 1198 is a good example: ". . . committimus vobis H. Navigaioso et A. Donato legatis nostris, ut, facta salutatione domino imperatori et nostris litteris presentatis, factoque sermonis vestri exordio de introitu eius sicut vobis providentia vestra suaserit, cum veneritis ad legationis radicem . . ." It then proceeds in great detail. Armingaud, *Venise et le Bas-Empire*, pp. 126-127, n. 1.

[83] Rymer, *Foedera*, IV, iv, 96-97.

[84] A.S.F., Dieci di Balia—Missive—Legazioni e commissarie, I, 88.

[85] Perret, *Relations de la France avec Venise*, I, 65. Perret cites another example where the ambassador was instructed that under certain circumstances he should say that he had no instructions and could only offer his personal views, but that he should try every means to sound out the other side. *Ibid.*, I, 410-411. Silence of instructions could lead to lengthy delays, which might or might not be desirable. *Ibid.*, II, 100.

[86] Maulde La Clavière, *La diplomatie au temps de Machiavel*, II, 120. In such cases, of course, there were often secret instructions also.

[87] A.S.V., Senato, Secreta, XXII, 4v (6v); Perroy, *Anglo-French Negotiations at Bruges (1374-1377)*, pp. 61-62, no. LIX.

[88] A.S.V., Maggior Consiglio, Capricornus, 69r (174r).

[89] Maulde La Clavière, *La diplomatie au temps de Machiavel*, II, 122-123.

[90] Bernard du Rosier, *Ambaxiator brevilogus*, pp. 13-14, Chap. XIII, and p. 16, Chap. XVI.

mission was not the real purpose at all, but only a pretext.[91] This might not even be known to all the ambassadors, or even to any of them, for secret instructions might be entrusted to one of their number or even to a member of the embassy of inferior rank.[92]

Naturally, instructions kept secret had no juridical effect upon the relationship between the principals. Even those revealed did not grant or withhold any powers, although any party who entered into an agreement with an ambassador contrary to the instructions of that ambassador as revealed to him obviously did so at considerable risk of repudiation of the agreement. Venetian ambassadors were made to swear to abide by their instructions, could be punished for failure to do so, and yet it appears they repeatedly did go beyond what they had been instructed to do.[93] A surprising Venetian decree of 1478 complains of "the most bad and harmful custom" of orators who "presume to undertake matters not committed to them, and to speak and to respond beyond or contrary to what they have in their mandates." The Senate enacted severe penalties upon those who should do so in the future.[94] The word *mandatum* probably should be interpreted here in its general sense, meaning "instructions," not in the specific legal sense, meaning "procuration." Juridically, a principal would be bound by an act within an ambassador's powers, even if in violation of his instructions. Of course there was no court to enforce such rights, but repudiation of them would be embarrassing and not conducive to maintaining the confidence upon which any future negotiations must rest.[95]

[91] Bakhrouchine and Kosminski, "La diplomatie au Moyen Age," p. 92, writing specifically of Byzantine diplomacy.

[92] Chaplais, *War of Saint Sardos*, pp. 140-142, in which two of the envoys received secret instructions about making concessions not mentioned in the instructions known to the rest of the embassy. Maulde La Clavière cites an embassy in which only the secretary was aware of the real objective of the mission, while its nominal head was deceived with spurious instructions. *La diplomatie au temps de Machiavel*, I, 374.

[93] Nicolini, *Il consolato generale veneto nel regno di Napoli*, p. 29. For a record the entire commission was copied with the substitution of sacramental phrases for the original imperatives. A.S.V., Avogaria di Comun, Capitolare, VII, 3r. The date is not given, but it is probably early fourteenth century. "Li Avogari sono tenuti placitar Li Oratori che non osservano Le Loro Commissioni. Cap° 62."

[94] A.S.V., Senato, Secreta, XXVIII, 104v (115v).

[95] In 1503, Ferdinand and Isabella refused to ratify the acts of their ambassador to France. One of their excuses was that, "although for the sake of his honor his mandate had been free and most ample, he had to refer to his instructions, which had been limited." The ambassador denied that his instructions were any less liberal than his powers, and insisted that the monarchs had placed the matter in his hands and had sworn to observe whatever he concluded. Francesco Guicciardini, *Storia d'Italia*, Giovanni Rosini, ed., 8 vols. (Pisa, 1822-1824), Lib. VI, cap. 1, III, 7. See also Juan de Mariana, *Historiae de rebus Hispaniae libri XXX* (Moguntiae, 1605), Lib. XXVII, cap. xix, pp. 545-547. In the Spanish ed., *Historia general de España* (Barcelona, n.d.), pp. 550-551. Guicciardini attributes the failure to Ferdinand's duplicity, while Mariana declares that the ambassador was intimidated and corrupted by the French.

In addition to the above documents, the diplomatic pouch often contained and sometimes bulged with copies of documents providing evidence in support of the envoy's mission. A departing ambassador might go armed with a large number of supporting documents, 27 in one case, for example, 35 in another.[96] These might include earlier letters of credence and procurations and records of the previous negotiations based upon them with the requests of one party and the responses of the other. Terms upon which they had reached tentative agreement would surely be included. The records of arbitrations into which they had entered and judgments rendered might be needed by the envoys. Similarly, previous truces and armistices, as well as prolongations of the same, treaties, alliances, and marriage contracts might provide them with needed evidence. Copies of papal bulls in support of the position of the principal were often found in the possession of envoys. So were acts of homage and fealty and significant renunciations. Guarantees were also important. Very frequently, also, the envoy bore lists of grievances against the opposite party. Envoys sent by William I, count of Hainaut (and of Holland), in 1304 to seek an alliance with France against Flanders, carried rolls marked "A" containing documents on the two marriages and two families of Countess Margaret. Those marked "B" had to do with arbitrations by Saint Louis in 1246 and 1256. The ill-fated investiture of Charles of Anjou with Hainaut was covered by documents in the rolls marked "C." "D" indicated rolls containing judgments of the German court in favor of John of Avesnes, William's predecessor.[97] Ambassadors also might be given drafts as a basis for negotiation of conventions into which they might enter. If these were not intended to be shown, signs or notations might indicate points upon which the ambassador could make concessions, but if they were to be revealed such information would be contained in the instructions.[98]

For their own protection envoys often received letters of protection and passports. Letters of protection were issued by the principal himself, taking under his protection the person of the envoy, his men, and his lands

[96] "Additions au Codex diplomaticus Flandriae," F. Funck-Brentano, ed., *Bibliothèque de l'École des Chartes*, LVII (1896), 382; *C.C.R., Edward I (1302-1307)*, pp. 105-107. Cuttino's account of the development of the office of the *custos processuum* as a sort of incipient foreign office is based upon the collection and use of documents pertaining to the persistent disputes over English holdings in France. Clerks were set to researching in the documents the points at issue. Chaplais, *War of Saint Sardos*, pp. 238-239.

[97] Duvivier, *Influences*, II, 572-573, no. CCCXXIII. The Venetian orator to Rome to treat concerning the protection of Djem received all reports from the Venetian secretary at the Ottoman capital concerning the unfortunate brother of the sultan. A.S.V., Dieci, Misti, XXVI, 68v (96v)–69r (97r); filze, VIII, 13.

[98] Maulde La Clavière, *La diplomatie au temps de Machiavel*, II, 137.

and goods during his absence. A clause called *volumus* also granted to the envoy immunity against most legal processes during his mission.[99] In a sense these acts were only peripheral to diplomacy, and they were probably not borne by the ambassador, but left in safe-keeping at home. Passports were also issued by the government sending the envoy to establish his identity and to request his protection and good treatment on his way.[100]

Often, also, it was felt necessary that an envoy should have a safe-conduct from the government to which he was accredited or from those through whose territory he passed. The principal would usually request letters of safe-conduct, but the request might also be made by a third party.[101] Lacking assurance of safe passage, an embassy might abort or be delayed.[102] Bernard du Rosier indicated that safe-conducts were sought when the principals were not upon friendly terms and that such assurance should not be denied. Once granted, moreover, it should not be infringed for any reason, regardless of the depth of enmity between the governments.[103] By a

[99] Cuttino, *English Diplomatic Administration*, p. 112. E.g., *C.P.R. Henry III (1247-1258)*, p. 486. Respite on debts due the king from an ambassador. *C.C.R. Edward III (1330-1333)*, p. 323. Letters of protection for a clerk sent as a messenger from the ambassador because the clerk, outlawed in a plea of debt, feared to approach the king with his message. *C.P.R. Richard II (1385-1389)*, p. 195. Absent ambassadors, however, were not always immune to suit. *C.R. (1251-1253)*, pp. 191-192. Revocation of letters of protection. *C.P.R. Henry VI (1429-1436)*, p. 326.

[100] Maulde La Clavière, *La diplomatie au temps de Machiavel*, II, 52-54. Rymer, *Foedera*, III, ii, 136. A very common Florentine type seems intended for use within Florentine territory. E.g., A.S.F., Signori—Carteggi—Missive—Legazioni e commissarie—Elezioni e istruzioni a oratori, XXI, 94v (95v). Maulde La Clavière distinguishes letters of recommendation, similar to passports, but taking the form of personal letters and sometimes requesting a more specific favor than simply safe passage and a good reception. He states that these were rarely used for ambassadors. *La diplomatie au temps de Machiavel*, II, 54-56. Cuttino writes of safe-conducts issued to one's own envoys (*English Diplomatic Administration*, p. 112) and Hill calls passports what I have classed as safe-conducts (*The King's Messengers*, pp. 96-97). A Florentine document describing a protest from the pope against the arrest of two *astigiani* merchants of the Roman curia bearing a "safe-conduct" also seems to equate safe-conducts with passports. A.S.F., Archivio diplomatico—Riformagioni—Atti publici, XVI, 63. In fact, the index to this collection refers to the same act as a *salvo condotto* and a *passaporto*.

[101] Kern, *Acta Imperii, Angliae et Franciae*, p. 18, no. 31. Not only ambassadors, but princes themselves, merchants, and others enjoyed the protection of safe-conducts. Henri Nowé, "Notes sur un manuscrit de l'abbaye de Saint-Pierre de Gand conservés aux Archives Nationales de Paris," in *Bulletin de la Commission Royale d'Histoire*, LXXXVII (1923), p. 20; *C.R. (1253-1254)*, p. 316; *Rotuli litterarum patentium in turri Londonensi asservati (1201-1216)*, Thomas D. Hardy, ed. (London, 1835), I, i, 99; *C.P.R., Edward III (1370-1374)*, p. 430. A Venetian order to the consul at Bruges to obtain new letters of safe-conduct for the galleys at as cheap a rate as possible. *Calendar of State Papers. Venetian*, p. 60, no. 223. An insufficient safe-conduct, for example, one issued by procurators lacking authority to do so, might be rejected by the intended benefactors. British Museum, PS 4, 5335, AD. MS 14820 C.

[102] Chaplais, *War of Saint Sardos*, p. 191; A.S.V., Senato, Secreta, VIII, 53r (54r).

[103] Bernard du Rosier, *Ambaxiator brevilogus*, p. 27, cap. XXVII. Sometimes they were refused, of course. A.S.V., Senato, Secreta, IV, 238v (238v) and 239v (239v). Ganshof, *Le Moyen Age*, p. 276, stresses the importance of safe-conducts for allowing ambassadors to return home safely after a rupture had occurred. On the other hand, requesting or offering a safe-conduct

statute of 1414, Henry V of England declared the violation of safe-conducts an act of high treason against the crown and established in each port a conservator of truces and safe-conducts.[104]

The Archives du Nord contain several prototypes of requests for safe-conducts and of safe-conducts which the clerks could follow in drafting specific documents.[105] A clearer and simpler example, however, is provided by Edward's safe-conduct for Bertrand de Got, the future Clement V, in 1295:

> The king, to all his ministers and faithful to whom the present letters come, greeting.
>
> Since the most holy father . . . may send the discreet man master Bertrand de Got, canon of Lyons, his chaplain, for certain difficult matters touching us and our kingdom, to our presence, desiring that safe and secure conduct, as much by land as by sea, within our dominion and power should be provided to the same, we order you, enjoining you strongly, that you should conduct and make to be conducted to us, etc., the aforesaid master Bertrand and his men and his entourage, of whatever nation they might be, together with all their things and goods, both coming and going, until the feast of Pentecost next.[106]

Examples of much simpler "licenses" given by the receiving government can be found, but it is doubtful whether they had the full value of a safe-conduct.[107]

Safe-conducts might be subject to any number of conditions. A limit might be put on the size of the retinue subject to the safe-conduct.[108] An envoy might even be offered an escort or provided with horses upon request.[109] A safe-conduct usually had a time limit.[110] A safe-conduct of

---

could be a first *démarche* in seeking peace. Maulde La Clavière, *La diplomatie au temps de Machiavel*, II, 49-50.

[104] Nys, *Origines du droit international*, p. 214.

[105] Archives du Nord, Lille, Chambre des Comptes, B 1561, nos. 505-508.

[106] Kern, *Acta Imperii, Angliae et Franciae*, pp. 66-67, no. 93. The order actually to conduct the envoys was not, however, essential to a safe-conduct. On occasion a safe-conduct could be issued for ambassadors whose names were unknown. For Burgundian envoys *quorum Nomina nobis non certificavit*. Rymer, *Foedera*, IV, ii, 154.

[107] "Dominus Paulinus ambaxiator Comunis Cremone cum uno socio et hoc duobus ratione habuit licentiam eundi Cremonam. data Mantua die XVIII Maii." Archivio di Stato, Mantova, Archivio Gonzaga, 2881 (Copialettere I, c. 29).

[108] Rymer, *Foedera*, IV, ii, 176. For the duke of Burgundy himself and up to 800 attendants. For a retinue of 50 horses. A.S.V., Senato, Secreta, IX, 146v (144v).

[109] Rymer, *Foedera*, I, iv, 136; Chaplais, *Treaty Rolls*, I, 105, no. 248.

[110] Lucas, "Machinery of Diplomatic Intercourse," p. 310. Nys reports that according to Muslim law a safe-conduct could not be valid for more than one year. Ernest Nys, *Études de droit international et de droit politique* (Bruxelles et Paris, 1896), p. 51.

1422 for deputies of the duke of Brittany for swearing to the treaty between England and France provided that they must have powers for taking such an oath.[111] Or a safe-conduct might provide that the ambassador should not undertake any matters other than those for which the protection was granted.[112] Or it might provide that the envoys be protected only on condition that they act well and honestly toward the grantor and his subjects.[113] An exception might also be made of those in the company who should be rebels or exiles from the country to which the mission is directed.[114]

By far the most spectacular documents borne by diplomats were blanks sealed in advance by the principal and left to be filled out by the envoys. Although scattered examples had been known previously, Joycelyne Dickinson undertook a systematic consideration of some fourteenth- and fifteenth-century examples for the first time in the *English Historical Review* of 1951.[115] Additional, earlier, and much more extraordinary examples can be cited.[116] Miss Dickinson pointed out that the words *au blanc* or *in albo* did not necessarily indicate parchments containing no writing, but only a seal,[117] yet evidence of such documents, subsequently filled in by the envoys or returned and destroyed, has been found.

The earliest example which we have is the oft-mentioned embassy of crusaders to Venice in 1201. The oaths taken by Villehardouin and his five colleagues for their principals state explicitly: "Therefore he gave to us this blank parchment furnished with his seal, in which should be written that the aforesaid count will hold firm and fast whatever we will have concluded for him with you."[118] Since each of the three crusading chiefs

111 Rymer, *Foedera*, IV, iv, 68.

112 *Ibid.*, I, i, 47-48. On one occasion the Venetian Senate raised the question whether safe-conduct applied to visits to castles and fortresses. A.S.V., Senato, Secreta, XIX, 212v (212v). In any case a safe-conduct did not excuse interference in the domestic affairs of the host. Maulde La Clavière, *La diplomatie au temps de Machiavel*, II, 39-40.

113 With a proviso that violation by any of the ambassadors or their retinue should not nullify the safe-conduct as regards those adhering to its conditions. Rymer, *Foedera*, V, iv, 26. Exception of *homicidio, furto, assassinaria et robaria.* A.S.V., Senato, Secreta, I, 117r (118r). Maulde La Clavière suggests that even without such a clause the safe-conduct is quite inconsistent with the idea of extraterritoriality. *La diplomatie au temps de Machiavel*, II, 57.

114 Chaplais, *War of Saint Sardos*, pp. 187-188.

115 Joycelyne G. Dickinson, " 'Blanks' and 'Blank Charters' in the Fourteenth and Fifteenth Centuries," *E.H.R.*, LXVI (1951), 375-387.

116 Donald E. Queller, "Diplomatic 'Blanks' in the Thirteenth Century," *E.H.R.*, LXXX (1965), 476-491. Consult this for a fuller discussion than can be given here.

117 Dickinson, "Blanks," pp. 377-379.

118 The oaths have been published in the following: Longnon, *Vie de Villehardouin*, pp. 181-183; Villehardouin, *Conquête de Constantinople*, I, 217-218; Tafel and Thomas, *Urkunden*, pp. 358-362; Tessier, *Quatrième Croisade*, pp. 254-255. Hodgson long ago pointed out the freedom these ambassadors had to determine the route to be taken on the crusade and to use "deeds already sealed to confirm any agreements they made on behalf of the barons." F. C. Hodgson, *The Early History of Venice* (London, 1901), pp. 352-353. In my article, "L'évolu-

was represented by two envoys, and each pair of envoys swore in the name of their principal, the use of at least three clearly labeled blanks is established.[119] Additional evidence afforded by Villehardouin proves the extent of the freedom enjoyed by the envoys in converting their blanks. They had authority to choose their own destination, to negotiate and conclude a treaty upon terms unforeseeable by their principals, to send it to Rome for confirmation, and to borrow money for the purpose of carrying it out, all without consultation with, reports to, or additional instructions from their principals.[120] Although it cannot be proved that the missing copy of the treaty in the names of the crusaders was redacted upon another blank, it is quite possible. Since the sending of a *nuncius* to Rome to gain confirmation and the borrowing of money to begin the execution of the treaty were less solemn acts, it is not likely that in these cases blanks provided with the principals' seals were used.[121]

In 1253, Countess Margaret of Flanders dispatched to Thomas of Savoy, widower of her sister, Countess Jeanne, and to Pope Innocent IV an embassy entrusted with sealed blanks. Their misuse, according to the countess, accounts for her subsequent complaint to the pope, which provides a lengthy description of the embassy.[122] The bishop of Cambrai and Egidius van Breedene, the titular head of the mission, received from the countess certain distinct and limited petitions in writing with conditions set down. The countess expressed orally to the bishop and Egidius, however, certain complaints upon which the whole execution of her will depended, but these were not given in writing because of the secret character of the business. Because of the difficulty and the magnitude of these secret negotiations, they received six blank parchments sealed by the countess. If agreement could be reached with Thomas and the pope in accordance with her requests, they could inscribe pacts and conventions and undertake obliga-

tion du rôle de l'ambassadeur," I have shown that the freedom they enjoyed was really fantastically great.

119 Miss Dickinson warned that direct evidence of blanks would be hard to find since, once converted, they would resemble a normal document. "Blanks," pp. 383-384. These, however, are plainly labeled.

120 Villehardouin, *Conquête de Constantinople*, Secs. 11-32. One may well note the character of the envoys, especially of Villehardouin and Conon of Béthune, ranking just under the crusading chieftains and frequently employed on diplomatic missions. Such flexibility might well be denied to lesser men.

121 The powers of the envoys seem to have been adequate for concluding such a treaty and swearing to uphold it in the names of their principals without the use of sealed blanks, but the seals of the principals provided extra ceremonial sanction.

122 Duvivier, *Influences*, II, 403-406, no. CCXXXV. Mission also described at some length in Eg. I. Strubbe, *Egidius van Breedene (11..-1270): Grafelijk ambtenaar en stichter van de abdij Spermalie* (Brugge, 1942), pp. 82-84.

tions upon those membranes. They promised upon their faith that the blanks would not be used unless those secret matters which the countess had entrusted to them should be accomplished according to her instructions. With this understanding, when they departed from the countess they received no procuratorial letters or patents whatsoever. The mission began to go awry when the envoys agreed with Count Thomas that he should join them in their mission to Rome in return for ten *livres tournois* a day upon the purse of the countess, concerning which, she complained, " . . . non habuerunt mandatum." What was wanting, however, was easily supplied by the use of one of the blank parchments.[123] Other blank parchments were used to borrow money in Rome, which, according to her version of her instructions to her envoys, was an abuse. The occasion of her complaint, upon which this account is based, was a papal order of 1255 to pay the Florentine bankers to whom Egidius had obligated her. One of these converted blanks can be positively identified. It is a procuration ostensibly given by Margaret at Sluis on 12 October 1253 and sealed with her seal, but actually written by her envoys at Rome, probably on 26 March 1254 upon one of the sealed blanks in the exact amount of a loan they had contracted.[124] Following the copy of the loan, this procuration is described: "Item: procuratorial letters of my lady upon the aforesaid loan. On this procuration we expended one schedule." The same note continues: "On a loan of 1,000 libr. we expended another. On a loan of 2,000 libr. a third. On the conventions with Count Thomas a fourth."[125] We also know that Arnold of Ghent and Thomas of Cambrai, canons of Liège, borrowed from Florentine bankers in the name of the countess, from whom they had a mandate for contracting such a loan.[126] This mandate was certainly another converted blank, perhaps the second or third just mentioned, perhaps another still. Margaret attested that she had supplied no procurations, so the procurators wrote their own—a rather risky business, as Margaret discovered. Her complaint was in support of an appeal to the papal court.[127]

[123] Duvivier, *Influences*, II, 367, no. CCXV, n. 1.

[124] Strubbe, *Egidius van Breedene*, pp. 228-229; Duvivier, *Influences*, II, 364, no. CCXII. Duvivier, apparently following Victor Gaillard, *Inventaire analytique des chartes des comtes de Flandre* (Gand, 1857), no. 508, gives the amount of the loan incorrectly in the headnote, although it is correct in the text. Both make the same error with regard to the loan itself as they do concerning the procuration. This is corrected, by the way, in the manuscript supplement to Gaillard in the Rijksarchief. Bigwood, observing the strangely uneven sum authorized by the procuration, interpreted it as a subsequent ratification by the countess, not having seen the complaint of the countess published by Duvivier. He also misdated it. Georges Bigwood, *Le régime juridique et économique du commerce de l'argent dans la Belgique du Moyen Age*, 2 vols. (Bruxelles, 1921-1922), I, 63-64.

[125] Duvivier, *Influences*, II, 367, no. CCXV, n. 1.

[126] *Ibid.*, II, 372-375, nos. CCXVIII-CCXIX.

[127] Rijksarchief, Gent, Gaillard, no. 508ter.

Three examples of the use of blanks by the court of Henry III can also be documented. The first two arose out of the endless negotiations concerning the affair of Sicily. The Calendar of Patent Rolls for 1254 records:[128]

> *Memorandum* that three void schedules sealed with the king's seal, have been sent by Robert Walrond, the steward, to Sir Peter of Sabaudia to do what he think fit about the affair of Scecil', and to send, if necessary, to Peter, Bishop of Hereford, at the court of Rome.
>
> Afterwards the said Robert sent to the bishop two of the said void schedules to make bonds thereof and procurations in the court of Rome in the king's name, and restored the third to the king at Windsor on 13 November, 40 Henry III (1255).

The bishop of Hereford also bore two blanks of a more limited type. One was a document appointing a new royal procurator in Rome with a space left for the bishop to insert the procurator's name. The other was a grant of 30 marks in favor of a papal clerk, whose name was to be inserted subsequently by the bishop.[129] When Peter of Hereford had completed his mission, he left behind him two procurators in Rome, presumably employing either the procuration with the blank space left for the name of a procurator (the appointment of two, rather than one, may have caused difficulties) or one of the void documents with which he had been entrusted.[130] One of the void schedules, we know, was returned to the king, and we may assume that it was destroyed. Two, presumably, were used by the bishop, but cannot be identified. As Miss Dickinson pointed out, used completed blanks, even if they survived, could be identified only by a remarkable stroke of luck.

Again in 1257, Henry III employed blanks in negotiations concerning Sicily. Simon de Montfort and Peter of Savoy, then occupied in Paris with negotiations with Louis IX, were commissioned, along with John Maunsell and the archbishop of Tarentaise, to seek from the pope a legate to facilitate the French negotiations and to negotiate in the hardest way for an amelioration of the papal demands regarding Sicily.[131] Simon and Peter, clearly the chief negotiators, were authorized either to go themselves or to send others in their stead. If they should send others, highly specific instructions were given, but if they should go themselves they simply re-

[128] *C.P.R. Henry III (1247-1258)*, p. 389.

[129] *Ibid.*, p. 343.

[130] *C.R. (1254-1256)*, p. 211.

[131] *C.P.R. Henry III (1247-1258)*, p. 567; Rymer, *Foedera*, I, ii, 28. See Margaret Wade Labarge, *Simon de Montfort* (London, 1962), p. 152; Charles Bémont, *Simon de Montfort, Earl of Leicester, 1208-1265*, new edn. trans. by E. F. Jacob (Oxford, 1930), pp. 132-133; Sir Maurice Powicke, *The Thirteenth Century, 1216-1307*, 1st edn. 1953, reprinted with corrections (Oxford, 1954), pp. 122-124.

ceived full powers for the whole business. How broad their powers were is indicated by a memorandum which states that a large number of documents on the Sicilian affair "with twenty white and void schedules, sealed with the seal of the king; and eight void schedules, sealed with the seal of the lord Edward; and ten void schedules, sealed with the golden bull, under the name of the lord Edmund, son of the king" were delivered to an envoy for transmission to Simon de Montfort and Peter of Savoy. If these two negotiators go to Rome, they should use these documents and blanks just as they deem expedient for the honor of the king and the affair of Sicily. If they do not wish to go, however, the blank schedules should be damaged (by slashing, presumably) and returned to the king. A letter to Simon and Peter confirms the contents of the above document and adds that they may make use of the blanks for procurations for other envoys if they are unable to go. They should handle the matter as seems best to them, "because we commit all these things totally to your discretion."[132] Although Simon de Montfort and Peter of Savoy did not accept the Roman mission and there is no evidence that they sent any procurators in their place, the enormous breadth of freedom granted to them by their full powers and the blank parchments is noteworthy. We have no record of the use or destruction of the numerous blanks, but they probably were destroyed.

At about this same time, Henry III had promised to send to Alfonso the Wise envoys to deal with threats which had recently developed endangering the Anglo-Castilian alliance.[133] This proved rather difficult. On 16 August the king placed the entire matter in the hands of John Maunsell, who had greater familiarity with Anglo-Castilian relations than any other and who had advised that someone must be sent to Castile.[134] The abbot of Shrewsbury had agreed to go, and with him the king had associated John of Sumercote. He asked that Maunsell should instruct them upon what they should say or do. Maunsell might also wish to write letters of his own to the king of Castile. *Et ad cautelam majorem* the king sent to Maunsell three blank schedules sealed with the royal seal and two sealed with the seal of the lord Edward. Along with these he sent procuratorial letters permitting the famous clerk to do whatever he thought best con-

[132] Rymer, *Foedera*, I, ii, 29; *C.P.R. Henry III (1247-1258)*, pp. 567-568. Powicke, *King Henry III and the Lord Edward*, I, 375, discusses these documents, mentions the sealed blanks of Edward and Edmund, but ignores those of Henry. The privilege of concession of Sicily to Edmund by Innocent IV was also sent to the envoys for possible surrender, but unless Simon and Peter themselves went to Rome it was to be returned. Rymer, *Foedera*, I, ii, 30.

[133] *C.R. (1256-1259)*, p. 135.

[134] Joseph O. Baylen, "John Maunsell and the Castilian Treaty of 1254: A Study of the Clerical Diplomat," *Traditio*, XVII (1961), 482-491.

cerning the Castilian matter. An addendum to the copy of the king's letter in the Close Rolls reveals that all the blanks were returned in mid-December and were torn up in the presence of witnesses.[135] In this case, of course, the blanks were not intended for the actual use of a diplomatic envoy, but of an adviser remaining in England.[136]

Blanks were thus used in the thirteenth century with incredible freedom and power of discretion on the part of the diplomatic envoy. He could make conventions, take oaths, borrow money, issue procurations, and do other things in his judgment suitable to carrying out the general objectives of the principal. This was an exceedingly risky device, entrusted only to the most trusted councilors, for allowing an envoy more freedom and authority than would have been possible in any other way. The thirteenth century remained an age of *ad hoc* embassies often entrusted to the ruler's intimates. Communication between the principal and the envoy was infrequent and slow, so that envoys were not only allowed the power to conclude, but occasionally even the possibility of redacting the most solemn acts over the seals of the principals.

Miss Dickinson's late fourteenth- and fifteenth-century examples suggest that, as the conditions of diplomatic intercourse evolved, blanks were used in a rather more limited and conservative manner. Her earliest example has the ambassadors of Hugh IV, duke of Anjou, presenting to the judge of Majorca "a white roll sealed with the seal of the said lord duke and signed with his own hand" upon which a notary made a copy in Latin of their letters of credence, which were written in French.[137] She discovered another example of blanks in the dispatch case of the ambassadors of the dukes of Berry, Orléans, Bourbon, and Alençon captured by king's men in 1412. Among other documents there were "four blanks sealed with four great seals and signed with four manual signs, namely of Berry, of Orléans, of Bourbon, and of Alençon, and in each blank were their names written above their seals in the margin, and there was not at all another thing written."[138] That it was still possible for blanks to be used in the fifteenth century as they had been used in the thirteenth is proved by Miss Dickinson's latest example. Ambassadors of Charles VII in 1441 were given various sealed and signed documents of the usual sort "with several blanks sealed and signed as has been said, by which letters and blanks the said ambassadors had power and authority to treat and negotiate upon the said

[135] *C.R.* (*1256-1259*), pp. 149-150.

[136] For evidence of the contemporary use of the papal bull appended to blank parchments to be sold for such purposes as the commutation of crusading vows, see Matthew Paris, *Chronica majora*, v, 527, 713, and Bémont, *Simon de Montfort*, p. 165.

[137] Dickinson, "Blanks," pp. 380-381.

[138] *Ibid.*, p. 376.

treaty of peace. . . ." The king, however, revoked these letters, fearing that they would fall into the wrong hands and that treaties, agreements, or other obligations might be made by virtue of them to his prejudice and harm.[139] It is the king's apprehensions which prove that blanks could still be used for the most serious and important undertakings.

Maulde La Clavière also knew of the use of blanks in diplomacy in the late fifteenth and early sixteenth centuries, although he offered no systematic treatment of them. He called attention to the blanks possessed by an ambassador of the duke of Brittany at the beginning of the War of the Public Weal. With them the ambassador "should make new (documents) and writings as the case required."[140] He cited another blank given by Charles VIII to his ambassador to the duke of Austria. The ambassador should present the letters of the king, "of which you have sent me a blank signed with your hand. . . ."[141] In 1505, also, Louis XII sent fifteen *lettres en blanc* to Du Bouchage which should be used by the count of Nevers as he deemed necessary.[142] A Florentine ambassador in 1508 demanded of his government instructions in cipher, a blank signature, and full powers in cipher, which he could copy himself upon the blank.[143] Finally, Maulde La Clavière also noted the existence of the other kind of blank, where open spaces were left only for the insertion of names.[144]

Any or all of the documents discussed so far, letters of credence, procurations, instructions, and blanks could be sent to the ambassador during the course of his mission, as well as given to him at its inception. Negotiations of any duration and complexity, especially after the thirteenth century, required correspondence from the ambassador informing his government of developments and new instructions sent from the government to him.[145] Ambassadors were as apt to complain of lack of instructions from their governments as the latter were to complain of lack of information from their ambassadors.[146] The response of the government to its ambassador might be

[139] *Ibid.*, pp. 379-380.

[140] *La diplomatie au temps de Machiavel*, II, 105-106 and 106, n. 1; Commynes, *Mémoires*, I, 17-18, Liv. I, Chap. II. Luzio also wrote of the authority given to Mantuan ambassadors to compose letters on the spot as their local experience indicated. The document of 1388 which he quotes does establish that this was done, but does not, I think, prove that it was a common practice. *L'Archivio Gonzaga*, II, 79 and n. 2.

[141] *La diplomatie au temps de Machiavel*, II, 115-116; Bibliothèque Nationale, Fr. 15, 541, no. 171.

[142] Bibliothèque Nationale, Fr. 2928, f°, 2.

[143] *La diplomatie au temps de Machiavel*, III, 133, n. 7.

[144] *Ibid.*, II, 115-116, and 116, n. 1. Bibliothèque Nationale, Fr. 20855, no. 55.

[145] True at an earlier date for Byzantine diplomacy. Bakhrouchine and Kosminski, "La diplomatie au Moyen Age," p. 92.

[146] Kervyn de Lettenhove, *Études*, p. 58; A.S.M., Archivio Sforzesco, Venezia, busta, no. 385, in which the Milanese ambassador complains mildly that he has not received a letter for eight days.

in the form of full powers authorizing him, for the first time, to conclude. This is the nature of the Venetian *sindicati*, the terms of which are usually based upon draft conventions already negotiated by the ambassadors and reported to the government. Communication between the government and the ambassador tended to be slow, and a number of letters were often saved up to be sent by means of a single courier. A letter from Florentine ambassadors of 24 January 1499, for example, reveals that on the preceding day they had received from their government letters dated 31 December, and 6, 8, 10, and 13 January.[147] A letter written by Louis XI on 18 November 1464 did not arrive in Venice until 6 March 1465.[148] The reason medieval diplomats at distant courts sometimes received discretionary powers far beyond those of their modern counterparts should be quite clear. Even if the information upon which a government based its decision was not already obsolete when the decision was made, such a decision might no longer conform to realities by the time it was communicated to the ambassador in the field.

Some of the communications directed to the ambassador were obviously not intended to be conveyed to the opposite party. A large part of the art of diplomacy lies in knowing what to reveal and what not to reveal. That ambassadors sometimes judged badly in these matters is indicated by a decree of the Venetian Senate in 1468 complaining about the bad custom of some orators of reading their letters to the rulers to whom they were accredited. This should henceforth be prohibited without the express mandate and license of the Senate.[149]

Communications between ambassadors and their governments had, of course, to flow in both directions. The remainder of this chapter will be devoted to the dispatches, reports, and relations of ambassadors. Governments repeatedly and strongly urged their ambassadors to write frequently. The Venetian Senate inveighed in 1478 against ambassadors who did not write concerning their dealings with the princes to whom they were sent, "which is among the first of the offices of a true and faithful orator."[150]

[147] A.S.F., Signori, Carteggi, Responsive originali, XI, 75r.

[148] Perret, *Relations de la France avec Venise*, I, 439.

[149] A.S.V., Senato, Terra, VI, 42v (43v).

[150] A.S.V., Senato, Secreta, XXVIII, 104v (115v). Ganshof, *Le Moyen Age*, pp. 278-279, reports that the earliest Venetian *dispacci* preserved date from 1379-1380, although they certainly existed before that date. Raimondo Morozzo della Rocca has published the minutes of some dispatches of Venetian ambassadors in Caffa in 1344-1346. "Notizie da Caffa," in *Studi in onore di Amintore Fanfani*, III (Milano, 1962), 267-295. A number of authors have claimed to find the first Venetian ambassadorial dispatch in the letter of Jacopo Tiepolo from Constantinople in 1219. Da Mosto, *L'Archivio di Stato di Venezia*, II, 25; Giuseppe Volpi, *La repubblica di Venezia e i suoi ambasciatori* (Milano, 1928), p. 50; Romanin, *Storia di Venezia*, II, 408. Tiepolo, however, was not strictly an ambassador in my opinion. Romanin's headnote refers to him as *bailo*, and in the letter he calls himself simply *potestas*.

Particularly in a time of crisis the government wanted to be kept *au courant.* Upon the death of the sultan in 1481 the Senate urged the orator and *baiulo* in Constantinople to keep them informed of everything occurring in the city, the provinces, and the Straits without sparing either persons or expense.[151] A Florentine ambassador to the duke of Milan in 1493 was told to write often and as fully and accurately as possible in order that the government might make its determinations to the greatest benefit of Florence.[152] The concern was quite legitimate, for the difficulty and slowness of communication was the basic problem of medieval diplomatic administration.[153]

How often an ambassador wrote to his government varied greatly. It would appear from the replies written by the Venetian Senate to its ambassadors that they sometimes wrote every few days, even on successive days, but sometimes they wrote rather infrequently. It seems that they wrote when they had something to report and not otherwise.[154] An English ambassador in 1418 was instructed to write at least once a week, but of course this does not establish any general rule.[155] A Mantuan ambassador to Hungary in 1395 wrote a dispatch on 24 November, two on 27 November, two on 28 November, and did not write another until December 30. Moreover, the last was canceled by slashing.[156] Letters written over a considerable period of time were sometimes retained to be sent by a single messenger, an unwisely parsimonious practice. Sanuto reports that on 5 May 1497 arrived much-desired letters from Spain of 12 January to 8

151 A.S.V., Senato, Secreta, xxx, 16v (26v).

152 A.S.F., Signori—Carteggi—Missive—Legazioni e commissarie—Elezioni e istruzioni a oratori, xxi, 109r (110r). In 1388 ambassadors sent to assist in making peace between Venice and Padua were admonished: . . . *E spessociavisate dogni cosa.* A.S.F., Dieci di Balia—Missive—Legazioni e commissarie, i, 88.

153 Of *administration,* not of diplomacy itself, which is beset by much more fundamental problems of ambition, hate, fear, and genuine conflict of interests. I would not have myself ranged with those who appear to believe that improved communication is the panacea for all the world's problems.

154 Reference to dispatches of three successive days. A.S.V., Senato, Secreta, vi, 20v (21v). Record of Francisco Venerio writing from Hungary on 13 and 14 June 1464, to which response was made on 29 June. On 22 July the Senate had not had further word from him. The Senate reprimanded him for this unaccustomed behavior and urged him to write daily. A.S.V., Senato, Secreta, xxii, 173v (175v). Bakhrouchine and Kosminski find Venetian orators writing once a week at first, then more frequently as the means of transport became better. "La diplomatie au Moyen Age," p. 15. Reumont wrote that Italian orators of the Renaissance were expected to write every two or three days if they were in Italy, but that as many as fifteen days might elapse between letters from ambassadors sent abroad. *Diplomazia,* p. 213. I have not found a consistent pattern, but improvement in the means of communication and the distance of the ambassador from home were undoubtedly factors. Machiavelli sent back 49 dispatches during 50 days on his first legation to Rome, but it is conceded that this was exceptional. Hale, "International Relations in the West," pp. 269-270.

155 Rymer, *Foedera,* iv, iii, 68-69.

156 Archivio di Stato, Mantova, Archivio Gonzaga, 533 (E. v. 3).

April.[157] Traveling time was always an important factor. Letters sent from Rome on 24 June 1298 arrived at Ghent on 19 July.[158] Nys reports as exceptional examples of speedy delivery a courier who promised to travel from Rome to Paris in thirteen days and another who left Blois on the seventh of the month to arrive at Venice on the morning of the fourteenth.[159] Dangers as well as delays beset messengers and messages in the Middle Ages. The Senate wrote to a Venetian orator in Rome that his messenger had almost been drowned and his letters were soaked, torn, and rubbed off so that the smallest part of them could scarcely be read.[160]

The contents of the dispatches were not restricted to a single subject, nor even to the purpose of the embassy or the place to which it was sent, but ranged across any subjects apt to be interesting or useful to the government.[161] A Florentine ambassador of the late fifteenth century was instructed:

> During the period of your legation you should observe and investigate diligently all those things that you esteem not only to be pertinent to our particular affairs but all that which generally should occur day by day. You should give to us in detail and often news of every event, frequenting the court and following continually his Excellency the Duke, when he goes any place to stay, in order that you can communicate and relate from this everything that happens day by day. And above all, you should write often and specifically about everything.[162]

Examples of newsworthy dispatches of this kind are readily found.[163] Much information appears to have been repeated in successive dispatches, sometimes even in two dispatches of the same day, presumably because of the danger of the dispatches not arriving or, because of some delay in transmission, their not arriving in the sequence in which they were written.[164]

157 Sanuto, *Diarii*, I, 615.

158 Kervyn de Lettenhove, *Études*, pp. 41-46.

159 Nys, "Le droit d'ambassade jusqu'à Grotius," p. 581.

160 A.S.V., Senato, Secreta, XII, 182r (189r).

161 Morozzo della Rocca, *Indice*, p. x; Quazza, *La diplomazia gonzaghesca*, p. 33.

162 A.S.F., Signori—Carteggi—Missive—Legazioni e commissarie—Elezioni e istruzioni a oratori, XXI, 143v (144v).

163 A.S.V., Lettere di rettori, I, no. 5. In 1388, Jacobus de Campana wrote to Mantua from Rome reporting his own activity, including the forging of a letter in the name of his principal, diplomatic news picked up from the ambassador of Perugia, and other news of the court. Archivio di Stato, Mantova, Archivio Gonzaga, 839 (E. XXV. 3). As ambassadors grew increasingly hungry for news for their own use or to be traded, the Venetian government sent out to them *avvisi* composed of information extracted from the dispatches of various diplomatic agents. Selmi, "Diplomazia stabile di Venezia," pp. 14-15.

164 Duplicates sent explicitly *ad petitionem regis* (King John) *propter pericula viarum*. "La prima relazione del cardinale Nicolò de Romanis sulla sua legazione in Inghilterra," Monsignore Angelo Mercato, ed., in *Essays in History Presented to Reginald Lane Poole*, H.W.C. Davis, ed. (Oxford, 1927), p. 286. The danger is also illustrated by the Venetian ambassador in

At least among the states of the Late Middle Ages with advanced diplomatic techniques, both governments and ambassadors kept files or registers of letters governing the embassy. In time of peril ambassadors were sometimes warned to be prepared to destroy their papers to prevent them falling into unfriendly hands.[165] The most shocking carelessness concerning diplomatic security occurred, however. A Venetian codification of 1477 of the many laws regulating the expenses of ambassadors provided that horsemen sent by the ambassador with messages to Venice must not be paid at a higher rate than was customary in the place.[166] Obviously, Venetian ambassadors were employing local couriers in order to communicate with Venice. Florentine ambassadors a few years later were instructed to send dispatches via the post of the king of Naples or the duke of Milan, although the caution was taken of providing a cipher for secret messages.[167] This laxity concerning security is especially surprising in light of the fact that as early as 1340 the lords of Mantua instructed ambassadors to send any letters containing secret messages only by way of Mantuan messengers, since they had recently received letters which had been opened.[168] In republican states it was sometimes necessary to address dispatches containing highly secret information to a restricted body, such as the Council of Ten.

In the late fourteenth and fifteenth centuries it was not uncommon to employ a cipher in an effort to maintain secrecy. Quazza reports that cipher was used in Gonzaga diplomacy from the middle of the fourteenth century.[169] Although evidence of earlier ciphering of documents exists, the first extant ciphered document in the archives at Venice dates from 1411, at Florence from 1414, at Milan from 1454 and at Genoa from 1481.[170] Since

---

1350 who provided his messenger with false letters to be shown in Lombardy, but to be ignored by the Senate. A.S.V., Senato, Secreta, B (C), 81v-82r.

165 Florence had a law that a register should be kept in which every orator's commission should be copied, after which should be added all letters written to him or received from him. Finally, the report at the end of the embassy should be copied so that the expectations and results of the mission could be seen at a glance. Vedovato, *Note*, pp. 53-54. Orders by the Venetian Council of Ten to ambassadors: (1) to be prepared to destroy their registers; (2) to burn all their papers. A.S.V., Dieci, Misti, XXVI, 127r (156r) and 129r (158r) (filze, VIII, 254 and 262), respectively.

166 A.S.V., Senato, Terra, VII, 174v (173v).

167 A.S.F., Signori—Carteggi—Missive—Legazioni e commissarie—Elezioni e istruzioni a oratori, XXI, 28r.

168 Archivio di Stato, Mantova, Archivio Gonzaga, 2881 (Copialettere I, c. 4). English ambassadors of the Late Middle Ages were accompanied by a regular messenger, but private messengers were also used. Hill, *The King's Messengers*, pp. 88-89.

169 *La diplomazia gonagescha*, p. 21.

170 P.-M. Perret, "Les règles de Cicco Simonetta pour le déchiffrement des écritures secrètes (4 juillet 1474)," *Bibliothèque de l'École des Chartes*, LI (1890), 519, n. 3.

the vast majority of the Venetian Documents useful for diplomacy are copies in registers of instructions, procurations, and letters from some governmental body to the ambassador, cipher is not obvious, although indications of its use do appear from time to time.[171] The *Archivio Sforzesco*, on the other hand, contains a large number of ciphered messages. Sometimes only key words were ciphered; entire letters written in cipher, including the date, the signature, and other standard material exist only rarely. Since cipher was a rather simple method of concealment involving the substitution of one or more letters, numbers, or other signs for others, the ciphering of dates, signatures, and formulas would expose the message to rather easy deciphering. A typical cipher given to a Mantuan ambassador to Hungary in 1395 has one character for each of the 23 letters of the alphabet.[172] There are added five characters marked *nichil relevantes* to be scattered here and there throughout the message to make deciphering without a key somewhat more difficult.[173] By the end of the Middle Ages there existed experts in the deciphering of messages.[174] Such a cipher as the one described from 1395 would not appear to have been very difficult to crack. Evidence also exists of surprising carelessness with ciphers. An ambassador of Margaret of Austria reported that he could no longer find the cipher that he had with her, so he was sending her another by the hands of a secretary.[175] Still, despite simplicity and carelessness, cipher was undoubtedly of considerable value to ambassadors and their principals.

Although in antiquity Roman ambassadors only reported orally upon their missions, written reports became customary in Byzantine diplomacy, and by the Late Middle Ages this custom was also adopted commonly in the West.[176] As early as 1268, Venetian ambassadors were required by law to submit written reports on their missions within fifteen days after their return.[177] Florentine orators were required to make written reports in their own hands, although not at such an early date. North of the Alps the re-

[171] To the first orator to the Turks after the fall of Constantinople: "Insuper vobis mittimus his insertam unam ziffram cum qua siquid secrete scribere volueritis. scribatis nobis, ac capitano generali." A.S.V., Senato, Secreta, XIX, 204 (204v).

[172] No distinct "j" or "v." Naturally no "w."

[173] Archivio di Stato, Mantova, Archivio Gonzaga, 533 (E. v. 3). Perret describes such ciphers with a few refinements. "Règles de Cicco Simonetta," pp. 518-520. Maulde La Clavière gives some examples of infantile codes, easily read—one could scarcely even say "broken"—by anyone with any interest in the matter. *La diplomatie au temps de Machiavel*, III, 132.

[174] Perret, "Règles de Cicco Simonetta."

[175] Maulde La Clavière, *La diplomatie au temps de Machiavel*, III, 134, n. 1.

[176] Serguiev, "La diplomatie de l'antiquité," p. 50; Ganshof, *Le Moyen Age*, pp. 43-44, 278-279.

[177] Cessi, *Deliberazioni del Maggior Consiglio*, II, 102. The statutory collection of Perugia of 1342 required of returning ambassadors a written report. Angelini, *La diplomazia comunale a Perugia*, p. 41.

quirement of a written report was not so firm.[178] The report could be a very brief and simple account of the response to the mission,[179] but a more complete narrative account became more common in the later period.[180] A *procès-verbal* was sometimes employed in lieu of a written report for especially formal proceedings.[181]

In Venice there became established an "ancient and laudable custom"[182] that a returning diplomat should deliver a rather special kind of report called his *relazione*. Venetian statesmen and modern scholars have found in these *relazioni* not just reports on specific missions, but comprehensive descriptions of political, economic, social, and military conditions of the states from which Venetian ambassadors returned.[183] The Republic was most anxious that as full an exchange of views and information as possible should occur between its envoys and the Senate,[184] and the *relazione* was the chief means by which the Senate gained access to a mass of background information not necessarily related directly to the specific mission. The anonymous French author of the *Traité du gouvernement de Venise* about 1500 noted with admiration how newly elected Venetian ambassadors could become well informed and instructed upon all things concerning the land to which they were assigned by reading the registers of *relazioni*.[185]

Unfortunately, not many *relazioni* prior to 1500 are extant. Until 1425 they probably were not registered, and the registers of written *relazioni*, which were required to be kept after that date, were in all likelihood among the documents destroyed in the tragic fires in the ducal palace in 1574 and 1577. Sanuto, however, gives us summaries of some *relazioni* from the very end of our period, and it is still hoped that a few copies or rough drafts retained by the ambassadors themselves may have survived in private collections of documents. It has been contended by some that a report of Marsilio Zorzi, *baiulo* in Syria from 1240 to 1243, constitutes the earliest

178 Degert, "Louis XI et ses ambassadeurs," p. 18.

179 Archives du Nord, Lille, Chambre des Comptes, B 1263, nos. 3680-3684; A.S.F., Signori—Carteggi—Rapporti e relazioni di oratori, I, 1r. The date of the Florentine document is 1385.

180 Maulde La Clavière, *La diplomatie au temps de Machiavel*, III, 382-383. E.g., A.S.F., Signori—Carteggi—Rapporti e relazioni di oratori, III, 2rv. Louis XI particularly liked detailed reports. Degert, "Louis XI et ses ambassadeurs," pp. 17-18.

181 Delcambre, "Recueil de documents relatifs aux relations du Hainaut et de la France," pp. 44-48.

182 Girolamo Donato, ambassador to Rome, began his *relazione* of 20 June 1499: "Secondo l'antiqua et laudabele consuetudine di questa ben instituta republicha, referirò serenissimo principe, la legatiom mia." Sanuto, *Diarii*, II, col. 835. Antonibon's date conflicts with Sanuto's.

183 Antonibon, *Relazioni di ambasciatori veneti*, p. 14. Also note quotations on p. 13, n. 1, from Reumont, Ranke, and Morandi on the value of the *relazioni*.

184 Ambassadors had temporary seats in the Senate from their nomination until their departure and for a period after their return. Da Mosto, *L'Archivio di Stato di Venezia*, p. 35.

185 Perret, *Relations de la France avec Venise*, II, 292.

surviving *relazione*.[186] In the first place, this argument rests upon the incorrect assertion that the *baiulo* was an ambassador.[187] In any case, the document on its face is not a true *relazione*. The headnote reads: "Marsilius Georgius, *baiulus* of the Venetians in Syria, narrates in order many things done in that place . . . ," and that is precisely what follows. He recounts in order his negotiations concerning the privileges of Venetians in Syria, which, by the way, is precisely the sort of negotiation which might be expected of a consul instead of an ambassador. There follows a list of the possessions and rights of Venice in Tyre.[188] This is a valuable document beyond doubt, but it lacks the generalized, didactic character of the later *relazioni*, which discuss geography, economics, personalities, and many other matters of general interest. Albèri on sounder ground accepted as the earliest surviving *relazione* that of Zaccaria Contarini in 1492 upon his return from France. It is preserved in a contemporary copy in the Museo Correr.[189] There can be no doubt concerning its character, and it is the earliest extant document that ought to be accepted as a true *relazione*.

The origin of the *relazione*, however, goes back to a law of the *Maggior Consiglio* of 23 December 1268 requiring returning ambassadors to have written within fifteen days the responses made to their mission and whatever they might have learned and heard said which they deemed to the profit and honor of Venice.[190] The *relazione*, at least insofar as it was unique to Venice and insofar as it has any unique importance, was not a mere report on the ambassador's activities, but a more generalized account of whatever information the ambassador could provide which might be useful to Venice. The next great milestone in the history of the *relazioni* was a Senatorial decree of 1425 repeating the requirement that *relazioni* must be given in

[186] Georg Martin Thomas, "Die ältesten Verordnungen der Venezianer für auswärtige Angelegenheiten," *Abhandlungen der philosophisch-philologischen Classe der Königlich Bayerischen Akademie der Wissenschaften*, XIII (1875), p. 144; Volpi, *Venezia e i suoi ambasciatori*, p. 50; Selmi, "Diplomazia stabile di Venezia," p. 13.

[187] *Supra*, pp. 80-82.

[188] Tafel and Thomas, *Urkunden*, II, 351-360.

[189] Albèri, *Relazioni*, serie I, IV, 2. Also Ganshof, *Le Moyen Age*, pp. 278-279, and Andreas, *Staatskunst und Diplomatie der Venezianer*, p. 66. Alfred von Reumont, *Dei diplomati italiani e delle relazioni diplomatiche italiane dal 1260 al 1550* (Padova, 1850), p. 53, was wrong on the earliest surviving *relazione*, but he corrected himself in the revised edition. Reumont, *Diplomazia*, pp. 71, 76.

[190] Cessi, *Deliberazioni del Maggior Consiglio*, II, 102. Hale misdates this document 1288, probably through a misprint. "International Relations in the West," p. 266. The idea that a *written* report was not required until the act of 1425 (Baschet, *Les archives de Venise*, pp. 346-347, and Andreas, *Staatskunst und Diplomatie der Venezianer*, pp. 65-66) is contradictory to the very words of the act of 1268. I can see only special pleading in Nicolà Nicolini's attempt to find in the reports of the consuls of Apulia the origin of the fifteenth-century *relazioni*. *Il consolato generale veneto nel regno di Napoli*, p. 60. According to her own words, the consul was required *riferire sinteticamente sul suo biennio di consolato*. This would constitute only a rather lengthy report, not a *relazione*.

writing and adding that the document should be turned over to the Chancellery to be copied in a volume devoted specially to that purpose. The background information contained in *relazioni* would thus become available to future statesmen, as well as those who were present at the reading.[191] Assuming that this decree was effective, copies of the *relazioni* from this date must have been destroyed in the sixteenth-century conflagrations.

In a republic as complex as Venice, the question of the recipients of the *relazioni* becomes almost as important as the fact that they were given. A law of 1296 complains that ambassadors had recently failed to conform to the custom that they should report upon their missions in the councils in which they had been commissioned, but had contented themselves with reporting before the doge and his councilors. Henceforth they must report in the council which had appointed them, and that council must hear them within fifteen days.[192] A senatorial decree of 1349 consolidating earlier legislation on the relationship between the doge and his councilors with *nuncii* provided that they might not hear *relazioni* without first summoning the heads of the Forty.[193] The ducal oath of the ill-fated Marin Faliero prohibited his hearing *relazioni* without the presence of at least four of the Council of Six and two of the three heads of the Forty, except that he and his councilors might proceed if the heads of the Forty failed to appear when summoned.[194] By 1401 the bad habit of reporting only to a restricted body, in this case the *Collegio* (doge, Council of Six, heads of the Forty, and the *sapientes*), had again prevailed. In order that the councils should be properly informed, the law again required that ambassadors and other *nuncii* sent abroad must give their reports in the councils in which they had been named. They were also required by law to return to the Republic all cor-

[191] A.S.V., Senato, Misti, LV, 117v (118v). Andreas calls attention to an act of 1533, outside the scope of this book, which repeated the requirement of written *relazioni*. *Staatskunst und Diplomatie der Venezianer*, pp. 65-66. The Venetians possessed a long-standing respect for records. This can be discerned in an act (nondiplomatic) of the Great Council in 1166. "Whenever affairs of such a kind are transacted that it is important to transmit the memory of them to posterity they should be tied down in the bond of writing, lest in the course of time according to the old habit of memory one should recall something in doubt with renewed spite and produce controversy from peace." Cessi, *Deliberazioni del Maggior Consiglio*, I, 247. For other examples see pp. 249 and 250.

[192] Cessi, *Deliberazioni del Maggior Consiglio*, III, 403; Thomas, "Die älteste Verordnungen," p. 107; A.S.V., Avogaria di Comun, Cerberus, 5v, no. 41. Antonibon regards this, not the act of 1268, as the beginning of the requirement of a *relazione* in writing. *Relazioni di ambasciatori veneti*, p. 13. Selmi believes that this is the beginning of the requirement of a *relazione* in any form, and that the act of 1425 first required it to be in writing. "Diplomazia stabile di Venezia," p. 16. The latter, however, was original only in requiring that a register be kept.

[193] A.S.V., Senato, Misti, xxv, 49rv (49rv).

[194] A.S.V., Maggior Consiglio, Novella, 30v (41v). In "Early Venetian Legislation Concerning Foreign Ambassadors," I have incorrectly dated this document 1314.

respondence connected with the embassy, lest such documents should fall into the hands of foreigners.[195] This law was honored, at least sometimes, for Sanuto records a summary of the *relazione* of Marco Dandolo, ambassador to Milan, delivered before the *Collegio* on 6 May 1497, then repeated in the Senate on 11 May. It was, he says, much praised. In 1449, he records another summary of a *relazione* given in the *Collegio* and the Senate for which the orator was praised "according to custom."[196] The "Traité du Gouvernement de Venise" reports that the doge responded to the *relazione* before the *Collegio* and the Senate by offering praise to the ambassadors if they deserved it, "a thing of which Venetian gentlemen take great account."[197]

As far as is known, the true *relazione* was unique in Venice.[198] Other ambassadors gave reports, of course, but nowhere else is found the synthetic description of the land to which the ambassador had been sent with all sorts of background information which would not only inform the policy makers of the results of the mission, but educate them in a much more comprehensive way. Maulde La Clavière claimed to have found *relazioni* in Florence, but did not provide documentation.[199] In the series called *Rapporti e Relazioni di Oratori* there are a number of documents called *relazioni*, but these are similar to those called *rapporti* and bear no resemblance to Venetian *relazioni*. Some of them indeed, especially those involving missions with a number of specifically assigned tasks, are in the form of lists, "*Prima* . . . , *Secondo* . . . , *Terzo* . . ." etc., containing the assignments and the results. Nothing could be further from a true *relazione*.

The French *Traité* written about the end of the Middle Ages gives an outline of the contents of a *relazione*:

> He speaks first of the things he has done and treated during the said embassy. Subsequently he speaks of the person of the princes and lords

[195] A.S.V., Maggior Consiglio, Leona, 118v (122v). We know that this last provision was not fully obeyed, for many such documents survived in private archives.

[196] Sanuto, *Diarii*, I, col. 615, and II, col. 923. The "Traité du Gouvernement de Venise" states that if there were two or more envoys, the youngest was responsible for reporting to the *Collegio*, the eldest to the Senate. Perret, *Relations de la France avec Venise*, II, 292. I have not verified this. Also, it was not necessarily the Senate (*Conseil de Priés*) in which the *relazione* was made, but in whatever council named the ambassador.

[197] *Ibid.*, II, 292.

[198] I share the view of Antonibon and other Venetian authorities. *Relazioni di ambasciatori veneti*, pp. 13, 17. Also Reumont, *Diplomazia*, p. 74.

[199] *La diplomatie au temps de Machiavel*, III, pp. 386-388. Perhaps one should hesitate to point out flaws in a work of such erudition, but the inadequacy of the apparatus is extremely annoying. J. E. Neale did find one English relation of 1609, but it was avowedly an imitation of Venetian models and did not set a precedent. "The Diplomatic Envoy," *History*, XIII (1928-1929), 216. Quazza also claims genuine *relazioni* for Mantua in the second half of the *Cinquecento*, which lies beyond the scope of the present study. *La diplomazia gonzaghesca*, p. 32.

> where they have been sent, of his wife and of his children, if he has any. Later he speaks of the intention and will, according to his opinion, which the said princes and lords have, as much towards the *Signoria* as towards others. He speaks also of their ordinary and extraordinary revenue, and similarly of their expenses, as much in time of peace as in time of war, of their council, of those who have some authority with the said princes and lords, and even of those who are loved. And they speak also of other lords who are under their jurisdiction and of the disposition that they have toward the said lords . . . .

The author adds that when an ambassador was appointed to a mission, he would read the registers of *relazioni* in order to go to his task "well informed and instructed concerning all things."[200] Francesco Antonibon reported another document originating in the Council of Ten in the sixteenth century and outlining for the benefit of orators what should be included in their *relazioni*. The influence of the Renaissance in Venice seems to have given the *relazione* by this time a more literary character. According to this document, it should describe the site of the province, giving both its ancient and modern names and its boundaries. Its subdivisions, its most important city, famous ports, fortresses, episcopal sees, principal rivers, mountains and forests should be described. One should treat of the climate, the temperature, rainfall, fertility, mines, animals. If the country is mountainous, forested, swampy, and if there is any noteworthy effect of nature, it should be reported. One ought to describe its inhabitants, their costumes, color, stature, disposition of mind and religion. The defenses by land and by sea must be described. Their crafts and their commerce and the riches of both nobility and people should be included. Finally, the orator ought to come to the prince himself: his ancestry, person, life, customs, income and expenses, whether he is loved by his subjects, the guard that he maintains, the grandeur of his court, and with what princes he has friendship or enmity.[201]

There is something of the Renaissance rhetorical exercise in the sixteenth-

[200] Perret, *Relations de la France avec Venise*, II, 292.

[201] *Relazioni di ambasciatori veneti*, p. 16. Volpi, *Venezia e i suoi ambasciatori*, pp. 48-49, derived much the same list of desired contents of the *relazione* from *commissioni*. Antonibon, *op.cit.*, p. 23, contrasts *relazioni* and *dispacci*. It is true that the *relazione* was a more public document, and some things, therefore had to be withheld. On the other hand, however, the *dispaccio* was concerned with the matter of the moment, and does not provide the overview characteristic of the *relazione*. Maulde La Clavière points out that Machiavelli recommended that experienced diplomats write seldom, but at length, providing a much broader picture than was typical of dispatches. *La diplomatie au temps de Machiavel*, III, 141-143. I do not regard this as good advice, and I am sure that governments would have appreciated more frequent correspondence.

century outline given above, but at least until the end of the fifteenth century *relazioni* contained little that was for display alone and much that could be useful. The earliest surviving *relazione* of 1492 is an excellent example.[202] Zaccaria Contarini, ambassador just returned from France, begins by saying:

> My duty . . . is to refer to your Sublimity all the comings and goings of this our legation. And because on the one hand I propose to touch upon all those things that I recognize as worthy and suitable of notice, and on the other I desire, in order not to be either lengthy or tedious, to use the most brief and restricted form of words which seems possible to me, therefore, without any exordium and divisions of speaking I will commence to speak as best I know to be able to satisfy your Sublimity.[203]

And this is precisely what Contarini proceeded to do, although the *relazione* as printed is 23 pages long and we do not even have a complete copy. He tells of his journey to Paris, and of his reception in Milan, Pavia, and Savoy on the way. A brief description of Savoy, its income and its military preparedness is included, but he does not give any details on Milan, because a Venetian ambassador was resident there. Then, after describing his reception in Paris, he undertakes to describe the persons of the king and the queen, the grandeur of the kingdom, the government, income and expenses, armies and other preparations for war, the enmities that the king has and the means he has for freeing himself of them, and finally of the parties and enmities that exist in the court. His description of Charles VIII is priceless:

> The Majesty of the King of France is twenty-two years of age, small and badly formed in his person, ugly of face, with eyes great and white and much more apt to see too little than enough, an aquiline nose much larger and fatter than it ought to be, also fat lips, which he continually holds open, and he has some spasmodic movements of hand which appear very ugly, and he is slow in speech. According to my opinion, which could be quite wrong, I hold certainly that he is worth too little both in body and in natural capacity.[204]

Contarini goes on to discuss the foreign problems of the king and, in particular, the relations between him and his potential enemies. In the long account he includes a list of pensioners of Charles VIII who would be prepared to betray their master in favor of Venice. Some of these he has

202 Albèri, *Relazioni*, ser. I, IV, 3-26.
203 *Ibid.*, p. 3.
204 *Ibid.*, p. 15.

met, others he has not, but he claims to be certain of the accuracy of his information.[205]

By the end of the Middle Ages the mission of an ambassador was documented from before his departure (with letters of credence, procurations, instructions, and safe-conducts), during its course (with letters and dispatches exchanged, and always with the possibility of new or revised credences, procurations or instructions), and after its conclusion (with reports and in Venice *relazioni*). Some of these were intended for the guidance of the ambassador, some to inform the other party of his appointment and powers, others to inform and enlighten the government and its servants, both at the present and in the future. The *forms* of communication seem quite adequate, in some cases superb; what was lacking was only an instrument for increasing the speed of communication.

[205] The summaries in Sanuto's *Diarii* prove that Contarini's *relazione* was characteristic of those of the last decade of the fifteenth century. For example, see the *relazione* of Alvise Sagudino, a secretary, returned from Constantinople in 1496. *Diarii*, I, cols. 397-400. See also *ibid.*, cols. 405-408 and 438, for a *relazione* of Francesco Foscari, ambassador to Germany. Some of the summaries in Sanuto listed by Antonibon as *relazioni* appear to me to be only reports of the more usual kind, informing the principal concerning the mission, but lacking the distinguishing characteristics of the Venetian *relazioni*. E.g., *ibid.*, I, cols. 735-736, 858-859. The same may be said of the so-called *relazione* of Francesco Barbaro in 1497. Domenico Malipiero, "Annali veneti, ordinati e abbreviati dal senatore Francesco Longo," in *Archivio storico italiano*, VII, ii (1844), 636-640. The document offered in translation as *A Relation, or rather a true account, of the Island of England; with sundry particulars of the customs of these people, and of the royal revenues, under King Henry the seventh, about the year 1500*, trans. from the Italian with notes by Charlotte Augusta Sneyd (London, 1847), is likely not a true diplomatic *relazione*. It is an amazing document, almost fifty pages long in print, filled with useful, well-organized information and idle gossip. The diplomatic envoy did not normally use his *relazione* to inform his hearers on the qualities of English ale and the virtues (or lack thereof) of English ladies.

CHAPTER VI

PERSONNEL AND EXPENSES

The manner of selection of diplomatic envoys differed, of course, according to the type of government and from one century to another. The ambassadors of monarchies were normally named by the king, often, but not necessarily, with the advice and consent of his council.[1] Among the Italian republics the process of selecting ambassadors was much more complex. A Florentine act of 1408, for example, provided that election by the Priors and the *Vexilliferum* of Justice was not sufficient, but that the *Gonfalonieri* of the Societies of the People and the twelve *boni viri* of the Commune (or at least two-thirds of them) must also participate. In 1494 it was required that orators should be elected by the *Signoria* and the *Collegi* and the two councils of the People and the Commune.[2] Under the Medici we also know that ambassadors officially representing the Republic and personal envoys chosen by the Medici functioned side by side. In Venice a great variety of methods of election prevailed. In the thirteenth century the Great Council, the doge and the Council of Six, the three Heads of the Forty and the Forty itself were often involved. In one case the Great Council determined that an ambassador should be elected by the "electors for the year."[3] From the fourteenth century onward the Senate gained a greater and greater role in diplomacy, while the Forty became exclusively a judicial council. By 1497 the Senate was so overburdened with elections that it provided that all elections except those for specified offices, among which were ambassadorships, should be treated in the Great Council.[4] Although it is clear that by this time most elections to ambassadorial office were conducted in the Senate, the laws requiring an ambassador to give his *relazione* in the council in which he was elected indicate that some variety remained. The Ten, for example, could also dispatch ambassadors. The responsibility for electing ambassadors could even be delegated to private citizens, as it was by the Great Council in 1311, when injured merchants received authority to name *nuncii* to represent the Commune before the king of Aragon and his Council to claim recompense for goods which had been seized.[5]

[1] Degert, "Louis XI et ses ambassadeurs," pp. 7-8. In both England and Scotland in the fifteenth century, the advice and consent of the council was usually sought.

[2] Maulde La Clavière, *La diplomatie au temps de Machiavel*, III, 425-428.

[3] Cessi, *Deliberazioni del Maggior Consiglio*, III, 234.

[4] A.S.V., Senato, Terra, XIII, 8v (10v).

[5] A.S.V., Maggior Consiglio, Presbiter, 39v (40v).

In considering those who were eligible to become ambassadors, a distinction should again be made between monarchical governments and those of the Italian city-states. Theoretically at least, the freedom of the monarch and his council to select envoys was absolute—though, as we shall see, an ambassador of insufficient social rank might be rejected by the recipient. Some discussion concerning the employment of clerics in secular diplomacy appears in the law books,[6] but there is no doubt whatsoever that churchmen very frequently appeared as ambassadors, especially of the non-Italian powers. In Venice the word "ambassador" was reserved for envoys drawn from the nobility and required to be at least 38 years old.[7] Envoys of lesser status, including the secretaries of the Chancellery who were often employed, were called *nuncii*. Holders of office in Venice were not allowed to accept distant embassies without yielding their offices. Venice also prohibited that ambassadors chosen for the same mission should be related to each other—probably a wise check on a possible conflict of interest.[8] Even women could function as ambassadors—although the only examples discovered involve wives or daughters of princely houses. Isabella of Portugal, duchess of Burgundy, was very active in diplomacy on her husband's behalf. Nys cites embassies of Lucrezia, wife of Piero de Medici, of Isabella d'Este, wife of Ludovico Sforza, and the accreditation of Catherine of Aragon to represent her parents before her father-in-law, Henry VII.[9] Even a captive was sometimes employed—after all, he was already in the presence of the enemy—and under such circumstances arose the anomaly of a solemn reception tendered to a prisoner.[10]

Medieval diplomacy only very gradually evolved from a personal to an institutional level. In the early Middle Ages the sense of national identity was weak, and although nationalism developed to a considerable extent in the fourteenth and fifteenth centuries, the feeling that a diplomat ought to be a subject of the state he represented came into being very slowly.[11] In

[6] E.g., Gondisalvus de Villadiego, *Tractatus*, Pars II, Q. I, p. 55.

[7] Antonibon, *Relazioni di ambasciatori veneti*, p. 12, n. 2; Reumont, *Diplomati italiani*, p. 47.

[8] Cessi, *Deliberazioni del Maggior Consiglio*, II, 45, no. VIII; II, 234; II, 250; A.S.V., Avogaria di Comun, Bifrons, 47v, no. I. Certain officials could not be elected under any circumstances. Rubric only. The original is lost, but its validity is documented by references in other documents. Cessi, *Deliberazioni del Maggior Consiglio*, II, 392. Law on relatives. A.S.V., Avogaria del Comun, Cerberus, 23v, no. 6; Buzzati, "Diritto diplomatico veneziano," p. 229, but dated November 31!

[9] *Origines du droit international*, p. 336; Rymer, *Foedera*, V, i, 161-163 and 175-176.

[10] Maulde La Clavière, *La diplomatie au temps de Machiavel*, I, 214.

[11] One can, of course, find much evidence of nationalism long before 1300. See, for example, the triumphant return toward Paris after the Battle of Bouvines of the army of Philip Augustus, leading in chains his captives to the accompaniment of the cheers and jeers of celebrating Frenchmen newly awakening to the emotional impact of nationalism. Luchaire, "Louis VII—Philippe-Auguste—Louis VIII," pp. 196-197. On the other hand, although the division of

early Russian diplomacy Alexander Riasanovsky calls attention to the "Scandinavian, Slavic (East and West), German, Anglo-Saxon, Turkic" ambassadors employed by Kiev, especially the Swedes of the famous mission of 838-839 of the *Annales Bertiniani*.[12] We know that foreigners were used frequently in the West also.[13] Sometimes there were special reasons of convenience for the accreditation of foreigners. The simplest case is that of the reverse letter of credence by which envoys were returned to their original principal as representatives of the original recipient.[14] Usually these fulfilled only the rather mechanical function of communication. Somewhat different from the simple reverse letters of credence was the role of those envoys whose true responsibility appears to be to both parties equally. Count Florence of Holland seems to have represented both sides in negotiating a treaty between Edward I and Adolf of Nassau, although he appears in an English procuration along with the bishops of Dublin and Durham and Hugh le Despenser, whose loyalties were clearly English.[15] A Scottish merchant, Henry Carwy, along with two other envoys, Jacques Louchard[16] and Gilles of Bruges, made a payment to the king of Scotland on the occasion of the marriage of the count of Flanders' daughter to the king's son on Christmas Day 1283. Two months later the king requested that additional payments be made to the same Henry Carwy.[17] Sometimes a mission was entrusted for the sake of convenience and economy to foreigners who were already present at the court of the recipient or on their way to it. In 1487 the Lord Prior of the English *langue* of the Hospitallers, on his way to

Europe behind the Roman and Avignonese popes during the Great Schism is often cited as a manifestation of strong nationalism in opposition to earlier values, Charles Leon Tipton recently has shown that Richard II and Henry IV offered no opposition to the adherence by the English *langue* of the Hospitallers to the French pope, but in fact defended the Hospitallers' papal policy. "The English Langue of the Knights Hospitallers during the Great Schism," unpublished Ph.D. dissertation (University of Southern California, 1964), pp. 47-54, 73-74. This would scarcely be characteristic of strong nationalism.

[12] Alexander V. Riasanovsky, "The Embassy of 838 Revisited: Some Comments in Connection with a 'Normanist' Source on Early Russian History," *Jahrbuch für Geschichte Osteuropas*, x (1962), 11-12.

[13] E.g., Musciato Guidi of Florence was employed frequently, especially on missions having to do with financial matters, by Philip IV. Ganshof, *Le Moyen Age*, p. 267; Delcambre, "Recueil de documents relatifs aux relations du Hainaut et de la France," p. 125; Funck-Brentano, *Philippe le Bel en Flandre*, pp. 254-255.

[14] Kern, *Acta Imperii, Angliae et Franciae*, p. 69, no. 99; A.S.F., Archivio diplomatico—Riformagioni—Atti publici, xvi, 59v (58v).

[15] Van den Berg, *Oorkondenboek*, ii, 404, no. 880.

[16] J. Lestocquoy, "Deux familles de financiers d'Arras, Louchard et Wagon," *Revue belge de philologie et d'histoire*, xxxii (1954), 61-66, discusses Jacques Louchard. See Georges Bigwood, "Les financiers d'Arras: Contribution à l'étude des origines du capitalisme moderne," *Revue belge de philologie et d'histoire*, iii (1924), 492.

[17] Archives du Nord, Lille, Chambre des Comptes, B 403, nos. 2530, 2543, and 2545; Queller, "Diplomatic Personnel," pp. 390-391.

France on a mission for the pope and the Grand Master of Rhodes, received credentials also from Venice.[18] Two Venetian nobles residing in London in 1496 not only received *sindicati* from their own government for completing an alliance with England, but also from the duke of Milan, who found it inconvenient to send his own procurators.[19] Although we have seen that even Venice was not adverse to the use of foreign envoys or to the use of Venetians as envoys by foreign powers, some hint of limitations upon the use of Venetian subjects by other states does appear. A law of 1394 prohibited those Venetians who became *potestates* in other cities to come to Venice as ambassadors. Also the Ventian *baiulo* in Cyprus was not allowed to undertake a mission for that king under color of prohibiting laws and ordinances of Venice.[20] A sense of the exclusive duty of the official toward the Republic was beginning to prevail.

More important than the nationality of an envoy was his social status. Bernard du Rosier pointed out that one should not be assigned an embassy if he was not "suitable" (*dignus*) and personally acceptable to the recipient, while Gondisalvus de Villadiego added that for important negotiations orators of excellent social standing should be sent, for the Holy Scriptures themselves give an example in the Annunciation, not by a mere angel, but an archangel.[21] An embassy of Henry VI to treat of a marriage alliance was headed by a cardinal, the duke of Burgundy, the archbishop of York, a bishop, two earls and a mere lord.[22] Venetians took care to send *sufficientes et solempnes* ambassadors on appropriate occasions.[23] In 1478 they argued in favor of sending joint envoys of high rank and prestige to the pope against their allies, Milan and Florence, who favored the appointment of those of the second order.[24] Venetian embassies are replete with the most illustrious names in Venice: Mocenigo, Contareno, Foscari, Mauroceno, Dandulo, Michael, Lauredano, Bragadino, Venerio, and others. Tommaso Mocenigo was elected doge while he was ambassador to the pope.[25] According to Baschet, no ambassador was named by Venice to any great lord

[18] *Calendar of State Papers. Venetian*, p. 168, no. 523.

[19] A.S.V., Senato, Secreta, XXXVI, 4v (16v).

[20] A.S.V., Maggior Consiglio, Leona, 78v; Senato, Secreta, XXI, 4r (5r).

[21] Bernard du Rosier, *Ambaxiator brevilogus*, p. 7. Gondisalvus de Villadiego, *Tractatus*, Pars II, Q. II, par. 2. "Angel," of course, has as its basic meaning "messenger."

[22] Rymer, *Foedera*, v, i, 30-31.

[23] ". . . prout semper solita est in similibus casibus providerit mittere suos ambaxatores solempnes . . . Vadit pars, ut dicti ambaxatores habeantur sufficientes et solempnes prout exigat conditio dicti facti . . ." A.S.V., Maggior Consiglio, Novella, 93v (104v). The word *solemnis*, often used of ambassadors and embassies, has no juridical significance, but was used only of those embassies involving considerable social and ceremonial value.

[24] Perret, *Relations de la France avec Venise*, II, 155.

[25] A.S.V., Maggior Consiglio, Leona, 231r (236r).

unless he had already received the dignity of the *savi grandi*.[26] Representatives of various classes of society played roles in diplomacy, however, for as Tout said, ". . . the practical medieval mind secured the happy mixture of good breeding and capacity . . . by putting a great nobleman at the head of a foreign embassy, while associating with him a bishop, who had, perhaps, begun life as a chancery clerk, to help out his intelligence, and a chancery clerk or two still on the make, to supply the necessary hard work and technical knowledge."[27] Simple clerks and others of low estate were not used exclusively in a subordinate capacity, however, but were increasingly employed as heads of missions to lesser powers and even on assignments to great powers if the ceremonial requirement was not controlling.[28]

When a mission required an ambassador of high rank who must, at the same time, have the complete trust of the principal, princely governments often solved the personnel problem by calling upon some member of the ruling house. Countess Margaret and Count Guy of Flanders in the thirteenth century made great use of the family for these reasons in conducting their diplomacy.[29] Romolo Quazza has indicated how membership in the Casa Gonzaga lent particular solemnity to orators drawn even from its collateral branches.[30] It is probable that no other choice of personnel could equal this in ceremonial value.

One of the most fruitful sources of diplomatic personnel was the clergy. The religious aura which surrounded medieval diplomacy called for participation of the clergy.[31] Until a well-educated class of laymen arose, moreover, clerics were chosen for this, as for other governmental tasks, because they were most qualified by education. The advanced secular culture of Italy, therefore, explains the relative lack of clerical ambassadors of Italian states other than the papacy. Ecclesiastics in government, of course, were in many cases simply bureaucrats by profession enrolled in Holy Orders as a means of reaping the reward of benefices for their labors. Those seeking ecclesiastical preferment were particularly eager to serve on embassies to Rome, where their advancement might be gained from the pope, as well as from the prince whom they served.[32] On some occasions the expense of

[26] Baschet, *Les archives de Venise*, pp. 383-384.

[27] Thomas Frederick Tout, *The Collected Papers of Thomas Frederick Tout*, 3 vols. (Manchester, 1932-1934), III, 203. Quoted in Cuttino, *English Diplomatic Administration*, p. 19.

[28] Queller, "Diplomatic Personnel," passim; Luchaire, *Manuel*, p. 535; Da Mosto, *L'Archivio di Stato di Venezia*, II, 25.

[29] Queller, "Diplomatic Personnel," pp. 97 and 421.

[30] *La diplomazia gonzaghesca*, p. 25.

[31] Frantz Funck-Brentano, "Caractère religieux de la diplomatie au XIIIe siècle," *Revue d'histoire diplomatique*, I (1887), 113-125.

[32] Quazza, *La diplomazia gonzaghesca*, pp. 24-25.

an ecclesiastical ambassador might be less,[33] although an embassy of any ceremonial importance was costly by nature, regardless of the character of its head. Ecclesiastical garb, moreover, offered an additional factor of safety along routes that were none too secure.[34] The cardinals themselves often represented their home states or others as ambassadors at the Roman curia. (Often also they received large retainers to see to the interests of secular powers in a less overt fashion.) Bishops were among the most common diplomats of high rank, but provosts and deans of chapters, cathedral canons, and chaplains also appear among the ambassadors of more modest status. Abbots served to combine high rank, a semblance at least of sanctity and a very significant guarantee of security against violence.[35] Simple monks also served as envoys—and some not so simple, witness Savonarola's embassy to Charles VIII.[36] Even Venice, possibly the most secular of medieval powers, on occasion employed monks in diplomacy, although without the title of ambassador and probably in an attempt to keep the state officially uncommitted in the initiation of negotiations for peace.[37]

Envoys were also selected from the various ranks of the lay nobility for appropriate missions. The greater nobles offered ceremonial value comparable to that of a bishop or a great abbot and were commonly found at the head of an embassy. Among these and especially suitable for such tasks were the great officers—marshall, grand butler, and the like—of a princely household. Lesser nobles also possessed prestige sufficient for all but the most solemn missions and were very commonly employed. Such people as castellans and *baillis* also served.

Men of the middle class grew increasingly important in diplomacy during the period under consideration. From the late thirteenth century—possibly earlier in Italy—legists and canonists began to play an important role, although they did not normally possess the social status to head major embassies, but served in a supporting capacity there or as the heads of less solemn missions.[38] Imperial or papal notaries also were used in their professional capacity, but not usually as heads of missions. Secretaries,

[33] *Ibid.*; Commynes, *Mémoires*, Liv. VIII, Chap. XXIII, II, 365-366. The author adds that clerics were also used through hypocrisy and pretence of religion.

[34] Cuttino, *English Diplomatic Administration*, p. 90.

[35] When Guy of Flanders finally decided to defy Philip IV in 1297, the bearers of the defiance were the abbots of Floreffe and Gembloux. Limburg-Stirum, *Codex diplomaticus Flandriae*, I, 132-133, no. 40. Professor Van Werveke called my attention to the fact that the location of their monasteries in Guy's marquisate of Namur, an imperial fief, not French, also added to their security.

[36] H.-François Delaborde, *L'expédition de Charles VIII en Italie* (Paris, 1888), p. 442.

[37] A.S.V., Senato, Secreta, XX, 3r (4r).

[38] E.g., Hugues de La Celle, lawyer of Philip IV. Funck-Brentano, "Documents relatifs aux formes diplomatiques aux XIIIe et XIVe siècles," p. 235, n. 2.

too, came to play an important part in diplomacy, both beyond the Alps[39] and in Italy. They were educated, trusted, dependent upon the state for their careers and, through their familiarity with the principal's correspondence, apt to be possessed of an unusual background in the matters under concern. To a lesser extent clerks possessed similar advantages and began to have a greater part in diplomacy from the late thirteenth century. Particularly for missions of a financial character, the clerk, usually called the receiver, who had risen to the head of the financial administration, was employed with advantage. Sometimes very minor members of the household were used, as when Charles IV, king of the Romans, sent two *jongleurs* to Strasbourg, or when Louis XI dispatched his barber to the Low Countries.[40] That merchants of the Italian republics served as ambassadors need hardly be mentioned, but among the princely states of the North they also had their role. In most cases their names are virtually unknown, but among the merchant-diplomats was the great Jacques Coeur.[41]

With the coming of the Renaissance and the new emphasis upon oratory, poets, scholars, and other men of letters became highly valued as diplomats. Among Italians we find Dante, Petrarch, Boccaccio, Latini, Machiavelli, and, as secretary of an embassy, Tasso. French kings employed Eustache Des Champs, the friend of Chaucer; Alain Chartier, the orator; Philippe de Commynes, so often cited in the present work, who should probably be classed as a professional diplomat and amateur historian; Guillaume Budé; and, as secretaries, Dolet, Ronsard, and Joachim du Bellay. The English used Chaucer, Sir Thomas Wyatt, and Sir Philip Sidney, while the Scots employed Sir David Lyndesay.[42]

If an ambassador of sufficient prestige was not named, it could be construed as disrespectful of the power to which he was sent and, since a lesser man required a smaller retinue, degrading penny-pinching on the part of the principal. When, in 1286, Edward I sent two insignificant persons in haste to Rome to gain confirmation of a treaty with Philip IV which the French king would not regard as binding until confirmed, Edward apologized for their insignificance, but explained that there had not

[39] L. B. Dibben, "Secretaries in the Fourteenth and Fifteenth Centuries," *E.H.R.*, xxv (1910), 431-433; Ganshof, *Le Moyen Age*, p. 279.

[40] Commynes, *Mémoires*, Liv. v, Chap. xiv, i, 408-409; Ganshof, *Le Moyen Age*, pp. 266-267.

[41] Perret, *Relations de la France avec Venise*, i, 186, n. 1.

[42] Jusserand, "The School for Ambassadors," pp. 9-10; Reumont, *Diplomati italiani*, pp. 12-15; Serguiev, "La diplomatie de l'antiquité," p. 73. It is interesting to note an eleventh-century prototype of the Renaissance orator: "Fuit autem in capella Johannis episcopi (of Moravia) clericus nomine Hagno, vir Teutonicus, philosophie domesticus, Tulliane eloquentie alumnus . . . ," assigned as an ambassador in 1072-1073. Cosmas of Prague, *Chronica Boemorum*, pp. 122-123.

been time to choose more solemn envoys.[43] Clement V on one occasion expressed his displeasure to Philip IV that the king had sent to him someone of humble status, who had traveled on foot, and warned him to send henceforth more suitable envoys.[44] Not only would additional time have been necessary to find magnates or prelates willing to go, but much more time would have been consumed in providing a suitable retinue with all the necessary trappings. Pius II simply rejected the imperial ambassadors sent to the Congress of Mantua, declaring that although they "were eminent enough, personally acceptable to the pope and invested with full powers," they lacked sufficient prestige for the occasion.[45] Edward III and his council took affront at Charles V's defiance sent by the hands of a kitchen varlet, for wars between great princes ought to be declared by prelates or barons or, at least, by knights.[46] One could scarcely reject an embassy of defiance, of course.

The social status of those selected as diplomatic envoys did tend to change with the rise of monarchy, bureaucracy, and the middle class. The transition has been discovered in Flanders, for example, in the course of the thirteenth century. A progressive transfer of diplomatic activity occurred from the hereditary members of the ancient feudal court to the new councilors freely elected by the ruler and to his professional administrators. Toward the end of the century the majority of missions were entrusted to professional civil servants. On the social plane, of course, this meant a transfer of responsibility from the great nobility to the middle class. Almost all the diplomatic agents of early thirteenth-century Flanders were drawn from among the members of the great houses. In mid-century an emphasis upon the use of lesser nobles, bishops, and, above all, simple clerks, can be noticed, while the great nobility almost disappeared. These trends increased by the end of the century, while new classes, townsmen, and professionally trained lawyers and notaries made their appearance.[47]

The *Risposti verbali di oratori* of Florence for a little over one-third of the fifteenth century provides an easy opportunity to study the status of

[43] Clifford, *Knight of Great Renown*, p. 91. In the same year Edward also apologized to the pope for sending to him a mere knight and a clerk, but the urgency of the business was again his excuse. *C.C.R.*, *Edward I* (*1279-1288*), p. 431. Henry III excused the fact that his envoys to the count of Toulouse were not *solempniores* only because of the peril of the roads. Rymer, *Foedera*, I, i, 96.

[44] Mollat, "La diplomatie pontificale," p. 507.

[45] Pius II, *Commentaries*, trans. by Florence Alden Gragg with introduction and notes by Leona C. Gabel, in Smith College Studies in History, XX (1 and 2), XXV (1-4), XXX, XXXV, XLIII (Northampton, Mass., 1937-), p. 204.

[46] Froissart, *Oeuvres*, VII, 305-308.

[47] Queller, "Diplomatic Personnel," p. 422. A detailed and quantitative analysis is given in the article and need not be repeated here.

ambassadors received in Florence. The following figures, however, provide only a sampling (and possibly not even a random sampling), for sometimes only the speaker is named while his colleagues are ignored and the title or status of those named is not always given. Nonetheless the figures are instructive. Twenty-nine (31 per cent) of those given some title were designated as jurisconsults or doctors of laws, while another two (2 per cent) were called knights and jurisconsults and yet another was both a doctor of laws and deacon of a church. Twenty-six (28 per cent) are designated as knights, which does not seem to mean much. It may indicate patrician status. Many of them are from Venice. Eight (9 per cent) were bishops, plus one archbishop. Five (5 per cent) were notaries. Three were counts and another three were secretaries. Two were called knights and doctors, two were doctors of medicine, and two chamberlains. One of each of the following appeared: a canon, a lector of a church, a brother, and a son of the principal, a nobleman, a judge and seneschal, a castellan, a doctor, and a merchant. Anyone of middle rank and above could be selected, it appears, and we have seen earlier that even a kitchen varlet might exceptionally be employed. The most striking factor in the list of ambassadors to Florence is the very large number of lawyers.[48]

Although there was an increasing tendency to rely upon professional bureaucrats as envoys, medieval governments did not evolve a professional and specialized foreign service. Certain men, naturally, were repeatedly employed in missions arising out of affairs of which they had experience and knowledge, and, in this sense, there was a sort of *ad hoc* specialization.[49] Commines demonstrates how easy it was for simple and inexperienced ambassadors to be hoodwinked by a clever opponent such as Louis XI.[50] The same names, therefore, appear again and again in diplomatic affairs. Geoffroi de Villehardouin, a skilled and experienced diplomat, appears repeatedly as an envoy of the count of Champagne and the army of crusaders.[51] Esther Clifford Rowland has recently devoted a good volume to Othon de Grandson, a Savoyard knight of middle rank, who spent a great part of his long and active life on diplomatic missions for Edward I and Edward II. She writes that ". . . during the first years of the reign (of

[48] A.S.F., Signori—Legazioni e commissarie: Risposti verbali di oratori. There are two registers covering April 1458 to February 1461 and May 1465 to July 1496. I have omitted from the calculations orators from the pope.

[49] Ganshof, *Le Moyen Age*, pp. 39, 122, 267; Quazza, *La diplomazia gonzaghesca*, p. 9; Cuttino, *English Diplomatic Administration*, p. 95. Bureaucratic specialization appears to have occurred earliest in financial and judicial affairs, which require a high degree of technical competence.

[50] Commynes, *Mémoires*, Liv. v, Chap. xv, I, 424-425.

[51] Queller, "L'évolution du rôle de l'ambassadeur," p. 482, n. 11.

Edward I), Othon was constantly leaving Westminster and returning to report on his success or failure, only to be briefed on a new appointment and sent off again."[52] Philippe de Commines, of course, was a master of the diplomatic art, and I think that we might legitimately call him a professional, although a professional foreign service had not yet become an institution. And ". . . that prince of negotiators and confidential clerks, John Mansel . . ." served Henry III on diplomatic missions of the highest importance all over Western Europe.[53] In its election in 1396 of Johannes Vido to the Venetian chancellorship, the highest office open to a Venetian commoner, the Great Council took note that ". . . from his infancy on he served our government faithfully and indefatigably and with the greatest perils and exertions going very frequently to diverse parts of the world and satisfactorily leading all things committed to him most adequately to the desired end."[54] A similar kind of career was enjoyed in the service of Ludovico Gonzaga by Bertolino Capilupi, who also rose to a chancellorship.[55] Chancery clerks, because of their familiarity with affairs through the process of copying and enrolling documents, were well suited for diplomatic tasks, especially for secondary roles, and many of them became somewhat specialized in foreign affairs. Lawyers, also, as we have noted, were found useful in diplomacy, and Venice is found hiring lawyers because of the great amount of business the Republic has with various communes, kings, and barons.[56] So, although the day of the institutionalized foreign service had not arrived, a number of more or less professional and specialized diplomats can be identified.

Although a few men might achieve successful careers in the diplomatic service of lords or communes, there was considerable resistance to undertaking diplomatic missions because of the sacrifices in time and money and the hazards of medieval travel. Some hint of the problem of finding suitable ambassadors is provided by Henry III's letter to John Maunsell in 1257, recalling that the powerful clerk had advised that someone must be sent to Castile in response to the embassy of the bishop of Jaen. It had been difficult, however, to find anyone willing to go except the abbot of

[52] Clifford, *Knight of Great Renown*, p. 46.

[53] E. F. Jacob, "England: Henry III," *Cambridge Medieval History*, vi, 1st printed, 1929 (Cambridge, Eng.: 1936), 267; Powicke, *The Thirteenth Century*, pp. 116, 118; *Dictionary of National Biography*, Sir Leslie Stephen and Sir Sidney Lee, eds., 22 vols. reprinted (London, 1949-1950), xii, 969-971; Bémont, *Simon de Montfort*, pp. 130-131; Matthew Paris, *Chronica majora*, v, 355.

[54] A.S.V., Maggior Consiglio, Leona, 87v (91v). Another election of a chancellor from among the notaries with mention of his services in diverse parts of the world. *Ibid.*, 145v (150v).

[55] De Tourtier, "Bertolino Capilupi," pp. 321-344.

[56] A.S.V., Maggior Consiglio, Fronesis, 47r (47r) canceled.

Shrewsbury, with whom the king had associated John of Sumercote. Maunsell was asked to instruct them upon what they should say or do.[57] Enthusiasts for medieval Venetian government have propagated a myth of the patriotic and selfless service of the Venetian nobility as ambassadors.[58] Yet the Venetian archives are full of documents proving the great difficulty which the government had in trying to coerce patricians to serve the state at the sacrifice of their own interests. The preamble to a defeated motion in the Senate in 1389 reveals that in spite of two centuries of legislation attempting to coerce nobles to accept offices, the majority of those elected refused.[59] An act of 1443 in the Great Council also complains of the refusal of embassies to the "great detriment and evident prejudice and peril of our state," and warns that the present inconveniences may in the future be of irreparable harm.[60] The series of extant acts by which Venice sought to compel its nobles to accept public office begins in 1185, and throughout the period considered here the effort to impose penalties and define acceptable excuses continued.[61] The dependence of Venice upon commerce for its economic life required that a nobleman could even be excused from his diplomatic duty in order to go abroad on a commercial venture.[62] Many

[57] *C.R.* (*1256-1259*), pp. 149-150. See Queller, "Blanks," p. 490. This is the document mentioning blank parchments sent to Maunsell for any letters he might wish directed to Alfonso.

[58] "Per servire degnamente la Repubblica non pochi 'oratori' n'ebbero dissestato il patrimonio familiare. Ma nessuno venne mai meno al proprio dovere. Amanti della patria, ligi agli ordini, compresi dell'importanza e della necessità dell'ufficio, noi li troviamo sempre alacri, diligenti e premurosi attendere ad esso con tutte le forze, superando disagi, dispendî, contrarietà e difficoltà." Volpi, *Venezia e i suoi ambasciatori*, pp. 45-46. This is typical of the tone of this terrible book. These are not the Venetian patricians known to Lazzarini or to me from the documents.

[59] ". . . pro maiori parte reffutant . . ." A.S.V., Senato, Misti, XL, 146v (151v).

[60] A.S.V., Maggior Consiglio, Ursa, 143v (149v). Also, *ibid.*, 188v (194v). Among published sources F. Nicolini's list of Venetian orators at Naples, 1450-1501, shows many refusals of the office. "Frammenti veneto-napoletani," pp. 9-19.

[61] Cessi, *Deliberazioni del Maggior Consiglio*, I, 252-253. The act does not specifically mention ambassadors, but *aliquo officio nostre curie vel servitio Venecie.* Vittorio Lazzarini devoted a most interesting article to this problem. "Obbligo di assumere pubblici uffici nelle antiche leggi veneziane," *Archivio veneto*, XIX (1936), 184-198. The act of 1185 is described on pp. 192-193. Illness of the elected ambassador or of his father, mother, wife, child, or brother was an acceptable excuse, according to a law of 1286. Cessi, *op.cit.*, I, 142-143; Buzzati, "Diritto diplomatico veneziano," p. 228. Reumont, *Diplomati italiani*, pp. 108-109, refers to an act of the *Maggior Consiglio* of 1280 establishing serious illness as the only excuse. I found no act of that sort in 1280 and it is not included in Cessi's list, *op.cit.*, II, 440-442. I believe he actually refers to the act of 1286. So does the Avogaria di Comun, Cerberus, 21v, no. 4. Ill health, as evidenced by the oath of the nobleman's physician, and advanced age were accepted as excuses. Cessi, *Deliberazioni . . . Rogati*, "*Mixtorum*," I, 250, no. 36; A.S.V., Maggior Consiglio, Stella, 1r (5r); Senato, Terra, VI, 38r (39r). Angelini points out that Perugia also imposed penalties upon those who refused ambassadorships from the mid-thirteenth century, although the penalties appear to have been fixed individually, rather than by general statute. *La diplomazia communale a Perugia*, pp. 50-51. The Perugian statute of 1279 provided that those elected should be compelled to accept if they were not impeded by some just cause. *Ibid.*, App., no. 1, p. 54.

[62] A.S.V., Maggior Consiglio, Spiritus, 116v (117v); Lazzarini, "Obbligo di assumere pubblici uffici," pp. 196-197.

nobles took advantage of this act, which required absence from the city for two months, by simply moving to Murano for that period. Lazzarini, in fact, attributes the fine patrician palaces of this famous island of glass-making to the exile which patricians enforced upon themselves in order to escape onerous offices.[63] At least one case can be cited—an effort to send an ambassador to England to protest Henry V's seizure of three Venetian ships for his invasion of France—of the cancellation of a mission because no nobleman could be found willing to serve as ambassador.[64] Although notable examples can be found of Venetian patricians spending their lives and their fortunes in the service of the Republic, the myth of selfless service to the state by the oligarchic caste should be laid to rest—in fact, Lazzarini's article of 1936 should have buried it. Difficulty in finding suitable ambassadors willing to accept the task was not peculiar to Venice, but Florence also shared it as Vedovato has shown. Enforced withdrawal from the political struggle at home, neglect of the family business caused by prolonged absence, the direct cost to the individual of embassies, the difficulty of medieval travel and the attendant risks of capture and injury—all multiplied by the duration and frequency with which a single individual could be asked to serve—militated against a willing acceptance of diplomatic assignments.[65]

An appalling lapse of time often occurred between the decision to send an envoy and his departure. There was much concern that embassies should set out as quickly as possible,[66] and when we examine the chronologies of some missions, such concern is readily understood. On 15 January 1444, for example, the Venetian Senate decided to send a secretary to congratulate the cardinal of San Angelo, the king of Poland, and the lord of Transylvania on their victory over the Turks. One of the advantages of employing a secretary-*nuncius* was that, as a more informal envoy not entitled to all the honors and the impressive retinue of an ambassador, he could be dispatched more easily and quickly. Yet on 28 January, when the Senate decided that the consequences of this victory justified the sending

[63] A.S.V., Senato, Misti, XL, 146v (151v). Another device was to remove to Murano when an election was impending and remain for three days after it. *Ibid.*, 147r (152r). Lazzarini, "Obbligo di assumere pubblici uffici," p. 191.

[64] *Calendar of State Papers. Venetian*, I, 58, nos. 214-215.

[65] Vedovato, *Note*, pp. 11-14; Maulde La Clavière, *La diplomatie au temps de Machiavel*, III, 428-429 and 432. James C. Davis in his interesting *The Decline of the Venetian Nobility as a Ruling Class* (Baltimore, 1962), pp. 86-88, underestimates the financial burden upon ambassadors and the difficulty in obtaining suitable ambassadors before 1500. The problem may well have been intensified during the last three centuries of the Republic, but it was serious enough at a much earlier date.

[66] Cessi, *Deliberazioni del Maggior Consiglio*, III, 399; A.S.V., Avogaria di Comun, Cerberus, 5v, no. 50, and 23v, no. 9; Buzzati, "Diritto diplomatico veneziano," p. 229; A.S.V., Senato, Secreta, B (C), 103r.

of a more formal ambassador, the secretary, who was still to precede the ambassador, had not yet departed. The ambassador was required to depart within ten days, but such requirements were not often met. On 3 March it appears that a specific secretary had not yet been named, but on 6 March, Johannes de Reguardatis received his commission, including instructions to depart with all possible speed.[67] I do not know when—or if—he or the ambassador actually completed their preparations and left Venice, for the Venetians did not record the date of departure as the Florentines did, but over a month and a half had passed between the decision to send a mere secretary and the receipt of his commission without any indication that such delay was extraordinary. Once resident embassies had become established, a new ambassador was supposed to enter upon his office at the end of the term of his predecessor, but we know from the frequent complaints of resident ambassadors awaiting their successors that this requirement was often not met. Again ample evidence exists that Florence also faced a problem in completing the preparations for an embassy and getting it on the way.[68]

The reluctance of medieval envoys to set forth on their journeys is understandable in the light of the dangers, hardships, and discomforts to which medieval travel was subject. King John in 1205 planned to send to Rome different *nuncii* bearing copies of the same letters "because of the various perils of the ways."[69] Numerous accounts of the mistreatment of ambassadors could be given, such as the complaint of two Venetian ambassadors sent to the emperor that they had been captured, robbed, kept in prison for more than twenty-two and a half months, hungry, thirsty, and subjected to many injuries.[70] Because of these dangers an ambassador, in addition to his diplomatic retinue, sometimes had be provided with a military escort.[71] In the face of such perils the Venetian state, at any rate, was extremely reluctant to accept even the financial risk of robbery or shipwreck. A law of 1265 placed the ambassador at his own risk once he left the safety of the lagoon, and a subsequent law provided that the state could not recompense ambassadors for damages except by action of all six councilors, 35 of the Forty and two-thirds of the Great Council.[72] On occasion the

[67] A.S.V., Senato, Secreta, XVI, 57v (57v), 58v (58v), 72r (72r), 73r (73r).

[68] Maulde La Clavière, *La diplomatie au temps de Machiavel*, III, 411-413, 420-421.

[69] Rymer, *Foedera*, I, i, 44.

[70] A.S.V., Maggior Consiglio, Novella, 83r (94r). They requested financial aid in consideration of their losses, carefully pointing out that others would be led to refuse embassies if such damages were not reimbursed. The Council granted them one-ninth of the amount requested. In the following chapter I shall deal with the immunities of ambassadors and their abuse.

[71] E.g., A.S.V., Senato, Misti, XXX, 102v (102v).

[72] Cessi, *Deliberazioni del Maggior Consiglio*, II, 383; A.S.V., Maggior Consiglio, Presbiter,

danger of capture was so great, however, that the state had to agree in advance to recompense the owner of the ship on which an ambassador was transported in the event that it should be seized.[73]

The risk of maltreatment of ambassadors was probably of less concern, however, than the unavoidable hardships of medieval journeys. Travel was slow: a mission from Flanders to Nuremburg in the late thirteenth century required fourteen days of traveling each way, in addition to the nine days spent at Nuremburg.[74] Since medieval courts were peripatetic, ambassadors could not count upon finding the lord to whom they were sent at a given place. The counts of Flanders, for example, had castles at Bruges, Ghent, Ypres, Courtrai, and Oudenaarde, and ambassadors sent to them had to seek them out at one of these places or elsewhere.[75] Moreover, even in the days of the so-called resident ambassadors, princes had a habit of moving about, and the ambassadors were expected to follow in their train.[76] An embassy might simply be stopped in its tracks by the rigors of winter.[77] The bishop of Carlisle, envoy of Henry III to the archbishop of Cologne, reported how he had been forced to abandon his ship because of a violent storm and to come ashore in a small boat without baggage and horses, which could not be brought off. With a single servant, he had then taken ship with other travelers for Gravelines, and, having borrowed two horses from a merchant who had crossed with them, they set out for Cologne by long daily stages. The pen of anyone, he reported, would scarcely be able to describe the adversities of the journey due to the hardness of the roads, the bad weather, continual fear, and illness. They lost several horses and spent all the money with which they had been provided.[78] The death of an ambassador before the completion of his embassy was sufficiently common that the law took cognizance of it by providing that a surviving colleague might act as if his deceased fellow were present.[79] On quite another plane of adversity, a law of the Great Council of Venice in 1318 required that

78v (79v); Avogaria di Comun, Capitolare, VII, 49r. In the late fifteenth century an ambassador was allowed to carry silver of his own worth 200 ducats at the risk of the Commune. A.S.V., Senato, Terra, IX, 36r (36r). Exceptions were frequently made by which the state assumed a greater risk. E.g., *ibid.*, IX, 71r (71r).

[73] Cessi, *Deliberazioni del Maggior Consiglio*, I, 94-95.

[74] Rijksarchief, Gent, Saint-Genois, no. 559.

[75] Lucas, "Machinery of Diplomatic Intercourse," p. 326. The castle of the counts at Lille had been a very important center of government, as Theo Luykx, *De grafelijke financiële bestuursinstellingen en het grafelijk patrimonium in Vlaanderen tijdens de regering van Margareta van Constantinopel (1244-1278)* (Brussels, 1961), p. 72, notes, but Lille was lost to Philip IV.

[76] Sanuto, *Diarii*, I, 406. In this instance the king ordered the ambassadors not to follow him for two days, since the lodgings along the way were not adequate.

[77] Maulde La Clavière, *La diplomatie au temps de Machiavel*, II, 202.

[78] Champollion–Figeac, *Lettres*, I, 45-48, no. XXXV.

[79] Bertachinus, *Repertorium*, p. 73.

each innkeeper should keep two rooms honorably prepared with four beds "honorably and suitably furnished" for each room, "in order that ambassadors, clerics and other solemn persons coming to Venice can be suitably entertained in them."[80]

During that period in the evolution of diplomacy when the financial resources of states were much more meager than they are at present, the expense of sending embassies was an important factor in public finance and much of the burden was placed upon private shoulders. Even the Romans at the height of their power had minimized the costs of embassies by providing ambassadors with rings of gold which entitled them to free transport and maintenance within the broad circle of the world subject to Rome. This method of providing for the needs of ambassadors by inhabitants along the route survived into the early Middle Ages, although it was less satisfactory because of the fragmentation of the Roman world.[81] In a later period, the thirteenth to fifteenth centuries, more of the Venetian laws dealing with ambassadors were concerned with expenses and expense accounts than any other matter. The Senate justified an effort to control expenses in 1371 with the explanation that "the greatest quantity of money of our commune is expended continually in embassies which are sent outside of Venice." A few years earlier the Great Council had complained of the "great and almost intolerable expenses" of ambassadors, incurred because of their "liberal consciences" in expending the wealth of the commune.[82] We have been told also of the strain upon the budget of Philip the Fair imposed by the expenses of his envoys.[83] There is, of course, another side to this problem, that of the suffering ambassador. The touching complaints of Machiavelli and other ambassadors of the Renaissance por-

[80] A.S.V., Clericus-Civicus, 145r (193r). One must be aware, however, that one bed in each corner of a large room also used for dining, living, and entertaining, was the customary arrangement in the houses of the wealthy at this time. Philippe Ariès, *Centuries of Childhood: A Social History of Family Life*, Fr. edn., 1960, trans. by Robert Baldick (New York, 1962), p. 395. In 1403 the Venetian Senate acted to remove a favored Genoese ambassador from an inn to house him in a more comfortable and honorable fashion. A.S.V., Senato, Secreta, I, 118v (119v). That late medieval ambassadors were often entertained sumptuously we know from the descriptions of their receptions by Johannes Burckhard and others. In 1488, for example, four orators of the King of the Romans to Rome were met and accompanied to their places of residence, "videlicet iuxta plateam Sancte Marie rotunde, quam quondam d. Sinibaldus de Spata, scriptor apostolicus, construi curavit, in qua prefatus episcopus orator hospitatus est, alii autem college in aliis domibus prope ipsam." *Liber notarum*, I, 221.

[81] Serguiev, "La diplomatie de l'antiquité," p. 50; Ganshof, *Le Moyen Age*, pp. 40-41.

[82] A.S.V., Senato, Misti, XXXIII, 104v (104v); A.S.V., Maggior Consiglio, Novella, 25v (36v). Additional complaints: . . . *maxima pecunia exit de bursa nostra* . . . A.S.V., Senato, Misti, XLIX, 120r (122r); . . . *cum maiore expensa nostri dominii* . . . A.S.V., Senato, Terra, VIII, 197v (198v). For these and many other legislative acts on ambassadorial expenses see my *Early Venetian Legislation on Ambassadors* (Geneva, 1966).

[83] Luchaire, *Manuel*, pp. 601-602.

traying their pitiable state due to lack of funds are well known, but the ambassadorial laments of the later age only echo those heard earlier.[84] On one occasion, at least, Venice voted a subsidy to an imperial ambassador whose condition has become so penurious that he could no longer remain without assistance.[85]

In varying measure the expenses of an embassy were often defrayed by the state receiving it. An embassy to Byzantium was accustomed to full maintenance at the expense of the emperor—as well as the close observation that went along with it. In the West, however, ambassadors could not be assured of hospitality, although they might hope for it in some measure. Sometimes an envoy was fortunate enough to receive payment for his expenses, at least in part, from the prince or state to which he had been sent.[86] At other times ambassadors were received as guests, like the Castilian *nuncii* housed at the New Temple under Henry III.[87] The undoubtedly sound and somewhat cynical advice of Philippe de Commines was that visiting ambassadors should be lodged in handsome apartments provided with discreet persons to spy upon them. He further declared it only honorable that one should feast them, pay their expenses, and make them presents.[88] The *ordini* of Milan of 1468 concerning the manner in which foreign ambassadors should be received according to their status provide valuable information on the entertainment of envoys at the expense of Milan. *Legati a latere* and other cardinals should receive their expenses and be lodged at San Ambrogio. Orators of the emperor and of the king of France should also receive expenses and lodging in the court. Legates other than cardinals remaining only two or three days should not receive expenses, but rather a gift of 25 to 30 ducats, according to their quality and the number of horses in their retinue, and they should be lodged at *lhostaria* or wherever it seems better. *Nuncii* of the pope should receive 15 or 16 ducats. The duke makes provision for the resident orator of King Ferdinand, but those who come from time to time should receive about 20 ducats, depending upon the number of persons and horses, and the same should be true for orators of non-Italian princes, including those of the imperial electors.

[84] E.g., letters of Michael as Clokettes, a Flemish ambassador in Rome in 1299, complaining of lack of money. Kervyn de Lettenhove, *Études*, pp. 61-62, 64-66.

[85] A.S.V., Senato, Misti, XXXVIII, 4v (5v).

[86] *Rotuli litterarum clausarum in turri Londonensi asservati*, Thomas D. Hardy, ed., 2 vols. (London, 1833-1844), I, 175; Funck-Brentano, *Philippe le Bel en Flandre*, p. 140.

[87] *C.R. (1254-1256)*, p. 114. Also see Commynes, *Mémoires*, Liv. III, Chap. VIII, I, 222. Or the Venetian ambassador on his way to France entertained handsomely in Milan "all'osteria dei Tre Re, preparata per lo allogiamento nostro, per mia fè onoratemente, delle tappezzerie del duca." Albèri, *Relazioni*, Ser. I, IV, 4.

[88] *Mémoires*, Liv. III, Chap. VIII, I, 222.

Venetian and Florentine orators should be given 25 to 30 ducats, while those of the duke of Modena should have 20 to 25. Orators of the marquis of Montferrat and the marquis of Mantua, on the other hand, should receive nothing, although a present of 300 pounds should be made to either of the marquises themselves, should they come to Milan. Twelve ducats should be given to orators of Siena, Bologna, Lucca, and the Swiss confederation, and Genoese orators should have the same, even though Genoa was subject to Milan. All lords and orators who have come to offer condolences for the death of the duchess, Bianca Maria, should receive their expenses, and if two or three orators come from the same principal, the gift must be doubled or tripled, at least in part, according to the discretion of the seneschal, the quality of the ambassadors, and the number of their horses. Other orators may be given expenses or gifts according to the same principles.[89] A Venetian ambassador in 1492, Zaccaria Contarini, remarked upon the hospitality of Milan and Pavia.[90]

Venice sometimes provided furnished houses, as well as expenses, for visiting ambassadors.[91] According to Sanuto, the Neapolitan ambassador in 1498 was lodged in the *Ca' Venier* in the *Calle delle Rasse* and provided with expenses for his first day, as was the custom. For French ambassadors a year later the *Ca' Dandolo*, also in the *Calle delle Rasse*, where the Florentine ambassador had been lodged, was prepared. They received monthly expenses.[92] The *Calle delle Rasse* may not actually have been an "embassy row," but it is convenient to the ducal palace and contained *palazzi* of some of the greatest Venetian families, so it was highly suitable for housing visiting ambassadors.

A series of Senatorial decrees from 1371 until the end of the fifteenth century attempted to limit the expenditures made by the Venetian republic upon foreign ambassadors, apparently without great success, for many exceptions were made.[93] In an effort to escape the burden of the expenses of foreign ambassadors, the Senate decreed that Venetian ambassadors abroad and foreign ambassadors in Venice should receive no expenses from the host—a rather modern notion. On at least one occasion a Venetian ambas-

[89] Maspes, "Ricevimento degli ambasciatori," pp. 148-149. Maulde La Clavière, *La diplomatie au temps de Machiavel*, II, 388, n. 4, describes the same document.

[90] Albèri, *Relazioni*, Ser. I, IV, 7.

[91] "Traité du gouvernement de Venise," in Perret, *Relations de la France avec Venise*, II, 287-288.

[92] Sanuto, *Diarii*, I, 906, and II, 835.

[93] A.S.V., Senato, Misti, XXXIII, 104v (104v); Secreta, XXII, 160v (162v); Terra, VII, 116v (115v)–117r (116r); Terra, XIII, 77v (79v). For a detailed account, see my *Early Venetian Legislation on Ambassadors*. Exceptions: A.S.V., Senato, Misti, XXXVIII, 96r (97r); Terra, V, 148r (148r); Secreta, XXXII, 108v (108v), and XXXVII, 117r (131r).

sador was sharply reprimanded by the Ten for accepting expenses from the queen of Hungary.[94] Nonetheless, until the end of the Middle Ages the practice of the host assuming some responsibility for the expenses of an embassy continued.

As the intensity of diplomatic activity increased, however, the state represented by an envoy increasingly assumed responsibility for his expenses. Provision by the state was almost always inadequate (as it is today), but by the end of the Middle Ages the state customarily assumed some burden of the cost. The amount provided varied according to the rank of the envoy, the size of his entourage, the duration and nature of the mission, the state of the treasury, and the generosity of the monarch or ruling body.[95] Marjorie Nice Boyer's two valuable studies on travel allowances in fourteenth-century France indicate that three methods of computing travel allowances were common: by the journey, by the day, and by expense account. The former was used primarily for messengers performing routine tasks the duration of which could be rather readily predicted. Even so, she finds that many men subsequently claimed additional reimbursement for expenses, although a fixed payment had been accepted in advance. The daily allowance and the expense account were more often used for men of greater rank and responsibility, but these methods also were unsatisfactory. The king complained that those with a daily allowance deliberately extended the necessary time and that others submitted padded expense accounts.[96] These methods of computation, of course, were used in other lands as well. They could be employed in various combinations also.[97] Diligent servants of a medieval state also hoped to receive recompense for their services in the form of ecclesiastical benefices, fiefs, rents, or other forms of remuneration.

A considerable body of Venetian legislation upon the expenses of ambassadors was passed, frightfully dull in its detail, but intriguing in the mass as a manifestation of the clash of public and private interests. On the one hand was a stingy state and on the other an oligarchy eager to reserve most responsibilities for itself as a class, but reluctant to assume such re-

94 A.S.V., Senato, Secreta, XXII, 160v (162v); A.S.V., Dieci, Misti, XXIV, 115v (154v); filze, III, 201.

95 Ganshof, *Le Moyen Age*, p. 277; Lucas, "Machinery of Diplomatic Intercourse," pp. 319-321; Marjorie Nice Boyer, "Travel Allowances in Fourteenth Century France," *Journal of Economic History*, XXIII (1963), 73; Marjorie Nice Boyer, "Status and Travel Stipends in Fourteenth Century France," *Speculum*, XXXIX (1964), 52. The variation according to status is well exemplified in a series of expenses for ambassadors of San Gimignano in 1282 ranging from two *solidi* to 18 *solidi per diem*. Kern, *Acta Imperii, Angliae et Franciae*, pp. 186-187, no. 254.

96 Boyer, "Status and Travel Stipends," pp. 46-47, and "Travel Allowances," pp. 72-73.

97 *C.C.R., Edward III (1343-1346)*, p. 495.

sponsibilities as individuals, and if compelled to accept them, determined to find some means of padding their expense accounts. The best single description of the Venetian custom with regard to the expenses of ambassadors, however, is not in the laws, but in the "Traité du gouvernement de Venise" written around the end of the fifteenth century or the beginning of the sixteenth and published by Perret.[98]

The Venetian state invariably provided directly for the expenses of the journey (*agoziorum*), such as horses, the cost of transport on ships, and any authorized military escort.[99] As Boyer has noted for fourteenth-century France,[100] the number of horses was crucial to the cost of an embassy, and in Venice, as in France, limitation of costs was achieved by specifying the number of horses, although the number of men might not be mentioned. In 1500 the Senate prohibited the spending of more than 50 ducats for the horse of an ambassador, more than 20 for the horse of the secretary of a mission, and more than 12 for the horses of servants. It was also required that horses returned from embassies should be sold promptly at public auction, although a prudent exception was quickly made in order to allow horses returned from one embassy to be used on another.[101] Provision was also made to prevent orators from requisitioning from rectors the best military mounts to the great damage of the state.[102] For those crossing the seas transport on ships was also directly provided. By the late fourteenth century the Senate prohibited that any fare should be charged to an ambassador or other *nuncius* taking passage on a merchant galley. Since embassies sent beyond the seas were customarily in the interest of those engaged in commerce, the shipowners were expected to bear this share of the entire expense.[103] If Venetian ambassadors had to go some place that was dangerous, so that a military escort was necessary for their safety, it was supplied at the cost of the *Signoria*.[104] Certain other costs were also commonly borne directly by the commune. Since the appearance of the

98 In Perret, *Relations de la France avec Venise*, II, 289-292.

99 Cessi, *Deliberazioni del Maggior Consiglio*, II, 101, no. I; Buzzati, "Diritto diplomatico veneziano," p. 227.

100 "Status and Travel Stipends," p. 50.

101 A.S.V., Senato, Terra, XIV, 87v (87v); 92r (92r). The codification of 1477 had earlier required the sale of horses at public auction. *Ibid.*, VII, 174r (173r)–175r (174r).

102 *Ibid.*, XII, 66v (66v).

103 A.S.V., Senato, Misti, XLI, 121r, written over 113 (124r). In England no fixed rule on the cost of transport across the sea seems to have existed. Order to the sheriff of Kent to have ships ready. *Calendar of the Liberate Rolls. Henry III (1226-1240)* (London, 1919-59), p. 37. Ambassador granted the costs of shipping. *C.C.R., Henry VI (1429-1435)*, p. 273. Ambassador taking ship at his own cost. *Ibid. (1422-1429)*, pp. 172-173. When a special effort was made to honor some foreign ambassador, passage for all or a part of his journey might be provided for him. *C.R. (1254-1256)*, p. 360.

104 "Traité du gouvernement de Venise," in Perret, *Relations de la France avec Venise*, II, 289.

ambassador reflected upon the prestige of the state, coverings, mantles, robes, and other trappings were often provided at public expense, as well as traveling bags in which to carry them.[105] With the exception of robes these items had to be returned to the commune at the end of the embassy.[106] On one occasion the Great Council even agreed to pay the costs of the burial of an ambassador who died while he was abroad, but there was mention of other sacrifices by his family which inspired this unwonted generosity.[107] In Venice other expenses were considered ordinary or *expense oris*, the cost of living during the embassy, and these were paid on the basis of an expense account.[108] For this reason the Great Council at an early date took precautions to see that the doge and his councilors and the heads of the Forty fixed the number of servants and horses, the amount of salary, if any, and other expenses which would be permitted. They subsequently added the additional requirement that the same officials must have found the money necessary for the embassy before electing an ambassador.[109] A decree of the Senate in 1353 stated that *nuncii* and notaries going abroad for the commune should not receive the same expenses as ambassadors, for ambassadors had many greater costs, and the expenses of a *nuncius* or notary with one servant and two horses could be relatively easily determined. They should be allowed, therefore, 30 *grossi* a day for everything except tolls, ships, or horses.[110] This act probably only made subject to rule a common practice of allowing less expenses to envoys of inferior rank. On the same day, the Senate also decreed for ambassadors a *per diem* allowance for *expense oris*, although in this case it must be determined for each embassy individually. Food and drink alone, moreover, should be counted

105 *Ibid.*, 289-292. Even shoes were allowed to some English envoys. *C.C.R.*, *Edward III (1339-1341)*, pp. 7 and 431. The Venetian Senate made an effort in 1500 to allow a fixed sum for chests, covers, household goods, and the like. A.S.V., Senato, Terra, xiv, 4v (4v). Attempts were made also to restrict the number of chests, valises, and so forth that ambassadors provided at their own expense, for these retarded their movements and added to the expense of transportation. A.S.V., Senato, Misti, xxvi, 126rv (127rv); A.S.V., Senato, Terra, xiii, 143v (145v). There are two documents on page 143v (145v) dealing with the same subject. The first lacks the customary marginal cross indicating passage, and although there were 48 votes for it and none opposed, I suspect that it failed for want of a quorum. Florence in 1408 prohibited the giving of clothing or anything else for displaying an embassy unless it was sent for the coronation of a pope, emperor, or king. Even then, all clothing provided by the state had to be returned to the *camera* and sold. Maulde La Clavière, *La diplomatie au temps de Machiavel*, iii, 426-427.

106 Cessi, *Deliberazioni del Maggior Consiglio*, ii, 102; Buzzati, "Diritto diplomatico veneziano," p. 227.

107 A.S.V., Maggior Consiglio, Presbiter, 20r (21r).

108 "Traité du gouvernement de Venise," in Perret, *Relations de la France avec Venise*, ii, 289.

109 Cessi, *Deliberazioni del Maggior Consiglio*, ii, 40-41, no. lxxxiiii; *Buzzati*, "Diritto diplomatico veneziano," p. 228; A.S.V., Maggior Consiglio, Capricornus, 12r (117r).

110 A.S.V., Senato, Misti, xxvi, 126rv (127rv). I consider this document significant for showing the difference in status between a Venetian ambassador and a *nuncius*.

as *expense oris*.[111] By 1470, Venetian ambassadors were accustomed to receive a half ducat a day for the *expense oris* of each man and horse, but at that time the allowance was cut to one-third ducat. Subsequent efforts were required to define extraordinary expenses which were not subject to this limitation.[112]

Attempts were also made to limit the salaries which ambassadors could pay at the expense of the state to servants in their retinues.[113] The large codification of legislation on expenses of ambassadors in 1477 allowed three ducats a month for the seneschal, two for the chaplain, the barber, and the master serving the horses, two and a half ducats for two personal servants, and ten *lire* each for others. Horsemen sent to Venice with messages should receive what is customary where the ambassador finds himself, unless it should be necessary to offer them more to obtain greater speed. For the entire course of the legation the ambassador could spend up to 25 ducats for trumpeters.[114] The Senate also limited the amount that could be given in gifts. If it was necessary for an ambassador to give a more costly gift, he had to receive permission from the *Signoria*, although this was freely given.[115]

The problem of obtaining accurate and understandable accounts submitted promptly after the conclusion of a mission was a persistent one. In 1254 the Great Council required that ambassadors and others must render their accounts within five days after their return and must return any goods of the commune remaining in their hands.[116] An act of 1273 required them to keep a day by day expense account with justification for each item.[117] Many ambassadors began the rendition of their accounts within the prescribed time, then failed to complete them, so a law of 1293 required that the accounting must be completed within three months.[118] By the fourteenth century it was customary for an *expensator* to be included in

111 *Ibid.*, 126rv (127rv). Senato, Misti, Rubriche, I, 77v, refers to an act limiting the expenses of *nuncii* and notaries going abroad on state service, but the page referred to has disappeared.

112 A.S.V., Senato, Terra, VI, 99r (100r); VII, 115v (114v)–116r (115r); 174r (173r)–175r (174r). Boat passage, rents, guards, salaries of servants, trumpeters, and mounted messengers were excepted.

113 A.S.V., Senato, Misti, XXVI, 126rv (127rv).

114 A.S.V., Senato, Terra, VII, 115v (114v)–116r (115r), and 174r (173r)–175r (174r).

115 *Ibid.*, VII, 174r (173r)–175r (174r); "Traité du gouvernement de Venise," in Perret, *Relations de la France avec Venise*, II, 289-292.

116 Cessi, *Deliberazioni del Maggior Consiglio*, II, 294-295.

117 *Ibid.*, II, 102-103; Buzzati, "Diritto diplomatico veneziano," p. 228; Reumont, *Diplomazia*, p. 237. How Reumont could have so consistently dated his documents incorrectly is somewhat surprising.

118 A.S.V., Avogaria di Comun, Cerberus, 23v, no. 4; Buzzati, "Diritto diplomatico veneziano," p. 229.

the retinue of an ambassador, but the ambassador himself was required to see and receive the accounts of his *expensator* at least every three days.[119] A senatorial decree of 1353 commanded the ambassador to oversee the accounts at least every other day and also required him upon his return to submit his written expense account to the *camerlenghi*, who should report it to the doge and the Small Council, who in turn should have it read in the Great Council.[120] The Senate required in 1456 that accounts had to be submitted to the officials of New Accounts within one day after returning to Venice, excluding feast days.[121] During the time of their absence, according to a decree of 1464, ambassadors should send reports of their expenses every two months.[122] Still ambassadors sent summary accounts which could not be understood, so the Senate attempted to require greater clarity in the daily reports and a rendering of the full account within eight days after return.[123] A new effort was also made to see that the notaries or secretaries of missions kept accurate accounts, clearly distinguishing *expense oris* from extraordinary expenses, and that they should be examined under oath by the officials of the New Accounts.[124] The daily records of the seneschals or *spenditori* also had to be presented after 1476.[125] The code on expenses passed in 1477 required the seneschal to keep careful notes on all expenses on the basis of which the notary must every evening record in a book provided for that purpose the expenses of the day. Penalties were imposed upon any ambassador who should command his seneschal or notary to falsify records. The raw notes and the expense book must be given to the officials of New Accounts.[126] It is obvious that all sorts of precautions had to be taken against cheating on expense accounts. Florence, Mantua, and other states also required expense accounts.[127] In England, at least for the fourteenth century, the accounting does not seem to have been as careful as in Venice, although we do possess some fairly detailed accounts.[128]

Some Venetian ambassadors, especially those who were subjected to the risks of long journeys and those to non-Christian princes, received salaries.[129]

119 A.S.V., Maggior Consiglio, Capricornus, 57v.

120 A.S.V., Senato, Misti, XXVI, 126rv (127rv).

121 A.S.V., Senato, Terra, IV, 23r (24r).

122 *Ibid.*, V, 83v (83v).

123 *Ibid.*, VI, 98r (99r).

124 *Ibid.*, VI, 104v (105v).

125 *Ibid.*, VII, 115v (114v)–116r (115r).

126 *Ibid.*, VII, 174r (173r)–175r (174r).

127 Maulde La Clavière, *La diplomatie au temps de Machiavel*, III, 413-418; De Tourtier, "Bertolino Capilupi," p. 327.

128 For a description of the typical technique of accounting, see Lucas, "Machinery of Diplomatic Intercourse," pp. 330-331. For examples of English accounts, see Charles Lethbridge Kingsford, "John de Benstede and His Missions for Edward I," *Essays in History Presented to Reginald Lane Poole*, H.W.C. Davis, ed. (Oxford, 1927), pp. 350-354, and pp. 354-359.

129 "Traité du gouvernement de Venise," in Perret, *Relations de la France avec Venise*, II, 289-292. E.g., a salaried ambassador to Sicily. Cessi, *Deliberazioni . . . Rogati*, *"Mixtorum,"* I,

The Senate in 1440 complained of "the great and excessive salaries" paid to orators and others sent abroad and imposed a limit "during the present war" of 50 ducats a month.[130] Florence similarly sought to limit salaries after 1408 to five florins a day for a knight or a doctor, eight florins for others.[131] A contrast among the amounts given to people of various classes may be gained from an English mission of 1324. The earl of Kent, brother of the king, received £640; the archbishop of Dublin, £230; Richard Grey, a banneret, £95; and William Weston, a clerk who departed perhaps twenty days ahead of the others, £37 13*s.* 4*d.*[132]

There was another less common, but simpler way of handling the costs of a Venetian embassy. The *Signoria* provided to each ambassador 30 ducats for coffers, chests, covers for horses and mules, and other necessary items. These did not have to be returned and no accounting for the 30 ducats was required. Beyond this each ambassador received a fixed sum of money according to the place to which he was going and the size of his authorized retinue. An ambassador sent within Italy, for example, with eleven horses received 100 ducats a month for which also no accounting was required. Those sent beyond Italy should receive 120 ducats. If an ambassador were authorized a greater or smaller retinue, the amount of money allotted was changed accordingly. The "Traité" tells us that twenty horses was normally the largest number to accompany each ambassador, ten the least, and fifteen the average and most common number. Ceremonial embassies of congratulation to a pope, emperor, or other great lord, however,

---

5, no. 25. An act of the Great Council of 1360 mentions ambassadors going abroad *sive cum salario, sive sine salario.* A.S.V., Maggior Consiglio, Novella, 75v (86v). An act of the College in 1381 denied a salary. Pien Collegio, Notatorio, I, at top 74 and 95, at bottom 110. In 1451 the Senate first voted that an orator should be salaried, then reversed itself. A.S.V., Senato, Secreta, XIX, 54r (54r). Behrens heaps scorn on legalistic-scholastic treatises which deal with such petty points as "whether an ambassador who approaches his destination by a circuitous route should be paid for the whole of his journey; whether he should be paid on Sundays or if he is ill; whether when he is accredited to the Papal Curia he can solicit benefices for his relations." "Treatises on the Ambassador," p. 617. Yet the practical Venetian government was concerned with just such issues. A.S.V., Avogaria di Comun, Cerberus, 23v, no. 1. A salaried ambassador in the fifteenth century could not be elected to any public office, but an ambassador without a salary was eligible and was often elected to the highest positions. "Traité du gouvernement de Venise," in Perret, *Relations de la France avec Venise*, II, 289-292. By the fifteenth century deliberations of the Great Council often specify that since an orator does not have a salary, an office to which he has been elected can be reserved until his return. E.g., an orator to Florence had membership on the Council of Ten reserved until his return. A.S.V., Maggior Consiglio, Ursa, 143r (149r).

130 A.S.V., Senato, Misti, LX, 239v (240v). The same limitation was imposed sometime between 1347 and 1349 according to the *Rubriche* (I, 4) for this series, but I am unable to find the document in the appropriate register. That salaries were excessive in fact is highly questionable.

131 Maulde La Clavière, *La diplomatie au temps de Machiavel*, III, 413-418, 426-427, 436.

132 Chaplais, *War of Saint-Sardos*, p. 181 and n. 1.

required a greater train, and sometimes they sent ten ambassadors with a total of more than 300 horses.[133]

Medieval governments were often constrained to resort to loans for the financial needs of their embassies. John, bishop of Metz, son of Guy of Flanders and his envoy to Rome in 1282, borrowed from Sienese bankers funds needed for his mission. His brothers, Robert of Béthune and Philip of Thiettes, and two councilors of the count similarly borrowed from Florentine bankers to support their ill-fated effort in Rome in 1298 to secure a place for Flanders in the Anglo-French settlement. A few months later at Besançon they borrowed more money.[134] Edward I and Edward III made use of the Lucchesi bankers and of the Bardi of Florence among others for support of their embassies.[135] The Venetians very commonly authorized their envoys to borrow money to carry out their embassies.[136] In 1498 the Ten issued a blanket guarantee to the banks which would honor the letters of exchange of its orators to Paris.[137]

In some cases, moreover, interested private parties were required to finance an embassy wholly or in part. In a commercial state, such as Venice, many embassies were in the interests of private houses as much as the state, and as early as 1260 the Great Council found it necessary to legislate against the sending of ambassadors in the interest of private persons at public expense.[138] For example, an envoy sent to the king of Hungary to recover goods seized from Venetian merchants should have his expenses repaid out of the recovered goods if he should be successful. Or, in a similar case, the merchants concerned should share with the Commune the expenses of a *nuncius*.[139] A variation on this principle is provided by the embassy to England in 1399 financed by a loan to be repaid through a .5 per cent levy on all Venetian vessels going to and from London.[140] An ambassador sent to London with two attendants in 1408 was to be transported and fed on board the galleys at the expense of the owners, and half of his salary of 100 ducats was also

133 "Traité du gouvernement de Venise," in Perret, *Relations de la France avec Venise*, II, 289-292. A.S.V., Senato, Terra, XIII, 145v (147v). The former specifies twelve horses in Italy, the latter eleven. I have followed the latter as the official document, although, since the "Traité" cannot be precisely dated, a change may have occurred. It should be noted that the expense of *cursores* was not limited, for the government could not allow the penury of the ambassador to restrict its access to information.

134 Rijksarchief, Gent, Saint-Genois, no. 310; Limburg-Stirum, *Codex diplomaticus Frandriae*, I, 231, no. 80; Kervyn de Lettenhove, *Études*, p. 51.

135 Clifford, *Knight of Great Renown*, p. 83; *C.C.R.*, *Edward III* (*1333-1337*), p. 628.

136 E.g., Cessi, *Deliberazioni del Maggior Consiglio*, III, 66 and 74.

137 A.S.V., Dieci, Misti, XXVII, 184r (227r); filze, XII, 166.

138 Cessi, *Deliberazioni del Maggior Consiglio*, II, 53; Buzzati, "Diritto diplomatico Veneziano," p. 228. Badly misdated.

139 Cessi, *Deliberazioni del Maggior Consiglio*, I, 68, and III, 400.

140 *Calendar of State Papers. Venetian*, p. 39, no. 134. A similar case. *Ibid.*, p. 55, no. 198.

to be paid by them.[141] This was not peculiar to Venice. Flemish envoys sent to England in 1291 in order to ransom certain merchants of Flanders who had been arrested there were to have their expenses from the merchants in question.[142]

When all the provisions for meeting the cost of an embassy are taken into consideration, they were still usually inadequate. Ambassadors themselves often had to absorb a considerable portion of their own expenses, which they might or might not eventually recover with profit through the grant of a prebend, fief, or rent, or election to some remunerative office. An embassy to a distant country was regarded by a family of the Venetian patriciate as a great misfortune, which many patricians sought frantically to escape. Maulde La Clavière has described the financial hardships of some Venetian ambassadors around 1500. Z. Badoer claimed to have left over 1,000 ducats of his patrimony in Hungary. Paul Capello claimed to have spent 2,900 ducats on a mission to Rome lasting over sixteen months. The money allowed him by the state did not nearly cover these costs.[143] If such sacrifices in the service of the state could lead to election as *baiulo* in Constantinople, however, the much-desired perquisites of that office could compensate for earlier losses.[144]

The hardship upon envoys was heightened by an illiberal rule from Roman law providing that losses suffered by a mandatory not having anything to do with the mandate could not be charged as expenses, even if they would not have occurred except for the mandate. Money or personal goods lost to robbers, for example, were not required to be replaced by the principal.[145] In order to persuade those elected as ambassadors to accept, Venice, in addition to penalties for refusal, found it necessary on many occasions to authorize ambassadors to carry a certain amount of their own wealth at the risk of the Commune.[146]

In the diplomacy of the Middle Ages all sorts of persons could be employed as diplomatic envoys, although ceremonial missions designed to demonstrate respect for the recipient had to be manned by ambassadors of high social rank. Princely families, other nobles, clergy of various ranks,

141 *Ibid.*, p. 48, no. 168. Another variation on the same theme. *Ibid.*, p. 49, no. 170.

142 Thierry de Limburg-Stirum, *La cour des comtes de Flandre. Leurs officiers héréditaires. I. Le chambellan de Flandres* (Gand, 1868) cxvi, no. LIII; Varenbergh, *Relations diplomatiques*, p. 166; L'abbé C. Dehaisnes, "Essai sur les relations commerciales de la ville de Douai avec l'Angleterre au Moyen Age," *Mémoires lus à la Sorbonne* (Paris, 1867), p. 111, no. XII. Dehaisnes published more accurately some of the documents published somewhat badly by Varenbergh.

143 Maulde La Clavière, *La diplomatie au temps de Machiavel*, II, 24.

144 Da Mosto, *L'Archivio di Stato di Venezia*, II, 25.

145 *D.* 17, 1, 26, 6; Buckland, *Textbook of Roman Law*, p. 517.

146 E.g., A.S.V., Senato, Terra, VI, 61v (62v).

and, in the later years especially, scholars and poets served as orators. Professional diplomats were not found, although professional bureaucrats and others with much experience in government and diplomacy were frequently employed. In many cases an ambassador undertook diplomatic service at considerable cost to himself and his family, so that it was often no easy task to obtain qualified personnel. Hardships, dangers, and discomforts also frequently beset them upon their way, and not a few were robbed, imprisoned, or killed. Medieval states were possessed of inadequate means to finance the costs of embassies, which gave rise to a continual and bitter struggle between ambassadors and their principals over money. The padded expense account was by no means unknown. In Venice, especially, vast amounts of complicated legislation sought to regulate the costs of embassies. This chapter has sought to cast some light on some very mundane problems besetting and distracting ambassadors in the developing stage of modern diplomacy.

CHAPTER VII

IMMUNITIES AND CEREMONIES

> Mankind by common agreement of every people and nation has resolved to promulgate rights among others for the public utility to accomplish and dispose well of difficult matters. Therefore it provides to all ambassadors especially security on their journies with all impediments to ambassadors of whatever kind removed. Because they are ambassadors and they exercise their office laudably and do not exceed it, it is considered that they should come freely.[1]

Not only do authors of treatises on ambassadors, such as Bernard du Rosier, justify the extraordinary security of ambassadors as a necessity for the conducting of diplomatic intercourse, but such reasoning finds place also in the official documents issuing from chanceries: ". . . among all nations the name of legates has always been worthy of respect, so that the protection of them both in war and in peace ought to be secure and safe, inasmuch as they bear the employment of the public good between princes and peoples."[2] This protection which ambassadors enjoyed consisted in the inviolability of their persons, their retinues and their goods. There were exceptions and violations of this immunity, of course, as there are of all the decencies which make civilized life possible and in some measure enjoyable, but in general diplomatic immunity was recognized and honored from an early age. Ganshof declares it an unwritten law of the Merovingian age that the persons and possessions of ambassadors were inviolable.[3] This may have been even more consistently true in the West than in the more civilized East, because of the Western rulers' habit of employing their most distinguished councilors on embassies.[4]

The sanctity of legates was well recognized in Roman and canon law. Pomponius declared that any act of violence against a legate was a violation of the *ius gentium*. Even if war should break out while the legate of the enemy was in Roman territory, he should remain free.[5] The *ius gentium* as redacted by the Roman jurisconsults also provided that he who com-

[1] Bernard du Rosier, *Ambaxiator brevilogus*, p. 23.

[2] Rymer, *Foedera*, v, iv, 26. This is a safe-conduct containing a proviso that the ambassadors should conduct themselves properly. If they do not, the punishment should be limited to the guilty. I mention this to make clear that extraterritoriality is another matter than "extraordinary security."

[3] "Merowingisches Gesandtschaftswesen," p. 181.

[4] Löhren, *Geschichte des gesandtschaftlichen Verkehrs*, p. 75.

[5] *D.* 50, 7, 18. Also see *D.* 48, 6, 7.

mitted violence against a legate should be delivered to the injured legate's principal for punishment.[6] Not unnaturally, the canon law, international by its very character, took up and extended the immunities of ecclesiastical and secular legates. Gratian noted that their residences must not be violated.[7] He also pointed out that one who interfered with the mission of a legate harmed not only the legate but the many whom his mission concerned and was deserving of deprivation by society of its benefits. By this he probably intended excommunication.[8] A famous instance, although not involving a secular diplomat, was the murder of Peter of Castelnau, legate of Innocent III, in 1208. Excommunication, interdict, and release of the subjects of the count of Toulouse from their fealty fell in rapid succession upon the unhappy count.[9] Durandus made a special point that the missions of envoys sent by enemies were to be deemed sacred.[10] Baldus, the great fourteenth-century doctor of both laws, declared anyone who killed an ambassador guilty of *laesa maiestas*.[11] In another place he pointed out that neither ambassadors nor their authorized companions could be subjected to the harsh medieval law of reprisals.[12] Martinus Garratus pronounced legates immune from the laws and anyone who injured a legate guilty of sacrilege.[13] These strictures protecting ambassadors found their way also into the *Siete Partidas* of Alfonso the Wise.[14]

The above principles gained incorporation in the great *De jure belli ac pacis* of Grotius and thence in modern international law: the sacred

[6] *D.* 50, 7, 18. Martinus Garratus said that Roman law made the violator of diplomatic immunity a slave of the ruler of the injured envoy. Garratus, *Tractatus*, p. 47.

[7] *Decretum*, 1, 9.

[8] *Ibid.*, 94, 2. Gratian also wrote: "Qui autem spernit eos, eum a quo missi sunt et cuius legatione funguntur, spernit, et ipse indubitanter spernetur a Domino." *Ibid.*, 21, 2. This probably was equivalent to excommunication. Ruess, *Die rechtliche Stellung des päpstlichen Legaten*, p. 185. This, at any rate, is the penalty specified by Durandus. *Speculum legatorum*, p. 33. So also according to Garratus, *Tractatus*, p. 47.

[9] Ruess, *Die rechtliche Stellung des päpstlichen Legaten*, p. 185.

[10] Durandus, *Speculum legatorum*, p. 32. Gregory X wrote to Charles of Anjou: ". . . jus gentium exigat ut et legati gentis cujuslibet securitate gaudeant et apud hostes . . ." *Les registres de Grégoire X (1272-1276), suivis du registre de Jean XXI (1276-1277)*, J. Guiraud and L. Cadier, eds., in Bibliothèque des Écoles Françaises d'Athènes et de Rome, 2e sér., XII (Paris, 1892-1960), p. 326, no. 770. Ganshof quotes a letter from Gregory X to Charles of Anjou which may be this one, although the Latin syntax is not identical. *Le Moyen Age*, pp. 277-278. See also Bertachinus, *Repertorium*, p. 76; Gambarus, *Tractatus*, p. 2.

[11] Baldus, *Commentaria*, ad *Libros Decretalium*, 1, *De officio legati*, 1, 7. See also Garratus, *Tractatus*, p. 48; Gambarus, *Tractatus*, p. 16; Alciati, *Opera*, col. 483.

[12] Baldus, *Commentaria*, ad *D.* 27, *De excusatio tutorum*, 44, 1. Also Garratus, *Tractatus*, p. 50. Bertachinus adds that this is true even in the lands through which they pass. *Repertorium*, p. 73.

[13] Garratus, *Tractatus*, pp. 48 and 52. They could not be cited for debts contracted prior to the embassy. Bertachinus, *Repertorium*, p. 71. For proof that the rule was actually practiced, see *infra*, p. 180.

[14] *Las Siete Partidas*, 3 vols. (Valladolid, 1587), 7, 25, 9.

character of legates; that they might not be violated for they are protected by extraterritoriality; at most an ambassador might be sent home with the demand that he be punished or surrendered to the offended state. If, however, a state sends a warning that ambassadors should not be sent, and, if sent, they are treated as enemies, the normal protection does not avail them.[15] Moreover, the law of inviolability, according to Grotius, does not of itself apply to ambassadors passing through the territory of a state other than the one to which they are accredited.[16] The suite of an ambassador and his effects share his inviolability, but whether his household offers the right of asylum depends upon the concession of the state in which he is residing and is not required by the law of nations.[17]

Certain special concessions were granted to ambassadors out of honor for the ambassador himself or the principal whose person he represented. The Venetian Great Council sometimes conceded to visiting ambassadors the extraordinary privilege of bearing arms in the city.[18] If an excommunicated ambassador were sent to the pope, it was customary to relieve him of that ban during the duration of his embassy.[19] The right of an ambassador of an alien faith to the private practice of his religion was undoubtedly also recognized.

The immunities of ambassadors represent not merely the lucubrations of lawyers, but the practice of princes and communes. When Mongol ambassadors arrived in France to demand of Louis IX earth and water in sign of subservience to the khan, the king of course refused, but he entertained them in Paris honorably and sent them on in peace to the pope.[20] Many centuries earlier the fierce Attila spared with a mere rebuke a Byzantine ambassador proved to have been sent to murder him.[21] An interesting discussion of the Venetian Council of Ten concerns an ambassador of Milan caught in the act of spying. He was in the habit of stationing him-

[15] Grotius, *De jure belli ac pacis*, I, 294, Lib. II, Cap. XVIII, Sec. I; I, 297, Sec. IV; I, 298, Sec. V.

[16] *Ibid.*, I, 298, Lib. II, Cap. XVIII, Sec. V. *Contra*, Bertachinus, *supra*, n. 12.

[17] Grotius, *De jure belli ac pacis*, I, 299, Lib. II, Cap. XVIII, Sec. VIII.

[18] Law of the Great Council, 7 January 1297, authorizing the doge and the Six to grant the privilege of bearing arms. Cessi, *Delizerazioni del Maggior Consiglio*, III, 416. A direct grant of permission for an ambassador to bear arms by the Great Council. A.S.V., Maggior Consiglio, Clericus-Civicus, 96r (144r).

[19] Nys, *Origines du droit international*, pp. 345-346.

[20] *Cronica S. Petri Erfordensis moderna*, p. 401.

[21] Bakhrouchine and Kosminski, "La diplomatie du Moyen Age," I, 84. When the sons of Guy de Dampierre reacted violently toward the envoys of Philip IV who laid hands on their father to summon him, the count restrained them, since the envoys were only performing their assigned job. *Istore . . . de Flandre*, I, 208. Even though this is a weak source, it does not here matter whether Guy actually did it or the author had heard or fabricated the story involving the principle. What the author believed to be true is as important as what actually happened.

self at appropriate places in the ducal palace to see and to hear all he could, a practice common to competent ambassadors, so nothing was said to him about it. When he disappeared from the city, however, and appeared *ad partes Clugie* viewing and counting the troops which Venice was about to send into Lombardy, the matter became more serious. Inquiry proved that other activities of his were subject of considerable suspicion. It was proposed that he should be seized and examined with torture. The surprising thing is that the proposal was defeated by a vote of ten to three with three abstentions.[22] One cannot argue safely that the Ten had this much respect for diplomatic amenities, for other factors, such as the desire to keep his activities under secret observation, may have played a role, but that an ambassador caught in the act of spying was not seized seems of some significance. When the bailiff of Dover arrested Thomas of Savoy's *nuncius*, Henry III ordered that he be released and allowing to go wherever he wished.[23] Not only could the state sending an ambassador take offense at any hindrance caused him along the way, but so could the state for which he was destined. The Venetian Senate protested to the marquis of Mantua in 1415 against the arrest of an ambassador from Cremona as he crossed Mantuan territory. If the marquis had reason, as he claimed, to seize all citizens of Cremona, the Senate conceded that such action was within his rights, but ambassadors must be excepted.[24] When reprisals were authorized against the citizens of another state, ambassadors were sometimes explicitly excepted from this punitive measure.[25] On one occasion Swiss ambassadors were received honorably in Milan although Milanese ambassadors had just been seized in Switzerland, threatened with death, and compelled through fear to enter into a convention which exceeded their powers.[26] If an ambassador were seized, however, and his letters opened,

[22] A.S.V., Dieci, Misti, XVII, 59r (101r).

[23] *C.R. (1237-1242)*, p. 29; Theo Luykx, *Johanna van Constantinopel* (Antwerpen and Utrecht, 1946), p. 375.

[24] A.S.V., Senato, Misti, LI, 66rv (68rv).

[25] A.S.V., Maggior Consiglio, Clericus-Civicus, 155v (203r); Senato, Misti, XLIII, 58r (57r). Nys stated that ambassadors were free from reprisals "sans exception." *Origines du droit international*, pp. 339-340. (See also Baldus, *supra*, p. 176.) The following document indicates that this was not completely true and is also interesting for the rationalization in the preface: "Cum usus et conversatio forinsecorum et vicinorum nostrorum Redundet in utilitatem et bonum civitatis nostre Venetie, ut omnibus patet, Et adhoc sit vigilandum In quantum est possibile. Vadit pars Quod Ambaxatores comitatis franchevile, contra quam est data represalia ad petitionem Nicoleti georgii civis nostri, possint libere et secure venire ad presentiam dominii nostri, et stare Venetiam ad tractandum super dicto facto, et super aliis, que eis viderentur se ponendis, usque per totum mensem Julii proximi non obstante represalia predicta. Et fiant litere affidantie sicut necessarie fuerit." A.S.V., Senato, Misti, XLII, 59v—over 58 (58v).

[26] Maulde La Clavière, *La diplomatie au temps de Machiavel*, III, 230, n. 1.

revealing information embarrassing to the power from which he was sent, it was this latter which was expected to be apologetic and not the officials who had violated the person and the letters of the ambassador.[27] The immunities of ambassadors, after all, were based upon their function of furthering good relations between states.

The immunities that we have been discussing were not generally recognized to be dependent upon safe-conducts. When King Ladislaus in 1406 desired from Venice a safe-conduct for a certain Guilielmus Pannono Gallico, the Senate replied that no such document was necessary, since, as a friend, he could come with his retinue and goods in all assurance of security.[28] On another occasion the Senate objected to Genoa that the latter's request for a safe-conduct for its legate was unnecessary, but since the Venetians themselves only recently had requested a safe-conduct from Genoa, they granted it reluctantly.[29] Sanuto reports how a Venetian ambassador returning from Milan was stopped and subjected to insults by a Milanese customs officer because he did not have a passport. The duke of Milan ordered the ambassador sent on his way and sent the offending officer to Venice for punishment, but the Venetian ambassador, having won his point, with great tact made the customs officer a small present and sent him home.[30] The honor in which the ambassador of even an enemy power was held is indicated by Commines' report that after the publication of the treaty of 1495 directed against his king, he remained in Venice almost a month and was as well treated as before.[31] And even though messengers did not enjoy all the immunities of ambassadors, in the 178-year period studied by Hill, she finds only one messenger killed on a mission and several injured, although a number had been imprisoned.[32]

Ambassadors were not even subject to judicial action for criminal or civil offenses of their own, at least not for those committed prior to their missions. Whether this immunity was extended to acts committed in the course of the mission was a debatable question.[33] An entry in the *Capitolare* of the *Avogaria di Comun* of 1315 states flatly: *Li ambasciatori non possono*

[27] *Ibid.*, III, 155, gives two good examples.

[28] A.S.V., Senato, Secreta, IV, 183r (183r). They did later grant the requested safe-conduct, still disclaiming the necessity for it. *Ibid.*, 185v (185v). Safe-conducts might, indeed, prove useful in time of war.

[29] A.S.V., Senato, Secreta, IX, 161r (159r). ". . . salvumconductum *et* nostras passus literas . . ." Italics mine. Two documents or redundancy? Since it appears that only a safe-conduct was requested, I think it is a redundancy.

[30] Sanuto, *Diarii*, I, col. 38.

[31] Commynes, *Mémoires*, Liv. VII, Chap. XX, II, 229.

[32] *The King's Messengers*, p. 112.

[33] Maulde La Clavière, *La diplomatie au temps de Machiavel*, II, 35-36.

esser citadi.[34] A most interesting series of mid-fourteenth century acts of the Great Council deal with whether an ambassador can be cited for debts contracted before his mission. On 17 January 1339 the Great Council accepted the argument of a foreign ambassador that he should be free from judicial action, "since our ambassadors, who go continually throughout the world, could continually encounter obstacles in this case, if an obstacle should be placed in the way of others by us." At one point this act was revoked by the *sapientes consiliorum*, but in 1355 the Great Council insisted that it be restored in its pristine form.[35] Even in a case of homicide ambassadors might be released.[36]

On the other hand, ambassadors who abused their status to work against the interests of their hosts did not always enjoy the immunity granted to them today.[37] In 1427 the Venetian captain at Brescia was ordered to proceed against *nuncii* of the duke of Milan who had entered that place to stir up trouble.[38] The Florentine ambassadors in Venice were instructed in 1447 to inform the Venetians of the arrest of a French ambassador to Milan, whose letters had already been seized (copies of which were sent to Venice) and who was being examined under torture to learn the whole truth concerning his mission.[39] The Venetians in 1494 even sought to explain to the pope why they had incarcerated and tortured a monk whom they believed to be an orator of the Turks to the king of Naples. They had not extorted any information from him, but they claimed to have proceeded upon evidence and to have had the concurrence of the patriarch of Venice.[40]

According to Maulde La Clavière, the idea of the extraterritoriality of ambassadors goes back to Roman times when the legate carried with him the Roman law.[41] Every student of the early Middle Ages has learned that during this period of the mingling of peoples each man was personally subject to the law of his own people, while the concept of a territorial law broke down. Even after territorial law revived, ambassadors continued to bear with them their own law and were even considered by a fiction not to have left the soil of their own land. Joanna II of Naples, confirming in

[34] A.S.V., Avogaria di Comun, Capitolare, VII, 3r. The reference is to Cap°. 496–C 204. This did not lead to any register of acts found in the archives.

[35] A.S.V., Maggior Consiglio, Spiritus, 92r (93r) and Novella, 41.

[36] Rymer, *Foedera*, II, iv, 119.

[37] Nys, *Origines du droit international*, p. 347.

[38] A.S.V., Senato, Secreta, x, 22r (26r). They did not have a Venetian safe-conduct. In 1473 we hear of a Venetian secretary in Moscow arrested by the duke because he was suspected of dealing with the Turks against Moscow. *Ibid.*, XXVI, 48r (58r).

[39] A.S.F., Signori—Missive—Originali, IV, 10r.

[40] A.S.V., Dieci, Misti, filze, VII, 249 and registri, XXVI, 63v (91v); filze, VIII, 20 and registri, XXVI, 72r (100r).

[41] *La diplomatie au temps de Machiavel*, II, 36-37.

1419 a house granted to the Venetian consul, granted that on feast days the consul might display *il vessillo col Leone*, the proud red- and gold-serrated banner of St. Mark. Nicolà Nicolini interprets this convincingly as a sign that the palace enjoyed extraterritoriality.[42]

The immunities of Christian ambassadors in Muslim lands and of Muslims in Christian countries was not very different from that enjoyed by those engaged in diplomacy among Christians. Relative security of ambassadors is essential to the effective conduct of relations between states, and nowhere was this more clear than in those states on the frontier between Christendom and Islam, such as Castile. In the *Siete Partidas*, Alfonso X established the inviolability of Moorish envoys in both their persons and their goods.[43] Maulde La Clavière incorrectly cites Christine de Pisan to the effect that a safe-conduct given to a Muslim was legally null. In her discussion, it is true, the position is stated that they are enemies of God, and even subjects of the king issuing the safe-conduct might violate it justly, but she continues that all Christians ought to honor safe-conducts given for a reasonable cause for two reasons. The first is that they should not gain a reputation as faithless, and the second is that they do not wish to incur retaliation upon Christian merchants and ambassadors in Muslim lands. Exception is made of those who bear letters under safe-conduct harmful to the interest of a king, but the exception applies to Christian, as well as Muslim, envoys.[44] On the other side, also, the inviolability of ambassadors was generally recognized. One exception, noted by Joinville, was that the protection offered by a safe-conduct lapsed with the death of the ruler who had granted it. A *nuncius* who encountered this state of affairs could be imprisoned and even enslaved.[45]

Law and fact, of course, are not identical, and a lengthy and lamentable list of violations of the immunities of ambassadors could be given. The complaints and retaliations—often of the most vehement sort—which violations of diplomatic immunity evoked, however, prove that immunity was the rule, violation its exception. In the late eleventh century Cuman ambassadors to Sviatopolk were arrested, and although they were later released, the enraged Cumans attacked Russia in force. After Sviatopolk

[42] Nicolini, *Il consolato generale veneto nel regno di Napoli*, p. 35. According to Maulde La Clavière, however, consuls lacked diplomatic immunity.

[43] *Siete Partidas*, 7, 25, 9; Rafael Bauzá a Bauzá, "Doctrinas juridicas internacionales de Ramón Llull," *Estudios lulianos*, III (1959), p. 183, n. 38.

[44] Maulde La Clavière, *La diplomatie au temps de Machiavel*, I, 16, n. 3. Christine de Pisan, *The Book of Fayttes of Armes and of Chyualrye*, trans. and printed by William Caxton, A.T.P. Byles, ed., in Early English Text Society, no. 189 (London, 1932), pp. 249-250.

[45] Nys, *Droit international et droit politique*, p. 72; Jean, sire de Joinville, *Histoire de Saint Louis*, Natalis de Wailly, ed. (Paris, 1874), Chap. LXXI, Sec. 363, p. 198.

made peace with them, Vladimir, who had not been a party to the peace, killed new Cuman envoys, and the war began anew.[46] Manuel Comnenus imprisoned ambassadors of Roger II of Sicily who had come to seek a treaty based upon recognition of Roger's royal title and equality in status with the emperor, a condition which the Byzantines were never willing to admit.[47] Frederick Barbarossa on crusade complained bitterly that Isaac II had cast his legates nude into prison. He did secure their release, by the expedient of burning and depopulating every place in his path, and Isaac was compelled not only to free them, but to indemnify them for their damages.[48]

Russians and Greeks, of course, had no monopoly upon the abuse of the rights of ambassadors. Perhaps the most famous seizure of legates in medieval history was Frederick II's capture of over 100 archbishops, bishops, *nuncii*, and procurators of prelates and ambassadors of the rebellious Lombard towns in 1241.[49] An outraged public opinion represented chiefly by St. Louis compelled him to release them. Florence objected to Perugia in 1387 against the seizure of its envoys and the opening of their letters, demanding to know the meaning of such acts "so that we can know how we have to live together in such a matter."[50] In 1417 the French objected bitterly to the arrest of a French herald by Henry V. The archbishop of Rheims presented a systematic argument against this violation of the rights of heralds:

> In the first place, because it is against the old and honest custom of arms; secondly, because it is against the force and effect of the safe-conduct of your lord the king, in which he conceded to us a certain number of servants, among which they have been included; thirdly, because, if chronicles and the old pages of treaties are looked back upon, it does not appear that in these hundred years any herald coming for holding solemn embassy between two kingdoms, especially for the good of peace, has been thus arrested; fourthly, because it is against the good and utility of this kind of

[46] George Vernadsky, *Kievan Russia* (New Haven, 1948), p. 88.

[47] Helene Wieruszowski, "Roger II of Sicily, *Rex-Tyrranus*, in Twelfth-Century Political Thought," *Speculum*, XXXVIII (1963), 62.

[48] *Historia de expeditione Friderici*, pp. 41, 47, and 66. Frederick had another occasion to complain that in the presence of his legates in Santa Sophia, the patriarch had publicly preached that whoever killed a hundred crusaders should receive indulgence for the homicides of ten Greeks. *Ibid.*, pp. 42-43.

[49] Letter of Frederick himself. Rymer, *Foedera*, I, i, 137-138. *Annales Stadensis auctore M. Alberto*, *M.G.H.*, *SS.*, XVI, I. M. Lappenberg, ed. (Hannoverae, 1859), p. 367.

[50] A.S.F., Dieci di Balia—Missive—Legazioni e commissarie, I, 60. See also a Venetian protest to Milan against seizing and torturing diplomatic messengers and opening, reading, and confiscating their letters. A.S.V., Senato, Secreta, XI, 43r (44r)–46r (47r).

> negotiation of peace for which we have come, in which we need the activities of the same heralds most urgently, if perchance, for any necessary cause it will be opportune to send some *nuncius.*

To this the English orator could only reply that he had no instructions, but that he knew that his master would not commit such an act without honest and reasonable cause.[51] A Venetian objection against the seizure of ambassadors within the territory of the duke of Austria also indicates some interesting facts concerning diplomatic immunity. The envoy to Austria should point out that the injury was principally to the duke, since the security of his roads and territories, which he and his father had always wished to be secure to all men, had been violated, and this was exceptionally harmful since the victims were ambassadors. Only then, after the general argument for the immunity of ambassadors, was it mentioned that they also bore the duke's letters of security, which the malefactors had dared to tear up. The envoy should beg the duke to secure the ambassadors' release, but he should also visit several other princes who might bring to bear some influence, and the ambassador to the emperor should seek his intervention, especially since the ambassadors had also borne imperial letters of security from which the culprits had disdainfully removed the seal.[52] Degert recounts the dreadful hardships suffered by Charles de Marigny, ambassador of Louis XI to Edward IV. He was overburdened with affronts, and Englishmen pillaged his household and half-destroyed it. His person was never secure in the face of threats of hanging or drowning. His domestics were constantly insulted in the streets. One of them was wounded and left for dead, and Edward IV did not even dare to punish the archer of his guard who was recognized responsible for the crime.[53] The eleventh-century philosopher and Ciceronian in the service of the bishop of Moravia mentioned in the last chapter unfortunately had his nose cut off and was threatened with death unless he turned back.[54] Even bearers of safe-conducts were sometimes murdered.[55] The Ten in Venice had a device for handling such cases which probably served as some sort of deterrent. Leonardo Venerio, a Venetian ambassador, had been killed in Milan by one Giovanni Stampa. The Milanese government did nothing about the matter, so the

[51] Rymer, *Foedera*, IV, iii, 25-28.

[52] A.S.V., Senato, Misti, XIX, 42v (42v). A Florentine ambassador sent to Giovanni Beltoft was seized by the pope in the territory of Perugia. Florence pressed claims against Perugia and urged the *condottiere* to do the same. A.S.F., Dieci di Balia—Missive—Legazioni e commissarie, I, 82-86.

[53] Degert, "Louis XI et ses ambassadeurs," p. 14.

[54] Cosmas of Prague, *Chronica Boemorum*, pp. 122-123.

[55] Perroy, *The Anglo-French Negotiations at Bruges, 1374-1377*, p. 81, Appendix, XI. Vengeance was later taken.

Ten offered 20,000 pounds, recall from exile (if he should be exiled for anything except rebellion), the opportunity to recall anyone else from exile if he should not himself be an exile, and the command of a force of lances or of infantry for life to anyone who would kill Stampa.[56] This is an enormous bounty, and the provisions concerning recall from exile indicate that it was directed in part, at least, to hardened cutthroats. Also, since the offer was open to any claimant, it must have been publicized in some way so as to render Stampa's life—whatever remained of it—somewhat unpleasant.

It is apparent that diplomatic immunity was not always observed during the three medieval centuries considered here, but just as many examples of violations could undoubtedly be collected from the middle of the seventeenth century to the present. It was taken seriously by legists, canonists, and statesmen, and when violations occurred satisfaction was demanded in the most urgent terms or even attempted unilaterally by lawless retribution. In the light (or should I say shadow) of the ink-splattered American embassies in 1965 and 1966, it is impossible to resist citing an episode in 1499 mentioned by Sanuto. A band of disguised youths composed of about 800 from the best families of Florence brought a cartful of excrement before the house of the Milanese orator and used it to wall up his door.[57] Murdering ambassadors, cutting off their noses, and bombing embassies is different in degree from plastering excrement and throwing ink, but in one degree or another the acts of barbarism against medieval diplomats were not so different from those known today and were about equally disapproved.

Undue emphasis, however, should not be placed upon occasional acts of diplomatic discourtesy. The high culture of the fourteenth and fifteenth centuries, as Huizinga observed, "found its most direct expression in all that constitutes ceremony and etiquette. The actions of princes . . . all assume a quasi-symbolic form and tend to raise themselves to the rank of mysteries. . . ."[58] What was true of princes was equally true of those who represented their persons for ceremonial purposes. Not only courtesy, but an etiquette exaggerated far beyond that employed in diplomacy today was the rule. An insulation of elaborate ceremony helped to protect the fragile thread of civilized intercourse against the violence and brutality still prevalent in European society. Occasional bizarre violations of the rules of courteous and civilized relations arose partly from the underlying crudity of a culture which was only recently and superficially (though extravagantly) polite

[56] A.S.V., Dieci, Misti, XIV, 4r (7r).

[57] Sanuto, *Diarii*, II, 407. This proves that civilization has progressed in sanitation, if not in sanity.

[58] Huizinga, *The Waning of the Middle Ages*, p. 41.

and partly from a deliberate perversion of the norms of behavior, which only proves the general acceptance of the rules which were perverted.

Not the least of the ceremonial factors involved in an embassy was its size: the greater the number of ambassadors, the more numerous their retinue and baggage, the greater was the honor paid to the recipient and the impression of the wealth and power of the principal. In the sheer size of the embassy the grandeur of both parties was symbolized in visible form.[59] The size of the retinue accompanying a medieval embassy varied from century to century, from state to state, and according to the importance and nature of the embassy.

Even in the thirteenth and fourteenth centuries embassies were usually relatively modest in size. A thirteenth-century Venetian embassy to Constaninople consisted of two ambassadors with six servants each, a bursar (*expenditor*) for the pair, a chaplain who should also be a notary, two trumpeters, and a cook. This would make up a retinue, excluding the ambassadors themselves, of seventeen persons.[60] A Venetian embassy to honor the accession of a new king of Hungary in 1291—an occasion calling for a considerable show of honor—numbered 24 horses.[61] For the coronation of an emperor in 1311 a retinue of 50 horses was allowed the Republic's ambassador, yet an ordinary embassy to Constantinople two years later numbered only a notary and six servants in the retinue.[62] English practice appears to conform approximately to that of Venice. Henry S. Lucas has collected a number of English examples from 1329 to 1336. Embassies headed by great persons numbered from 32 to 107 men and from 22 to 83 horses. Those headed by clerks, notaries, and others of lesser estate were accompanied by one to four persons and up to five horses.[63]

Maulde La Clavière contends, however, that by the late fifteenth century a special embassy to a major court ought to number at least 150 horses, although even powerful city-states, such as Milan and Venice, would accept royal embassies of 80 horses or 55 horses and 25 footmen as showing sufficient respect.[64] Some embassies indeed were huge. A safe-conduct issued by Henry VI to French ambassadors in 1440 permitted to the archbishop of Rheims 80 persons and horses; to John, bastard of Orléans and

[59] *Ibid.*, p. 28. Roman ambassadors, usually two or three to an embassy, were also accompanied by quite a retinue of secretaries, interpreters, bakers, butchers, and others. Serguiev, *La diplomatie de l'antiquité*, p. 50.

[60] Cessi, *Deliberazioni del Maggior Consiglio*, III, 50. I assume that a *cenamelam* must be a cook.

[61] *Ibid.*, III, 306. The size of an embassy was often given in number of horses.

[62] Cessi, *Deliberazioni . . . Rogati*, "*Mixtorum*," I, 136, nos. 111-112, and I, 140, no. 152.

[63] "Machinery of Diplomatic Intercourse," pp. 321-323.

[64] *La diplomatie au temps de Machiavel*, I, 379-380.

count of Dunois, 120; to the archbishop of Narbonne, 60; to the bishop of Poitiers, 60; to master Guille le Tur, 25; to master Jacques Jennenel, 15; to master André de Beuf, secretary of the adversary, 12; and to master Nicole Aymer, also 12. The total was 384.[65] A year later a safe-conduct was issued for 25 French ambassadors with a preposterous retinue of 1,340 persons and horses.[66] Yet Maulde La Clavière appears to be somewhat excessive in his estimate of the minimum number necessary to make a decent show, for there was no more solemn diplomatic occasion than an embassy of obedience to a new pope, yet those sent to honor Nicholas V were on the order of 150, 170, 120, etc.[67]

In Venetian records even of the fifteenth century I find no evidence of such enormous retinues as some of those just named. Presumably an oligarchic republic, rich as it was, felt no compulsion to rival royalty in conspicuous display of wealth in this particular way. Yet Venice, too, felt compelled sometimes to add members to an orator's entourage "in order to augment the prestige of the orator on account of the importance of the embassy."[68] Still, prestige and costs had to be balanced. As early as 1371 the Senate began passing a series of decrees attempting to establish a fixed limit for the size of all embassies. The first attempt restricted the embassy to a single ambassador with four servants, a notary with his own servant, and two stableboys. An exception was made for the coronations of popes, emperors, and kings, popes and emperors being allowed three ambassadors and kings two, with each of the ambassadors, however, restricted to the retinue named above.[69] An act of 1461 again tried to impose a limit of eight upon the retinue accompanying an ambassador.[70] The limit was raised to twelve horses in 1483, including those of the ambassador, the notary, and their servants, but in addition they should be allowed two lackies.[71]

[65] Rymer, *Foedera*, v, i, 93-94. The bishop of Tournai, representing the duchess of Burgundy, also received safe-conduct for sixty persons. The Burgundian party was permitted to come armed for their security, which was not said of the ambassadors of France.

[66] *Ibid.*, v, i, 107-108.

[67] Ludwig Freiherrn von Pastor, *Geschichte der Päpste seit dem Ausgang des Mittelalters*, 1st edn., 1884-1933, 12th edn. 16 vols. in 22 (Freiburg, 1955-), I, 395-396.

[68] A.S.V., Senato, Terra, VIII, 87rv (88rv). Also Maggior Consiglio, Leona, 157v (162v)–158r (163r). Ambassadors sent to congratulate Louis XI on his accession, for example, each had 25 horses. Sanuto, *Diarii*, I, col. 987. Incidentally, a retinue of horsemen was not always and entirely for ceremonial purposes, but for protection on the way. A.S.V., Senato, Terra, v, 39r (40r).

[69] A final clause permitted exceptions by an extraordinary majority of the Senate. A.S.V., Senato, Misti, XXXIII, 104v (104v). Maulde La Clavière indicates that three or four ambassadors were commonly employed to honor a papal coronation, but one to twelve were known. *La diplomatie au temps de Machiavel*, I, 112.

[70] A.S.V., Senato, Terra, IV, 165v (166v).

[71] *Ibid.*, IX, 46r (46r). Sixteen years later the limit was lowered by one. *Ibid.*, XIII, 109r (111r).

The composition, as well as the size, of the ambassador's retinue is of interest. To begin on a negative note, wives did not normally accompany their husbands on embassies. Economy, the necessity for preserving secrecy, and the hardships of the way were probably the factors contributing to this practice. In Venice, at least, it was explicitly prohibited by law that an ambassador should take his wife on the mission.[72]

Various specialists in chancery practices, accounting, and law were sometimes important members of an ambassador's entourage. A secretary generally wrote the dispatches and kept necessary records other than the financial ones. Only in the case of especially important communications was the ambassador likely to write in his own hand, though he probably signed all dispatches. In case of the absence or death of the ambassador, a secretary would be in charge of the mission.[73] In Venice these functionaries were drawn from the chancellery and were designated notaries. They accompanied ambassadors at least as early as the thirteenth century.[74] In view of the continual controversy over the expenses of Venetian ambassadors, it is not surprising that each embassy included a bursar.[75] Lawyers were also extremely useful specialists, particularly for certain types of missions, to inform and advise the ambassadors on points of law.[76] In a decree of 1483 the Senate stated that for certain types of missions it was not only appropriate and honorable, but utterly essential to include those skilled in civil and canon law.[77] Roman and canon lawyers were of particular value in medieval diplomacy, of course, since these two systems of law had common currency.

[72] Cessi, *Deliberazioni del Maggior Consiglio*, III, 214; A.S.V., Avogaria di Comun, Cerberus, 23v, no. 3; Buzzati, "Diritto diplomatico veneziano," pp. 228-229.

[73] Maulde La Clavière, *La diplomatie au temps de Machiavel*, I, 372-373. Venetian secretaries also were probably intended to serve as a check or restraint upon the ambassadors, for it was required that in all dealings of the ambassador the secretary must always be present. "Traité du gouvernement de Venise," in Perret, *Relations de la France avec Venise*, II, 292.

[74] Cessi, *Deliberazioni del Maggior Consiglio*, III, 306; A.S.V., Avogaria di Comun, Cerberus, 23v, no. 8; Buzzati, "Diritto diplomatico veneziano," p. 229. Jusserand declared that the French first established a salaried corps of secretaries suitable for use as secretaries of embassies in 1711. "The School for Ambassadors," pp. 41-42. This does not seem credible, since the English, as well as Italians, possessed them centuries earlier. Cuttino, *English Diplomatic Administration*, p. 107.

[75] *Expensator* or *expenditor*. A.S.V., Maggior Consiglio, Capricornus, 57v; Cessi, *Deliberazioni del Maggior Consiglio*, III, 50.

[76] "Quia alias, quando nostrum dominium misit suos ambaxatores ad curiam, specialiter pro factus, in quibus et circa quam occurrere dubia Iuris, reperitur, quod dominacio providit, per tempora in mittendo ad curiam, cum Ambaxatoribus suis aliquem, vel aliquod Iuris peritos, cum quibus Ambaxatores possint in agendis habere consilium, et plenius Informari . . ." A.S.V., Senato, Misti, XXIV, 90v (90v).

[77] A.S.V., Senato, Secreta, XXXI, 41r (41r). In the two instances under consideration the lawyers received their own letters of credence and instructions and were to be treated by the orators already appointed as colleagues. These are among the rare instances of recognition of anyone outside the patrician caste as orators.

Because there was also a language of common currency in Western Europe, on the other hand, translators or interpreters were not necessary for embassies within that area. Although some diplomatic documents exist in the vernacular tongues, many of these are letters between the principal and the ambassador, and the communication between states was conducted in Latin or in some vernacular language common to the states in question—French for Anglo-French relations, for example. Venice, which stood between two worlds, however, often required interpreters for its ambassadors.[78] The Venetian chancellery was provided with persons competent in the languages of the various states with which Venice had to deal.[79] The Great Council in 1481 rewarded one Hermanuelis Turzimani, who had performed many services in many places, some at the risk of his life. Among them he had served before Ussonus Cassanus, with the Venetian orator in Constantinople and on various borders with the Turks. He had command of a number of languages.[80] Vernadsky tells the amusing story of Friar William Rubruck at the Mongol court and his difficulty in understanding because his interpreter got drunk. Or perhaps the fault was not entirely that of the interpreter, for the good friar suspected that the khan was also a bit inebriated.[81]

From quite early times, a priest with the title of chaplain was attached to major deputations for the purpose of performing the religious ceremonies connected with diplomacy.[82] A chaplain was not, however, invariably a member of a quattrocento embassy. As the garb of diplomacy shifted from the ecclesiastical vestments fashionable in the Middle Ages to the legal robes it has worn in modern times,[83] the role of the chaplain diminished as that of the lawyer increased.

The retinue of an ambassador also normally included a number of persons of more menial status. Many important embassies, especially those of ceremonial character, included trumpeters, and very honorable ones might

[78] E.g., A.S.V., Senato, Secreta, v, 134r (136r), and xxiii, 12r (14r).

[79] "En ladite chancellerie sont beaucoup qui seullement ne sont pas instruitz en la langue ytalique et latine, mais aussy sont instruitz a la langue grecque et en tout aultre langaige, en telles manieres que toutes le lettres qui sont escriptes a ladicte Seigneurie de Venise, en quelque langue que ce soit, sont leues et enterpretées par ceulx de ladicte chancellerie, sans pourchasser aultres gens de dehors." "Traité du gouvernement de Venise," in Perret, *Relations de la France avec Venise*, ii, 279.

[80] A.S.V., Maggior Consiglio, Regina, 15r (19r).

[81] Vernadsky, *The Mongols and Russia*, p. 68.

[82] Funck-Brentano, "Caractère religieux de la diplomatie," p. 117.

[83] At least until a few decades ago. I sometimes fear that the legal garment is falling into tatters and that diplomacy may soon stand denuded of any covering of religion or law. Perhaps it may even be for the best that we see it as it is without trappings.

be expected to include an orchestra of minstrels, lute players, and trumpeters.[84] A cook was frequently included,[85] partly to provide the household, as nearly as possible, with the types of food to which it was accustomed, partly to enable the ambassador to entertain, and, in all honesty, partly to prevent the ambassador from being poisoned. Household servants were, of course, allowed, not only to the ambassadors, but in reduced number to the accompanying notary.[86] Stableboys also were permitted, and on more solemn occasions when larger embassies were sent, a marshall might be placed in charge of all the embassy's horses.[87] I have already noted that Mantuan embassies as early as 1340 were instructed to send dispatches only by way of Mantuan couriers, who presumably made up part of an ambassador's original retinue, while Venetians at a much later date relied unwisely upon foreign couriers.[88]

By the end of the fifteenth century Florentine law required that every ambassador should be accompanied by a subambassador—a youngish man from 24 to 40 years—in order that the latter might gain experience.[89] Occasionally the Venetians did the same, but it was not a regular practice. In 1407 a major embassy was sent in which each orator was allowed to take along a younger noble because it would lend added prestige to the embassy and because it was also "good and useful that our noble young men should observe the ways and practices of the world for the events of future times."[90] Normally an ambassador was not permitted to take his son, but the Senate granted special permission to Giovanni Gradonico for a mission to Hungary in 1449.[91] Because the Senate wanted its embassy to the Congress of Mantua to be more impressive than those of other states, it provided that the orators should be accompanied by sixteen of the most suitable youths, well clothed and with fine horses, from each of the subject cities of Verona, Vicenza, and Padua, and twenty such young

[84] Maulde La Clavière, *La diplomatie au temps de Machiavel*, I, 379-380. The Venetian Senate in 1477 approved ". . . erogandas pecunias nostri dominii in donis tubetarum, piffarorum, et aliorum huiusmodi hominum . . ." A.S.V., Senato, Terra, VII, 176v (175v).

[85] E.g., as early as 1291. Cessi, *Deliberazioni del Maggior Consiglio*, III, 306.

[86] Four for each ambassador and one for the notary, in this example. A.S.V., Senato, Secreta, XXII, 35r (37r). A notary acting as head of a mission, of course, was also allowed a servant, but still customarily only one.

[87] *Ragocios*, *ibid.*, or *stapherios*, A.S.V., Senato, Terra, XIII, 109r (111r). *Marescalchum*, A.S.V., Senato, Secreta, III, 84r.

[88] Archivio di Stato, Mantova, Archivio Gonzaga, 2881 (Copia-lettere I, c. 4). A.S.V., Senato, Terra, VII, 174v (173v). *Supra*, p. 140.

[89] Act published, Vedovato, *Note* (Appendice: Codicetto, c. 20 and 20t), pp. 67-68; Maulde La Clavière, *La diplomatie au temps de Machiavel*, III, 432-433.

[90] A.S.V., Senato, Secreta, III, 84r. Another example a half century later. *Ibid.*, XXII, 35r (37r).

[91] A.S.V., Senato, Misti, XXV, 52r (52r).

men from Venice. Those from the subject cities should remain only until the orators' visitation upon the pope and the cardinals, while the Venetian youths should remain for two more days.[92]

From all that has been said, the importance of prestige and ceremony in medieval diplomacy is apparent. Still today diplomacy remains circumscribed with ceremony, and so it was also in antiquity. The Roman *fetiales* wore special costumes and performed rigorously prescribed ceremonies for negotiating, making peace, or declaring war.[93] In the Middle Ages ceremonies range from the minimal to the most elaborate and from the highly religious to those quite secular. The ambassador, as we have said, personified his principal, and therefore the ceremony which was lavished by and upon ambassadors manifested the respect of the principals for each other.[94] Probably at no time in history has ceremony been more important, in diplomacy and elsewhere, than at the end of the Middle Ages. Johannes Burckhard's *Liber Notarum* provides us with a magnificent source on diplomatic ceremonial at this time, for Burckhard was the papal master of ceremonies, the expert in such matters. Yet practicing diplomats and the governments which sent them also furnish ample evidence of the importance of ceremony in diplomacy. Commines stresses the importance of making the visiting ambassador welcome, entertaining him, making presents to him, always treating him honorably, even if there is cause for suspecting him of enmity toward the government.[95] The Venetian Senate expressed the value of ceremony very well, declaring that it was appropriate to honor the person of the Portuguese ambassador with all suitable honors so that the reciprocal friendship between Venice and his royal majesty of Portugal might be apparent to all.[96] Froissart, who loved such things, tells of an ambassador instructed by his king to remember to maintain such state as became a royal ambassador—promising that he would defray all expenses. True to his charge, the ambassador lived most magnificently. Gold and silver implements he used as profusely as a prince. His dinner was announced by music. Whenever he went out, a handsome sword, richly emblazoned with his arms, was carried before him. For everything he bought his servants paid well.[97] It seems that he enjoyed his mission—as Froissart enjoyed it vicariously—and it is entirely possible that his master received the desired return upon his investment.

[92] A.S.V., Senato, Terra, IV, 120v (121v)–121r (122r).

[93] Serguiev, *La diplomatie de l'antiquité*, pp. 48-49.

[94] Antonibon, *Relazioni di ambasciatori veneti*, 11, n. 1; Cuttino, *English Diplomatic Administration*, p. 85.

[95] Commynes, *Mémoires*, Liv. III, Chap. VIII, I, 222.

[96] A.S.V., Senato, Secreta, XXXIII, 1v (11v).

[97] Froissart, *Oeuvres*, IX, 124.

Often in the Middle Ages diplomacy was encompassed with religious ceremonies. Negotiations were opened with religious rituals and the raising of prayers. Solemn acts were brought to conclusion in a church, chapel, episcopal palace or abbey, sanctified by the performance of Mass and the sound of organs, chants, and songs. Censers smoked, the *Te Deum* sounded, and relics were brought forth to solemnize diplomatic acts. If possible, the most important acts were performed on feast days.[98]

Even the dress of an ambassador ought to reflect the solemnity of the occasion and the dignity of his master. Prelates, of course, took advantage of full pontifical garb. Lay diplomats, also, sought to impress by their appearance. We hear of the magnificent splendor of the raiment of the logothete Gregory, *nuncius* of Michael Paleologus to the Council of Lyons. On the same occasion, *nuncii* of the Tartars appeared "glittering in garments interwoven with gold."[99] Accounts of ambassadors claim expenses for such things as cloths and plumes.[100] Even the stingy Venetians often provided crimson robes for their ambassadors.[101]

Other furnishings, as indicated by Froissart's luxury-loving envoy, were also important. Tapestries, tableware, and other accouterments all helped lend stature to the ambassador and his mission. The Venetian Great Council in 1329 felt it necessary to forbid the worked silver goods of the commune to ambassadors except those sent to popes, kings, cardinals, and princes, although wine bowls and cups might be allowed to all.[102]

As a ceremonial representative of his principal, on the other hand, an ambassador ought not only to be received upon his entry with great honor, but it was customary, at least by the end of the period studied, to go forth or send forth to meet him.[103] As early as 1284, Venetian law required that when a *legatus* came to Venice four *ambaxatores* should be sent to meet him to learn the cause of his coming so that whatever would be suitable might be done. These were no mere messengers, but two of them should be ducal councilors, the third one of the heads of the Forty, and the fourth

[98] Funck-Brentano, "Caractère religieux de la diplomatie," pp. 115-118.

[99] *Cronica S. Petri Erfordensis moderna*, p. 407.

[100] Limburg-Stirum, *Codex diplomaticus Flandriae*, I, 272-273, no. 104.

[101] A proposal to send ambassadors to Milan with condolences on the death of the duke in 1402 was defeated, but it happened to provide for black clothes. A.S.V., Senato, Secreta, I, 78r (79r). The three paintings in Carpaccio's St. Ursula cycle depicting ambassadors do not show them invariably in robes of red, but reveal considerable variety. Although the ambassadors were supposed to be from Britain a millenium before Carpaccio's day, it is common knowledge and perfectly obvious that his settings and costumes were those of Venice in the late fifteenth century.

[102] A.S.V., Maggior Consiglio, Spiritus, 37v (38v).

[103] Antonio Maria Bettanini, "Note di ceremoniale diplomatico," in *Studi dedicati alla memoria di Pier Paolo Zanzucchi dalla Facoltà di Giurisprudenza* (del' Università Cattolica del Sacro Cuore) (Milano: n.d.), p. 8.

one of the Advocates of the Commune, all officials of the greatest prestige.[104] Throughout the fifteenth century Venetian law reveals some difficulty in obtaining appropriate particians to go to meet and to accompany visiting ambassadors and other dignitaries. Such visitors made their appearence every day, according to the preamble of a senatorial decree, and the refusal of patricians to perform their duty meant that many of these honored guests either had no company or not so much as was suitable.[105] At the court of Milan a codification of 1468 determined the requisite reception according to rank. The duke himself, accompanied by an appropriate retinue of course, should always go to meet orators of the pope, the emperor, and the king of France. He should also personally go out to meet orators of other kings, cardinals (even if not legates), imperial electors, the duke of Modena, the marquis of Mantua, the marquis of Montferrat, and other princes. Two of the duke's brothers, the council, and additional gentlemen should be sent to greet legates of the pope who were not cardinals and other worthy orators. Even to orators considered less honorable, some gentlemen should be sent.[106] Zaccaria Contarini, Venetian ambassador to France, later described to the Senate his reception in Milan. Giovan Francesco Pasqualigo with two councilors and about 40 horsemen met him about two miles from Milan, greeted him, and rode with the Venetians to the gate. There they were greeted by the Secret Council and the Council of Justice, who had come out to meet them, and all rode together to the *osteria dei Tre Re* prepared honorably for their lodging and furnished with the tapestries of the duke himself. The bishops of Como and Novara, chief of the councilors, together with Bartolomeo da Calco, secretary of state and *un uomo colto*, accompanied Contarini to his room, where the bishop of Como apologized that the *signori* (Gian Galeazzo and Ludovico il Moro) had not greeted him personally, since they were out of the city.[107] Later three distinguished councilors with eight or ten horses rode with them to Pavia, where the duke, his uncle Ludovico, the ambassadors of Florence, Ferrara, and Montferrat, and all the court met them. Contarini with the duke on his right hand and the Florentine ambassador on his left rode into the city at the head of the procession, followed by his colleague Francesco Capello with

[104] The greeting was not only honorific, however, for the visitors were required to wait outside the city until the Venetian *ambaxatores* reported and appropriate action had been determined. Cessi, *Deliberazioni del Maggior Consiglio*, III, 59.

[105] A.S.V., Senato, Terra, VIII, 198r (199r), and I, 138r (139r).

[106] Maspes, "Ricevimento degli ambasciatori," p. 148. The codification published here took no particular account of orators of Venice and other major Italian states, or else did not offer sufficient honors to them, as will appear in the following sentences in the text.

[107] Albèri, *Relazioni*, Ser. I, IV, 4. Maspes was aware that the dukes themselves were accustomed to go forth *berreto in mano* to meet Venetian ambassadors. "Ricevimento degli ambasciatori," p. 146.

Ludovico on the right and the ambassador of Ferrara on the left. They were accompanied to their place of lodging, and the next morning many of the councilors came to lead them to the *castello* for their formal audience.[108]

On certain occasions also, the papal court of the late fifteenth century sent retainers of the pope and the cardinals to meet orators and to accompany them to the place assigned for their habitation. On this Burckhard is invaluable. The papal court, as the most exalted in Western Christendom, showed more restraint in showering honorable receptions upon orators at their entry than was elsewhere customary. After debate it was determined in the late fifteenth century that the pope should order his retainers and those of the cardinals to be sent out of the city to greet only those orators summoned to Rome by the pope or those coming to offer obedience to a new pope.[109] On other occasions, however, when the papacy wanted especially to manifest honor to another power, retainers of the pope and of some friendly cardinals might be sent out.[110] An interesting and complicated case arose in 1485 concerning orators dispatched from France to offer obedience. On February 8 the cardinal of Anjou returned to Rome as the chief of eight French orators. He had originally been sent to France as legate by Sixtus IV, but had not been received as such. Innocent VIII ordered the cardinals themselves to go forth to meet him, as was the custom when one of their own number returned from a legation. Burckhard without success objected on three grounds: (1) the cardinal of Anjou had not been received in France as a legate; (2) just as an orator he ought not to be solemnly received by the college; (3) the college should not go out to meet a cardinal without conducting him directly to the consistory. On the following day the seven ambassadorial colleagues of the cardinal of Anjou entered the city, and the pope and the cardinals sent retainers to meet them in the accustomed manner. The cardinal of Anjou, however, personally rode outside the gate to greet his colleagues. He then rode at the right of the count of Montpensier to his own house. The other orators followed, the next two flanked by prelates of the palace, the others between a prelate of the palace on the right and one of the foreign orators in Rome on the left. The cardinal of Anjou dismounted at his own house, and the other orators were accompanied to theirs in the accustomed manner. The elements of a solemn entry of envoys in Rome are present here, but in a rather confused state on account of the ambiguous position of the cardinal of Anjou—member of the college, abortive legate to France, and head of the embassy.

108 Albèri, *Relazioni*, Ser. I, IV, 5-6.
109 Burckhard, *Liber notarum*, I, 241, 309.
110 *Ibid.* I, 241.

Burckhard notes that the cardinal went beyond the gates to meet his ambassadorial colleagues on his own authority, beyond the decree and ordination of the pope, and that for this act he was criticized justly by many.[111] The entry of a Turkish ambassador was handled differently and in a more secular manner. In 1492 a Turkish orator, bearing as a gift to the pope the alleged iron of the sacred lance, came to Rome. Francesco Cibo, son of the pope and captain of the church, accompanied by armed retainers of the cardinals but not by prelates or chaplains, went to meet him. Burckhard records his very brief welcome: *Siate ben venuto: Nostro Signore et li cardinali ce mandano le loro famiglie a farvi honore. Siate il ben venuto.* The Turk had an interpreter, who translated this welcome and the orator's response.[112] Solemn entries like those described were accorded only to special ambassadors. Such receptions, in principle, were not granted to residents, or even to special embassies dependent upon a resident. It almost goes without saying that a secretary or other figure of minor rank was not honored in this way.[113]

Soon after the reception of envoys they were customarily granted an audience.[114] Burckhard continues to give a full description of the French embassy of obedience in 1485. Before the hour set for the audience with the pope, the other seven French orators came to the house of the cardinal of Anjou, and together they rode to the papal palace in the same order and with a similar company as on the occasion of their entry. The retinue sent to accompany them, according to the master of ceremonies, was not customary and from his viewpoint therefore not desirable, but was the work of the bishop-elect of Tournai, who had not gained possession of his church and was currying the favor of the king of France.[115] The cardinal of Anjou joined the other cardinals in attendance upon the pope at the palace, entered the consistory with them, and took his accustomed seat.[116] The other orators, admitted to the consistory, went through the usual ceremony of kissing the foot, the hand, and the mouth of the pontiff. The

[111] *Ibid.*, I, 107-108. Vernadsky recounts that in Russia, until the time of Peter the Great, a foreign envoy was met at the border by a special official (*pristav*). *Pristav* and the foreign envoy dismounted simultaneously to exchange greetings. On the journey to Moscow the *pristav* rode on the ambassador's right. Western ambassadors objected violently to this procedure, but to no avail. *The Mongols and Russia*, pp. 387-388.

[112] Burckhard, *Liber notarum*, I, 363.

[113] Maulde La Clavière, *La diplomatie au temps de Machiavel*, II, 195. In fact one of the advantages of sending a secretary was the avoidance of attention.

[114] When, for one reason or another, an audience was long delayed, this was ground for grievous complaints and laments by ambassadors.

[115] Burckhard, *Liber notarum*, I, 223. Three years later, for the same purpose, he had similar honors extended to ambassadors from Germany.

[116] Owing to the ambiguous role of the cardinal of Anjou, Burckhard errs in describing the entry of the ambassadors into the papal consistory, but he quickly corrects himself.

cardinal of Anjou then presented to the pope letters from the king of France in the French tongue, and the count of Montpensier presented letters written in Latin. The seven orators then took their seats on a bench behind the cardinal-presbyters. The letters were read aloud by the bishop of St. Jean de Maurienne and the archbishop of Benevento, respectively. The orators then performed the customary ceremony of obedience in the name of their king. An oration was made by the bishop of Orange. The members of the ambassadorial retinue were also allowed to kiss the papal foot, and when the pope departed for his own chamber, the count of Montpensier received the honor of bearing the papal train.[117] Sometimes ambassadors received their audience in secret consistory, a practice to which Burckhard objected.[118] Occasionally, even at Rome, an envoy of minor rank bearing a message was received. In 1490 a herald accompanied by a single servant came from the emperor Frederick with letters from Maximilian, king of the Romans. His letters were read in consistory, and Burckhard had to translate the reply of the pope, since the herald knew neither Latin nor Italian. Naturally he was not received with the ceremonies due to orators.[119]

From the same period we again have the Venetian Contarini's relation of his audience with the king of France. He and his colleagues also were accompanied to their audience by a large company of *uomini di conto.* They were presented to the king in a hall about half the size of the Senate chamber of the ducal palace at home. At one end the king sat upon a dais, with a curtain behind his back and a canopy of Alexandrian velvet embroidered with the arms of France above his head. Along the side of the hall to the right of the king was a bench occupied by barons of the blood and on the opposite side one occupied by prelates resident in the court. These made up the secret council of the king. At the end of the hall opposite the king was a bench reserved for the ambassadors, upon which the king wished that they should sit and expose to him the purpose of their embassy.[120] We know that in Venice ambassadors were received in the *sala duarum Napparum* (*Sala del Collegio*) or in the little hall next to the White Chamber. There they awaited the doge, and when he came they customarily descended to the basilica for the usual rites.[121] The Venetian doge was extremely circumscribed by law in his relations with foreign ambassadors. He could neither receive them in private audience nor give any response to them on his own authority. The Council of Six (or at least a

[117] *Ibid.*, I, 108-110. The place of the oration in the order of events is not quite clear.
[118] *Ibid.*, I, 211. [119] *Ibid.*, I, 294-295.
[120] Albèri, *Relazioni*, Ser. I, IV, 12.
[121] A.S.V., Maggior Consiglio, Regina, 37v (43v)–38r (44r).

certain number of its members) had to be present at any audience, and the heads of the Forty must at least be given the opportunity to be present. The restrictions upon giving any definitive response to ambassadors were quite stringent.[122]

Since ceremony symbolized the mutual respect of the parties, unpleasantness could arise over ceremonial questions. The Muscovites, following Mongol custom, had a rule concerning ambassadors, which many Westerners resented, requiring that they not be armed when received in audience. Since a Western feudal lord considered his sword part of his usual formal attire, he frequently objected, but all were compelled to comply.[123] Burckhard reports an urgent conference held among himself and four cardinals when it was learned that the Neapolitan ambassador planned to appear sword in hand at vespers on the eve of Pentecost.[124]

The ambassador, or one of the group of ambassadors, always had to make a polite opening. In the earlier part of our period this seems to have been quite simple. Instructions of English envoys to France in 1324 are illustrative of this simplicity: ". . . after they will have greeted the king and recommended our lords and ladies, the king, the queen and their children, and described their health, which is good, thanks be to God, and the desire that they have to learn of their health . . ." they should get right down to the matter of the embassy.[125] The exchange of pleasantries about the health of one party and the other was quite customary and—as in the case of our "How do you do?"—the report seems to have been expected always to be favorable.

Under the influence of humanism the opening oration by an ambassador took on great importance as an item of prestige, and skilled orators therefore found themselves much in demand as diplomats.[126] The ambassador who delivered the oration might not be the leader of the embassy,[127] and in fact might have been sent for the sole purpose of his oration. Enthusiasts for the Renaissance, however, may have made of diplomatic oratory some-

[122] A.S.V., Maggior Consiglio, Novella, 30v (41v); Fronesis, 113v (114v)–114r (115r); Regina, 37v (43v)–38r (44r); Senato, Misti, xxv, 49rv (49rv); Senato, Terra, I, 28r. For a fuller exposition of these restrictions on the doge see, Queller, "Early Venetian Legislation on Foreign Ambassadors," pp. 9-12.

[123] Vernadsky, *The Mongols and Russia*, pp. 387-388.

[124] Burckhard, *Liber notarum*, I, 309.

[125] Chaplais, *War of Saint Sardos*, p. 182.

[126] Much the same had been true under the Roman Empire due to the influence of the schools of rhetoric. Serguiev, *La diplomatie de l'antiquité*, I, 73-74.

[127] ". . . orationem fecit Guillelmus prior Ecclesie cantuariensis, quintus in ordine oratorum . . ." There were ten. Burckhard, *Liber notarum*, I, 197. The "Traité du gouvernement de Venise" holds that the younger of two ambassadors always made the first *exposicion* of the embassy. Perret, *Relations de la France avec Venise*, II, 288-289.

thing more significant than it actually was. We know that Doge Andrea Vendramin was required to add to his ducal oath the promise that he would not hear "those long orations," which were not considered to comport with the dignity and gravity of the *Signoria* nor with the efficient use of time.[128] The *Diarii* of Marino Sanuto also include occasional expressions of annoyance with long-winded orations. The Venetian governing class, at any rate, while appreciative of speeches full of useful matter, appears intolerant of loquacity out of proportion to the content.

The words of ambassadors were not always polite. Burgundian orators to Venice in 1409 used words which were "improper and not good," because the Senate was stalling on a claim that the Republic owed the duke of Burgundy 100,000 ducats.[129] An ambassador of Ferrara in Venice in 1495, outraged because a captain of a *sestiere* had taken a poniard away from one of his servants at night, burst out with an offensive attack on the Venetian official before the Senate: ". . . your captain of the *sestiere*, could not be the son of a gentleman, but he is a bastard, son of some slave, male or female, and he could not be anything but a coward." The ambassador did not confine himself to saying this once, but repeated it several times. He also added that the poniard was not worth more than three ducats, and if the offending official had so much need of three ducats, he, the ambassador, would have given them to him. However just his complaint might have been, it was presented in such a disrespectful manner that the Ten debated whether they should request his recall and replacement by another, although this was voted down by a margin of nine to six.[130] Insults could be calculated acts by the principal, also. The letters of credence from Philip IV borne by the bishops of Puy and Amiens to Guy of Dampierre in 1297, and which, naturally, were read before the count, addressed him as "Guy of Dampierre, marquis of Namur, bearing himself, so it is said, as count of Flanders." A note in a contemporary hand on the back of the document preserved in Ghent remarks that this failure to give the count his proper title was harsh,[131] as indeed it was. The diplomatic exchanges of

[128] "Et non audiat sermones, sive compositas illas longas orationes, Quoniam non sunt enim dignitate gravitateque nostri Dominii, neque cum commodo rerum nostrorum temporis utilioris Indigentium." The preceding passage refers specifically to orators from subject cities, but I believe this provides some light upon a general Venetian attitude toward oratory. A.S.V., Maggior Consiglio, Regina, 155v (163v).

[129] A.S.V., Senato, Secreta, IV, 57r (57r). Negotiations continued, however. *Ibid.*, 58v (58v)–59r (59r) and subsequent documents.

[130] ". . . nos in cuius conspectu et facie hec dicta sunt atque atque adeo omnis Senatorius ordo noster et offensus, et Indecenter ac procaciter dehonestatus fuerit." A.S.V., Dieci, Misti, XXVI, 189v (218v). The Council of Ten, by the way, had an ordinary membership of seventeen.

[131] Funck-Brentano, "Documents relatifs aux formes diplomatiques," pp. 92-96; Rijksarchief, Gent, Saint-Genois, no. 859.

earlier centuries probably lacked the refinement that was at any rate expected in the fifteenth. We have a record of a rough, but not angry, interchange between King John—scarcely noted for his tact, in any case—and two ambassadors of the count of Flanders. When John heard that Ferrand had arrived in England, he called the two envoys to inform them. "And what are you waiting for then," said Robert of Béthune, "that you do not go immediately to meet him?" "Oh," said the king, "this Fleming! He seems to think that this is some great matter of his lord, the count of Flanders." "By St. James," Robert replied, "I am right that it is that." The king laughed and ordered horses prepared to go to meet the count with honor.[132] This sort of rough banter is difficult to imagine amidst the formalities of the fifteenth century.

In that later period, Maulde La Clavière indicates that ambassadors, too, were entitled to a respect manifested in honorific titles. A lay ambassador was usually addressed with the adjective *magnificus*, less often *spectabilis*. In Venice they addressed him as *clarissimo orator*. An ecclesiastic was called *reverendus*, a bishop always *pater*.[133]

Various other signs of respect were granted to ambassadors. A rather common way of honoring an ambassador at the papal court was to accord him the privilege of bearing the papal train.[134] At a papal mass, orators to whom special honor was to be shown brought to the pontiff, one by one, the water for the ceremonial washing of his hands.[135] Occasionally, quite extraordinary honors were bestowed upon ambassadors. The story has been told—but bears retelling—how the son-in-law and envoy of Ludovico il Moro proudly reported that the French king had led him into the apartment where the royal mistresses were kept, had taken one of them by the hand and presented her to the ambassador, had chosen another himself, and then they had amused themselves for two hours. Sforza replied that he was highly honored that the king had introduced his son-in-law to his domestic pleasures.[136]

The conclusion or proclamation of a treaty was an occasion for rather elaborate diplomatic ceremonies. Commines gives a marvelous description of the ceremonies accompanying the anti-French treaty of Venice of 1495:

> After dinner all the ambassadors of the league met together in boats upon the water (which in Venice is their chief recreation); the whole

[132] Michel, *Histoire des ducs de Normandie et des rois d'Angleterre*, pp. 139-141.
[133] Maulde La Clavière, *La diplomatie au temps de Machiavel*, III, 399 and n. 2.
[134] ". . . caudam pluvialis pape more solito deferente." Burckhard, *Liber notarum*, I, 223.
[135] *Ibid.*, I, 229.
[136] Maulde La Clavière, *La diplomatie au temps de Machiavel*, III, 5-6.

> number of their boats (which are provided at the charge of the Signory, and proportioned to every man's retinue) was about forty, every one of them adorned with the arms of their respective masters; and in this pomp they passed under my windows with their trumpets and other instruments of music. . . . At night there were extraordinary fireworks upon the turrets, steeples, and tops of the ambassadors' houses, multitudes of bonfires were lighted, and the cannon all around the city were fired. I was in a covered boat, rowing by the wharves to see this triumphal sight, about ten o'clock at night, especially before the ambassadors' houses, where there was great banqueting.
>
> But this was not the day on which the league was proclaimed; for the pope had sent to them to defer it for some days, till Palm Sunday, at which time he had ordered that every prince in whose dominions it was published, and all the ambassadors then with him, should carry an olive-branch in their hand, in token of their alliance and peace; and that upon the same day it should be published both in German and Spanish. At Venice they made a gallery of wood a good height above the ground (as they are wont to do at the inauguration of their Doges), which reached from the palace to the end of the piazza of St. Mark; upon which (after mass had been sung by the pope's nuncio, who absolved all people who were present at the solemnity) they marched in procession; the Signory and the ambassadors all very splendidly dressed, several of them in crimson velvet gowns which the Signory had presented to them, at least to the Germans; and all their retinue in new gowns, but these were a little of the shortest. After the procession was ended, a great many pageants and mysteries were presented to the people: first of all, Italy, and then the allied kings and princes, and the queen of Spain. At their return, at a porphyry stone, where such things are usually done, proclamation was made, and the alliance was published.[137]

Villehardouin's description of the conclusion of the crusader-Venetian treaty of 1201 (almost three centuries earlier) shows a greater emphasis upon ceremonial sanctions of a religious nature and rather less secular pomp. After the treaty had been negotiated, the envoys from the North came into the basilica to seek the consent of the people. Mass was said, and then Villehardouin himself made a short speech imploring Venetian aid, whereupon all six crusader-envoys knelt weeping before the people, while the doge and the people lifted up their hands and shouted their approval. Dandolo

[137] Commynes, *Mémoires*, Liv. VI, Chap. XX, II, 227-229. I have used the Scoble translation. II, 180-181.

then addressed the assembly eloquently. When the treaty was redacted and sealed and presented to the doge and his Council of Six in the ducal palace, Dandolo knelt weeping and swore upon the Gospels to uphold it, as did his councilors and the envoys. The shedding of tears was copious.[138] In Russia the kissing of the cross appears to have been a conventional ceremony for adding sanction to treaties.[139]

On other solemn occasions also ambassadors played a prominent part. Marriages between princely families called for a great display of ambassadors, not only those of the participating parties, but those of friendly states as well. Multiple ambassadors with large retinues, richly garbed and bearing fine gifts, were commonly sent by friendly states to grace these solemnities. Another example of an occasion of ambassadorial prominence was the famed wedding of Venice to the Adriatic on the day of the Ascension. Sanuto described it in 1499. The doge in the usual manner went in *il Bucintoro* to marry the sea just beyond the castles marking the straits of San Nicolò, then proceeded to hear mass at the church of the same name. Present were orators from Naples, Milan, Florence, Ferrara, Montferrat, but by some inadvertence the orator from Rimini was not present in his place.[140]

The proper place was an important factor in diplomatic ceremonial. It was recognized by all and sanctioned by law that the envoy (*legatus*) of a greater prince ought to precede that of a lesser, but it was equally well known that disputes frequently occurred over which prince or city-state was the greater.[141] Such disputes could be relatively mild, as when orators of Montferrat ascribed to themselves precedence over those of Mantua at Milan in 1471. The Mantuans felt it inappropriate to contest the issue on the spot, but obtained from the emperor a ruling that no precedent should be established by this submission, but that the order of precedence should be as it had been formerly.[142] Celano, the editor of Burckhard, notes that

[138] Villehardouin, *Conquête de Constantinople*, Secs. 25-31, I, 26-32. For translation of "sainz" as "Gospels," see p. 32, n. 1.

[139] Vernadsky, *The Mongols and Russia*, p. 171. I cannot resist repeating the story of the envoy sent to complain to Vladimir, prince of Galitch, of his failure to abide by a treaty he had confirmed by kissing the cross of St. Stephen. He replied that it was only a very small cross! The envoy stated that its force was great and that it was a miraculous cross, and warned the prince of impending death before he was summarily dismissed. Bakhrouchine and Kosminski, "La diplomatie du Moyen Age," p. 117.

[140] Sanuto, *Diarii*, II, col. 695.

[141] Garratus, *Tractatus*, p. 49; Nys, *Origines du droit international*, p. 330. Nys points out that questions of precedence very much concerned diplomats and publicists of the sixteenth to eighteenth centuries. *Droit international et droit politique*, p. 212. It was of some concern also in the fifteenth century, but not much before that.

[142] Archivio di Stato, Mantova, Archivio Gonzaga, 506 (E. II. 4).

questions of precedence were frequent, lively, and often bitter, causing a steady flow of dissertations and treatises on the subject.[143] Burckhard's notes, indeed, are filled with such disputes.[144]

Although there was no common code prescribing the order of precedence of orators of various states, almost everywhere the same general order was followed. The envoys of the pope, whether legates or *nuncii*, had precedence over all Italian diplomats. After them the Venetians had place. Among the orators of non-Italian powers, naturally those of the emperor had the highest standing, followed by those of France and Spain.[145] In an age when, as Maspes says, "appearance symbolized power,"[146] states and their orators took this matter of precedence most seriously. In 1452 the Venetian Senate ordered its ambassadors to take every possible measure to see that their customary precedence over the orators of Sforza should be preserved at both imperial and papal courts. To this end they should also seek the aid of the Venetian cardinals.[147]

We have spoken of the participation of ambassadors in a papal mass through the presentation of the water for washing the pontiff's hands. On Christmas day, 1485, the Venetian orator had the honor of presenting the water first; the nephew and orator of the king of Portugal second; Lord Robert, *gonfaloniere* of the church third; the orator of the emperor fourth. It is not clear that there was any rank value in the order. Burckhard received complaints, however, because the Portuguese stood a step above the *gonfaloniere*, but the pope accepted his expert's judgment.[148] A most interesting dispute arose in 1488 when the French orator claimed precedence over the orator of the king of the Romans, since his master was the first king in Christendom and ought to cede only to the emperor. It was decided against him on the grounds that the king of the Romans was the future emperor. The dispute continued, however, when another orator of France requested through Burckhard that he not be required to stand at mass below the orator of the king of the Romans, and he was allowed

[143] Burckhard, *Liber notarum*, I, 109, n. 2.

[144] I had hoped to find in this connection some discussion of the relative rank or representative character of the various kinds of envoys, but the disputes involve only orators and occasional personages who were not diplomats. Undoubtedly the precedence of the orator or ambassador over other types of envoys was so well established that no questions arose which might have enabled a modern historian to define more clearly just how an orator or ambassador differed from a *nuncius* or procurator.

[145] Maspes, "Ricevimento degli ambasciatori," p. 147. Nys has proved that the regulation of precedence of 1504 given by Paris de Grassis was not an official act of general application, but simply the arrangement the master of ceremonies could make for the occasion of the English embassy of obedience to Julius II in 1504. *Droit international et droit politique*, pp. 211-218.

[146] "Ricevimento degli ambasciatori," p. 147.

[147] A.S.V., Senato, Secreta, XIX, 123r (123r).

[148] Burckhard, *Liber notarum*, I, 135-136.

another position removed from, though not as high, as that of the German. Less than a month later the quarrel became violent when the French orator, the bishop of Lescar, occupied the first place after the cardinals in a papal procession. Georgius de Turre, the German orator, demanded his rightful place. The bishop, unwilling to cede, rode upon the German with his horse. The latter grabbed the bishop by his hood and mantle, and threw him out of the coveted spot, occupying it himself with the other German orators. The bishop subsequently demanded of the pope at mass that Georgius de Turre be excommunicated for laying violent hands upon him. The pontiff replied that he would allow the offender to remain for mass and would consider the matter afterwards, but while he was speaking the German orators walked out.[149] Obviously precedence was a matter of considerable account.

When his tasks were completed, an envoy naturally was expected to take polite leave of his host and obtain license to depart. Failure to do this was a shocking display of discourtesy. The Venetian doge in 1283 expressed his astonishment to the pope that the envoy of the latter, the bishop of Grosseto, having arrived in Venice on 3 June, having been received by the doge and his Small Council on the following day, and having read the pope's letters on the sixth, had disappeared on the ninth without awaiting the verbal response of the doge or the letters which he wished to send to Rome.[150] The departure from Venice without leave of a *nuncius* from Ferrara was probably a calculated insult, since the message sent by the Senate to Ferrara after him was in effect an ultimatum.[151]

An ambassador properly licensed to return home could depart in honor, sometimes with considerable ceremony. A fifteenth-century Venetian ambassador licensed to depart from Milan was entitled to a guard of honor and escort by all the court.[152] A way in which a host could break off dealings—or threaten to do so unless new proposals were made by the other side—was to inform a visiting ambassador that he could go or stay according to his pleasure.[153] Departure without honors would presumably be the rule in case of such a disdainful dismissal.

An envoy departing in peace and with honor was accustomed to receive

149 *Ibid.*, I, 223, 225, and 230. For certain ceremonies there was an advantage in precedence in having prelates as orators in Rome. There may well have been other advantages also.

150 ". . . sine mea scientia, sine responsione, sine litteris, et aere prodigaliter in pluvias resoluto." Cessi, *Deliberazioni del Maggior Consiglio*, III, 31.

151 A.S.V., Senato, Misti, XXIII, 18r (18r).

152 Maspes, "Ricevimento degli ambasciatori," p. 146.

153 A.S.V., Maggior Consiglio, Capricornus, 52v (157v). I have seen other examples in the Ventian documents. Maulde La Clavière found Louis XII using the same device. *La diplomatie au temps de Machiavel*, III, 356.

a gift from his host. The exchange of gifts between ambassadors and the princes to whom they were sent was an ancient and widespread usage.[154] Even the tight-fisted Venetians recognized the need for their envoys to offer gifts to their hosts and for the Venetian government to give something to a visiting envoy.[155] Maulde La Clavière mentions chains or collars of gold and clothing of rich material as suitable presents. Money, he says, not entirely correctly, was considered suitable only for ambassadors of middle rank.[156] Silver vessels of one sort or another were also considered in good taste. The failure to offer these or other gifts was taken as an insult.[157] Philip VI even gave great gifts and fine cloth to a herald sent to bear a challenge to battle.[158]

Clothing was probably the most common gift to an ambassador, although a great variety of gifts are revealed on occasion. The king of the Romans in 1496 gave to Foscari, the departing Venetian ambassador, cloth of gold for a robe.[159] A few years later the gift given by the Senate to a German ambassador was enough black velvet for a robe.[160] Venetians were always anxious either to destroy or to placate the Turks. Liberal gifts were therefore often given to Turkish ambassadors. In 1484 a Turkish ambassador received from the Senate a robe of cloth of gold and 200 ducats, while each of his servants was given a scarlet robe—an extraordinary example of diplomatic extravagance.[161] Luzio's profound knowledge of the *Archivio Gonzaga* led him to believe that for reasons both of economy and of good taste the Gonzaga princes preferred to give objects of art. They found, however, that certain greedy and rude foreigners preferred jewels or *danaro sonante*.[162] It has appeared already that money was not an inappropriate gift for honored orators. On at least two occasions in 1483 the Venetian Senate

[154] Serguiev, *La diplomatie de l'antiquité*, p. 51; Vernadsky, *The Mongols and Russia*, pp. 387-388.

[155] A.S.V., Senato, Secreta, VI, 93r (94r) and XXXVIII, 144v (145v). Maggior Consiglio, Ursa, XXII, 131v (137v), placing restrictions upon giving away the lands, goods, or money of the Commune, makes explicit exception of gifts customarily made to ambassadors and other foreigners.

[156] Maulde La Clavière, *La diplomatie au temps de Machiavel*, III, 370-371.

[157] *Ibid.*, III, 368 and n. 5. Centuries earlier *nuncii* of Barbarossa reported how the Greek emperor had insulted them by giving to envoys of Saladin horses better than theirs. *Historia de expeditione Friderici*, pp. 48-49.

[158] Froissart, *Oeuvres*, III, 38; Anthony R. Wagner, *Heralds and Heraldry in the Middle Ages*, 1st edn., 1939, 2nd edn. (London, 1956), p. 37; Maulde La Clavière, *La diplomatie au temps de Machiavel*, III, 373 and n. 3.

[159] Sanuto, *Diarii*, I, cols. 396-397.

[160] A.S.V., Senato, Secreta, XXXVII, 117r (131r).

[161] *Ibid.*, XXXII, 104r (104r).

[162] Luzio, *L'Archivio Gonzaga*, II, 82. Between 1371 and 1384 the Venetian Senate appears to have decreed that no gift of money could be made to a visiting *nuncius* or ambassador. The act cited is not the decree, but an explicit exception to it. A.S.V., Senato, Misti, XXXVIII, 96r (97r). It became a dead letter.

offered 200 ducats to orators who were bishops, envoys of the duke of Burgundy and of the emperor.[163] On the other hand, honors without cost, such as titles, could be conferred.[164]

It was generally conceded that the gift made to an ambassador was his own[165]—except in Venice. There all gifts made to diplomatic envoys had to be turned over to the state.[166] Sometimes, it is true, the ambassador was allowed to retain his gift, and *relazioni* of the sixteenth century normally conclude with a request for this privilege, but the law establishing the proprietary right of the Commune was not a mere formality, as Reumont believed.[167] Venetian legislation on this score goes back to 1268, and from later evidence we learn that such gifts were sold at public auction.[168] That gifts given to the representative of a state should be turned over to the state is a principle that can be defended, although we have seen that most medieval diplomatic representatives had a just claim to additional compensation in one form or another. Had ceremonial gifts to Venetian ambassadors been given to the treasury of St. Mark, there would be less cause for criticism, but the sale at public auction of ceremonial gifts does really strike a discordant note in the elaborate formalities of late medieval diplomatic usage.

In fairness to the *Serenissima*, however, it must be admitted that valuable gifts made by foreign powers to ambassadors clearly raised a conflict of interest and invited outright corruption. The large majority of the documents dealing with ceremonial gifts do not suggest any but the noblest motives of honoring the ambassador and the principal represented by him. Some few, however, make it clear that a price was being paid for influence over the ambassador. In 1442 the Senate gave a generally negative

[163] A.S.V., Senato, Secreta, XXXI, 35v (35v), and 41v (41v). Naturally, a gift to envoys of lower status was smaller, 20 ducats, for example, to messengers from Milan bearing good news in 1391. A.S.V., Senato, Misti, XLII, 18r—16 crossed out (18r).

[164] A.S.V., Senato, Secreta, XIX, 49r (49r).

[165] Garratus, *Tractatus*, p. 49; Maulde La Clavière, *La diplomatie au temps de Machiavel*, III, 373.

[166] "Traité du gouvernement de Venise," p. 289. In Florence the noble young men elected to accompany ambassadors for the purpose of training them for the future were required to give gifts received by them to the state, but I have seen no evidence that ambassadors had to do the same. Vedovato, *Note*, p. 34.

[167] Reumont, *Diplomazia*, pp. 225-226. Maulde La Clavière states that decisions varied in Venice whether or not such gifts belonged to the ambassador. *La diplomatie au temps de Machiavel*, III, 17. Although the ambassadors sometimes were allowed to retain them, I find no question whatsoever concerning the proprietary right of the state. See also Baschet, *Les archives de Venise*, p. 354.

[168] Cessi, *Deliberazioni del Maggior Consiglio*, II, 101; Buzzati, "Diritto diplomatico veneziano," p. 227. Also, A.S.V., Avogaria di Comun, Capitolare, VII, 3r. A.S.V., Senato, Misti, XLIV, 146r (146r).

reply to the requests of an ambassador of the king of the Romans, a man with a name which seems borrowed from old-fashioned melodrama or a very bad comic strip, Gaspar Slik. In order to maintain a useful connection, however, they voted 1,000 ducats to him—a gift out of all proportion to customary practice.[169] A Venetian ambassador, Paolo Capello, in 1497 dutifully reported to the Senate that he had refused the king of Naples' offer of a yearly grant of 400 ducats to himself and to his heirs.[170] Obviously, this practice of giving valuable gifts to ambassadors was wide-open to tremendous abuses.

The act of 1268 requiring Venetian ambassadors to turn over their gifts to the state was based quite explicitly on their duty "to devote themselves to the interest and honor of Venice."[171] An act of 1305 (which suggests that the earlier legislation was something less than totally successful) prohibited an ambassador from receiving for himself or anyone else any provision, gift, or recompense from the lords or communes to which he was sent.[172] A broader prohibition of 1375 provided that no citizen should hold a provision, gift, or loan from any signory or commune under the penalty of perpetual deprivation of all offices, benefices, and councils of the Commune of Venice in addition to other penalties already established.[173] In 1403 a still more wide-sweeping act—at least insofar as native-born nobles were concerned—was passed prohibiting them from receiving from any prince or commune any fief, provision, loan, gift, stipend, procurations, lands or houses at rent. Anyone who already possessed such a benefaction must dispose of it within a year.[174] Largely repetitive legislation passed by the Senate and the Great Council in 1482 and 1483 denied to ambassadors that they should solicit any favors for themselves or for others, unless,

[169] A.S.V., Senato, Secreta, xv, 151r (152r).

[170] Sanuto, *Diarii*, I, col. 627.

[171] Cessi, *Deliberazioni del Maggior Consiglio*, II, 101. By an act of 1271 the Great Council forbade the *baiulo* of Constantinople to accept any gift from the emperor within a year after giving up his office. *Ibid.*, II, 401.

[172] A.S.V., Maggior Consiglio, Magnus, 94r (95r). An index reference to what appears to be this document is dated 24 August, although the copy in the register is dated 31 August. A.S.V., Avogaria di Comun, Capitolare, VII, 3r. The prohibition was supposed to be placed in the commissions of all ambassadors. This was rarely done, although it was done on occasion. A.S.V., Senato, Misti, XXVIII, 26r (26r). If the chancellery had conformed to all legal requirements concerning matters that should be contained in the commissions of ambassadors, those documents would have become most unwieldy.

[173] Molmenti, "Relazioni tra patrizi veneziani e diplomatici stranieri," p. 39.

[174] *Ibid.*, pp. 40-41. In 1406 an exception was made for papal benefactions. *Ibid.*, p. 43. In 1406, however, the Avogaria di Comun broke the exception as in opposition to the earlier act, an interesting example of the power of the Maggior Consiglio to bind itself with regard to future action. *Ibid.*, p. 44.

of course, this was contained in their instructions.[175] An ambassador received a severe reprimand from the Ten in 1489 for accepting 400 ducats from the queen of Hungary.[176]

With regard to conflict of interest, Rome, the fount from which benefices flowed, posed a particular problem. Perhaps this is one reason why Venice avoided the use of ecclesiastics as ambassadors. As early as 1238 the Great Council saw fit to act against *nuncii* to Rome who received any petitions of private persons without special permission.[177] Certain ambassadors sent to Rome later were permitted to seek prebends or benefices, but only as private persons, not as ambassadors, and it was specified that no precedents might be drawn from these exceptional cases.[178] The prohibition against seeking benefices was extended in 1328 to ambassadors sent to the court of a papal legate, though this was a special act, not generalized legislation.[179] Another special act took precautions against the chancellor or other member of the retinue of an ambassador seeking favors in Rome on the ambassador's behalf.[180] The author of the "Traité du gouvernement de Venise" found the rule against ambassadors' seeking benefices in Rome worthy of note and added that no one could be elected ambassador to that place if he had a close relative who was a priest or a religious.[181]

Ambassadors holding possessions within the territories of other states might also have their interest in the public welfare undermined by self-interest, so in 1271 the Great Council provided that those who held possessions in the marquisates of Treviso or Ferrara or the county of Rovigo should not be sent as ambassadors to those places.[182] So far as is known the prohibition was never extended to other territories, but it certainly does reflect a legitimate concern.

Another conflict of interest of a different sort arose from ambassadors drawn in Venice from among the great mercantile families who mixed private business with their diplomatic missions. Galleys bearing ambassadors to Alexandria were prohibited in 1302 from carrying money or goods

175 A.S.V., Senato, Terra, VIII, 181r (182r); A.S.V., Maggior Consiglio, Stella, 32rv (36rv).

176 Lamansky, *Secrets d'état de Venise*, pp. 198-199.

177 Cessi, *Deliberazioni del Maggior Consiglio*, II, 44. Nys dates this document incorrectly by two years and errs slightly concerning its contents. "Le droit d'ambassade jusqu'à Grotius," XV, 579. The act was confirmed in 1303. A.S.V., Magnus, 54v (56v). The question of concern in this act is another upon which Behrens wrongly heaps scorn. "Treatises on the Ambassador," p. 617. See also Garratus, *Tractatus*, p. 36.

178 A.S.V., Maggior Consiglio, Clericus-Civicus, 60r (108r); A.S.V., Senato, Misti, XV, 2r (2r).

179 Cessi, *Deliberazioni . . . Rogati, "Mixtorum,"* I, 371, no. 139.

180 A.S.V., Senato, Terra, V, 148v (148v).

181 "Traité du gouvernement de Venise," p. 289.

182 Cessi, *Deliberazioni del Maggior Consiglio*, II, 61; Buzzati, "Diritto diplomatico veneziano," p. 228 (misdated). Exceptions were sometimes made. Cessi, *op.cit.*, III, 87.

from Venice, Crete, or elsewhere to Alexandria or from that city on the return.[183] *Nuncii* sent to Rome in 1348 were refused permission to engage in any business of their own or of others, but were required to tend strictly to affairs of state.[184] This feeling that the ambassador ought to concentrate exclusively upon the affairs of the commune was written into a generalized decree in 1396. Ambassadors and others who served outside the city were denied the privilege of doing business, either for themselves or through others, in the places where they served. An exception was made in favor of ambassadors who already had business affairs under factors in some place where they were subsequently sent as ambassadors. The factors could carry on as before, but the ambassador could not enter into any new enterprise.[185] Ambassadors or *nuncii* from Cyprus carrying the yearly tribute to Egypt came under special scrutiny a century later, for the April galleys sent for that purpose had become so overburdened with merchandise that they had been unable to enter the Damietta mouth of the Nile. No ambassador, secretary, or *nuncius* to the sultan, therefore, should be permitted to carry with him any merchandise, especially wine, either going or returning, except for what was necessary for the journey.[186]

Although the foregoing discussion of conflict of interest has centered upon Venice, we know that other states also were concerned about it, particularly that conflict which tempted ambassadors to Rome.[187] Edward II denounced one *nuncius* as a *pseudo-nuncius* because he had pursued his own interests rather than those of the king, by seeking for himself the bishopric of Winchester, which the king desired for another.[188] Vedovato quotes Savonarola on the many temptations besetting an ambassador, and the noted Florentine friar calls attention not only to the problems of envoys at the papal court, but to some of the other possibilities of conflict of interest against which Venice tried to protect itself.[189]

The position of the ambassador, as we have seen, was hedged about with immunities and ceremonies. His specially protected status, his sacrosanctity, if you will, was recognized in both laws and with some exceptions in

[183] A.S.V., Maggior Consiglio, Magnus, 22r.

[184] A.S.V., Senato, Misti, XXIV, 99v (99v).

[185] A.S.V., Senato, Misti, XLIII, 121v (120v). An ambassador to be sent to London in 1408 was to be allowed to trade either personally or through factors. *Calendar of State Papers. Venetian*, I, 48, no. 168. Special inducement may have been necessary to find an ambassador for this distant assignment.

[186] A.S.V., Dieci, filze, IX, 145; Misti, XXVI, 179v (208v).

[187] Maulde La Clavière, *La diplomatie au temps de Machiavel*, II, 394-395.

[188] Rymer, *Foedera*, II, ii, 82.

[189] ". . . non soggiornare per alcuno caso fuori di quello, cioè nè per faccenda sua nè d'altri, nè provedere cose nuove nè fare mercatantia nè altri sua fatti, nè commessi d'altri, nè impetrare grazie, benefici, presenti, utilità, nè comodo alcuno in suo profitto o acconcio, o di sua amici o parento . . ." Vedovato, *Note*, p. 11.

diplomatic practice. One might almost say that it was recognized of necessity, for medieval lawyers and medieval governments understood that only by a free and secure exchange of envoys can diplomatic activity of any degree of intensity and complexity be conducted. The ambassador was protected—theoretically, at least—against lawless violence and legal process, at least as long as he behaved himself in the course of his embassy. Some notion of the extraterritoriality of ambassadors existed, although not so clearly as at present. Many and vivid were the violations of sacrosanctity, but infinitely more frequent surely were the unmentioned, because customary, observations of it.

Since an ambassador represented his principal, he was expected to be personally worthy of that exalted status and to make an appearance which would do honor to his master. The size and composition of his retinue became increasingly important for this purpose, as did such details as his and their dress, and the furnishing of his temporary residence. On the other hand, the princes or heads of government receiving an ambassador were expected to manifest their respect for his principal by honoring him. Thus, by the fifteenth century it became customary in Italy to go out to meet an ambassador or, at any rate, to send a distinguished group of persons to meet him. The visitor was received in audience in a solemn and honorable manner. Honors or gifts of one sort or another were customarily bestowed upon ambassadors as a mark of respect, both for the envoy and his principal. Any failure to observe the respect due to an ambassador was cause for serious complaint, as was any affront arising out of the relative degree of honor due to an ambassador of one state as against that of another. Diplomacy in the more pragmatic twentieth century has lost much of the ceremonial of late medieval diplomacy, although some vestiges of it remain.

CHAPTER VIII

RATIFICATION

Although the thesis of this chapter on ratification is in conflict with most authorities on medieval diplomacy, it follows from what has been shown of the characters of the different types of diplomatic envoys and is supported by the medieval evidence. This thesis is that under certain common circumstances subsequent ratification by the principal of the acts of his envoys was not necessary to the conclusion of binding covenants.

Ratification as a discretionary act by which the state might give or withhold its consent to be bound by the acts of its diplomats is a modern development.[1] According to J. Mervyn Jones in his book on *Full Powers and Ratification*, treaties and other international covenants in the seventeenth and eighteenth centuries were regarded as personal contracts between monarchs, full powers were simply unlimited powers of attorney, and ratification was merely a formality "obligatory according to the rules of diplomatic practice." It was the American and French revolutions which marked the watershed between the personal diplomacy of the seventeenth and eighteenth centuries under the forms of private law and the constitutional diplomacy of the nineteenth and twentieth centuries under the forms of international public law.[2] All of Jones's evidence quite properly was drawn from seventeenth- to twentieth-century sources, but his conclusions are complementary to those of the present chapter. Diplomacy in the Middle Ages was conducted under the forms of private law, as in the seventeenth and eighteenth centuries, but subsequent ratification had not yet become obligatory or even customary, even as a mere formality, although it was being increasingly employed.

The terms *ratificare* and *ratum habere* have a much broader significance during this period than just the subsequent affirmation of the act of an agent by his principal without which the act of the agent would be juridically incomplete. For example, ". . . rati enim habitio mandato comparatur"[3] originally referred to the subsequent act by which a principal could

[1] Still, world opinion was not prepared for the failure of President Wilson, having negotiated the Treaty of Versailles, to obtain ratification of it by the Senate. Wilson, of course, was no mere diplomat.

[2] The thesis of the book is summarized on p. 12.

[3] *D.* 46, 3, 12, 4; *D.* 50, 17, 152; *C.* 4, 28, 7; William of Drogheda, *Summa aurea*, CII, in Wahrmund, *Quellen*, II, ii, 98; *Sext.* 5, 12, *De regulis juris*, 10; Dinus de Rossonibus de Mugello, *Commentarius in regulas iuris pontificii*, bound with Philippus Decius (Lugduni, 1570), p. 74.

validate what someone *without* authority to conclude had done on his behalf. We have seen, however, that a *ratihabitio* (or *ratum habere*) clause came to be included in the mandate itself and was considered by some legal writers, both medieval and modern, as essential to the grant of a power to conclude.[4] In this sense also it became equivalent to a subsequent ratification.

Acts of medieval diplomatic envoys lacking full powers did require subsequent ratification. Any agreements made by *nuncii*, legates, ambassadors, or orators without full powers could become binding covenants only upon formal approval by the principals. Thus legates of Venice and Ferrara in 1226 after lengthy negotiations arrived at agreements which they submitted for the approval of their governments.[5] Other documents dealing with diplomatic envoys contain such clauses as: ". . . but it can not in any way be completed except in this Council. . . ."[6] Obviously, also, when a plenipotentiary knowingly exceeded his powers, and this was known also to the other party, he would subject his dealings to his principal for ratification before they became conclusive. A Milanese ambassador to France in 1446-1447 made covenants of this sort with the king, stipulating that those which exceeded his powers should be subject to ratification, although the others should be considered binding in any case.[7] Maulde La Clavière indicates several cases where rulers subsequently ratified the acts of those who had simply taken upon themselves to negotiate peace.[8] In juridical terms there was really no difference between the acts of such self-appointed individuals and regularly appointed envoys lacking full powers, although in practical terms one could easily disavow the efforts of the former, while refusal to ratify the acts of the latter, though lawful, was necessarily a matter of diplomatic embarrassment.

Even treaties negotiated by plenipotentiaries sometimes included the provision that the principals should take an oath personally in support of the

[4] *Supra*, pp. 119-120, n. 55.

[5] Cessi, *Deliberazioni del Maggior Consiglio*, I, 173.

[6] A.S.V., Maggior Consiglio, Magnus, 89r (90r).

[7] Osio, *Documenti diplomatici*, III, 457, no. CCCLXXIII, and III, 464-466, no. CCCLXXVIII. The instructions are printed in Bernardino Corio, *Storia di Milano*, riveduta e annotata dal Egidio de Magri, *et al.*, 3 vols. (Milano, 1855-1858), II, 759. Perret, *Relations de la France avec Venise*, I, 184-186. The case of the *nunciis et procuratoribus* with power of confessing the excesses of Louis of Bavaria against the church may be another example of plenipotentiaries exceeding their powers. Louis rejected the penance which Clement VI wished to impose upon him and refused to ratify the acts of his envoys. There is no clear indication in the chronicle that they had full powers to accept penance. In any event, it is not surprising that subsequent *nuncii* sent to Clement VI were not successful. Even if juridically defensible, repudiation of one's envoys bears a price. Heinricus Surdus de Selbach, *Chronica*, Harry Bresslau, ed., in *M.G.H.*, *Script. rer. Germ.*, *N.S.*, I (Berlin, 1922), 53-58.

[8] *La diplomatie au temps de Machiavel*, II, 88.

conventions.[9] The often mentioned crusader-Venetian treaty of 1201 was one of these.[10] The word "ratify" does not necessarily appear in such documents, although an oath by the principal probably amounted to a ratification in its most solemn form. In a treaty of 1261 between Genoa and Michael Paleologus, the Genoese envoys promised that the *podestà*, captain, and the eight noble *anciani* of Genoa would swear to implement it and by oath would confirm and ratify it.[11] Later documents are more likely to specify a formal written ratification than an oath, another example of the increasing substitution of legal forms for religious.[12]

Procuratorial letters sometimes included specifically the authority to promise subsequent ratification by the principal.[13] From the beginning of the fourteenth century such clauses were common enough.[14] The procurator might be authorized to promise that the principal would ratify "without delay."[15] Other principals would ratify if necessary or if requested.[16] That a procurator was authorized to promise subsequent ratification did not prevent him, of course, from making conventions which lacked such a promise.[17]

Often by the terms of a treaty an exchange of ratifications was required.[18] Under the terms of a Venetian-French treaty of 1484, the Venetians promised ratification within four months, upon the receipt of which the French king should cause his own letters of ratification in similar form to be dispatched. The Venetian ratification was sent to Antonio Loredano, orator in France, with an admonition to be sure that he received the reciprocal ratification.[19]

A common and obvious condition was that accords should be ratified within a certain time—by the next feast of the Nativity of St. John the Baptist, by Christmas, or within four months.[20] An Anglo-French treaty

[9] E.g., Chaplais, *Treaty Rolls*, I, 106, nos. 249-250.

[10] Longnon, *Vie de Villehardouin*, pp. 179-181; Tessier, *Quatrième Croisade*, pp. 252-254; Tafel and Thomas, *Urkunden*, I, 362-368.

[11] It was so ratified with great ceremony and was at the same time ratified by ambassadors of the emperor. *Liber Iurium reipublicae Genuensis*, I, col. 1350, no. DCCCCXLV.

[12] Rymer, *Foedera*, III, iv, 7, and V, iv, 13; A.S.V., Senato, Secreta, XXVIII, 132v (138v).

[13] Ganshof, *Le Moyen Age*, pp. 123 and 275.

[14] A few fourteenth-century examples: Rymer, *Foedera*, II, i, 106; II, iv, 176; III, ii, 117; III, ii, 208; III, iv, 35; III, iv, 74-75. I cannot, however, agree with Maulde La Clavière that such a clause was usual. *La diplomatie au temps de Machiavel*, II, 89.

[15] *Indillate*. Osio, *Documenti diplomatici*, I, i, 203, no. CXXXVII.

[16] Rymer, *Foedera*, II, iv, 62; IV, i, 122-123 and 129; IV, iv, 140-141.

[17] *Ibid.*, IV, i, 123-124; *C.C.R.*, *Henry IV (1405-1409)*, p. 306.

[18] E.g., Rymer, *Foedera*, II, iii, 75-76.

[19] A.S.V., Senato, Secreta, XXXII, 82v (82v), and 80v (80v)–81r (81r).

[20] Chaplais, *Treaty Rolls*, I, 259-263, no. 660; Rymer, *Foedera*, II, ii, 138, and V, iii, 11-12; A.S.V., Senato, Secreta, XXXII, 81v (81v). Benedict XII suspended the interdict upon Bergamo in May 1335 on condition that the Bergamese ratify before the Nativity of the Virgin and transmit before All Saints the agreement made by their envoys to withdraw support from Louis of

of 1327 provided that if the English king did not transmit his ratification to the king of France before the Tuesday after the Octaves of Easter, the treaty "should be null, of no value, just as if it had not been negotiated, and that the previous treaty should remain in full force."[21]

Although, as has been shown in a previous chapter,[22] a plenipotentiary had the power to conclude an agreement within the limitations of his mandate, a clause requiring subsequent ratification could be included within the conventions. If it were, it became as integral to the conventions as any other clause, and failure to abide by it was sufficient reason for the opposite party to regard the conventions as void. This did not need to be stated in the conventions; it is obvious. It was stated in the one example given merely to underline the point that the previous conventions should in that case remain in force. Juridically valid agreements voided for nonperformance, however, are quite different from agreements incomplete *ab initio* for want of ratification. Treaties, truces, and other covenants made by medieval plenipotentiaries were complete and valid without subsequent ratification by the principal.

This is contested by many authorities. Nicolson states of fifteenth-century treaties that it was taken for granted that a sovereign could not refuse to ratify a treaty negotiated by an ambassador having full powers.[23] In fact he was not required to ratify unless, of course, his plenipotentiary had promised that he should, but he was nonetheless bound to carry out such a treaty. Dickinson contrasts the necessity in diplomacy of subsequent ratification of the acts of a plenipotentiary by the principal with the lack of such necessity in common or civil law.[24] Fifteenth-century diplomacy, however, continued to function under the forms of private law, and ratification remained nonessential. Maulde La Clavière also regarded the ratification as "an indispensable formality."[25] Lucas, writing of fourteenth-century Eng-

---

Bavaria and the anti-pope in favor of a papal alliance. Archivio Secreto Vaticano, AA. Arm. I-XVIII, nos. 6202-6204.

21 Rymer, *Foedera*, II, ii, 180-181. The particular reason for this strong phrasing was the obvious intention to preserve the former treaty if the more recent one was not ratified.

22 *Supra*, pp. 36-37.

23 *Evolution of Diplomatic Method*, p. 41.

24 *The Congress of Areas*, p. 193. She cites Jones, and, as I have indicated, his documentation is from the seventeenth century on.

25 Stated flatly. *La diplomatie au temps de Machiavel*, III, 196. Elsewhere, III, 278-279, he states that a clause that an alliance should commence at once "does not dispense from the ratification and from the oath by the sovereign, within the delay stipulated . . ." If a time limit is established, then there must have been a clause requiring ratification in the covenant, and this has nothing to do with the necessity of ratification *per se*. Yet elsewhere, III, 163-164, he seems to acknowledge that some "articles" could be rendered definitive by the plenipotentiary. Maulde La Clavière's vast erudition never led him to an understanding of full powers.

land, declared that it was customary to ratify all agreements or treaties even when made by plenipotentiaries, although he seems to recognize that it was not juridically necessary.[26]

Mattingly stands on much firmer ground. He finds the normal result of ambassadorial negotiations to be a draft requiring subsequent ratification by the principal. No principal could be bound merely by the force of the ambassador's credentials or instructions. If the ambassador's agreements were to have any juridical standing in their own right, he must be the holder of a specific mandate resembling a power of attorney. Usually such a mandate merely authorized the ambassador to affix his signature to a text already approved by the principal. Less often it indicated possible changes in a draft or the essential terms of a possible covenant. Still less often was an ambassador authorized to sign any agreement which he considered consonant with his instructions. Even when ambassadors were authorized to sign and to ratify, governments generally preferred formal subsequent ratification by the principals. The extent of the powers of the ambassador was generally in inverse proportion to the importance of the negotiations in which he was engaged.[27]

A few qualifications may be added to Mattingly's opinion. It is true that by the fifteenth century, in Venice at least, and probably throughout Italy, a draft treaty submitted to the principal was the typical result of ambassadorial relations.[28] This was not infallibly true even in fifteenth-century Venice, however, and was less true in the thirteenth and fourteenth centuries and in the fifteenth century north of the Alps. Quite often a mandatory was given reasonably broad authority to conclude and, occasionally, quite surprisingly sweeping powers. Governments probably did prefer subsequent ratification of highly important covenants by the other principal, but the total number of subsequent ratifications found among the documents is relatively small compared to the total number of covenants negotiated by plenipotentiaries.

An indication that ratification was not necessary is provided by procurations which expressly concede the power "to conclude" and by covenants

[26] "The Machinery of Diplomatic Intercourse," p. 329.

[27] *Renaissance Diplomacy*, pp. 42-43. The procuration, of course, not only resembled but *was* a power of attorney or proxy. Ruess recognized that the pope did not have to ratify the acts of his legates. *Die rechtliche Stellung des päpstlichen Legaten*, p. 9. I am not knowledgeable in Byzantine sources, so cannot really criticize the assertion that early medieval Byzantine envoys had to have their acts ratified. Löhren, *Geschichte des gesandtschaftlichen Verkehrs*, pp. 74-75, and Bakhrouchine and Kosminski, "La diplomatie du Moyen Age," p. 93. I would want to see it proved rather rigorously.

[28] It was common Venetian practice to appoint envoys lacking full powers, receive from them draft covenants for approval, then forward to the envoys full powers for concluding the covenants.

in which ambassadors declare that they "effectively obligate" their principals.[29] One procuration is especially interesting, for it contains full powers for making a peace or a truce, including the *ratihabitio* clause, then proceeds: "And *nevertheless*, we promise to transfer to the said adversaries whenever requested our letters patent, confirmed with our own hand and sealed with our leaden seal."[30] That *nichilominus* indicates once more that the full powers were in themselves sufficient for a juridically binding compact. The subsequent ratification had another purpose. The same is suggested by the ratification of covenants already long in force[31] or by periodic oaths in support of a single covenant.[32] Another procuration contains the promise that the principal will ratify "any time" that he will be requested,[33] and another still "however often" he will be requested.[34] The repetition of ratification implies that it was not ratification that made a covenant binding, but full powers. If it were not so, a single ratification would surely suffice. Ratification reiterated upon request can only be construed as an extrajuridical expression of good faith. Also significant is the procuration in which the *ratihabitio* clause is modified to read, ". . . from this time we approve and we ratify. . . ."[35] Even more so is the procuration containing a normal *ratihabitio* and the additional statement, ". . . from now, just as from then, we ratify and approve by the present (letters)."[36]

Sometimes pairs of documents are found, one containing full powers with a *ratihabitio* and lacking any mention of subsequent ratification, the other lacking full powers and containing a clause by which draft agreements should be submitted to the principal for approval.[37] The clear implication is that subsequent ratification was not necessary if the procuration with *ratihabitio* was used. Such sets of double documents for the same purpose suggest, moreover, that the requirement of ratification did not come through any desire on the part of the principal to limit his envoys, but rather from the desire of the other party for subsequent personal ratification.

The authority to publish treaties and truces, which was often specifically granted to plenipotentiaries, strengthens the argument that subsequent ratification by the principal was not essential.[38] Sometimes this authority to publish the covenants was linked with the authority to promise that the

[29] Manaresi, *Atti . . . di Milano*, pp. 327-328, no. CCXXXI; Rymer, *Foedera*, III, ii, 60.
[30] Italics mine. Rymer, *Foedera*, III, iv, 40.
[31] *Ibid.*, V, iii, 24.
[32] Yearly oath. Cessi, *Deliberazioni del Maggior Consiglio*, II, 199-200.
[33] *Toute fois.* Rymer, *Foedera*, III, iv, 33-34.
[34] *Quotienscumque. Ibid.*, IV, ii, 81.
[35] Rymer, *Foedera*, III, iii, 202.
[36] *Ibid.*, III, i, 149.
[37] *Ibid.*, II, iv, 106, 107, 121, 147.
[38] *Ibid.*, III, i, 22; III, iii, 28; III, iv, 83-84; V, i, 13-14.

principal would ratify.[39] The ratification in such cases obviously followed the publication and so would seem to have had no effect upon the validity of the agreements.[40] In July 1363 a *baiulo* departing for Constantinople was instructed to obtain the oath of John Paleologus in support of the truce which his ambassadors had concluded and had redacted in public instruments four months earlier.[41]

It is even more conclusive that other measures were taken under the terms of covenants which were to be ratified, but had not yet received ratification. The crusader-envoys of 1201 sent their covenants to the pope for confirmation and borrowed money for beginning construction of the desired fleet before reporting to their principals. Only subsequently was the treaty ratified by the barons at Corbie.[42] In 1425 the Venetian consul at Bruges was ordered to seek from the duke of Burgundy ratification of a truce already published. In addition he was given 7,000 ducats for the remaining payment due under that truce.[43] A payment obviously had been made before ratification. The Treaty of Paris, 20 May 1303, provided that the English king should come to Amiens in September to confirm and swear to the treaty. It was published on 2 June. By 10 June the French king was required to appoint barons who would hasten to carry it out. The king of England ratified it on 10 July.[44] English envoys to treat with France in 1438, while receiving authority to promise ratification by their king, also had direct authority to order his subjects to carry out its terms.[45] On 4 August 1370, Edward III ratified a recent treaty with Flanders, since the count had sent a copy of it to the English captain at Calais, assuming it to be in effect. The count himself did not ratify it until 27 April 1371.[46] In the ratification by Lucca of an agreement with the papacy in 1341 is included the text of a bull of Benedict XII in which he had already lifted the excommunications

[39] *Ibid.*, III, iv, 95; IV, ii, 113; V, i, 133; V, i, 134.

[40] Anglo-French truce, 25 September 1413, in which the plenipotentiaries state that they have ordered publication. *Ibid.*, IV, ii, 48-49. Ratification by the king of England, 21 October 1413. *Ibid.*, IV, ii, 53.

[41] A.S.V., Sindicatus, I, 98v. A similar *sindicatus*, I, 106r.

[42] Queller, "L'évolution du rôle de l'ambassadeur," pp. 496-500. Villehardouin does not mention the assembly at Corbie. Our chief source is Robert of Clari, *La conquête de Constantinople*, Ph. Lauer, ed. (Paris, 1924), p. 8, sec. 8. Ernoul has a confused account. Ernoul et Bernard le Trésorier, *Chronique*, Louis de Mas Latrie, ed. (Paris, 1871), pp. 338-340. See my article, *op.cit.*, p. 499, n. 3, for a discussion of various modern opinions on it.

[43] A.S.V., Sindicati, II, 1r. Identical document for a different consul two years later. *Ibid.*, II, 9v. The first one must have failed for some reason.

[44] Chaplais, *Treaty Rolls*, I, 159-164, no. 394-395; Rymer, *Foedera*, I, iv, 28.

[45] Rymer, *Foedera*, V, i, 55.

[46] *Ibid.*, III, ii, 172 (*C.C.R.*, *Edward III* [*1369-1374*], p. 300), and III, ii, 182 (*C.C.R.*, *Edward III* [*1369-1374*], p. 300). See also *C.C.R.*, *Edward III* (*1369-1374*), p. 302.

and other penalties imposed upon its citizens.[47] Some covenants made by plenipotentiaries simply declare that they will be immediately effective, even though they have not yet even been published.[48] It is quite apparent that a considerable variety of acts were performed upon the assumption of the complete validity of covenants made by procurators with full powers regardless of the ratification of those acts by the principals.

Still clearer proofs that ratification was not necessary can be found if needed. Ambassadors of duke Leopold of Austria in Venice in 1406 insisted that their agreements with Venice "must be bulled with bulls of either party," and to that end it would be necessary to send a copy to Austria. The Senate replied that it considered the pacts to be in good form, and they were willing to do as the Austrians wished, but that meanwhile the agreements should be considered sufficient and adequate. Any additions or diminutions could be made subsequently by agreement of the parties.[49] Later Leopold tried to back out of the agreements on the grounds of the changed succession in his family as a consequence of the death of duke William. The Venetians objected strongly that his plenipotentiaries had entered into a binding compact.[50] The Venetians were naturally cautious in subsequent dealings with Austria on this matter, insisting that the envoys must have full powers and also the seal or bull so that at the same time and in the same place the agreements and the confirmations could be made and sealed.[51] In 1421 the Senate removed from the draft of a league with Milan a provision that unless it was ratified by both parties within fifteen days it should be considered null. Instead they substituted a clause saying that it should be regarded as binding upon both parties, but that nevertheless they should ratify it within the prescribed time for the sake of greater firmness.[52] At the very end of the period under study here, in 1499, the Venetians still did not consider subsequent ratification of the acts

[47] Archivio Secreto Vaticano, AA. Arm. I-XVIII, no. 6074.

[48] Rymer, *Foedera*, III, i, 74 and 133.

[49] A.S.V., Senato, Secreta, III, 34v (34v). [50] *Ibid.*, III, 48v (48v)–49r (49r).

[51] *Ibid.*, III, 65v (65v). See also the refusal of Ferdinand and Isabella to ratify the conventions made by their plenipotentiary with France in 1503. Of course there was no way to compel them to abide by the conventions, although both the French king and the Spanish ambassador considered themselves betrayed and the Catholic kings foresworn, so the French turned again to military operations. Guicciardini, *Storia d'Italia*, Lib. VI, cap. 1, III, 6-8.

[52] "Reformetur dictum capitulum in hec forma. Quod hec lega facta conclusione habeatur pro firma per ambas partes. Et quod nichilominus ad maius robur ambe partes teneantur omnino infra dictum terminum eam ratificare et approbare per publica et auctentica instrumenta.

"Et ex nunc sit captum quod contentante ambassiatore predicto cum capitulis, modis et conditionibus suprascriptis, in nomine Jesu Christi, ac gloriose virginis Marie et beatissimi Marci evangeliste, dicta liga et confederatio concludi et firmari debeat et fieri instrumenta necessaria cum clausulis opportunis." A.S.V., Senato, Secreta, VII, 207v (208v).

of plenipotentiaries to be necessary. Requested by the king of France to ratify the treaty between them, the Senate replied that "although in the clauses of the said treaty it was not declared that the parties should be held to ratify and approve it within a certain time, nor do we deem it necessary," they would do it to oblige him.[53]

On a few occasions, however, ratification appears to have been required despite the possession of full powers by the envoys. The "plenipotentiaries" of Edward II in 1316 for treating with Norwegian envoys were required to refer their negotiations to the king before they could be confirmed. Although these documents were called "full powers," however, they lacked a *ratihabitio* clause.[54] Despite a few examples previously indicated[55] of the apparent conveyance of power to conclude without the *ratihabitio* clause, legal opinion seemed to demand it, it was customarily used, and its omission at least casts doubt upon the powers of the envoys. Other procurations including the *ratihabitio*, however, also require that the negotiations be referred to the principal.[56] This also can be easily explained within the context of an argument that denies in general terms the necessity of subsequent ratification. The procuration formed a voluntary relationship between the principal and the procurator, and the principal might limit his consent in any way he wished. One such limitation might be required referral to the principal of any agreements before he could be bound. The other party or his representatives would pay close attention to an examination of the procuration in order to determine the precise limits of the powers of the plenipotentiary. One might argue, indeed, that if reference to the principal were required *per se* the requirement would probably not have been stated. Apparent exceptions to the rule that the acts of plenipotentiaries did not require subsequent ratification, therefore, can be interpreted instead as confirmation of it.

The acts of plenipotentiaries were subsequently ratified, in fact, in many instances where no juridical necessity for such ratification existed. It was not necessary in general, and it was not required by the powers or by the conventions specifically. *Gli Atti del Comune di Milano* for the twelfth and early thirteenth centuries is full of ratifications of the acts of ambassadors, some of which were clearly plenipotentiaries. Manaresi's observation that

[53] *Ibid.*, XXXVII, 87v (101v). Since Venice agreed to ratify, they should be sure to obtain reciprocal ratification from the king.

[54] Rymer, *Foedera*, II, i, 94. According to some of our sources, *supra*, pp. 119-120, such envoys were not plenipotentiaries. In some cases it was obviously not the intention to allow the envoys any freedom to act, and no mention of procuration, full powers, or *ratihabitio* is to be found. *Ibid.*, II, iv, 199; *C.C.R., Edward III (1346-1349)*, p. 67.

[55] *Supra*, p. 119, n. 55.

[56] Rymer, *Foedera*, II, iv, 125; III, i, 66.

treaties of peace which were not written by notaries of the commune in the offices of the commune had to be ratified by an act in simple notarial form is undoubtedly true, but reflects no defect in the powers of plenipotentiaries.[57] This was not a necessity of law or of diplomacy, but merely of Genoese diplomatics. The collection in the *Archivio di Stato di Venezia* called *Miscellanea di atti diplomatici e privati* contains many ratifications of conventions concluded by foreign plenipotentiaries—from Ferrara, Ravenna, Pola, and Ragusa, for example.[58] North of the Alps in France and England, in the fifteenth century as in the thirteenth, the kings sometimes ratified acts of their envoys in the same manner.[59]

There may be several reasons why ratification was sometimes desired, even though not necessary. Papal ratification of the grant of Sicily to Henry III's son Edmund indicates one of them, the wish to remedy any unknown defect of the original covenant.[60] The Venetian Senate also noted that it was "expedient" that they should ratify their pacts with Lombardy.[61] The extrajuridical desirability of subsequent ratification sometimes depended upon the social status of the plenipotentiary or the importance of the conventions. A special mandate given to the count of Hainaut and Holland for seeking allies and negotiating alliances for Edward III on the eve of the Hundred Years War did not contain a clause requiring ratification, while the otherwise similar document in favor of a knight and a lawyer did promise ratification.[62] The lesser status of the latter envoys made ratification more important—though not, of course, essential. The acts of the envoy of great estate were more convincing in themselves and had less need of supportive acts by the principal. Repudiation in such a case was extremely unlikely. English envoys, for making peace with the Scots in 1342, received one procuration containing full powers and a *ratihabitio* clause and another document directed to the same end, but omitting the above clauses and adding a requirement for subsequent ratification. The same envoys also carried full powers containing a *ratihabitio* for making a truce, but not a second document for this purpose.[63] It may be concluded that ratification was more likely to be desirable in connection with the more important

[57] *Atti . . . di Milano*, cv.

[58] Busta II, nos. 92 and 99; busta III, nos. 107 and 120.

[59] Chaplais, *Treaty Rolls*, I, 14, no. 27 (Rymer, *Foedera*, I, i, 121; *C.P.R.*, *Henry III* [*1232-1247*], p. 135); Chaplais, *Treaty Rolls*, I, 141-142, no. 367 (Rymer, *Foedera*, I, iii, 192); Rymer, *Foedera*, V, i, 39-40; V, ii, 108. Maulde La Clavière reports from the Milanese archives an instance of conventions extorted by the Swiss from Milanese mandataries upon fear of death. The promises exceeded their mandates and were also of no validity because extorted by force, but they were ratified anyway. *La diplomatie au temps de Machiavel*, III, 230, n. 1.

[60] Rymer, *Foedera*, I, i, 182.

[61] A.S.V., Senato, Misti, XVIII, 34v (34v).

[62] Rymer, *Foedera*, II, iii, 157.

[63] *Ibid.*, II, iv, 122.

act, the treaty. In 1450 "ambassadors and procurators" for the relatively routine task of obtaining a prorogation of a truce submitted their agreements "humbly for the ratification, approbation, and consent of our kings and lords, in order that due honor and reverence justly should be offered to them and their royal seats."[64] Given the ability of a properly empowered procurator acting within the limits of his procuration to conclude agreements juridically binding his principal, subsequent ratification was intended to give added security to the opposite party. On the one hand, it gave security against unknown defects in the procuration or the covenant. On the other hand, and more importantly, it gave added extralegal force to the act of the procurator through personal commitment of the principal and added publicity. Although diplomacy employs the forms of law, the relations among sovereign and quasi-sovereign states are only superficially subject to law. It is for this reason that various devices in excess of those required by law were used in an effort to ensure compliance with covenants in a field which is ultimately lawless.

Since the purpose of ratification of the acts of plenipotentiaries was not juridical, but to obtain whatever additional sanction could be obtained from a solemn act of the principal, the act of ratification of important covenants was given as much publicity and surrounded by as much ceremony as possible. We have a Milanese account of their own ratification of the alliance by which Lodi was brought into the Lombard League in 1167. (Unfortunately, the alliance does not make clear the character of the envoys who made it.) Otto Dulcianus, judge and consul of Lodi, read the conventions in a public assembly of Milan. The people were asked by the consul of Milan if they would have the conventions published and corroborated or attested by witnesses, and if they would have them redacted into a public instrument. The people confirmed the conventions by shouting very often: "Sia, sia, sia, sia, sia, sia, sia, sia, sia!" The covenants were then redacted—ironically enough—by an imperial notary.[65] A treaty which Venetian syndics brought back from Aragon in 1356 was ratified by the doge and the appropriate councils, summoned by ringing of the bell of the campanile in the accustomed manner. The doge swore in the hands of a public notary, who then made a public instrument, sealed with the doge's seal.[66] The Milanese ambassador, Leonardo Botta, recounted the publication of the Franco-Venetian alliance of 1499. Ambassadors and other dignitaries assembled in the piazza San Marco. A mass was said, then a procession

[64] *Ibid.*, v, ii, 23.
[65] Manaresi, *Atti . . . di Milano*, pp. 80-81, no. LIV.
[66] A.S.V., Senato, Misti, XXVII, 79v (80v).

marched about the piazza to the sound of the campanile and other instruments, and finally the alliance was proclaimed.[67] The Senate in 1480 wrote to Cardinal Foscari, who was acting as its intermediary with the pope, that it had hastened to ratify a treaty with the pope so that it could be solemnly published on Ascension Day, "which everywhere, but especially in our city, is most celebrated." It was hoped that the treaty could be published in Rome on the same day. The Senate wrote to officers throughout Venetian territories that on Ascension Day (12 May) they should publish the treaty with a solemn procession everywhere and with bonfires and other signs of rejoicing continuing for three days. In Venice itself public rejoicing was to begin on the very day of the letter, 9 May, and to continue three days after the publication of the treaty. The publication was to be performed at the time when the doge, according to custom, proceeded in the *Bucintoro* to the wedding of the sea, when the doge would be surrounded with neighboring dignitaries and orators and with great numbers of the people and nobles of Venice. The procession in Venice and the "devoted supplication" would be postponed until Pentecost (21 May), because the piazza on Ascension Day would be cluttered with booths and other accessories of the fair associated with that date.[68]

Other means of achieving the same ends of publicity and ceremonial sanction were possible. In 1475 the kings of England and France agreed to meet at the heads of their forces in full battle array and, by means of envoys passing from one to the other, to establish, proclaim, and publish the agreement which had been reached.[69] We also have an account in the Vatican Archives of the ratification of the Peace of Italy in 1443 by emissaries of the various powers. They exchanged hands and offered kisses to one another as a sign of peace. Then the pope admitted them as sons of peace to the kissing of his foot, his hand, and his mouth to the accompaniment of the solemn chanting of the *Te Deum* and of a prayer. Then all the notaries and clerks present were asked to compose instruments so that the act might be preserved in perpetual memory.[70] The form of the ceremonies, it is apparent, might vary, but the purpose was always that expressed in the papal document just mentioned, "for the firmness and strength of the aforesaid."

When covenants were ratified, the act need not necessarily be performed by the principals, but, as in the Peace of Italy of 1443 and many other ex-

[67] A.S.M., Archivio Sforzesco, Venezia, busta 385. The Venetian love of processions is well known.

[68] A.S.V., Senato, Secreta, XXIX, 95r (105r) and 98r (108r).

[69] *Calendar of State Papers. Venetian*, pp. 132-133, no. 446.

[70] Archivio Secreto Vaticano, AA. Arm. I-XVIII, no. 1443, p. 46r.

amples, it could be performed by envoys.[71] Sometimes the negotiations had been done by earlier envoys (presumably without full powers), and subsequently new envoys were sent to ratify.[72] In one example a Venetian secretary is authorized to ratify promises made in the name of Venice by a German orator for the purpose of hiring Swiss mercenaries.[73] On other occasions plenipotentiaries were empowered to ratify their own acts.[74] In 1436 the Senate wrote to its orator in Florence that, although they had hoped the treaty between themselves and Florence and Genoa could be concluded in the presence of the pope, or immediately after its conclusion ratified in his presence, they now wish it concluded as quickly as possible in Florence. Afterwards the orators of all three cities should go before the pope to ratify it.[75]

Since a primary purpose of ratification was to gain added publicity and ceremonial sanction, it was sometimes performed by some assembly, so that knowledge of it would be more widespread and broader-based acceptance of it might be assured. Lucas gives examples of English treaties ratified in parliament in 1328, and this was also done in 1365.[76] The Treaty of Troyes was ratified by the three estates of both kingdoms and was confirmed by their oaths.[77] In France treaties had been registered in Parlement since the origins of that body in the mid-thirteenth century, although such registration was not considered obligatory. By the reign of Louis XI, however, it was done consistently. The purpose again was to obtain greater public knowledge and more force.[78] The Venetian Senate in 1445 was demanding that the envoy of the cardinal-patriarch of Aquileia receive a mandate authorizing

[71] A.S.V., Senato, Secreta, IX, 137r (135r). In 1449 the Senate complained that Sforza did not fulfill the covenants ratified by his ambassadors with *amplissimo mandato ratificando* and finally broke relations with him over the issue. Gianni Zippel, "Ludovico Foscarini ambasciatore a Genova nella crisi dell'espansione veneziana sulla Terraferma: 1449-1450," *Bulletino dell'Istituto Storico Italiano per il Medio Evo e Archivio Muratoriano*, LXXI (1959), p. 242. See also p. 246.

[72] A.S.V., Maggior Consiglio, Spiritus, 6r (7r); Senato, Secreta, A, 12r.

[73] A.S.V., Senato, Secreta, XXXVI, 49rv (61rv).

[74] Rymer, *Foedera*, I, i, 316-318; III, iv, 23. Degert tells of an ambassador of Louis XI to Sixtus IV, who found that he lacked powers to ratify. The king, not pleased with the agreements, claimed that he was not bound. "Louis XI et ses ambassadeurs," p. 15. Unfortunately his reference to Delaborde, *Charles VIII en Italie*, p. 219, is erroneous.

[75] A.S.V., Senato, Secreta, XIII, 231v (231v).

[76] Lucas, "Machinery of Diplomatic Intercourse," pp. 303 and 330; *Rotuli parliamentorum Anglie hactenus inediti, MCCLXXIX-MCCCLXXIII*, H. G. Richardson and George Sayles, eds., in Camden Third Series, no. LI (London, 1935), p. 276. I am not convinced that Cuttino can rightly say "in 1365, when it could be said that treaties were ratified in parliament." *English Diplomatic Administration*, p. 105. I, at least, read and noted this as a generalization. If it is not, then 1328 could equally well be used, and possibly an earlier date. If it is, it may be true, but I should like more evidence.

[77] Rymer, *Foedera*, IV, iv, 47-48. Also the treaty of 1496. *Ibid.*, V, iv, 98.

[78] Felix Aubert, *Histoire du Parlement de Paris de l'origine à François Ier, 1250-1515*, 2 vols. (Paris, 1894), I, 352 and 357.

him to promise that the cathedral chapter of Aquileia could be convoked for the purpose of giving more strength to conventions with the cardinal.[79] In Venice this matter, like all other governmental affairs, could be terribly complex. In 1304 the Great Council (clearly sovereign at this time) delegated to the Council of Twenty the commissioning of envoys to deal concerning Padua. This council, with the heads of the Forty, could assume jurisdiction over negotiations, but no peace or truce should be completed without the participation of the Senate and the Forty.[80]

For similar reasons ratification was sometimes offered by nobles and towns.[81] A truce between Hungary and Venice in 1348 required ratification by the king and twenty Hungarian nobles and by the doge and twenty Venetian nobles.[82] In Flanders the nobles and towns were frequently called upon to ratify conventions made by the count or his representatives.[83] The original version of the Treaty of Melun for the release of Ferrand of Portugal was in fact rejected by them, although when the financial demands of France were modified they approved.[84] Their consent was important since ultimately it was they who would have to bear the financial burden. Edward I required ratification of a treaty with Guy of Dampierre from the count's sons, as well as the barons and towns of Flanders.[85] The real importance of sons, nobles, and towns, especially when the ruler was weak, was very likely to find reflection in such ceremonial roles as ratification.

Ratification was also employed to obtain the adherence of third parties to conventions. Many examples of this can be found in the *Secreta* of the Venetian Senate. Sometimes the principal adversaries made peaces or truces and their adherents were asked to ratify. On the other hand, in 1421 the duke of Milan inquired of the Senate whether the allies of either party should ratify the league into which he had entered with Venice, and the Senate replied that it was not necessary.[86]

The form of a ratification was customarily quite simple. It was customary in England and in France to incorporate the full text of the conventions to be ratified in the act of ratification, and in at least one truce between the two powers the agreement specified that it be incorporated

[79] A.S.V., Senato, Secreta, XVI, 143v (143v).

[80] A.S.V., Maggior Consiglio, Magnus, 68r. I concede that the use of "sovereign" may be a bit anachronistic.

[81] Rymer, *Foedera*, III, i, 101. I cannot subscribe to Luchaire's statement that a treaty or truce could have solidity in the eyes of the contracting parties only if it was sanctioned and sworn by the barons. *Manuel*, p. 498.

[82] A.S.V., Senato, Secreta, B (C), 54r.

[83] Warnkoenig–Gheldolf, *Histoire de la Flandre*, III, 350 and 352.

[84] *Ibid.*, I, 233.

[85] Chaplais, *Treaty Rolls*, I, 130-131, no. 348; Rymer, *Foedera*, I, iii, 173.

[86] A.S.V., Senato, Secreta, VIII, 4r (5r).

word for word.[87] If an oath were included in the ratification, which was not necessarily the case, a king or an emperor was not likely to swear in person, but to have someone else do it for him and in his presence.[88] The count of Flanders affected similar airs.[89] On occasion the clause requiring ratification could stipulate that it should be accomplished in the presence of the prince's councilors, prelates, barons, nobles, and others.[90] A ratification by Edward I informs Adolph, king of the Romans, that he has ratified their agreements and given his hand upon them to Eustace de Pomerio.[91] Since the northern powers consistently included the conventions in the ratification, the latter sometimes took the form of a *vidimus*.[92] Oddly enough, the Venetians were much more casual about the form of ratification. Perhaps the lack of a royal power in Italy deprived this act of some of its ceremonial value and, as we have seen, if the conventions had been concluded by plenipotentiaries, ratification had no juridical value. At any rate, in 1478, Louis XI was disappointed to find that the Venetian ratification of their treaty did not include the treaty *in extenso*. He regarded this as an irregularity and explained that it was a constant usage in France to include the entire document ratified. He begged the Venetians not to regard his scruples as mistrustful, but as respectful of the traditional usages of his chancery and desirous of surrounding the act of peace with all formalities. The *Signoria* approved his request and the doge transmitted a ratification in the form desired.[93] The less formal manner of the Venetians in this instance was not unique. In 1442 the Senate ratified conventions with an orator of the cardinal-patriarch of Aquileia in the following terms: "Since the instrument of agreement by the said Serafino and our syndics has now been called up for vote in an agreed form and according to the intention of this council: *Vadit pars* (the customary Venetian phrase of enactment) that the instrument now made should remain firm, as it was brought up for vote."[94] The Great Council in 1228 ratified an agreement with Ortona, saying, ". . . just as that agreement holds, so it ought to be done and to be observed."[95] This is the simplest possible form of ratification.

[87] Perret, *Relations de la France avec Venise*, II, 114; Rymer, *Foedera*, III, iv, 39-42.

[88] Ganshof, *Le Moyen Age*, p. 281. E.g., Chaplais, *Treaty Rolls*, I, 37-40, no. 103 (Rymer, *Foedera*, I, ii, 45); Chaplais, *Treaty Rolls*, I, 166-167, no. 395 (Rymer, *Foedera*, I, iv, 110); Rijksarchief, Gent, Saint-Genois, no. 863.

[89] Rymer, *Foedera*, I, ii, 851-852; Limburg-Stirum, *Codex diplomaticus Flandriae*, I, 114, no. 30.

[90] Rymer, *Foedera*, III, ii, 174.

[91] Chaplais, *Treaty Rolls*, I, 102, no. 238; Rymer, *Foedera*, I, iii, 140; *M.G.H.*, *Const.*, III, 498-499.

[92] Chaplais, *Treaty Rolls*, I, 259-263, no. 660; Rymer, *Foedera*, II, ii, 138, and III, ii, 7-8.

[93] Perret, *Relations de la France avec Venise*, II, 114.

[94] A.S.V., Senato, Secreta, xv, 120v (121v).

[95] Cessi, *Deliberazioni del Maggior Consiglio*, III, 216.

Although binding covenants between states could be accomplished by envoys without subsequent ratification, it was used in many cases. J. Mervyn Jones has traced the development of ratification from the obligatory ceremony of the seventeenth century to the discretionary ratification of the period after the American and French revolutions. In the Middle Ages, however, the *ratum habere* of a plenipotentiary's procuration constituted a ratification in advance, making the subsequent ratification unnecessary.

The acts of an envoy who was not a plenipotentiary, of course, had to be ratified in order to obligate the principal. The terms of agreements made by plenipotentiaries also might require subsequent ratification, in which case such requirement became integral to the compact concluded by the plenipotentiary. A failure to ratify, where ratification had been agreed upon by properly empowered envoys, was a failure to carry out a valid contract, not a defect in the conventions themselves.

Throughout the period studied here the plenipotenitary could bind his principal without any act on the part of the principal subsequent to the issuance of the procuration. Many scholars have held that ratification was essential in diplomacy, though not in private law, but the evidence proves that binding covenants were concluded definitively by plenipotentiaries.

Some of the confusion on the subject of ratification arises because many conventions were ratified, even though ratification was not required. The purpose of adding a legally superfluous act was sometimes to guard against unknown defects in the preceding acts. More often, however, the objective was to gain additional publicity and informal sanction for the covenants ratified. To this end ratification was surrounded with pageantry of church and state, chants, relics and solemn oaths, processions, heraldry, and fine costumes.

Ratification was sometimes performed by assemblies or councils to increase public knowledge of the act and to gain broader support for it. For similar reasons nobles and towns were often required to give acts of ratification. Third parties, especially weaker allies, sometimes became parties to covenants by their ratifications.

The form of ratification itself was relatively simple, consisting in the principal's affirmation of his intent to carry out the conventions made by his envoy. By this act a principal accepted obligations arising from negotiations by an envoy lacking full powers or reaffirmed obligations already accepted for him by a plenipotentiary.

CHAPTER IX

SUMMARY

In the course of the more than three centuries during which the ambassadorial office has been considered here, great changes were wrought in that office in conformity with sweeping changes in the fabric of a society in the process of transformation from feudal to modern. In the mid-twelfth century governments were relatively poor financially, bureaucracies were only beginning to develop, specialists in judicial and financial affairs were emerging from the undifferentiated *curia*, and diplomatic dealings among states were infrequent. By about the end of the fifteenth century, however, modern states were conducting frequent or continuous diplomatic relations very much as we do now.

The evolution of the ambassadorial office during this period begins with the simple *nuncius* of the period before the introduction of Roman procuration into diplomacy. The *nuncius* or *missus* was simply a messenger sent from one principal to another, merely a means of communication, a living letter. All sorts of persons sent and received diplomatic *nuncii*, for the concept of sovereignty was not yet highly developed, and the *droit d'ambassade* belonged to whomever possessed sufficient power to make use of it. No clear line existed between public and private or between diplomatic and political. Whatever could be accomplished through correspondence could be done also through *nuncii*. As a messenger the *nuncius* conveyed the will of his principal and could not act upon his own will so as to commit his principal. He could negotiate conventions in the form of a draft, but these could not be made obligatory upon the principal without their referral to him and an expression of his will to be bound. Whatever a *nuncius* could do was conceived to be done directly by the principal. He acted in the person of his principal in such a manner that direct relationships were established with the principal, not with the *nuncius*. In an age when diplomatic dealings were quite infrequent, the *nuncius* was a reasonably adequate instrument of diplomacy. Diplomatic negotiations normally were conducted by the rulers themselves, or else negotiations were conducted by letters or messengers, and culminated in a meeting of the rulers. Since diplomatic relations were largely limited to neighboring states, "summit" meetings were relatively easy to arrange. Even in the absence of a meeting of the principals, negotiations had to be concluded by a meeting of the minds of the principals themselves.

The broader field of diplomatic relations of the great states of the High Middle Ages, coupled with continued slowness of communication, made a more flexible instrument of diplomacy a desideratum. This was found in the Roman law procurator armed with *plena potestas*. The plenipotentiary acted in his own person, exercising his own will, in the name of his principal. By the act of a procurator within the powers granted in his mandate, the principal was bound. Without reference to the principal the procurator could negotiate and conclude. The principal, however, was not present in the person of the procurator, and therefore the procurator did not possess the ceremonially representative character of the *nuncius*. Since procuration was a private law institution, procurators could be appointed by private as well as public persons. Diplomacy remained open to all those possessing sufficient stakes to play the game. The *nuncius* did not pass out of use with the advent of the procurator in diplomacy. The two institutions were used concurrently, and the same envoy was often *nuncius* and procurator so that he could have the representative character of the *nuncius* along with the discretionary power of the procurator.

Diplomatic envoys came to be called ambassadors only in the High and Late Middle Ages, but even then this usage was not consistent, for the word "ambassador" had no very specific meaning. An ambassador was merely one sent on a mission, and such a person could equally well be called *legatus* or *nuncius*. *Ambaxator*, or its equivalent, *orator*, commonly came to be used for diplomatic envoys of high status, however, although throughout the period in question we occasionally find *ambaxatores* sent by nonsovereign entities on missions which were sometimes not diplomatic. As the frequency of diplomatic intercourse increased, there developed a tendency toward resident ambassadors. As this occurred the function of the ambassador tended to change. Whereas the chief occupation of earlier envoys had been the conveying of messages or negotiation between states, the resident was chiefly employed as a collector of information and ceremonial representative. An ambassador could, of course, be furnished with procuratorial full powers making him a plenipotentiary. As the exchange of envoys became more frequent, or as they became resident and communicated frequently with their governments through messengers, the granting of great discretionary authority became less common. Full powers were given, but usually only after the principal himself had agreed, at least in principle, to the specific obligations to which he was to be bound. The older practice of promising in advance of negotiations to hold firm whatever was promised by one's envoy, however, was not entirely abandoned.

Whereas in the very early Middle Ages an envoy might be sent without any written documents, by the end of the fifteenth century the exchange of ambassadors usually was accompanied by a considerable amount of writing. The document which was commonly required to constitute a *nuncius* or an ambassador was a letter of credence asking the recipient to have faith in what was said to him by the envoy on behalf of his principal. A letter of credence was not essential, however, if the envoy was a procurator, although envoys often did bear both letters of credence and procurations. Sometimes phraseology typical of both letters of credence and procurations is found mingled in the same document. This would presumably constitute the envoy as *nuncius* and procurator. Letters of instruction were not essential to the medieval diplomat, but became increasingly common. These were less formal documents affecting, not the relationship of one state to another, but the relationship of principal and envoy. An envoy might also be provided with documents, or copies of documents, providing evidence in support of his mission. He also sometimes received letters of protection, passports, and safe-conducts. On rare occasions we have even found diplomatic envoys provided with sealed, but otherwise blank parchments, upon which they could write agreements binding upon their principals. The diplomatic envoy might bear any or all of the above documents with him or they might be sent to him during the course of his mission. The latter procedure came to be commonly employed for procurations in the later part of the period studied. Diplomats had to send reports and requests for instructions to their governments, as well as receive communications from home. A returned diplomat by the Late Middle Ages also customarily made a written report. In Venice this took the unique form of the *relazione*, not so much a report on the mission as an essay on the country to which the envoy had been assigned.

All sorts of persons of the upper and middle classes manned medieval diplomatic missions, although the more ceremonial the character of the mission the more appropriate it appeared to send ambassadors of high social rank. Since the sense of national identity was weak, the use of foreigners as envoys was not unknown. Ecclesiastics were frequently used (though not in Venice), partly because of the protection afforded by their garb, partly because of their education, and partly because of the religious aura which surrounded diplomatic intercourse. Great nobles were useful when a mission had to be headed by someone of considerable social prestige. When technical knowledge was required more than social standing, legists, canonists, or professional bureaucrats were apt to find employment. As Renaissance humanism gained the field and the oration became a significant exercise, poets and scholars appeared more frequently as diplomats. Since diplomatic service was sometimes dangerous, filled with hardship, time-consuming and ill-paid, it was difficult to find qualified men of the higher ranks to fill diplomatic posts. The financing of embassies was no small problem to medieval states. Sometimes the state receiving an embassy was expected to bear part, at least, of the expense. Progressively, however, the state sending an envoy had to bear the cost of the embassy or compel the envoy himself to do so. The records are full of the laments of hard-pressed envoys against their governments and of efforts by the governments to prevent envoys from transferring more of the financial burden to the state.

Theoretically, at least, the diplomatic envoy was protected in his person, his retinue, and his goods. To a great extent, also, the diplomat was protected in practice, for if envoys could not come and go in security, diplomatic intercourse would be brought to a standstill. Of course, the immunities of ambassadors were sometimes infringed, but these cases were the notable exceptions. Diplomatic envoys were usually treated not only with respect, but with great courtesy. Ceremony, then as now, played a large role in diplomacy. Embassies of great ceremonial importance were very large and elaborate. Such embassies had to be received with considerable show of honor. A failure to display what was considered proper respect for an ambassador, because of his representative character, was regarded as a direct affront to his principal. Thus ambassadors of various powers struggled for precedence, especially in Rome.

Although most authorities have found subsequent ratification by the principal necessary to the conclusion of a treaty or other juristic act, this is only true of acts negotiated by envoys lacking full powers. Of course, subsequent ratification of the act concluded by a plenipotentiary might be given for various reasons, but it was not necessary in order to bind the principal, who had agreed in advance to hold firm his procurator's acts. When subsequent ratification was given, it was for the sake of publicity and added ceremonial sanction and was performed so as to attract as much attention as possible.

By the end of the fifteenth century the modern ambassadorship was formed in its essential outlines out of the raw material of the venerable *nuncius* and of *plena potestas*. With the great changes in society, these combined in different fashions and with different emphases—as they have done subsequently. The *nuncius* served adequately an age of very limited diplomatic intercourse with near neighbors. Full powers vesting great discretion in the procurator were useful in an age when intercourse was still infrequent, but missions were likely to be to distant powers. By 1500 the resident ambassador existed, chiefly for news-gathering and ceremonial purposes, but he was able to negotiate and conclude if provided with full powers for the purpose. One institution did not supplant the others, but existed alongside its predecessors, each used according to need.

BIBLIOGRAPHY

MANUSCRIPTS

Brussels
Archives du Royaume, Trésor de Flandre
Florence
Archivio di Stato
Archivio diplomatico—Riformagioni—Atti publici
Dieci di Balia—Missive—Legazioni e commissarie
Signori—Carteggi—Missive—Legazioni e commissarie—Elezioni e istruzioni a oratori
Signori—Carteggi—Missive—Minutari
Signori—Carteggi—Rapporti e relazioni di oratori
Signori—Carteggi—Responsive originali
Signori—Legazioni e commissarie—Risposti verbali di oratori
Signori—Missive—Originali
Signori—Missive—Prima Cancelleria
Ghent
Rijksarchief
Chronologisch supplement
Gaillard
Saint Genois
Stadsarchief, Van Duyse en De Busscher
Lille
Chambre des Comptes de Lille
London
British Museum
Mantua
Archivio di Stato, Archivio Gonzaga
Milan
Archivio di Stato
Archivio Sforzesco
Registri ducali
Paris
Bibliothèque Nationale
Vatican
Archivio Secreto Vaticano, AA. Arm. I-XVIII
Venice
Archivio di Stato
Avogaria di Comun, Capitolare

Dieci, Misti
Lettere di rettori
Maggior Consiglio
Miscellanea di atti diplomatici e privati
Pien Collegio, Notatorio
Senato, Misti
Senato, Secreta
Senato, Terra
Sindicati

PRIMARY SOURCES—DOCUMENTS

Acta Aragonensia: Quellen zur deutschen, italienischen, französischen, spanischen, zur Kirchen-und Kulturgeschichte aus der diplomatischen Korrespondenz Jaymes II, 1291-1327. Heinrich Finke, ed. 3 vols. Berlin and Leipzig, 1908-1922.

Acta Imperii, Angliae et Franciae ab anno 1267 ad annum 1313. Fritz Kern, ed. Tübingen, 1911.

Acta Imperii inedita. Eduard Winkelmann, ed. 2 vols. Innsbruck, 1880-1885.

Acta Imperii selecta. J. F. Böhmer, J. Ficker, eds. Innsbruck, 1870.

"Additions au Codex diplomaticus Flandriae," F. Funck-Brentano, ed. *Bibliothèque de l'École des Chartes*, LVII (1896), 373-417 and 529-572.

Anglo-French Negotiations at Bruges (1374-1377), The. Edouard Perroy, ed., in *The Camden Miscellany*, XIX (Camden Third Series, LXXX), (London, 1952).

Atti del Commune di Milano fino all'anno MCCXVI, Gli. C. Manaresi, ed. Milano, 1919.

Calendar of State Papers and Manuscripts, Relating to English Affairs, Existing in the Archives and Collections of Venice, and in Other Libraries of Northern Italy. R. Brown, *et al.*, eds. 38 vols. to date (London, 1864-1947).

C(alendar of the) C(lose) R(olls Preserved in the Public Record Office). Edward I. 5 vols. London, 1900-1908.

C(alendar of the) C(lose) R(olls) . . . Edward II. 4 vols. London, 1892-1898.

C(alendar of the) C(lose) R(olls) . . . Edward III. 14 vols. London, 1896-1913.

C(alendar of the) C(lose) R(olls) . . . Richard II. 6 vols. London, 1914-1927.

C(alendar of the) C(lose) R(olls) . . . Henry IV. 5 vols. London, 1927-1938.

C(alendar of the) C(lose) R(olls) . . . Henry V. 2 vols. London, 1929 and 1932.

C(alendar of the) C(lose) R(olls) . . . Henry VI. 6 vols. London, 1933-1947.

Calendar of the Liberate Rolls. Henry III. 4 vols. London, 1919-1959.

C(alendar of the) P(atent) R(olls Preserved in the Public Record Office). Henry III. 6 vols. London, 1901-1910.

C(alendar of the) P(atent) R(olls) . . . Edward I. 4 vols. London, 1893-1901.

C(alendar of the) P(atent) R(olls) . . . Edward II. 5 vols. London, 1894-1904.

C(alendar of the) P(atent) R(olls) . . . Edward III. 16 vols. London, 1891-1914.

C(alendar of the) P(atent) R(olls) . . . Richard II. 6 vols. London, 1895-1909.

C(alendar of the) P(atent) R(olls) . . . Henry VI. 6 vols. London, 1901-1910.

Capitularia regum Francorum, in *M.G.H., Capit.* A. Boretius and V. Krause, eds. 2 vols. Hannoverae, 1883-1897.

C(lose) R(olls of the Reign of Henry III). 14 vols. London, 1902-1938.

Codex diplomaticus Flandriae, 1296-1327. Thierry de Limburg-Stirum, ed. 2 vols. Bruges, 1879-1889.

Constitutiones et acta publica imperatorum et regum, in *M.G.H., Legum sectio IV.* L. Weiland, *et al.*, eds. 7 vols. Hannoverae, 1893-1926.

Constitutiones et acta regum Germanicarum, in *M.G.H., LL.*, II. Hannoverae, 1837.

Deliberazioni del Consiglio dei Rogati (Senato) Serie "Mixtorum." Vol. I. R. Cessi and P. Sambin, eds. Vol. II, R. Cessi and M. Brunetti, eds. Venezia, 1960-1961.

Deliberazioni del Maggior Consiglio di Venezia. Roberto Cessi, ed. 3 vols. Bologna, 1931-1950.

Diplomata regum et imperatorum Germaniae, in *M.G.H.* 7 vols. to date. Hannoverae, *et al.*, 1879-1931.

Diplomatic Correspondence of Richard II, The. Edouard Perroy, ed. in Camden Third Series, XLVIII. London, 1933.

Diplomatic Documents Preserved in the Public Record Office. Vol. I, 1101-1272, Pierre Chaplais, ed. (London, 1964), did not appear in time for consultation for the present work.

Documenti diplomatici tratti degli Archivi Milanesi. Luigi Osio, ed. 3 vols. in 6 parts. Milano, 1864-1877.

"Documents concernant l'Angleterre et l'Écosse anciennement conservés à la Chambre des Comptes de Lille (XIIe-XVe s.)," Pierre Chaplais, ed., *Revue du Nord*, XXXVIII (1956), 185-210.

Documents historiques inédits tirés des collections manuscrites de la Bibliothèque Royale et des archives ou des bibliothèques des departements. Jacques J. Champollion-Figeac, ed. 4 vols. Paris, 1841-1848.

"Documents relatifs aux formes diplomatiques aux XIIIe et XIVe siècles," Frantz Funck-Brentano, ed., *Revue d'histoire diplomatiques*, XI (1897), 76-101, 234-262, 369-386.

Epistolae illustrium virorum, clericorum vel laicorum ab a. 1060 ad a. 1180, la Congrégation de S. Maure, ed., in *H.F.*, XVI, 1st printing, 1813. Paris, 1878.

Foedera. Thomas Rymer, ed. 10 vols. Hagae Comitis, 1739-1745.

Foedera. Thomas Rymer, ed. Record Commission. 4 vols. in 7 parts. London, 1816-1869.

Groot charterboek der graven van Holland, Zeeland en heeren van Vriesland. F. van Mieris, ed. 4 vols. Leyden, 1753-1756.

Historia critica comitatus Hollandiae et Zeelandiae. Adriaan Kluit, ed. 4 vols. in 2. Medioburgi, 1777-1782.

Influences françaises et germaniques en Belgique au XIIIe siècle; la querelle des d'Avesnes et des Dampierres. Vol. II, Preuves, Charles Duvivier, ed. Bruxelles, 1894.

Layettes du Trésor des Chartes. Alexandre Teulet, Joseph Delaborde, and E. Berger, eds. 5 t. in 6 vols. Paris, 1863-1909.

Lettres de rois, reines, et autres personnages des Cours de France et d'Angleterre depuis Louis VII jusqu'à Henri IV tirés des archives de Londres par Bréquigny. Jacques J. Champollion-Figeac, ed. 2 vols. Paris, 1839-1849.

Liber Iurium reipublicae Genuensis, Vols. I and II. Vols. VII and IX in *Monumenta historiae patriae* (Torino, 1854-1857).

"Liste analytique des documents concernant l'histoire de la Belgique qui sont conservés au *Record Office*," Ernest van Bruyssel, ed., *Bulletin de la Commission Royale d'Histoire*, 3e sér., I (1859).

Monuments pour servir à l'histoire des provinces de Namur, de Hainaut et de Luxembourg. De Reiffenberg, J. J. De Smet, L. Devillers, Ad. Borgnet, E. Gachet et Liebrecht, eds. 8 vols. Bruxelles, 1844-1874.

"Notes sur un manuscrit de l'abbaye de Saint-Pierre de Gand conservé aux Archives Nationales de Paris," Henri Nowé, ed., *Bulletin de la Commission Royale d'Histoire*, LXXXVII (1923), 1-38.

Oorkondenboek van Holland en Zeeland. L. Ph. C. van den Bergh, ed. 2 vols. Amsterdam, 1866-1873.

"La prima relazione del cardinale Nicolò de Romanis sulla sua legazione in Inghilterra," Monsignore Angelo Mercato, ed., in *Essays in History*

Presented to Reginald Lane Poole, H.W.C. Davis, ed. (Oxford, 1927), pp. 274-289.

Proceedings and Ordinances of the Privy Council. Sir N. H. Nicolas, ed. 7 vols. London, 1834-1837.

"Recueil de documents inédits relatifs aux relations du Hainaut et de la France de 1280 à 1297," Étienne Delcambre, ed., *Bulletin de la Commission Royale d'Histoire*, XLII (1928), 1-163.

Recueil des actes de Philippe Auguste, roi de France. H. F. Delaborde, ed. 1 vol. (1179-1194) appeared (Paris, 1916).

Regesta Imperii. Johann Friedrich Böhmer, ed. New edn. by Mathilde Uhlirz, II (Sächsische Haus, 919-1024) (Graz and Köln, 1956).

Regestum Innocentii III papae super negotio Romani Imperii. Friedrich Kempf, ed., in *Miscellanea historiae pontificiae*, XII (Roma, 1947).

Register Papst Innocenz' III. über den deutschen Thronstreit, Das. Walther Holtzmann, ed. 2 vols. in 1. Bonn, 1947.

Registres de Grégoire X (1272-1276), suivis du registre de Jean XXI (1276-1277), Les. J. Guiraud and L. Cadier, eds., in Bibliothèque des Écoles Françaises d'Athènes et de Rome, 2e sér., XII (Paris, 1892-1960).

Relation, or rather a true account, of the Island of England; with sundry particulars of the customs of these people, and of the royal revenues, under King Henry the seventh, about the year 1500, A. Trans. from the Italian with notes by Charlotte Augusta Sneyd. London, 1847.

Relazioni degli ambasciatori veneti al Senato durante il secolo XVI, Le. Eugenio Albèri, ed. 15 vols. Firenze, 1839-1863.

Rotuli litterarum clausarum in turri Londonensi asservati. Thomas D. Hardy, ed. 2 vols. London, 1833-1844.

Rotuli litterarum patentium in turri Londonensi asservati (1201-1216). Thomas D. Hardy, ed. London, 1835.

Rotuli parliamentorum Anglie hactenus inediti, MCCLXXIX-MCCCLXXIII. H. G. Richardson and George Sayles, eds., in Camden Third Series, LI (London, 1935).

Treaty Rolls: Preserved in the Public Record Office. Pierre Chaplais, ed. 1 vol. to date. London, 1955.

Urkunden Heinrichs III, Die. H. Bresslau and P. Kehr, eds. in *M.G.H., Dipl. reg. imp. Germ.*, V (Berlin, 1931).

Urkunden zür älteren Handels-und Staatsgeschichte der Republik Venedig. G. L. Fr. Tafel and G. M. Thomas, eds. 3 vols. in *Fontes rerum austriacarum*, zweite abtheilung, Banden XII-XIV (Wien, 1856-1857).

War of Saint Sardos, 1323-1325. The Gascon Correspondence and Diplo-

matic Documents. Pierre Chaplais, ed., in Camden Third Series, LXXVII (London, 1954).

PRIMARY SOURCES—LAW

Aegidius de Fuscararius. *Ordo iudiciarius*, in Wahrmund, *Quellen*, III, i.

Alberico de Rosate. *Vocabularius utriusque juris*. Lugduni, 1535.

Alciati, Andrea. *Index locupletissimus D. Andreae Alciati super commentariis Codicis Iustiniani imperatoris*. Lugduni, 1536.

———. *Iudiciarii processus compendium*. Venetiis, 1543.

———. *Reliqua D. Andreae Alciati opera, quae typis nostris hactenus non fuerant excusa*. Lugduni, 1548.

Andreas (de) Barbatia (Siculus). *Tractatus de cardinalibus legatis a latere*, in Hrabar, *De legatis*, pp. 42-44.

Arnulphus, Magister. *Summa minorum*, in Wahrmund, *Quellen*, I, ii.

Azo. *Summa*. Lugduni, 1576.

Azo. *Summa*. Venetiis, 1594.

Azo. *Summa Codicis*. Venetiis, 1610.

Baldo degli Ubaldi. *Baldi Ubaldi Perusini . . . in Corpus iuris civilis . . . Commentaria*. 10 vols. Venetiis, 1615-1616.

Barbarus, Hermolaus. *De officio legati*, in Hrabar, *De legatis*, pp. 65-70.

Bartolus à Saxoferrato. *Commentaria*, in *Opera omnia*. 11 vols. in 6. Venetiis, 1602-1603.

Beaumanoir, Philippe de. *Coutumes du Beauvoisis*. Am. Salmon, ed. 2 vols. Paris, 1889-1890.

Bernardus Papiensis. *Summa Decretalium*. E.A.T. Laspeyres, ed. Reprint of the 1860 edition (Graz, 1956).

Bertachinus, Joannes. *Repertorium*, v° *Ambasiator*, in Hrabar, *De legatis*, pp. 70-76.

Bibliotheca juridica Medii Aevi. Augustus Gaudentius, ed. 3 vols. Bononiae, 1888-1901.

Boncompagnus. *Rhetorica novissima*, in Gaudentius, *Bibliotheca juridica*, II, 249-297.

Corpus juris canonici. Aemilius Friedberg, ed. 1st edn. 1881, reprinted, 2 vols. (Graz, 1955).

Corpus juris civilis. Paul Krueger and Theodor Mommsen, eds. 2 vols. Berlin, 1888-1889.

Corpus juris civilis, . . . commentariis Accursii. Venetiis, 1591.

Curialis, in Wahrmund, *Quellen*, I, iii.

Decretales D. Gregorii Papae IX . . . cum glossis. Venetiis, 1600.

"Dekretglossen des Cod. Stuttgart, hist. f. 419, Die," Franz Gillmann, ed., *Archiv für katholisches Kirchenrecht*, CVII (1927).

De Maino, Giasone. *Repertorium copiosissimum*, in *Omnia Jasonis Mayni Mediolanensis juris consulti clarissimi commentaria*. Augustae Taurinorum, 1573.

Dinus de Rossonibus de Mugello. *Commentarius in regulas iuris pontificii*, bound with Philippus Decius. Lugduni, 1570.

Dolius. *Glossae*, in *Iuris interpretes saec. XIII*. E. M. Meyers, ed. Neapoli, 1924.

Durandus, Gulielmus. *Speculum juris*. 2 vols. Augustae Taurinorum, 1578.

——. *Speculum juris*. Francofurti, 1612.

——. *Speculum legatorum* (in eius *Speculo iuris*. Rubrica *De legato*), in Hrabar, *De legatis*, pp. 31-41.

Établissements de Saint Louis, Les. Paul Viollet, ed. 4 vols. Paris, 1881-1886.

Gambarus, Petrus Andreas. *Tractatus de officio atque auctoritate legati de latere*. Venetiis, 1571.

Gar(r)atus (de Caratis sive Caraziis) Laudensis, Martinus. *Tractatus de legatis maxime principum*, in Hrabar, *De legatis*, pp. 45-52.

Gondisalvus de Villadiego. *Tractatus de legato*, in Hrabar, *De legatis*, pp. 53-70.

Gratia Aretinus. *Summa de iudiciario ordine*, in *Pillii, Tancredi, Gratiae libri de iudiciorum ordine*, Fridericus Bergmann, ed. Gottingae, 1842.

Grotius, Hugo. *De jure belli ac pacis libri tres*. James Brown Scott, ed. Vol. I, reproduction of edition of 1646; vol. II, trans. by Francis W. Kelsey *et al*. Washington, 1913-1925.

Hostiensis, Henricus de Segusio, Cardinalis. *Summa*. 1st printed (Lyon, 1537); reprinted (Darmstadt, 1962).

——. *Summa super titulis Decretalium*. Lugduni, 1548.

Hrabar, Vladimir E. *De legatis et legationibus tractatus varii*. Dorpat, 1906.

Irnerius. *Summa Codicis*. Hermann H. Fitting, ed. Berlin, 1894.

——. *Yrnerii formularium tabellionum s. XIII in. In novam formam redactum*, G. B. Palmieri, ed., in Gaudentius, *Bibliotheca juridica Medii Aevi*, I, 201-229.

Libellus de verbis legalibus, in *Juristische Schriften des früheres Mittelalters*. Hermann H. Fitting, ed. Halle, 1876.

Martinus de Fano. *Formularium*, in Wahrmund, *Quellen*, I, viii.

Ordo judiciarius "Scientiam," in Wahrmund, *Quellen*, II, i.

Petri exceptionum legum Romanorum appendices, in *Juristische Schriften des früheres Mittelalters*. Hermann H. Fitting, ed. Halle, 1876.

Quellen zur Geschichte des römisch-kanonischen Processes im Mittelalter. Ludwig Wahrmund, ed. 5 vols. Innsbruck, 1905-1931.

Rainerius de Perusio. *Ars notaria,* A. Gaudenzi, ed., in Gaudentius, *Bibliotheca juridica Medii Aevi,* II.

Ricardus Anglicus. *Summa de ordine iudiciario,* in Wahrmund, *Quellen,* II, iii.

Rogerius. *Summa Codicis,* G. B. Palmieri, ed., in Gaudentius, *Bibliotheca juridica Medii Aevi,* I.

Rosier, Bernard du. *Ambaxiator brevilogus,* in Hrabar, *De legatis,* pp. 3-28.

Siete Partidas, Las. 3 vols. Valladolid, 1587.

Summa notariae annis MCCXL-MCCXLIII Aretii composita, Carolo Cicognario notario, ed., in Gaudentius, *Bibliotheca juridica,* III, 283-332.

Summa notariae Belluni composita, Arthuro Palmerio, ed., in Gaudentius, *Bibliotheca juridica,* III, 353-367.

Tancred. *Ordo iudiciarius,* in *Pillii, Tancredi, Gratiae libri de iudiciorum ordine,* Fridericus Bergmann, ed. Gottingae, 1842.

William of Drogheda. *Summa aurea,* in Wahrmund, *Quellen,* II, ii.

PRIMARY SOURCES—NARRATIVES

Annales Fuldensis, M.G.H., SS., I (Hannoverae, 1826), 337-415.

Annales Stadenses auctore M. Alberto, M.G.H., SS., XVI, I. M. Lappenberg, ed. (Hannoverae, 1859), 271-379.

Burckhard, Johannes. *Liber notarum ab anno MCCCCLXXXIII usque ad annum MDVI,* Enrico Celano, ed., in *Rerum italicarum scriptores, t.* XXXII. 2 vols. Città di Castello, 1906-1911.

Commines, Philip de. *The Memoirs.* Andrew R. Scoble, trans. 2 vols. London, 1889-1890.

Commines, Philippe de. *Mémoires.* J. Calmette and G. Durville, eds. 3 vols. Paris, 1924-1925.

Commynes, Philippe de. *Mémoires.* B. de Mandrot, ed. 2 vols. Paris, 1901-1903.

Continuatio anonymi, to *Ottonis Morenae Historia Friderici I,* F. Güterbock, ed., in *M.G.H., Script. rer. Germ., N.S.,* VII (Berlin, 1930), pp. 177-218.

Continuatio Claromariscensis, to *Flandria generosa auctore monacho S. Bertini,* L. Bethmann, ed., *M.G.H., SS.,* IX (Hannoverae, 1851), 326-334.

Continuatio monachorum Sancti Petri, to *Annales Sancti Rudberti Salisburgensis,* W. Wattenbach, ed., *M.G.H., SS.,* IX (Hannoverae, 1851), 837-843.

Cosmas of Prague. *Chronica Boemorum*, B. Bretholz and W. Weinberger, eds., *M.G.H., Script. rer. Germ., N.S.*, II (Berlin, 1923).

Cronica S. Petri Erfordensis moderna, O. Holder-Egger, ed., *M.G.H., SS.*, XXX (Hannoverae, 1896), 335-457.

Ernoul et Bernard le Trésorier. *Chronique.* Louis de Mas Latrie, ed. Paris, 1871.

Fredegarius Scholasticus. *Chronicarum*, Bruno Krusch, ed., *M.G.H., Script. rer. Mer.*, II (Hannoverae, 1888), 1-168.

Froissart, Jean. *Oeuvres.* Kervyn de Lettenhove, ed. 25 vols. in 26. Bruxelles, 1867-1877.

Gesta archiepiscoporum Magdeburgensium, Continuatio altera, Guill. Schum, ed., *M.G.H., SS.*, XIV (Hannoverae, 1883), 361-486.

Gesta episcoporum Eichstetensium continuata, L. Bethmann and G. Waitz, eds., *M.G.H., SS.*, XXV (Hannoverae, 1880), 590-609.

Gesta Ludovici VIII, Francorum rex, auctore anonymo, ab anno 1223 ad annum 1226, in *H.F.*, XVII, 302-310.

Gilles Le Muisit. *Chronicon majus*, J. J. De Smet, ed., in *Corpus chronicorum Flandriae*, 4 vols. (Bruxelles, 1837-1865), II, 93-293.

Gregory of Tours. *Historia Francorum*, Wilhelmus Arndt, ed., *M.G.H., Script. rer. Mer.*, I (Hannoverae, 1885), 1-450.

Guicciardini, Francesco. *Storia d'Italia.* Giovanni Rosini, ed. 8 vols. Pisa, 1822-1824.

Heinricus Surdus de Selbach. *Chronica*, Harry Bresslau, ed., in *M.G.H., Script. rer. Germ., N.S.*, I (Berlin, 1922).

Hilary, bishop of Poitiers. *De Trinitate*, in *Patrologia latina*, J. P. Migne, ed., 221 vols. (Parisiis, 1841-1864), X, cols. 25-472.

Hincmar of Rheims. *Annales*, in *M.G.H., SS.*, I (Hannoverae, 1826), 455-515.

Histoire des ducs de Normandie et des rois d'Angeterre, 1181-1218. Francisque Michel, ed. Paris, 1840.

Historia de expeditione Friderici imperatoris, A. Chroust, ed., *M.G.H., Script. rer. Germ., N.S.*, V (Berlin, 1928).

Hugo Pictavinus. *Historia Vizeliacensis monasterii*, Martin Bouquet, ed., in *H.F.*, XII, 1st printing, 1781 (Paris, 1877), 317-344.

Istore et croniques de Flandre. Kervyn de Lettenhove, ed. 2 vols. Bruxelles, 1879-1880.

Jacques de Guyse. *Annales Hannoniae.* De Fortia d'Urban, ed. and trans. 22 vols. Paris, 1826-1838.

Joinville, Jean, sire de. *Histoire de Saint Louis.* Natalis de Wailly, ed. Paris, 1874.

Malipiero, Domenico. *Annali veneti*, ordinati e abbreviati dal senatore Francesco Longo, in *Archivio storico italiano*, VII, i (1843), 3-586, and VII, ii (1844), 589-720.

Mariana, Juan de. *Historia general de España*. Barcelona, n.d.

———. *Historiae de rebus Hispaniae libri XXX*. Moguntiae, 1605.

Mathias de Nuwenburg. *Chronica*, Adolf Hofmeister, ed., *M.G.H., Script. rer. Germ., N.S.*, IV (Berlin, 1924-1940).

Matthew Paris, monk of St. Albans. *Chronica majora*, H. R. Luard, ed., in *R.S.*, no. 57, 7 vols. (London, 1872-1883).

Memorials of St. Edmund's Abbey, T. Arnold, ed., in *R.S.*, no. 96, 3 vols. (London, 1890-1896).

Mousket, Philippe. *Chronique rimée*. De Reiffenberg, ed. 2 vols. Bruxelles, 1836-1838.

Pisan, Christine de. *The Book of Fayttes of Armes and of Chyualrye*. Trans. and printed by William Caxton, A.T.P. Byles, ed., in Early English Text Society, no. 189. London, 1932.

Pius II. *Commentaries*. Trans. by Florence Alden Gragg with introduction and notes by Leona C. Gabel, in Smith College Studies in History, XXII (1 and 2), XXV (1-4), XXX, XXXV, XLIII (Northampton, Mass., 1937——).

Robert of Clari. *La conquête de Constantinople*. Ph. Lauer, ed. Paris, 1924.

Roger of Hoveden. *Chronica*, W. Stubbs, ed., in *R.S.*, no. 51, 4 vols. (London, 1868-1871).

Roger of Wendover. *Flores historiarum*, Henry Hewlett, ed., in *R.S.*, no. 84, 3 vols. (London, 1886-1889).

Rolandinus Patavinus. *Cronica in factis et circa facta marchie Trivixane (1200 cc.-1262)*, A. Bonardi, ed., in *Rerum italicarum scriptores*, VIII, i (Bologna, 1905-1908).

Sanuto, Marino. *I diarii*, F. Stefani, G. Berchet, N. Barozzi, eds. 42 vols. Venezia, 1879-1894.

"Traité du gouvernement de la cité et seigneurie de Venise," in P.-M. Perret, *Relations de la France avec Venise*, 2 vols. (Paris, 1896), II, 239-304.

Villehardouin, Geoffroi de. *La conquête de Constantinople*, Edmond Faral, ed. and trans. 2 vols. Paris, 1938-1939.

SECONDARY WORKS

Allen, Alice M. *A History of Verona*. London, 1910.

Andreas, Willy. *Staatskunst und Diplomatie der Venezianer. Im Spiegel ihrer Gesandtenberichte*. Leipzig, 1943.

Angelini, Sergio. *La diplomazia comunale a Perugia nei secoli XIII e XIV*. Firenze, 1965.

Antonibon, Francesca. *Relazioni a stampa di ambasciatori veneti.* Padova, 1939.

Ariès, Philippe. *Centuries of Childhood: A Social History of Family Life.* Fr. edn., 1960, trans. by Robert Baldick. New York, 1962.

Armingaud, J. *Venise et le Bas-Empire: Histoire des relations de Venise avec l'Empire d'Orient,* extrait: *Des archives des missions scientifiques et littéraires,* T. IVe–2e sér. Paris, 1868.

Aubert, Felix. *Histoire du Parlement de Paris de l'origine à François Ier, 1250-1515.* 2 vols. Paris. 1894.

Bakhrouchine, S., and E. Kosminski. "La diplomatie du Moyen Age," Vol. I, part 2, *Histoire de la diplomatie,* Vladimir P. Potemkin, ed. Trans. from the Russian edition of 1941 by X. Pamphilova and M. Eristov. Paris, 1946.

Baschet, Armand. *Les archives de Venise: Histoire de la Chancellerie Secrète.* Paris, 1870.

Bauzá a Bauzá, Rafael. "Doctrinas juridicas internacionales de Ramón Llull," *Estudios lulianos,* III (1959), 181-184.

Baylen, Joseph O. "John Maunsell and the Castilian Treaty of 1254: A Study of the Clerical Diplomat," *Traditio,* XVII (1961), 482-491.

Behrens, B. "Treatises on the Ambassador Written in the Fifteenth and Early Sixteenth Centuries," *E.H.R.,* LI (1936), 616-627.

Bémont, Charles. *Simon de Montfort, Earl of Leicester, 1208-1265.* New edn. trans. by E. F. Jacob. Oxford, 1930.

Berger, Adolf. *Encyclopedic Dictionary of Roman Law,* in *Transactions of the American Philosophical Society,* N.S., XLIII, 2 (1953).

Bettanini, Antonio Maria. "Note di ceremoniale diplomatico," in *Studi dedicati alla memoria di Pier Paolo Zanzucchi dalla Facoltà di Giurisprudenza* (del' Università Cattolica del Sacro Cuore) (Milano, n.d.).

Bigwood, Georges. "Les financiers d'Arras: Contribution à l'étude des origines du capitalisme moderne," *Revue belge de philologie et d'histoire,* III (1924), 465-508, 769-819; IV (1925), 109-119, 379-421.

———. *Le régime juridique et économique du commerce de l'argent dans la Belgique du Moyen Age.* 2 vols. Bruxelles, 1921-1922.

Black's Law Dictionary. 1st edn., 1891; 3rd edn. (St. Paul, 1933); and 4th edn. (St. Paul, 1951).

Bloch, Marc. "Les formes de la rupture de l'hommage dans l'ancien droit féodale," *Nouvelle revue historique de droit française et étranger,* XXXVI (1912), 143-177.

Boyer, Marjorie Nice. "Status and Travel Stipends in Fourteenth Century France," *Speculum,* XXXIX (1964), 45-52.

———. "Travel Allowances in Fourteenth Century France," *Journal of Economic History*, XXIII (1963), 71-85.

Bréhier, Louis. *L'église et l'orient au Moyen Age*. Paris, 1928.

Buckland, W. W. *The Main Institutions of Roman Private Law*. Cambridge, 1931.

———. *A Textbook of Roman Law from Augustus to Justinian*. 2nd edn. Cambridge, 1932.

Buzzati, Giulio Cesare. "Diritto diplomatico veneziano del sec. XIII," in *Studi giuridici dedicati a Francesco Schupfer* (Torino, 1898), II, 223ff.

Carboni, Michele. "Sul concetto di 'Nuntius,'" in *Scritti giuridici dedicata a Giampietro Chironi* (Milano, Torino, Roma, 1915).

Cessi, Roberto. "Ambasciatore," *Enciclopedia italiana* (1929 edn.), II, 2, pp. 782-784.

———. "Venezia e la quarta crociata," *Archivio veneto*, ser. 5, XLVIII-XLIX (1951), 1-52.

Chaplais, Pierre. "The Making of the Treaty of Paris (1259) and the Royal Style," *E.H.R.*, LXVII (1952), 235-253.

Clarke, Maude V. *Medieval Representation and Consent*. London, 1936.

Clifford, Esther Rowland. *A Knight of Great Renown: The Life and Times of Othon de Grandson*. Chicago, 1961.

Corio, Bernardino. *Storia di Milano*. Riveduta e annotata dal Egidio de Magri *et al.* 3 vols. Milano, 1855-1858.

Cuttino, George P. *English Diplomatic Administration, 1259-1339*. London, 1940.

———. "The Process of Agen," *Speculum*, XIX (1944), 161-178.

Da Mosto, Andrea. *L'Archivio di Stato di Venezia*. 2 vols. Roma, 1937-1940.

Davis, James C. *The Decline of the Venetian Nobility as a Ruling Class*. Baltimore, 1962.

Degert, Antoine. "Louis XI et ses ambassadeurs," *Revue historique*, CLIV (1927), 1-19.

Dehaisnes, L'abbé C. "Essai sur les relations commerciales de la ville de Douai avec l'Angleterre au Moyen Age," *Mémoires lus à la Sorbonne* (Paris, 1867), pp. 79-117.

Delaborde, H.-François. *L'expédition de Charles VIII en Italie*. Paris, 1888.

Dept, Gaston. *L'influence anglaise et française dans le comté de Flandre au début du XIIIe siècle*. Gand, 1928.

De Tourtier, Chantal. "Un ambassadeur de Louis de Gonzague, seigneur de Mantoue: Bertolino Capilupi," *École française de Rome. Mélanges d'archéologie et d'historie*, LXIX (1957), 321-344.

Dibben, L. B. "Secretaries in the Fourteenth and Fifteenth Centuries," *E.H.R.*, xxv (1910), 430-444.

Dickinson, Joycelyne G. "'Blanks' and 'Blank Charters' in the Fourteenth and Fifteenth Centuries," *E.H.R.*, LXVI (1951), 375-387.

——. *The Congress of Arras, 1435*. Oxford, 1955.

Dictionary of National Biography. Sir Leslie Stephen and Sir Sidney Lee, eds. 22 vols. reprinted. London, 1949-1950.

Du Cange, Charles du Fresne, sieur. *Glossarium mediae et infimae latinitatis*. New edition by Leopold Favre, 1883-1887, reprinted, 10 vols. Paris, 1937-1938.

Düll, Rudolf. "Über Ansätze direkter Stellvertretung im fruhrepublikanischen romischen Recht," *Zeitschrift für Savigny-Stiftung für Rechtsgeschichte, Romanistische Abteilung*, LXVII (1950).

Duvivier, Charles. *Les influences françaises et germaniques en Belgique au XIIIe siècle; la querelle des d'Avesnes et des Dampierre*, 2 vols. Bruxelles, 1894.

Edwards, J. G. "The Plena Potestas of English Parliamentary Representatives," *Oxford Essays in Medieval History Presented to Herbert Edward Salter* (Oxford, 1934).

Ernst, Fritz. "Über Gesandtschaftswesen und Diplomatie an der Wende vom Mittelalter zur Neuzeit," *Archiv für Kulturgeschichte*, XXXIII (1950), pp. 64-95.

Firpo, Luigi. Description of *Relazioni di ambasciatori veneti al Senato*, in *Catologo 91, Jura et Medievalia, Bottega d'Erasmo*. Torino, 1963. P. 22.

Fourgous, J. *L'arbitrage dans le droit français aux XIIIe et XIVe siècles*. Paris, Toulouse, 1906.

Funck-Brentano, Frantz. "Caractère religieux de la diplomatie au XIIIe siècle," *Revue d'histoire diplomatique*, I (1887), 113-125.

——. *Les origines de la Guerre de Cent Ans: Philippe le Bel en Flandre*. Paris, 1897.

Gachard, Louis Prosper. *La Bibliothèque Nationale à Paris. Notices et extraits des manuscrits qui concernent l'histoire de Belgique*. 2 vols. Bruxelles, 1875-1877.

Gaillard, Victor. *Inventaire analytique des chartes des comtes de Flandre*. Gand, 1857.

Ganshof, François L. "Merowingisches Gesandtschaftswesen," in *Aus Geschichte und Landeskunde. Forschungen und Darstellungen. Franz Steinbach zum 65. Geburtstag gewidmet von seinen Freunden und Schülern* (Bonn, 1960), pp. 166-183.

——. *Le Moyen Age.* Vol. I in *Histoire des relations internationales.* Pierre Renouvin, ed. Paris, 1953.

Gierke, Otto von. *Das deutsche Genossenschaftsrecht.* 1st edn., 1881, reprinted, 4 vols. (Graz, 1954).

Guessard, F. "Pierre de Mornay, chancelier de France," *Bibliothèque de l'École des Chartes,* v (1843-1844), 143-170.

Guichenon, Samuel. *Histoire généalogique de la royale maison de Savoye.* 2 parts, 1660; new edition, 4 t. (Turin, 1778-1780).

Hale, J. B. "International Relations in the West: Diplomacy and War," *The New Cambridge Modern History,* I., G. R. Potter, ed. (Cambridge, 1957), 259-291.

Hayes, Carlton J. H. "Medieval Diplomacy," in *The History and Nature of International Relations,* Edmund A. Walsh, ed. (New York, 1922).

Herbomez, Armand d'. "Philippe le Bel et les Tournaisiens," *Bulletin de la Commission Royale d'Histoire,* 5e sér., III (1893), 17-197.

Hill, Mary C. *The King's Messengers, 1199-1377.* London, 1961.

——. "King's Messengers and Administrative Developments in the Thirteenth and Fourteenth Centuries," *E.H.R.,* LXI (1946), 315-328.

Hodgson, F. C. *The Early History of Venice.* London, 1901.

Huisman, Georges. "Un compte de réparations effectuées à l'hôtel du comte de Flandres à Paris (1374-1376)," *Bulletin de la Société de l'Histoire de Paris et de l'Ile de France,* XXXVII (1910), 257-272.

Huizinga, Johan. *The Waning of the Middle Ages.* 1st edn. in Dutch, 1919; trans. and adaptation from 2nd edn. by F. Hopman, 1924, reprinted (New York, 1954).

Ilardi, Vincent. "Fifteenth-Century Diplomatic Documents in Western European Archives and Libraries (1450-1494)," *Studies in the Renaissance,* IX (1962), 64-112.

Isaacs, N. "The Influence of Judaism on Western Law," in *The Legacy of Israel,* planned by I. Abrahams and ed. by Edwyn R. Bevan and Charles Singer, 1st edn. 1927 (Oxford, 1948), pp. 377-406.

Jacob, E. F. "England: Henry III," *Cambridge Medieval History,* VI, 1st printed, 1929 (Cambridge, Eng., 1936), 252-284.

Jolowicz, Herbert F. *Historical Introduction to Roman Law.* Cambridge, Eng., 1952.

Jones, J. Mervyn. *Full Powers and Ratification.* Cambridge, Eng., 1949.

Jusserand, J. J. "The School for Ambassadors," in *The School for Ambassadors and Other Essays* (New York and London, 1925), pp. 1-61.

Kervyn de Lettenhove. *Études sur l'histoire du XIIIe siècle. Recherches sur la part que l'ordre de Citeaux et le comte de Flandre prirent à la lutte de Boniface VIII et de Philippe le Bel.* Bruxelles, 1853.

———. *Histoire de Flandre*. 6 vols. Bruxelles, 1847-1850.

Kingsford, Charles Lethbridge. "John de Benstede and His Missions for Edward I," in *Essays in History Presented to Reginald Lane Poole*, H.W.C. Davis, ed. (Oxford, 1927), pp. 332-359.

Krauske, Otto. *Die Entwicklung der ständigen Diplomatie*. Leipzig, 1885.

Labarge, Margaret Wade. *Simon de Montfort*. London, 1962.

Lamansky, Vladimir. *Secrets d'état de Venise*. St. Petersburg, 1884.

Lane, Frederick C. "Venetian Merchant Galleys, 1300-1334: Private and Communal Operation," *Speculum*, XXXVIII (1963), 179-205.

Lazzarini, Vittorio, "Obbligo di assumere pubblici uffici nelle antiche leggi veneziane," *Archivio veneto*, XIX (1936), 184-198.

Le Glay, Edouard. *Histoire de Jeanne de Constantinople, comtesse de Flandre et de Hainaut*. Lille, 1841.

Lestocquoy, J. "Deux familles de financiers d'Arras, Louchard et Wagon," *Revue belge de philologie et d'histoire*, XXXII (1954), 51-76.

Limburg-Stirum, Thierry de. *La cour des comtes de Flandre. Leurs officiers héréditaires. I. Le chambellan de Flandres*. Gand, 1868.

Löhren, Alfred. *Beiträge zur Geschichte des gesandtschaftlichen Verkehrs im Mittelalter. I. Die Zeit vom vierten bis zum Ende des neunten Jahrhunderts*. Marburg, 1884.

Longnon, Jean. *Recherches sur la vie de Geoffroy de Villehardouin, suivies du catalogue des actes de Villehardouin*. Paris, 1939.

Lucas, Henry S. "John of Avesnes and Richard of Cornwall," *Speculum*, XXIII (1948), 81-101.

———. "The Machinery of Diplomatic Intercourse," in *The English Government at Work, 1327-1336*, James F. Willard and William A. Morris, eds. (Cambridge, Mass., 1940), I, 300-331.

Luchaire, Achille. "Louis VII—Philippe Auguste—Louis VIII," vol. III, in *Histoire de France*, Ernest Lavisse, ed. (Paris, 1901).

———. *Manuel des institutions françaises. Période des Capétiens directs*. Paris, 1892.

Luykx, Theo. *De grafelijke financiële bestuursinstellingen en het grafelijk patrimonium in Vlaanderen tijdens de regering van Margareta van Constantinopel (1244-1278)*. Brussel, 1961.

———. *Het graafelijk geslacht Dampierre en zijn strijd tegen Filips de Schone*. Louvain, 1952.

———. *Johanna van Constantinopel*. Antwerpen and Utrecht, 1946.

———. "De strijd van Margareta van Constantinopel, gravin van Vlaanderen en Henegouwen, voor het behoud van hare rijksgebieden," *Gedenkschriften van de Oudheidkundigen Kring van het Land van Dendermonde* (1950), 1-31.

Luzio, Alessandro. *L'Archivio Gonzaga di Mantova: La corrispondenza familiare, amministrativa e diplomatica dei Gonzaga.* Vol. II. Verona, 1922.

Mas Latrie, Le comte de. *De l'empoisonnement politique dans la république de Venise.* Paris, 1893.

Maspes, A. "Prammatica pel ricevimento degli ambasciatori inviati alla corte di Galeazzo Maria Sforza," *Archivio storico lombardo,* XVII (1890), 146-151.

Mattingly, Garrett. "The First Resident Embassies: Medieval Italian Origins of Modern Diplomacy," *Speculum,* XII (1937), 423-439.

———. *Renaissance Diplomacy.* New York, 1955.

Maulde La Clavière, M.A.R. de. *La diplomatie au temps de Machiavel.* 3 vols. Paris, 1892-1893.

Menzel, Victor. *Deutsches Gesandtschaftswesen in Mittelalter.* Hanover, 1892.

Mollat, Guillaume. "La diplomatie pontificale au XIVe siècle," in *Mélanges d'histoire du Moyen Age dédiés à la mémoire de Louis Halphen* (Paris, 1951), pp. 507-512.

Molmenti, Pompeo. "Le relazioni tra patrizi veneziani e diplomatici stranieri," in *Curiosità di storia veneziana* (Bologna, 1919), pp. 25-63.

Morozzo della Rocca, Raimondo. *Dispacci degli ambasciatori al Senato. Indice.* Venezia, 1959.

———. "Notizie da Caffa," in *Studi in onore di Amintore Fanfani,* III (Milano, 1962), 267-295.

Naz, Raoul. *Dictionnaire de droit canonique.* Paris, 1935——.

Neale, J. E. "The Diplomatic Envoy," *History,* XIII (1928-1929), 204-218.

Nicolini, Fausto. "Frammenti veneto-napoletani," estr. dal vol. *Studi di storia napoletana in onore di Michelangelo Schipa* (Napoli, 1926).

Nicolini, Nicolà. *Il consolato generale veneto nel regno di Napoli (1257-1495).* Napoli, 1928.

Nicolson, Harold. *The Evolution of Diplomatic Method.* London, 1954.

Nys, Ernest. *Études de droit international et de droit politique.* Bruxelles et Paris, 1896.

———. "Les origines de la diplomatie et le droit d'ambassade jusqu'à Grotius," *Revue de droit international et de législation comparée,* XV (1883), 577-586, and XVI (1884), 55-70 and 167-189.

———. *Les origines du droit international.* Harlem, 1894.

Oxford English Dictionary. Sir James A. H. Murray, ed. 10 vols. Oxford, 1888-1928.

Paradisi, Bruno. *Storia del diritto internazionale nel Medio Evo: L'età di transizione (dal sec. V al sec. IX).* Napoli, 1950.

Pastor, Ludwig Freiherrn von. *Geschichte der Päpste seit dem Ausgang des Mittelalters.* 1st edn., 1884-1933; 12th edn., 16 vols. in 22 (Freiburg, 1955—).

Perret, Paul-Michel. *Histoire des relations de la France avec Venise du XIIIe siècle à l'avènement de Charles VIII.* 2 vols. Paris, 1896.

———. "Les règles de Cicco Simonetta pour le déchiffrement des écritures secrètes (4 juillet 1474)," *Bibliothèque de l'École des Chartes,* LI (1890), 516-525.

Pieper, A. *Zur Entstehungsgeschichte der ständingen Nuntiaturen.* Fribourg-en-Brisgau, 1894.

Poncelet, E. "La guerre dite 'de la Vache de Ciney,'" *Bulletin de la Commission Royale d'Histoire,* 5e sér., III (1893), 275-395.

Post, Gaines. "Parisian Masters as a Corporation," *Speculum,* IX (1934), 421-445.

———. "Plena Potestas and Consent in Medieval Assemblies," *Traditio,* I (1943), 355-408.

———. "Roman Law and Early Representation in Spain and Italy, 1150-1250," *Speculum,* XVIII (1943), 211-232.

———. *Studies in Medieval Legal Thought: Public Law and the State, 1100-1322.* Princeton, 1964.

Powicke, Sir Maurice. *King Henry III and the Lord Edward.* 2 vols. Oxford, 1947.

———. *The Thirteenth Century, 1216-1307.* 1st edn. 1953; reprinted with corrections (Oxford, 1954).

Quazza, Romolo. *La diplomazia gonzaghesca.* Milano, n.d.

Queller, Donald E. "Diplomatic 'Blanks' in the Thirteenth Century," *E.H.R.,* LXXX (1965), 476-491.

———. "Diplomatic Personnel Employed by the Counts of Flanders in the Thirteenth Century," *Revue belge de philologie et d'histoire,* XXXIV (1956), 68-98 and 385-422.

———. "Early Venetian Legislation Concerning Foreign Ambassadors," *Studies in the Renaissance,* XII (1965).

———. *Early Venetian Legislation on Ambassadors.* Geneva, 1966.

———. "L'évolution du rôle de l'ambassadeur: Les pleins pouvoirs et le traité de 1201 entre les Croisés et les Vénitiens," *Le Moyen Age,* LXVII (1961), 479-501.

———. "Innocent III and the Crusader-Venetian Treaty of 1201," *Medievalia et humanistica,* fasc. XV (1963), 31-34.

———. "Thirteenth-Century Diplomatic Envoys: *Nuncii* and *Procuratores,*" *Speculum,* XXXV (1960), 196-213.

Raulich, Italo. *La caduta dei Carraresi, signori di Padova.* Padova-Verona, 1890.

Reumont, Alfred von. *Dei diplomati italiani e delle relazioni diplomatiche italiane dal 1260 al 1550.* Padova, 1850.

———. *Della diplomazia italiana da secolo XIII al XVI.* Firenze, 1857.

Riasanovsky, Alexander V. "The Embassy of 838 Revisited: Some Comments in Connection with a 'Normanist' Source on Early Russian History," *Jahrbuch für Geschichte Osteuropas,* x (1962), 1-12.

Romanin, Samuel. *Storia documentata di Venezia.* 10 vols. Venezia, 1853-1861.

Ruess, Karl. *Die rechtliche Stellung des päpstlichen Legaten bis Bonifaz VIII.* Paderborn, 1912.

Schmutz, Richard. "The Foundations of Medieval Papal Representation," unpublished Ph.D. dissertation (University of Southern California, 1966).

Selmi, Paolo. "L'inizio ed il primo sviluppo della diplomazia stabile della Repubblica di Venezia," unpublished thesis (Padova, 1960).

Serguiev, V. "La diplomatie de l'antiquité," 1, in *Histoire de la diplomatie,* Vladimir P. Potemkine, ed., trans. from the Russian edn. of 1941 by X. Pamphilova and M. Eristov (Paris, 1946).

Serrao, F. *Il Procurator.* Milano, 1947.

Sohm, Rudolph. *The Institutes: A Textbook of the History and System of Roman Private Law.* 3rd English edn. Oxford, 1907.

Strubbe, Eg. I. *Egidius van Breedene (11?-1270): Grafelijk ambtenaar en stichter van de abdij Spermalie.* Brugge, 1942.

Sturler, Jean de. *Les relations politiques et les échanges commerciaux entre le duché de Brabant et l'Angleterre au Moyen Age.* Paris, 1936.

Table chronologique des chartes et diplômes concernant l'histoire de Belgique. Alphonse Wauters, ed. 11 vols. Bruxelles, 1866-1907.

Tessier, Jules. *Quatrième Croisade. La diversion sur Zara et Constantinople.* Paris, 1884.

Thomas, Georg Martin. "Die ältesten verordnungen der Venezianer für auswärtige Angelegenheiten," *Abhandlungen der philosophisch-philologischen Classe der Königlich Bayerischen Akademie der Wissenschaften,* XIII (1875), 97-147.

Tipton, Charles Leon. "The English Langue of the Knights Hospitallers during the Great Schism," unpublished Ph.D. dissertation (University of Southern California, 1964).

Tourtoulon, Charles Jean Marie, Baron de. *Don Jaime I, el conquistador, rey d'Aragon, conde de Barcelona, señor de Montpeller, segun las crónicas y documentos ineditos.* 2 vols. in 1. Valencia, 1873.

Tout, Thomas Frederick. *The Collected Papers of Thomas Frederick Tout.* 3 vols. Manchester, 1932-1934.

Varenbergh, Émile. "Épisodes des relations extérieures de la Flandre au Moyen Age: Trois filles de Gui de Dampierre," *Annales de l'Académie d'Archéologie de Belgique*, 2e sér., XXIV, iv (1868), 607-642.

———. *Histoire des relations diplomatiques entre le comté de Flandre et d'Angleterre au Moyen Age.* Bruxelles, 1874.

Vedovato, Giuseppe. *Note sul diritto diplomatico della repubblica fiorentina.* Firenze, 1946.

Vernadsky, George. *Kievan Russia.* New Haven, 1948.

———. *The Mongols and Russia.* New Haven, 1953.

Volpi, Giuseppe. *La repubblica di Venezia e i suoi ambasciatori.* Milano, 1928.

Von Heckel, Rudolf. "Das Aufkommen der ständigen Prokuratoren an der päpstlichen Kurie im 13 Jht.," *Miscellanea Francesco Ehrle*, II (Roma, 1924).

Wagner, Anthony R. *Heralds and Heraldry in the Middle Ages.* 1st edn., 1939; 2nd edn. (London, 1956).

Warnkoenig, Leopold A. *Histoire de la Flandre jusqu'à l'année 1305.* A. E. Gheldolf, trans. 5 vols. Bruxelles, 1835-1864.

Wasner, Franz. "Fifteenth Century Texts on the Ceremonial of the Papal 'Legatus a Latere,'" *Traditio*, XIV (1958), 295-358.

Watson, Alan. *Contract of Mandate in Roman Law.* Oxford, 1961.

Weckmann, Luis. "Les origines des missions diplomatiques permanentes," *Revue générale de droit international public*, LVI (1952), 161-188.

Wenger, Leopold. *Institutes of the Roman Law of Civil Procedure.* Trans. by Otis H. Fiske from the German edn. of 1925. New York, 1940.

Wieruszowski, Helene. "Roger II of Sicily, *Rex-Tyrannus*, in Twelfth-Century Political Thought," *Speculum*, XXXVIII (1963), 46-78.

Zippel, Gianni. "Ludovico Foscarini ambasciatore a Genova, nelle crisi dell'espansione veneziana sulla Terraferma: 1449-1450," *Bulletino dell'Istituto Storico Italiano per il Medio Evo e Archivio Muratoriano*, LXXI (1959), 181-255.

INDEX